READING BIBLES, WRITING BODIES

D1559514

The Bible, a religious text, is also often said to be one of the foundation texts of Western culture. The present volume explores how religious, political and cultural identities, including ethnicity and gender, are embodied, often problematically, in biblical discourse. Following the authors, we read the Bible with new eyes: as a critic of gender, ideology, politics, and culture. We ask ourselves new questions: about God's body, about women's roles, about racial prejudices and about the politics of the written word.

Reading Bibles, Writing Bodies crosses boundaries. It questions our most fundamental assumptions about the Bible. It shows how biblical studies can benefit from, and contribute to, the mainstream of Western intellectual discourse, throwing up entirely new questions and offering surprising answers. Accessible, engaging, and moving easily between theory and the reading of specific texts, this volume is an exciting contribution to contemporary biblical and cultural studies.

Timothy K. Beal is Assistant Professor of Religious Studies at Eckerd College, Florida. **David M. Gunn** is A.A. Bradford Professor of Religion at Texas Christian University. He recently co-authored *Narrative in the Hebrew Bible* (1993). Both have published on the interface of critical theory and biblical studies.

BIBLICAL LIMITS

We have to move beyond the outside–inside alternative; we have to be at the frontiers. Criticism indeed consists of analyzing and reflecting upon limits.
– Michel Foucault ('What is Enlightenment?')

This series brings a variety of postmodern perspectives to the reading of the familiar biblical texts. Books in the series will bring the traditional field of biblical studies face to face with literary criticism, anthropology and gender-based approaches, thus reaching new ways of understanding biblical texts.

EDITORS

Danna Nolan Fewell
Southern Methodist University, Dallas, Texas

David M. Gunn
Texas Christian University, Fort Worth, Texas

Gary A. Phillips
College of the Holy Cross, Worcester, Massachusetts

ALSO IN THIS SERIES

Jesus Framed
George Aichele

READING BIBLES, WRITING BODIES

Identity and The Book

Edited by
Timothy K. Beal and David M. Gunn

London and New York

First published 1997
by Routledge
11 New Fetter Lane, London EC4P 4EE

Simultaneously published in the USA and Canada
by Routledge
29 West 35th Street, New York, NY 10001

Typeset in Garamond by
BC Typesetting, Bristol

Printed and bound in Great Britain by
TJ Press (Padstow) Ltd, Padstow, Cornwall

British Library Cataloguing in Publication Data
A catalogue record for this book is available from the British Library

Library of Congress Cataloguing in Publication Data
Beal, Timothy K. (Timothy Kandler),
    Reading Bibles, Writing Bodies: Identity and The Book/edited by
Timothy K. Beal and David M. Gunn.
        p.   cm. – (Biblical limits)
    Includes bibliographical references and index.
    1. Bible. O.T.–Hermeneutics.   2. Bible. O.T.–Criticism,
interpretation, etc.   3. Body, Human–Biblical teaching.   4. Bible
as literature.   5. Bible. O.T.–Feminist criticism.   I. Gunn, D.
M. (David M.)   II. Title.   III. Series.
BS476.B43   1996
221.6–dc20   96-1112

ISBN 0-415-12664-9
          0-415-12665-7 (pbk)

CONTENTS

Part III Textual Bodies

NOTES ON CONTRIBUTORS

Timothy K. Beal is Assistant Professor of Religious Studies at Eckerd College in St Petersburg, Florida. His interests lie in the relation of critical theory to Hebrew Bible studies; he also teaches and writes in gender studies and environmental studies. He is chair of the Reading, Theory, and the Bible Section of the Society of Biblical Literature. He has contributed essays to several books and to the journals *Biblical Interpretation* and *Semeia*. He is currently finishing his own book on the politics of identity and subversion in Esther.

Daniel Boyarin is Taubman Professor of Talmudic Culture at the University of California at Berkeley. A prolific writer, most recently he is the author of *Carnal Israel: Reading Sex in Talmudic Culture* and *A Radical Jew: Paul and the Politics of Identity* (both University of California Press). The present chapter will form part of a chapter in his current work-in-progress, *Judaism as a Gender; or, the Rise of Heterosexuality and the Invention of the Jewish Man: an Autobiography*.

Athalya Brenner is Professor of Feminism, and Christianity/Judaism Chair, at the University of Nijmegen, The Netherlands, and Associate Professor in the Department of General Studies, The Technion, Haifa, Israel. Among her recent writings is *On Gendering Texts: Female and Male Voices in the Hebrew Bible* (E. J. Brill), co-authored with Fokkelien van Dijk-Hemmes. Editor of the Feminist Companion Series (Sheffield Academic Press), her main interests are in feminist biblical criticism and Semitic philology.

Claudia V. Camp is Professor of Religion at Texas Christian University in Fort Worth. Author of *Wisdom and the Feminine in the Book of Proverbs* (Almond/Sheffield Academic Press), she has written extensively on the Bible's wisdom literature and feminist biblical interpretation, including contributions to the recent *Women's Bible Commentary* (Westminster/John Knox) and *Searching the Scriptures* (Crossroad). The present essay is part of a larger on-going project on the image of the strange woman in the Bible.

Howard Eilberg-Schwartz is Associate Professor and Director of Jewish Studies at San Francisco State University and a Guggenheim Fellow. His work on ancient Judaism draws on anthropological and gender theory to rethink Judaism as a religious culture. His books include *The Savage in Judaism* (Indiana University) and *God's Phallus and Other Problems for Men and Monotheism* (Beacon); and he is co-editor with Wendy Doniger of *Off With Her Head: The Denial of Women's Identity in Religion, Myth and Culture* (University of California).

Danna Nolan Fewell is Associate Professor of Hebrew Bible at Perkins School of Theology, Southern Methodist University in Dallas, Texas. She has written *Circle of Sovereignty: Plotting Politics in the Book of Daniel* (Abingdon) and co-authored with David Gunn several books of literary and feminist criticism, including *Narrative in the Hebrew Bible* (Oxford University Press) and *Gender, Power, and Promise: The Subject of the Bible's First Story* (Abingdon). She is editor of *Reading Between Texts: Intertextuality and the Hebrew Bible* (Westminster/John Knox).

Mark K. George, a recent graduate of Princeton Theological Seminary, teaches Hebrew Bible at Iliff School of Theology in Denver, Colorado. He is interested in questions of power and the cultural systems that produced the biblical texts, and is presently revising his dissertation, an analysis of the text's "rhetoric of the body" as a strategy of power employed in the construction of community identity.

David M. Gunn is A. A. Bradford Professor of Religion at Texas Christian University in Fort Worth, after teaching at the University of Sheffield, England, and Columbia Theological Seminary in Atlanta, Georgia. He has edited the Bible and Literature Series (Almond/Sheffield Academic Press) and Literary Currents in Biblical Interpretation Series (Westminster/John Knox), the latter with co-author Danna Nolan Fewell. His next book is on the figure of David in Western culture, *David and Goliath's Head: Sex, Politics, and the Authority of the Bible* (Routledge).

L. Daniel Hawk is Associate Professor of Old Testament and Hebrew at Ashland Theological Seminary, in Ashland, Ohio. He is the author of *Every Promise Fulfilled: Contesting Plots in Joshua* (Westminster/John Knox). His current projects include a commentary on 1–2 Samuel and a monograph on sacrifice as metaphor in the Former Prophets which includes a comparative study of the Saul–David–Solomon story and the Oresteia of Aeschylus.

David Jobling is Professor of Old Testament at St. Andrew's College in Saskatoon, Canada. A former president of the Canadian Society of Biblical Studies, he co-chairs the Ideological Criticism Group of the Society of Biblical Literature. He has written *The Sense of Biblical Narrative* (*I* and *II*; JSOT/Sheffield Academic Press) and is one of the authors of *The Postmodern Bible* (Yale University Press) as a member of the Bible and Culture Collective. Currently he is completing a book on 1 Samuel (Liturgical Press).

Kyle Keefer holds degrees in English from Baylor University in Texas and an M.Div. from Princeton Theological Seminary. He is currently a Ph.D. candidate in New Testament at Emory University, writing a dissertation on the interpretation of John in the early church. His interests include early Christianity, the relationship of hermeneutics to ecclesial concerns, contemporary literary theory, and American pragmatism.

Tod Linafelt is Assistant Professor of Biblical Studies at Georgetown University in Washington, D.C., after studying at Emory University in Atlanta. He holds a Graduate Diploma in Jewish studies from the University of Oxford. Post-holocaust biblical hermeneutics figures prominently in his research interests. He has published articles recently in the journals *Semeia*, *Biblical Interpretation*, and *Horizons in Biblical Theology*.

Carol A. Newsom is Professor of Old Testament at Candler School of Theology, Emory University. She has been closely involved in the Society of Biblical Literature, including terms as secretary-treasurer and program chair. Her writing includes a recently completed commentary on Job for the *New Interpreter's Bible*; and she is currently at work on other projects in wisdom literature, a book in Qumran studies on the construction of the self in the language of prayer and pedagogy, and contributions to *Discoveries in the Judaean Desert* (Oxford University Press).

Ilona N. Rashkow is Associate Professor of Comparative Literature and Women's Studies at the State University of New York at Stony Brook. Her writings include *Upon the Dark Places: Sexism and Anti-Semitism in English Renaissance Biblical Translation* (Almond/Sheffield Academic Press) and *The Phallacy of Genesis: A Feminist-Psychoanalytic Approach* (Westminster/ John Knox Press). Her current projects are a literary study of Esther and Ruth, and a book on the literary representations – and their cultural afterlife – of the dysfunctional family in the Hebrew Bible and other ancient texts.

Jan William Tarlin is Assistant Professor of Religious Studies at Montana State University, Bozeman. His dissertation, "Troubling Israel: Performing Gender and Power in the Reading of the Elijah Cycle," begins an exploration of the construction of masculinity in the reading of the Hebrew prophets. His work has appeared in the *Feminist Companion to the Bible* (Sheffield Academic Press) and *Literature and Theology at Century's End* (Scholars Press).

ACKNOWLEDGEMENTS

Athalya Brenner, "The Hebrew God and His Female Complements," is re-printed by permission of HarperCollins Publishers Limited from *The Feminist Companion to Mythology* edited by Carolyne Larrington (London: Pandora [1992], pp. 48–62).

Howard Eilberg-Schwartz, "The Problem of the Body for the People of the Book," was originally published in *Journal of the History of Sexuality* 2 (1991): pp. 1–24, under the title, "People of the Body: The Problem of the Body for the People of the Book," and is reprinted by permission of the University of Chicago Press.

Danna Nolan Fewell and David M. Gunn, "Shifting the Blame: God in the Garden," was originally published in their *Gender, Power, and Promise: The Subject of the Bible's First Story* (Chapter 1). Copyright © 1993 Danna Nolan Fewell and David M. Gunn. Used by permission of the publisher, Abingdon Press.

David Jobling, "Transference and Tact in Biblical Studies," was originally published in *Studies in Religion/Sciences Religieuses* 22/4 (1993): pp. 451–62. Copyright © Canadian Corporation for Studies in Religion. Reprinted by permission.

Carol A. Newsom, "Woman and the Discourse of Patriarchal Wisdom," is reprinted by permission from *Gender and Difference in Ancient Israel* edited by Peggy L. Day (pp. 142–60). Copyright © 1989 Augsburg Fortress.

PREFACE

Biblical studies exists in a ghetto. Isolated within the academy, the main body of biblical scholarship is not an active conversational partner within mainstream intellectual discourse. This was not always the case. There was a time when biblical scholars actively engaged other disciplines – classics and philosophy, for example. With the emergence of a positivist historical consciousness in nineteenth-century scholarship, however, biblical studies grew dissociated from the wider intellectual discourse as practitioners pursued ever more singlemindedly the mechanics of their new program. Ironically, with the freedom to read the Bible in a radically fresh way – as a text like any other – came the gradual imposition of new disciplinary limits, as the "historical-critical method" became the measure of legitimate thinking about the text and scholars pressed on toward completing the scientific (*wissenschaftlich*) understanding of the Bible. The outcome today is an insular guild, clinging to the bequest of nineteenth- and early twentieth-century scholars, reluctant to acknowledge the deep problems confronting the positivist historical-critical enterprise, and inclined to view biblical research as a matter of refining method and filling in gaps.

Yet such a story, while compelling, is hardly the only one that could be told. Particular critics and critical phases in modern biblical studies have periodically disturbed the move to isolation. Hermann Gunkel, for example, brought folklore studies and biblical texts into creative play in the early decades of this century. The last twenty years in particular have seen dramatic changes. Some biblical scholars have been adopting models from neighboring fields, especially literary criticism, sociology, anthropology, and feminist thought. Some scholars in cognate fields, notably in English and comparative literature (see, for example, the Indiana Studies in Biblical Literature series) have been making contributions to biblical studies. The extent of the changes being wrought within the guild can be seen in a nutshell in the program of the annual professional meeting of the Society of Biblical Literature. Along with the emerging variety of program units and session topics is, strikingly, and not unconnected, the growing participation of previously excluded voices, most prominently to date those of women and

African-Americans. Indeed, two women, feminist scholars, one a literary critic of the Hebrew Bible, have in recent years held the office of society president.

On the other hand, two points could be made. First, it would be hard to deny, when the flagship journals are surveyed, the graduate curricula laid out to view, and the professional placements tallied, that the opening story bears repeating. Second, while creative boundary crossing has become a feature of some contemporary biblical criticism, appropriations beyond the traditional limits have tended to be one way and *ad hoc*, with few established channels for substantive exchange with cognate scholarship. Viewed from "inside," it might be wished that those outside the field who have made the Bible a subject of inquiry would, more often than is the case at present, sustain and deepen their engagement with contemporary biblical scholarship (as Mieke Bal, for one, has done to considerable end).

Does biblical criticism have a place in the contemporary intellectual debate? That can only happen if the means for conversation are enlarged. At present the heavy dependence of biblical scholarship upon denominational/religious publishing, especially in the United States, reinforces the ghetto. That is one of the political "facts of life" in the current sociology of (biblical) knowledge. Biblical scholarship that reflects upon and transcends existing critical boundaries needs publication that undermines and reconstructs existing publishing boundaries. It needs publishers with lists in critical theory and cultural studies directed toward a wide array of readers – readers interested in the boundary questions of our time, in religion, ethics, politics, economics, gender, sexuality (to start a list). In short, we see both the series which this present volume helps initiate and the volume itself as playing a small role in the second of our stories, namely the dissolution of the ghetto or, to put it otherwise, the enlargement of the conversation through an expanded body of writers and writing on "the biblical."

The aim of the present book is to problematize some of the "identities" that have worn the label "biblical" and to do so in a way that responsibly engages both academic biblical criticism and broader discussions involving cultural criticism and the politics of identity. The book raises, we think, some important questions (which we are not the first to ask!). What is the relation between the Bible and identity in the West? Can or should one even talk of biblical identity at all? Does the Bible offer a system or blueprint for building a particular social order – a politics of identity? Does the biblical God, biblical law, or "The Book" itself for that matter, offer any sort of foundation or guarantee for building a particular self and for marking others clearly as "not-selves," shoring up an "I" over against an "other," an "us" over against "them"? Is it univocal (all of one voice, single minded) in providing such a system? How are references to "the biblical" in popular political discourse (biblical values, biblical morality, etc.) related to the texts themselves? Can "the biblical" ever backfire on those who invoke it in political discourse?

Apparently, for many people in North America the answers are obvious: yes, the Bible defines and prescribes a particular biblical subject and a politics of identity which marks that subject's "other" very clearly (for marginalization at best and oblivion at worst); and yes, references to biblical character, biblical values, biblical morality, and so on in contemporary political discourse are safely and securely grounded in the Bible itself, which is univocal and unambiguous as a guide for developing and maintaining one's identity in ways that will ensure that one is right with God, its Author and Guarantor. For many, the question is not what is "biblical" and what is not, since agreement is assumed, but whether one accepts or rejects the "biblical" as having some mandatory power in one's life or the life of the community.

The present book finds the questions themselves more compelling than the answers so often given. Indeed, when addressed honestly and self-critically, with careful attention to biblical texts, such questions about the assuredness of "the biblical" often lead not to any particular answers but rather to more questions. The chapters in this volume open "The Book" in precisely this way, engaging both critical biblical scholarship and contemporary critical theory in hopes of encouraging academic discussions, inside and outside the field of biblical studies, to develop a more critically rigorous and responsible theorizing of "the biblical" as it relates to contemporary politics of identity.

The book has three interrelated areas of focus, or bodies of concern: Part I, "Divine Bodies" (focusing on the character and problematics of divine identity, even God's body, in the Hebrew Bible); Part II, "Human Bodies" (focusing on the relations between God, biblical discourse, and the body politic, including issues of religious identity, national identity, sexual identity, and the place of otherness); and Part III, "Textual Bodies" (focusing more specifically on the body of the text itself – its status in the West, and the often problematic assumptions on which that status depends). Within each section the chapters cover a wide spectrum of topics, yet do so in ways that we believe produce engaging possibilities of inter-reading and signal to those unfamiliar with biblical scholarship something of the savor of current thought.

The sections themselves are frames to contour reading. They are also frames that challenge transgression, that manifest the implausibility of frames.

Claudia Camp (Part I) explores how language works as power and as theology. She takes Woman Wisdom (Sophia) and the Strange Woman as powerful female images producing a surplus of power that eludes the control of their (male) fashioners. Her study both resonates with and diverges from Athalya Brenner's (Part I) survey of the Hebrew God's relation to the divine female, a discussion which spans the Bible and its pervasive single-gender images of God and which presses the question of cultural consequences. In different ways, both critics analyze religious politics as gender politics and partner Carol Newsom's (Part II) discussion of biblical text as patriarchal discourse. Newsom asks what role – both in enabling men's speech and rendering it problematic – does sexual difference play in the symbolic world of a text (Proverbs 1–9) where the subject position of the reader is male but talk about women and women's speech predominates.

Ilona Rashkow (Part I) analyzes the relationship of Moses and another divine image, God's rod, in terms of the Oedipal conflict, and she traces, in the process, both the sacralization of Israelite male sexuality and the feminization of the Israelite male by circumcision. Her study resumes an issue, the theological problem of (dis)embodiment, which is central to Howard Eilberg-Schwartz's exploration of the tension that arises when the impulse to monotheism and a disembodied and sexless God is coupled with the conviction that humans are created in the likeness and image of God – and human bodies become problematic. Theological tension likewise emerges in Danna Nolan Fewell and David Gunn's (Part I) reading of God in the creation and garden story – a creative tension of separation and sameness where good and evil, man and woman, God and humankind, like most of the story's discriminations, turn out to be sliding terms. At the same time all three chapters share important interests with Daniel Boyarin's (Part II) politico-cultural rereading of Freud's *Moses and Monotheism*. By locating Freud's account of biblical religion specifically within Freud's own political situation as a male Jew in early twentieth-century Europe, Boyarin reads this classic work as a deeply ambivalent rewriting of (feminine) Jewish identity as (masculine – and Protestant) Aryan. Freud splits Moses, and thus Judaism, in two. In turn, threads in Boyarin's chapter will take the reader to David Jobling's (Part III) reflection on psychoanalysis in biblical interpretation as an entry into the question of how to read two texts, two "testaments," without acquiescing in the dominance (and anti-Semitism) of one. *Violence* Dan Hawk (Part II) examines the account of Israel's conquest of Canaan in the Book of Joshua as a text telling of the execution of an ancient program of divinely sanctioned ethnic cleansing – yet a text "configured by contradiction." Danna Nolan Fewell, too, writes in Part II on the conflicted nature of ancient Israelite identity building, where the "face" of post-exilic reconstruction demands the denial of Israel's Canaanite mothers and the rewriting of Genesis by Judges. (Questions of gender/ethnicity alignment recur throughout this volume, in Camp, Eilberg-Schwartz and Rashkow among others.) But Fewell also, by what she *does* as she writes her reading, invites us to consider her work in terms of the transference and tact to which David Jobling calls attention, and the complicating enrichment of subjectivity that takes place in Tod Linafelt's (con)scription of Edmond Jabès on the (inter)-textual margins of the Book of Lamentations (Part III).

With insights from Michel Foucault, Mark George (Part II) looks at the body as political metaphor in one of the Bible's great foundation myths, the story of David. His discussion of homoerotic and homosocial desire in ancient Israel intimates a theme concerning Freud and the cultural politics of modern Europe. And in remarking the equivalence of the king's body and God's body, he points us back once more to Eilberg-Schwartz's and Rashkow's (Part I) explorations of the divine body. So, too, do these writers beckon us when we consider Jan Tarlin's (Part II) reading of pornography, a violent God, and a masochistic prophet in the Book of Ezekiel – a study of the workings of the body metaphor and the politics of the male subject. Tarlin's venture into film criticism reminds us of Newsom's (Part II) interest in "Fatal Attraction" as biblical exemplar; and his discriminating appropriation of Kaja Silverman prompts our observation that an engagement with psychoanalytic theory is a hallmark of a number of the present chapters.

The volume is opened with Tim Beal's invitation to practice biblical studies as an "exegesis of the limit," a reading that feels carefully along the edges of the text and the edges of the reading process itself, looking for fissures that might open new spaces for understanding or reopen old ones for thinking anew. The final chapters by Kyle Keefer and David Gunn press the question of what *is* this text – what precise books, sentences, words? Keefer opens to view the canonical boundary blurring that the ancient writings of the Pseudepigrapha manifest; and, as Linafelt argues that the margins of Lamentation have been – and will go on being – inscribed, Keefer observes that the interpretive process that germinated the Pseudepigrapha is with us, and spawning texts, yet. À *la lettre* (as Jobling might put it), David Gunn's final chapter begins with one small piece of writing, David's decapitation of the giant Goliath, in order to pose the radicality of Beal's invitation (what edges shall we choose?) and to underscore what together these essays manifest, namely that reading the Bible is a performance of the body politic (what Bible shall we choose?). This chapter marks an attempt to close the book on an open note and yet close it with a point (*un point final?*). If an exegesis of the limit discloses an unstable Bible, what difference does that make? We believe that the chapters in this volume already suggest some of the ways this question might be followed.

Unless otherwise indicated, translations of biblical and other ancient texts are those of the individual authors. Throughout, however, we have tried to ensure that anyone will be able to follow the discussions of translation and textual criticism without having any background in Hebrew or other ancient languages. One should have no trouble, furthermore, cross-referencing individual translations with any of the widely published English Bibles.

There are two issues of academic practice, both concerning proper names, that are worth singling out at this time. First, the name of God: in Hebrew Scripture it is, literally, unreadable. Scribal tradition made the vowels inscribed with the name incompatible with its consonants, *y-h-w-h* (the tetragrammaton). This practice instructed the reader to avoid pronouncing the divine name, and instead to read "Adonai" ("my lord") following the clue of the vowels rather than the consonants. The name "Jehovah" in older English Bibles was the misconceived result of trying to vocalize the consonants of the one word with the vowels of the other. Interestingly enough (and consonant with a theme of this volume), no consensus among scholars has ever emerged on how to refer to this unreadable name. Hence our authors will refer to it, variously, as "Adonai," "LORD" (in small capitals, as in the New Revised Standard Version [NRSV]), "YHWH," "Yahweh" (a standard scholarly reconstruction), "the deity," or simply "God" (although there are other Hebrew words translated as "God").

Second, there is the question of what to name the text itself (or, for that matter, the texts themselves). This body of writing does not name itself, and no particular name for it throughout the history of its interpretation has won out entirely over others. In this volume different authors will refer to it as "Bible," "Hebrew Bible," "Jewish Bible," "Scripture," "Hebrew Scripture," "Jewish Scripture," or "Old Testament." As is the case with the divine name, each naming practice indicates something (although it is not always clear what) of how one interprets it. We have chosen to maintain this diversity of naming, both for the text and the deity it inscribes, because to do so is to resist erasing precisely the sorts of identity ambiguities that our readings disclose as characteristic of this writing. The Bible is not an easily boundaried ghetto. The Bible is not one story but many.

We wish to acknowledge and thank several people who have been instrumental in bringing this book to press. Richard Stoneman, senior editor at Routledge, has offered encouragement, helpful suggestions, and kept a critical eye on the process. Texas Christian University has given crucial financial support, as has Eckerd College, and we are deeply indebted to our colleagues at both schools for their friendship, support, and provocation. We thank Claudia Camp and Ed McMahon of the Department of Religion at TCU, and Brian McCormick of Columbia Theological Seminary, for reviewing parts of the manuscript and for constructive criticism. The support and consultation of series editors Danna Nolan Fewell and Gary Phillips is also much appreciated. We thank Shirley Davis, Cyndi Child, and Stephanie Gemperline of Eckerd College for editorial assistance. Jodi O'Rear at TCU has come to our aid on numerous levels and at many stages in the process, and we are most grateful to her. We much appreciate Kathryn Kolb's talent and generosity in creating for us the cover photo. Finally, we thank our families and especially our spouses, Clover and Margaret, for important suggestions, for key conversations, and for caring enough to voice or curb their exasperations, depending on what was needed at the time.

Timothy K. Beal
Eckerd College

David M. Gunn
Texas Christian University

OPENING:

Cracking the binding

Timothy K. Beal

It's not a question of drawing the contours, *but what escapes the contour*, the secret movement, the breaking, the torment, the unexpected.

(Cixous 1993: 96)

As signs of a postmodern condition appear with increasing frequency, we find ourselves returning once again to a familiar crossroads in the study of religion. Perhaps we have never left. Perhaps we can never leave. Perhaps the dilemma it poses is as inherent in the study of religion as it is in the word itself: in what sense is religion a kind of *binding* (from the Latin, *religāre*), a being bound to a web of principles, doctrines, certainties, and in what sense is it a *process of reading again*, as Cicero suggested (*relegĕre*, "to read over again [and again]"), a continuing engagement with texts, a way of articulating, by reading/writing, the most profound questions about life and death, identity and otherness? Is religion about asserting answers or crafting questions? Throughout most of modern history, at least in the West, it mostly has been about the former, and this view has typically been favored by modern scholars of religion as well. How might it be conceived according to the "postmodern"? What new possibilities, which at the same time may be very, very ancient, will be opened?

Similar questions are arising in the study of the Bible specifically.[1] In what sense are the texts we study religious? We are all well versed at reading them in terms of their binding, that is, the binding of Scripture (literally, "writing") into The Book, The Book of books, by which its monolithic and univocal Author/Father founds a politics of religious, national, and sexual identity, and claims binding authority over all His subjects. We know about reading the binding, and groups such as the Christian Coalition, with their explicit agenda of establishing one single founding voice in Bible and in politics alike, are always there to remind us lest we forget. But is that all there is to it – the binding? As we once again open the question, the book, and the question of The Book, might that binding begin to break? Might we find not only that Scripture can provide a binding social/symbolic order, a politics of identity, but that it also opens to the possibility of its own – and our own –

1

(self) interrogation, to its own – and our own – unsettling, to "what escapes"? Is it conceivable that it does not simply serve the formation of the subject within a particular system or politics of identity? Might it also articulate a crisis in identity, a crisis that is capable of opening to new possibilities for political transformation which at the same time may be very, very ancient?

EXEGESIS OF THE LIMIT

How to open, to read again, to crack the binding? The practice that has emerged recently in biblical studies in response to these kinds of questions might be described as a kind of *deconstruction in exegesis*: through close attention to the details of the text, one may watch and document meaning undoing itself. From a distance one can see only the binding. But the closer one gets the more tiny cracks and fissures become visible – so many that one might begin to wonder whether it is about the binding or the breaking.

This sense of exegesis as a way of encountering deconstruction happening is close to Jacques Derrida's construal of deconstruction in writings such as his "Letter to a Japanese Friend" (1985: 1–8), where he describes it not as a critical practice or method (one does not deconstruct a text), but as a phenomenon of textuality.

> Deconstruction is not a method and cannot be transformed into one. . . . It must also be made clear that deconstruction is not even an *act* or *operation*. . . . Deconstruction takes place, it is an event that does not await deliberation, consciousness or organisation of a subject, or even of modernity. *It deconstructs itself.*
>
> (1985: 5)

The practice this insight invites, then, is primarily exegetical: learning how to watch it happen in texts, and being self-reflective about the process.

In biblical studies, such critical practice might be called *exegesis of the limit*. Drucilla Cornell (1992) has argued for thinking of deconstruction as "the philosophy of the limit," by which she suggests a mode of criticism that attends to the very limits of philosophical understanding and metaphysical reflection – a kind of feeling carefully along the edges of the system, from the inside, looking for cracks that might open to otherness within the Logic of Sameness. While that is a very appropriate conception of deconstruction for philosophy, deconstruction's epiphanies in biblical studies, as already noted, tend to have more to do with questions of textuality and close textual analysis. Thus I suggest that it be considered here as an *exegesis* of the limit. Indeed, I would argue that this was the greatest force of now classic deconstructions by Jacques Derrida on, for example, Hegel's prefaces and Plato's *Phaedrus* in his *Dissemination* (1981: 1–59, 61–171), where he simply reads carefully, paying close attention to the text and reflecting on the process.

The same holds true for Luce Irigaray's careful analysis and interrogation of Plato's and Freud's texts on female sexuality in her epochal *Speculum of the Other Woman* (1985: 11–129, 243–364), along with many others. By such exegetical studies these writers have offered important philosophical reflections, but they have not developed any philosophy *per se*. Much of the secondary writing on their work (in translator's prefaces, introductions, and guides) nonetheless continues trying to build comprehensive interpretations (GUTs, "grand unifying theories") of the "Derridean" or "Irigararian." That is, they attempt to bind their writing into a book.

When it comes to common assumptions about the biblical (which do not seem to be able to see deconstruction happening), it is precisely an exegesis of the limit that is critically missing, whether these assumptions come from within the field of biblical studies (if it can even be called a field anymore) or ostensibly outside it, in cultural studies, gender studies, literary theory, psychoanalysis, or whatever. The discussions in the present book, which this chapter is "opening," share a concern for analysis of such assumptions through close engagement with biblical texts, and with texts that read biblical texts. My "opening" here is not so much a conventional introduction, aimed at leading readers in and through the "main body" of the book. Rather, it is a more modest first opening of a space for such an analysis and (self) reflection – an initial opening of a field of questions that will lead inevitably toward opening what many seem to assume is a closed question: the question of The Book.

BIBLE, SYSTEM, AND SPEAKING SUBJECT

In *New Maladies of the Soul* (1995), Julia Kristeva returns to the Bible, to read it again, and proposes an approach that is particularly suggestive with regard to an exegesis of the limits of biblical discourse (both within biblical texts and in contemporary discourses about them).[2] While drawing from many of the insights offered by structuralist analyses (whether anthropological, such as Douglas's, or more "semiological," such as Soler's), she criticizes them for not going beyond "specifying the profound logic" (i.e., the system) of the text as a network or encodement of differences to attend to "the linguistic subject of the biblical utterance." When one analyzes not only the system but also its speaking subject, one discovers

> a subject who is not at all neutral and indifferent like the subject described by modern theories of interpretation, but who maintains a specific relationship of *crisis*, *trial*, or *process* with his God.
>
> (Kristeva 1995: 117)

When approached in this way, biblical literature presents not only a "profound logic" but also a speaking subject, in the form of a biblical narrator, who is by no means a "neutral" or "impenetrable point that guarantees the universality of logical operations" (1995: 117), but is, rather, a "subject on trial," in the process of its own formation and susceptible to breakdown, fracture, dislocation. This "new space" of the speaking subject, Kristeva proposes, is the "subjective" and therefore "analyzable space" of the text (1995: 118).

By the Bible, it should be noted, Kristeva refers here primarily and almost exclusively to the discourse on abominations in Leviticus, as she did in *Powers of Horror* (1982, on which see Beal 1994; for a brilliant analysis of Song of Songs, see Kristeva 1987). In these Levitical texts, the speaking subject is "delineating the precise limits of abjection (from skin to food, sex, and moral codes)," and thus is marking the borders of the inside and the outside, self and not-self. Like psychoanalysis, then, this literature sees "abjection as necessary for the advent of the subject as a speaking being" (Kristeva 1995: 118). In this particular biblical discourse, the reader is allowed to watch the emergence and gradual formation of identity through speech (the biblical narrator's, as speaking subject) within a particular social and symbolic order, "a true archeology of the advent of the subject" (1995: 119).

By approaching biblical discourse in this way, moreover, focusing on the trials of a subject in process, one recognizes that the subject was not always already solid or securely located within the system, and therefore that identity is always in certain ways fragile, vulnerable to breakdown and collapse. Thus, for example, Kristeva suggests that elsewhere in the Bible, particularly in Isaiah which she reads as a "mutation of abjection," the reader finds the Levitical system breaking down and the abject collapsing back in on the prophet as speaking subject and on the people of Israel as a whole (1982: 108).

Kristeva's proposal and interpretation are very compelling, and demonstrate the continuing value of engaging psychoanalytic approaches within biblical studies. Yet I do not believe that this approach goes far enough as an exegesis of the limit, because it inadvertently protects the Bible's *theological* dimensions from trial and even crisis, and therefore protects the binding from the most remarkable kind of fissuring and self-interrogation.

On Kristeva's reading, which is very much in line with both Freud and Lacan in its construal of biblical theology, the social and symbolic order of the Bible has as its centerpiece, foundation, and guarantor the One God, whose divine prohibition against the mother (the Law/No of the Father) is the basis for the formation of identity. In this way biblical monotheism is understood in traditional psychoanalysis primarily as "the imposition of a *strategy of identity*" (Kristeva 1982: 94). Such a reading can allow the reader to reflect on the biblical narrator's identity crisis, but it may not be able to allow reflection on representations in the Bible of the *divine speaking subject on trial*. Therefore I propose to follow the path mapped by Kristeva further than she has taken it, perhaps further than it can be taken in accord with psychoanalytic orthodoxy, into the analyzable space of the divine speaking subject of the text.

Kristeva rightly argues that Leviticus "delineates the precise limits of abjection" and thereby offers an archeology of the advent of identity in biblical discourse. Other biblical texts, however, especially the prophets, articulate a crisis in that identity, as the Levitical order begins to fracture and lose its holding power. Insofar as *God's identity is bound up with Israel's identity*, in Levitical discourse and in other order-creating "legal" texts, such prophetic texts often represent the *undelineation* of order and meaning to such an extent that crisis and even disolution occur for the divine speaking subject as well as for the prophet.

GOD AND ABJECTION

There are multiple levels of subjectivity in biblical discourse. It should be remembered that in Leviticus, Kristeva's speaking subject, the biblical narrator who is "manifested in the figure of the text itself" (Kristeva 1995: 117), is narrating the voice of another speaking subject, namely YHWH.[3] So are the prophets. Thus this discourse also offers an archeology of the advent of the *divine* speaking subject, whose identity within the world of the text (even from an orthodox Jewish or Christiain theological perspective) is taking form in covenantal relation with Israel through this very same order-creating speech. Insofar as an analytic approach continues to keep a theological space, the space of divine speaking subject in the Bible, unanalyzable, closed off from such interrogation, it cannot comprehend the full impact of the subjective crisis articulated by the Bible.

Consider, for example, Micah 1:8–9:

> Over this I will lament and howl;
> I will go stripped[4] and naked;
> I will make lament like the jackals;
> and mourning like the ostrich.
> For her disease is incurable.
> Indeed, it has come as far as Judah;
> it has touched even as far as the gate of my people – as far as
>   Jerusalem.
>
> (translation mine)

In an earlier essay (Beal 1994), I showed how this passage can be read as a representation of the divine speaking subject on trial, in a profound crisis brought about by the fracture of that subject's covenantal relation with the people of Israel. In this prophetic discourse, abjection – which is externalized and pushed outside the borders of the camp (and therefore of identity) in Leviticus – collapses back into the system, touching even the divine center, and spoiling the borders. To make this argument, however, I had to argue first that this passage is in fact the prophet's representation of divine speech rather than his own reaction to the divine speech of the preceding verses (from "All her idols I shall lay waste . . . as the wages of a prostitute they shall again be used" [verse 7] to "Over this I shall lament and wail . . ." [verse 8]). With the remote exception of Saint Jerome, scholars have invariably identified the speaking subject as the prophet,[5] positing a shift from YHWH (who has been speaking since verse 5) to Micah at verse 8, introduced by the phrase 'al – zo't ("over this"). The subject of the first-person verbs ("I will lament ['espedah] . . . howl ['elilah] . . . go ['elkah] . . . make lament and mourning ['e'eseh misped . . . we'ebel]"), as well as of the possessive in the phrase "my people" ('ammî), is the prophet, and verse 8 is the beginning of a new utterance, which will continue through the end of Chapter 1.

Yet the text gives such little support for this identification of the prophet rather than YHWH as the speaking subject of verses 8–9 that I am led to conclude that its motivation can only be a theological restriction which makes it impossible to imagine such dirge-like, anomalous behavior in the character of YHWH. That is, the constraints on such a reading are found in the culture of biblical interpretation rather than in the text itself. In his lectures on thinking (Was Heisst Denken? Lecture IV), Heidegger suggested that one read Nietzsche as a scream. I would suggest that one read this and other prophetic passages as divine screams.

Is the passage Micah's speech or the prophet's representation of divine speech? First, the only explicit argument offered in support of the former view depends upon assimilating this passage to a literary set piece, the "prophetic reaction to bad news" (Jeremiah 6:24; 30:5–6; 49:23; 50:43; Isaiah 13:1–8; 21:3–4; Habakkuk 3:16; and Ezekiel 21:11–12; see Hillers 1965: 86–90; and 1984: 23). But the passage contains none of the four principle elements typical of this convention (Beal 1994: 179), where, moreover, there is always a clear transition from the bad news to the prophet's reaction (usually introduced by "When I/they/he heard . . ."), and where the reaction is typically narrated as a past event. In Micah 1:8, by contrast, the speech continues uninterrupted in the first person of future action (Hebrew "imperfect"), as it did throughout YHWH'S speech in the preceding verses, with no comment that anyone has "heard" and will now react.[6]

Second, the phrase that begins verse 8, 'al – zo't ("over this"), does not typically mark a shift from one speaker to another (see, e.g., Amos 8:8; Jeremiah 4:28; 5:9; 5:29; 9:8; Isaiah 57:6; 64:11; cf. Psalm 32:6), but more commonly marks a transition within a single speech, from the speaker's description of the state of things to that speaker's declaration concerning what will happen as a result.[7] (It is worth noting that the more common phrase in prophetic literature, 'al – ken, usually translated "therefore," also marks transition in a single speech more frequently than it does a shift from one speaker to another.)

Third, the first clear instance of the prophet as subject (using first-person speech) in Micah is not found until 3:8, where he justifies his prophetic task by the claim that he is filled with the power of YHWH's spirit. (All previous first-person speech is most easily read as the prophet's narration of divine speech.) Fourth, the phrase "gate of my people" in verse 9 occurs only one other time in the prophetic literature (Obadiah 13), and there it is spoken by YHWH. "My people" ('*ammi*), moreover, is nearly always spoken by YHWH; of the 109 times it occurs in the prophetic literature, it refers clearly to the *prophet's* people only five times.[8]

Finally, the fact that there is some theological anxiety concerning our passage is attested by the variant readings in other ancient (non-Masoretic Hebrew) versions of the text. The Greek Septuagint, for example, puts the verbs in the third-person feminine singular ("she will lament and howl"), whereas the Targum (an Aramaic revision/translation) uses third-person plurals ("they will lament and howl"). The Syriac version, on the other hand, uses second-person feminine singular imperatives ("lament-ye [Samaria], and howl"). In each case the variant achieves the same end: verses 8–16 are rendered as a continuation of YHWH's speech in verses 5–7, so that a shift from YHWH to the prophet at verse 8, and then back to YHWH again by verse 15, is no longer needed; and ambiguity concerning who the one lamenting might be is significantly diminished. That is, in each of these versions, a reading of YHWH as the one lamenting and wailing is no longer possible (YHWH is the speaker but tells someone else to lament, howl, wail, etc.). In the other versions, then, one finds traces of anxiety concerning who the "I" of this text might be. And the more one focuses on these traces, the more ruptures emerge in the dominant reading.

There are, then, no ostensible markers for a shift in speaking subject, from YHWH's voice to the prophet's, at verse 8. In the material preceding verses 8–9, one reads of YHWH's coming and YHWH's description – all in first-person verbs – of the violent destruction that will be brought to Samaria. This first-person description leads straight into verse 8, without so much as a *ne'um yhwh* ("an oracle of YHWH"), an *'amar yhwh* ("says YHWH"), or any other concluding remark. YHWH now laments and wails, going stripped and naked. In relation to the previous verses, this reveals a radical ambivalence in the divine speaking subject.

As we continue into verse 9 to open this new space further,[9] it becomes clear that YHWH's wailing and lamenting and mourning are linked to the lamentable state of YHWH's people. As will soon be seen, although most translators render verse 9 in terms of YHWH's destructive behavior described in the previous verses (thus *'anushah makkoteyha* is translated "her incurable wound" or emended to the "blow of YHWH," and *naga'* is "reached," suggesting the forward movement of YHWH's affront, from Samaria through Judah to Jerusalem), the more common senses – plague-related "disease" for *makkoteyha*, and "touched" for *naga'* – elicit an entirely different sense.

The discussion of skin diseases in Leviticus 13–14, where "leprous disease" is described as a "*touch [nega']* of leprosy," opens up some suggestive intertextual relations. *Mikwat*, which is identical to "disease" (*mkwt*) in our text in its unvocalized written form, refers to a certain kind of "leprous touch" in Leviticus 13 (cf. Hosea 4:2, where "bloods upon bloods spread/ touch [again *naga‘*]"). Thus we are closer to Kristeva's primary text for analysis (Levitical discourse on abjection) than we might have initially imagined.

In this light, a strong link emerges between YHWH's wailing, lamenting, and mourning in verse 8 on the one hand, and the *abject state* of YHWH's people in verse 9 on the other. YHWH laments, going stripped and naked among the people, for they are plagued. An incurable disease is spreading. It has spread so far as to touch (*naga‘ ‘ad*) the gate of YHWH's people, Jerusalem. The abject, which is pushed outside the camp in Leviticus, has returned, and threatens the entire social order. It has reached the center. Abject and subject stumble over one another in pandemonium. Order collapses. The divine speaking subject of that order dirges.

YHWH's dirge is described by two similes which push this sense of abjection so far as to touch even the one who wails: YHWH will "make lament like the jackals" and "mourning like the ostriches." Noisy jackals are pictured elsewhere in the prophets as the only survivors of destruction, notably in Isaiah and most powerfully in Jeremiah, where the uninhabited ruins of Jerusalem, Babylon, and Hazor become lairs for jackals (9:11; 10:22; 49:33; 51:37; cf. 14:6). That YHWH will lament like the jackals, then, conjures up the earlier scene of devastation and ruin. Like the jackals, YHWH will roam through the cities, among the piles of unclean corpses, his howls echoing through the barren buildings.

In Isaiah, the presence of jackals in the city carries the same connotation (13:22; 35:7). Twice, moreover, they are depicted along with ostriches (34:13; 43:20). Such usage, of course, intensifies the connotation of ruin and destruction in Micah 1:8. But with the ostrich, an additional sense is suggested. Aside from Isaiah, Micah, and Jeremiah, two of the three other references to these birds are in lists of "unclean" (*tame’*) birds (Deuteronomy 14:15 and Leviticus 11:16).[10] A generally accepted reason for abominating these birds is that they – like jackals – eat·carrion. YHWH is crying out like such an "unclean" creature, a devourer of the dead. The sense of the abject in YHWH's behavior is accentuated. Stripped and naked, YHWH howls among the carrion – YHWH, God. The dirge is unordinary (unorderly, anomalous). As the abominable disease spreads, as the structure begins to collapse, YHWH internalizes abjection.

NEW SPACE

I have read YHWH as the ambivalent speaking subject of an abjectionable dirge over the disease-ridden Judah. As such, the divine character in this prophetic discourse is rendered entirely ambivalent, sweeping through and among the people with all the rage and all the grief of absolute disorientation. And why not? The people have abandoned the structure that YHWH established, within which YHWH is the principle subject. YHWH has been *dispositioned*. Understood thus, the book of Micah opens with a theophany of, in Kristeva's terms (1986a: 30), a "subject on trial," brought about by the "fracture of a symbolic code which can no longer 'hold' its (speaking) subjects." When this reading of Micah 1 is placed in relation with Kristeva's reading of the discourse on abjection in Leviticus, one finds the very character of God breaking down, threatening total break down in the entire biblical symbolic order. A tremor runs through The Book.

The "analyzable space" of the divine speaking subject I have opened here is certainly very strange, and estranged, even disconcerting. It is also radical within Hebrew Scripture, and yet not without compare. When Micah 1:8–9 is read with YHWH as the speaking subject, texts that are often cited as "parallel" prophetic discourses (where the prophet reacts to bad news announced by YHWH; e.g., Jeremiah 8:23 and Isaiah 22:4) fall away, and a new intertextual space for analysis emerges. Perhaps the most obvious parallel is Jeremiah 48:30–33:

> Therefore [*'al ken*] I howl [*'elil*] for Moab;
> I cry out for all Moab; for the people of Kirhe'res I mourn;
> More than for Ja'zer I weep for you, O vine of Sibmah!
> Your branches crossed over the sea, and reached as far
> as [*naga'u 'ad*] Ja'zer...
>
> (verses 31–32a)

In this text we find the only other instance in the Hebrew Bible, besides Micah 1:8, of "howl" (*'elil*; root, *y-l-l*) in the first person, and it is clearly YHWH who speaks it. Moreover, there are several formal similarities between this text and Micah 1:8–9.[11] First, YHWH's announcement that YHWH will howl, cry, mourn, and weep is introduced by *'al ken*, which, while not identical to *'al zo't*, serves a similar rhetorical function within the passage. Second, the howling/lament is preceded by YHWH's claim against those whom the lament concerns (cf. Micah 1:5). Third, the howling/lament is followed by YHWH's statement that the branches of Sibmah have "reached as far as" (*naga'u 'ad*) Ja'zer; similarly, YHWH's bewailing in Micah 1:8 is followed by a declaration that the plague "has touched as far as" (*naga' 'ad*) Jerusalem. And finally, this divine wailing over Moab stands in tension with the wrathful decimation YHWH readily admits to bringing on in the preceding verses; this is clearly the case in Micah as well. Thus, in both of these intensely passionate prophetic discourses, we find YHWH making radical shifts between devastating wrath on the one hand and wild dirge-like lament on the other. As YHWH's subject position shifts back and forth, a profound divine ambivalence erupts.

9

Another parallel, I suggest, is the first-person declaration by YHWH in Isaiah 42:14. Here, as Phyllis Trible masterfully puts it, "historical chaos becomes divine labor pains" (1978: 64).

> Now I will cry out like a woman in labor;
> I will gasp and pant.

The previous image of YHWH in Isaiah 42 is as a mighty warrior, "crying out" and "shouting aloud," stirring up fury (verse 13). Thus here, as in Micah 1:8, there is an abrupt shift in metaphorical description, suggesting subjective ambivalence. Isaiah has earlier used the image of a woman crying out in labor to describe the reactions of the people of Babylon (13:6–8) and the prophet (21:3–4) to YHWH's judgment. Now, as in Micah 1:8–9 (see verses 11 and 16), there is a reversal in which YHWH does what the people and prophet have been (or should have been) doing. Both passages (dirge-like lamenter and woman in labor) are uncommon in relation to YHWH, and both describe a physical state that is in some way liminal or unordinary.

For Kristeva, as noted earlier, it is precisely the prohibition of access to and identification with the mother that is at the heart of biblical monotheism's "strategy of identity" with the Law of the Father. "I have come to realize that the object excluded by these rules [in Leviticus], whatever form it may take in biblical narrative, is ultimately the mother" (1995: 118; cf. 1982). Texts in which the prophet conceives of himself as having birth pains, in Isaiah and elsewhere, would support Kristeva's reading of the prophetic texts as "mutations of abjection," insofar as the mother is the ultimate object that stands behind the biblical system of abjection. That God would be represented in such a way, however, pushes this "mutation" much further, into theological space, the space of the divine speaking subject. This representation gives voice to a more radical disorientation than can be saved by a return to the Father, whose epiphany here is literally as the *speaking subject in travail*.

SHUDDER TO THINK

In returning to read the Bible again, Kristeva opens a new and at the same time very ancient space for analysis – beyond strict focus on the system to analysis of the speaking subject of that system (i.e., the biblical narrator). I have tried to open this new space onto another, contingent theological space – that of the divine speaking subject as represented in biblical discourse. In this new intertextual, theological space of the divine speaking subject, one may reflect on the most radical articulations of subjective crisis and trial, articulations that touch and even destabilize the very foundations of "biblical monotheism" as sometimes imagined in psychoanalytic theory – and, for that matter (not without irony), in biblical fundamentalism as well.

In what sense is this religious literature? Is its "sacred value" only, or even primarily, to be found in its cathartic, purifying capacity, locating and identifying me, providing "a place that gives meaning to these crises of subjectivity" (Kristeva 1995: 119)? Or can there be sacred value in its ungrounding, unbinding spaces as well? Is it simply an ingenious network or web of meaning, or does it also evoke, as Kierkegaard put it in his reading of the binding of Isaac in *Fear and Trembling*, a "shudder of thought"?

What, or where, is the sacred space of texts? In binding or loosing, filling or emptying, settling or unsettling, meaning or the shudder? Or is there always some endlessly uncomfortable and profoundly ambivalent oscillation between the two?

The chapters in this book open important spaces for analysis and interrogation in biblical discourse, both within the text itself and in discourses "on" the Bible. Although they each negotiate the binding and the cracking differently, collectively they call common assumptions and simplistic readings of "the biblical" (God, law, "The Book" itself) into question.

We will do well to read again, to risk opening new spaces and reopening old ones (which we thought we knew) for analysis and reflection. To watch closely what happens in these spaces, to think hard, to be self-reflective and to allow the text to be self-reflective too. To resist panicked flight from the hall of mirrors as it emerges, and to wonder why we would want to flee.

NOTES

1 My colleague Brent Plate is following a strikingly similar line of thinking in his religious (re)reading of Blanchot's re-citations of the limit (Plate forthcoming).

2 I am thankful to Danna Nolan Fewell for referring me to this new work, which both reiterates and builds on Kristeva's study of Leviticus in *Powers of Horror* (1982). See also Fewell in this volume. For a fuller discussion of Kristeva's earlier work on the Bible and abjection, see Beal (1994: 171–89). Thanks also to Jim Goetsch for the Heidegger reference (see below).

3 Both the biblical narrator and YHWH are, of course, such textual "manifestations."

4 I am reading the Qere. The sense is close to the verb *shalal*, "plunder," which then relates well with the previous description.

5 Among these scholars are: Allen (1976: 274–75); Budde (1917/18: 79–81); Calvin (1950 [1559]: 171–72); Cheyne (1882: 20); Elliger (1934: 136–39); Fretheim (1984: 135, 161); Hagstrom (1988: 46); Hillers (1984: 22–23); Keil (1954 [1885]: 429–30); Mays (1976: 50–56); Nowack (1903: 209–10); Rudolph (1975: 42–43); Shaw (1990: 64, 68); Smith (1928: 381–82); Stansell (1988: 41); Ungern-Sternberg (1958: 32–34); Weiser (1959: 240); and Wolff (1990 [1982]: 58–59). As Rudolph notes (1975: 42 n. 18), one isolated exception is Jerome's *Commentaria in Michaeam Prophetam* (in Migne's *Patrologiae cursus completus, Series Latina* 25), who reads verse 8 as divine speech.

6 The other set of parallels cited by Hillers (1984: 23) is equally problematic. In Isaiah 22, it is not at all clear that YHWH was speaking before the prophet describes (again in the perfect tense) his reaction. There is no first-person speech in the previous oracle. In fact, the scene from 22:1 on appears to be spoken in its entirety as an oracle from the prophet himself. Finally, there are no substantial lexical connections

between this passage and Micah 1. Neither are there any lexical or formal parallels between Micah 1:8–9 and Jeremiah 8:23. Indeed, this text is particularly problematic as a parallel, because while the previous speech is clearly YHWH's (concluding with *ne'um yhwh*, "an oracle of YHWH," verse 17), the subsequent lament contains additional speech that is most easily read as YHWH's – namely, "Why have they provoked me to anger with their foreign idols?" (Jeremiah 8:19).

7 The only exception I have found is Jeremiah 31:26, in which Jeremiah awakes from a dream after receiving a hopeful vision from YHWH. Here there is a clear shift; however, it is not a dialogical shift from YHWH to Jeremiah, but rather a shift from YHWH's speech to a past-tense narration of Jeremiah's action ("Thereupon I awoke and looked . . .").

8 Of these five instances, four occur in Jeremiah 8:18–9:2 (English trans., 8:18–9:3), a text whose speaker, as we have already noted, is extremely difficult to identify. The only other clear usage of *'ammî* by a prophet is found in Isaiah 22:4 (Isaiah 10:2 is marginal).

9 Given the rhetorical flow of the text (*'al – zo't . . . ki*, "on account of this . . . because"), it is important to read verse 8 together with verse 9.

10 The other occurrence is in Job 30:29, where Job claims that ostriches and jackals are his only companions. This suggests a sense similar to that in Isaiah and Jeremiah. Note also that Job's state, after being "touched" (again, *naga'*, 2:5) by a horrible skin disease "from the sole of his foot to his head" (2:7), might well be characterized in terms of abjection.

11 It is further noted that the action verbs used in Micah 1:8 ("wail/howl [*yll*]," "lament" [*spd*], and "mourn" [*'bl*]) occur primarily in the third-person plural form. They occur with the prophet as their subject very rarely, and then only as second person imperatives from YHWH (Jeremiah 4:8; Ezekiel 21:12, 24:16, 23; 30:2). *'bl* is somewhat exceptional, in that it is often used to describe the mourning of the land as a result of the people's transgressions.

PART I

GLEANINGS

In a sense the humans have led God out of paradise. Why does God follow? . . . There is no return to simplicity, for human beings or for God.

Danna Nolan Fewell and David M. Gunn

The human body, then, was the site at which conflicting cultural impulses met and clashed. It was that conflict that made the Jews more than just a People of the Book. They also became a People of the Body.

Howard Eilberg-Schwartz

The Father's disappointment in his children appears to be mirrored by his daughters' disappointment in him! Ironically, the information concerning this muted (minority?) view of the 'daughters' is preserved by the patriarchal YHWH opposition to it.

Athalya Brenner

Moses may wield God's rod, but never its power. For Freud, Oedipus wrecks. So too for Moses.

Ilona N. Rashkow

To call God Sophia is not on the same level as calling God a mother hen. Sophia is a powerful naming, a root metaphor, that names God with the same fullness as the name Jesus Christ.

Claudia V. Camp

DIVINE BODIES

This part focuses on questions concerning the characteristics and problematics (and problematic characteristics) of God's identity in biblical literature and in the religious communities that read it. What is "the image of God"? What are the implications of putting God into writing? Insofar as biblical texts often use metaphors that involve language of the body, what are the implications of God's incorporation into Scripture? Is God's inscription (being put into writing) also God's embodiment (a "theological corpus")? Relatedly, how is divine subjectivity entangled in issues of sameness and difference? How does biblical literature struggle with these conundrums? How do "people of the Book" struggle with them? How do such problematics constrain and/or empower theological discourse in contemporary politics?

1

SHIFTING THE BLAME

God in the Garden[1]

Danna Nolan Fewell and David M. Gunn

And God created humankind in his own image, in the image of God he created it, male and female he created them. And God blessed them, and God said to them, "Be fruitful and multiply, and fill the earth and subdue it; and subjugate . . ." And God saw everything that he had done, and behold, it was very good.

(Genesis 1:27–28, 31)

Then YHWH God said, "It is not good that the human should be alone; I will make it a helper, a counterpart for it."

(Genesis 2:18)

And the human said: "This at last is bone of my bones and flesh of my flesh; this shall be called 'woman,' because from man was this taken." (Hence a man forsakes his father and his mother and cleaves to his woman, so that they become one flesh.)

(Genesis 2:23–24)

And God said: "Have you eaten from the tree of which I said not to eat?" The man said, "The woman whom you gave to be with me, she gave me fruit of the tree, and I ate." And YHWH God said to the woman, "What is this that you have done?" And the woman said, "The serpent beguiled me, and I ate." And YHWH God said to the serpent. . . .

(Genesis 3:12–14)

For good and evil, Genesis 1–3, perhaps more than any other biblical text, has influenced the way men and women relate to one another in the Western world. For good and evil – because good and evil have a way of changing their spots, as this text invites us to see.

The story is about the origins of humankind. It is also a story about the divinity, God, or YHWH God, as the narrator goes on to call him (we use the masculine pronoun advisedly) in chapter 2. Indeed we could say

16

that God is the dominant character in this story of origins. Yet curiously, while commentators over the centuries have had an overabundance of observations to make about the character of the humans, and especially of Eve, whose failings have provided them with rich pickings, they have been remarkably reticent regarding the character of YHWH and, in particular, notably reluctant to put the deity under the same kind of critical scrutiny as the humans.

As any family therapist worth their salt would want to ask, however, how can you understand the children without understanding something of the parents and the interrelational dynamics of all? Families are systems. So here we have a story of what appears to be a single parent family, a family which, the narrator suggests, enjoys a measure of dysfunction (which some theologians have termed "The Fall"). If we wish to understand the daughter and son, Eve and Adam, it makes sense to take a searching look at this curious figure who seems to function as their father, namely God.

He is a talker. He talks the world into existence.

He appreciates the need for rest. Sabbath marks the culmination of creation.

He has a strong penchant for order. The story begins in Genesis 1 with a strong bias towards the binary. God divides up the world in clear categories: light and dark, day and night, wet and dry, plants and animals, heaven and earth. We see a desire to divide, differentiate, categorize and, in a word, name. Of course, differentiation could be said to be indispensable to creation. Certainly separation, division, difference is indispensable to meaning. Meaning *is* difference. A world that is no longer simply *tohu vabohu* ("a formless void," New English Bible) is a world of difference. Naming, the shaping of the world in language, is the manipulation of difference. Naming is the prerequisite of a meaningfully ordered world. Naming, as is often observed of this account, may also be an expression of control.

On the other hand, when the account reaches a climax with the creation of humankind, that is, the creature in the image of God (Genesis 1:26–30), we see movement against that desire to differentiate. Blurring the binary poles, God desires to create likeness or sameness, to recreate self, a desire impossible to achieve.

Equally interesting are the sharp edges of God's naming. The binary impulse is there very clearly. Yet in all this careful defining, separating, and opposing there is a curious slippage. God "himself" is unsure whether he is plural or singular, echoing the narrator's grammatical confusion of a plural name (*'elohim*, which may or may not be a proper noun!) and a singular verb (Genesis 1:26–29):[2]

Then God(s) [or "divinity"] said [sing.] "Let us make humankind in our image, after our likeness" ... So God(s) created [sing.] humankind in his own image, in the image of God(s) he created him, male and

17

female he created them . . . And God(s) said, "Behold, I have given you
[pl.] . . . ."

Significantly the slippage extends from the God(s) to the human(s) created
in his/their image. While humankind is one (him/it) it is also plural – male
and female (them).

Thus, despite the appearance of a world ordered and sustained by exclusive and fixed definitions, God's own blurred and slipping self-definition
suggests that things might be otherwise. This world might in fact be as
inherently indeterminable as the identity that creates it.

Within this system of divisions and separations, God begins to institute a
hierarchy of dominion: the greater light is to rule over the day, the lesser
light over the night. At the creation of the human, however, the language of
dominion grows stronger (1:26–28, 31):

> And God said, "Let us make humankind in our own image, after our
> likeness; and let them subjugate [*radah*: trample, put under foot] the
> fish of the sea and the birds of the air, and the cattle, and all the earth,
> and every creeping thing that creeps upon the earth." And God created
> humankind in his own image, in the image of God he created it, male
> and female he created them. And God blessed them, and God said to
> them, "Be fruitful and multiply, and fill the earth and subdue it
> [*kabash*: bring into bondage]; and subjugate all fish of the sea and birds
> of the air and every living thing that moves upon the earth." . . . And
> God saw everything that he had done, and behold, it was very good.

Rule, subjugate, subdue. The language is, disturbingly, the language of totali-
tarian power, as others have observed. It would be at home, for example, in
the Assyrian imperial annals. Humankind's first mandate is to subdue the
earth and subjugate every living thing that moves upon it. Not to cooperate
with, be partners with, share with, but bring into bondage and subjugate.
On the other hand, God seems to envision this subjugation as a blessing for
the humans, along with being fruitful and multiplying and filling the earth,
which lead to the instruction to subjugate.

"And God saw that it was good." That constant refrain speaks of discovery. This creator God is plainly not, as Christian theology would have it,
omniscient. He does/says something new, observes it, and remarks upon his
discovery: "it is good!" God is experimenting. God desires to explore. God
desires something new and greets with enthusiasm each new discovery of his
own handiwork. By the same token we suspect that there may come a point
when he will exclaim "it is not good!" And indeed God does so in chapter 2:
"It is not good," he finally admits, after trying out a single human being,
"that the human [*ha'adam*] should be alone." This, too, is a discovery on
God's part.

18

The very phrase, "not good," however, reminds us that meaning cannot simply be confined within binary terms. The true opposite of "good" is "evil." Intriguingly, the narrator manages in chapter 1 to insist repeatedly that God's creative differentiations are good without ever mentioning the term evil. That is kept out of sight until chapter 2. Some readers, on the other hand, may have already begun to wonder whether, in the face of such protestations of goodness, somewhere there must be evil, even if only in the imagination of God's heart (cf. the discussion within Jewish mysticism [Kabbalah]). They might also have begun to wonder whether evil is already latent in that ordered world as an expression of God's desire for himself to have dominion over the earth and for his viceroy, the creature made in his image, to subjugate all living things. The desire to subjugate is an ethically ambiguous one, for it may mean the desire to subjugate good (where subjugation is evil) or to subjugate evil (where subjugation is good).

> And YHWH God planted a garden in Eden, in the east, and put there the human whom he had formed. And he made grow from the ground every tree that is pleasant to look at and good to eat – and the tree of life was also in the midst of the garden, and the tree of the knowledge of good and evil.
>
> (Genesis 2:8–9)

So the story confirms that this discriminating God does indeed know good and evil, though clearly his eagerness to proclaim his own work as "good" suggests that he desires good rather than evil.

In Genesis 1 (through 2:4a) the narrator has opened up a broad and highly schematized view of creation. From 2:4b, the account takes a different shape and the focus falls upon a particular category of creation: the human.[3]

> On the day that YHWH God made the earth and the heavens . . . YHWH God formed the human, dust of the ground, and blew into its [his] nostrils the breath of life, and the human became a living being . . . And YHWH God took the human and put it [him] in the garden of Eden to till it and tend it.
>
> (Genesis 2:4, 7, 15)

Although the new episode goes on to present the human divided into its binaries, man and woman, it deals little with *biological* difference. In 1:26–30, the narrator has recounted the creation of the male and female of humankind in order to show how humankind as a species is to be fruitful and multiply – so as to fill the earth and subjugate it (cf. Bird 1981). In Genesis 2–3 it is gender that is under construction: here the *social* roles of man and woman are being defined. And what we shall discover is that, as usual, binaries are less equal than they at first appear. The apparent (biological) equity of Genesis 1:27 ("in the image of God he created them; male and female he created them") dissolves under closer scrutiny. Simple binaries in fact lend themselves to hierarchies. One term becomes Subject and Norm, the other becomes Object and Other. And hierarchy has a cunning way of ordering, of putting and keeping things – and people – in their "proper" place.

Let us trace the story further as it tells of God and humankind in the garden. Two trees grow at the center of the garden. The fruit from the tree of life is at first freely available (though it is not clear that the human knows of it). The other tree's fruit has not been put at the human's disposal. God's first words to the human, therefore, are characteristically authoritarian. He permits and prohibits (2:16–17).

> And YHWH God commanded the human, "You may certainly eat from any tree of the garden, but from the tree of the knowledge of good and evil you shall not eat, for the day you eat from it you shall certainly die."

The forbidden tree has been put before the human and named: the knowledge of good and evil. But to what purpose? This, after all, is a highly ambiguous gesture by God. Some have answered that the point is to instill trust. Perhaps so. But we could equally as well identify the action – as Francis Landy (1983: 188) suggests in his wonderfully rich (and, for us, influential) reading between the texts of Genesis 2–3 and the Song of Songs – as temptation. "Do not seek this knowledge," God tantalizes, "trust me!" "Stay ignorant – or seek it at your own risk!"

Of course, one might argue that God has no well-conceived plan for either of the trees. The narrator seems reluctant to implicate God in their planting. While God plants every tree that is a delight to see and good to eat, the narrator says, somewhat remotely, "the tree of life was in the midst of the garden as well as the tree of the knowledge of good and evil." God himself says that the latter tree is *not* good for food – "if you eat of it you will die" – thus further distinguishing it from the trees God is said to have planted. Perhaps God's control of the design and contents of this garden is less than complete. Certainly the serpent's later behavior will suggest this to be the case.

For most commentators, however, the issue is not one of control but of authority. As Walter Brueggemann (1982: 46) puts it:

> There is a *prohibition* (v. 17). Nothing is explained. The story has no interest in the character of the tree. What counts is the fact of the prohibition, the authority of the one who speaks and the unqualified expectation of obedience.

We are less sure than Brueggemann about the story's lack of interest in the tree. The tree is specifically labeled an intriguing name, by both the narrator (2:9) and God (2:17). Moreover, it turns out that to eat of it is not only to acquire the knowledge of good and evil but to "become *like God*, knowing good and evil" (3:22). Those characteristics are not incidentally mentioned, but proposed in due course by the serpent in a key speech (3:4) and confirmed by God (3:22). On the contrary, then, the character of the tree may be, for some readers, far from inconsequential. To block the question about the tree is to block a troubling question about God. Why does God put (or allow) this particular tree in the garden in the first place? We shall return to this question in due course.

After he has formed and placed the human in the garden, YHWH God then decides that

It is not good that the human should be alone; I will make it [him] a helper, counterpart [keneged; "like–opposite"] for it [him].

(2:18)

Despite God's own presence, despite the fact that the human, made in God's image, is arguably the deity's counterpart (like–opposite him), the deity deems the human to be alone. The implication, of course, is that God is deeming himself to be still alone.[4]

God's sense of the creature in his own image is ambivalent. Is it like or unlike him? Is the human a suitable counterpart for God or not? Or, to put it the other way around, is God a suitable counterpart for the human or not? Either way, God decides not. The sense of separation wins over the sense of sameness. Is that because the human is silent before God's commands? Does God seek response – or diversity in unity, like himself? (Of course, another reason why a helper is sought might be in order to produce fruitfulness and multiplication through division into male and female.)

God therefore forms the animals and parades them before the human, like gifts before a monarch, "to see what it [he] would call them." Confident that the human will replicate God's own desire to name, God is not disappointed. Yet the experiment fails in its main purpose, for a counterpart is not found. Perhaps the human is unwilling (or unable) to recognize the animals as counterparts because, like God, the human desires its own image. God reverts, therefore, to division. Man and woman are created. Likeness is conjured by separation. Male and female. Opposite and alike. Difference and sameness. Other and self.

So YHWH God caused a deep sleep to fall upon the human [ha'adam], and while he slept took one of its [his] sides and closed up its place with flesh; and the side which YHWH God had taken from the human he made into a woman and brought her to the human. And the human said:

"This at last is bone of my bones and flesh of my flesh;
this shall be called 'woman' ['ishshah]
because from man ['ish] was taken this."

(Genesis 2:21–23)

21

In other words, the effect of this new experiment is spectacular. The man formed from the human claims the woman, also formed from the human, as his own. Presumably he finds in her a suitable helper (partner?) because she is, as he puts it, bone of his bones and flesh of his flesh. On the other hand, as Landy wryly observes, this experiment, too, is a failure: though woman successfully supersedes the inadequate animals, she *is* the human. The human is thus still alone (Landy 1983: 234)! The desire for relationship with a like–opposite is therefore both fulfilled and unfulfilled, fulfillable and unfulfillable, in the case of the human as in the case of God.

The passage invites us to ponder the character of God a little further. We may by this stage in the story have decided that the deity's uncertain self-perception about being singular or plural may have been settled when the narrator begins (from Genesis 2:4 on) to use a name that pushes toward singularity: YHWH God. Yet identity slippage emerges again in connection with the differentiated human. Following God's point of view we see the human divided and a woman formed whom he brings to the human. But, of course, the one to whom he brings her is in fact the man, and it is the man, not the undifferentiated human, who then speaks. The narrator mirrors for us a striking confusion of categories. Is that because God has a problem recognizing singularity or plurality in his image? Or is it because he automatically assigns a hierarchy to his creation? He brings the newly formed woman before the man, as earlier he had brought the animals before the human. But he nevertheless nominates the man as still (or also?) the original inclusive being, the "Human." Thereby the human becomes *both* the human *and* the man. The woman is merely the woman.

The man is not slow to give human expression to the divine desire to name and control (if not subjugate). He moves a step beyond YHWH God and objectifies the woman. He does not address her as "you" or even refer to her as "she." Rather she is "this" (Landy 1983: 228). She is "this" in fact three times within a handful of words. Moreover, the man, like God in Genesis 1, is allowed the privilege of discovery. Though he does not pronounce her "good," he declares that she is appropriate. His standards, it seems, are likeness and lineage. He claims *her* as bone of *his* bones and flesh of *his* flesh. The direction of his claim for control is as clear as it is perverse: "wo-man" (*'ish-shah*) was taken out of "man" (*'ish*). Apart from his perverse interpretation of the wordplay (apparent to anyone who just listens to, or looks at, the words), there is the crowning perversity of his claim to be her progenitor. The woman (strictly the "side" from which she was formed) was taken out of the human, not the man. The man, however, claims the past (and Humanity) as his own dominion. And flying in the face of what every reader knows to be reality, he claims that woman comes out of man – claims for himself, that is, woman's biological function of childbearing. A breathtaking claim, indeed! In all this he asserts authority over the woman as a

22

parent over a child. For this moment, at least, God and man form the same perceptions, make the same moves, desire the same ends.

But what may we say of the woman? Had she, rather than the residual man, been allowed the role of discoverer in her introductory scene, might we have heard a somewhat different perspective? Would she have recognized the man to be flesh of her flesh and bone of her bone? Would she have decided to call him "man" because he had once been part of "woman"? Upon meeting her new companion, would she have been impressed? Disappointed? Ambivalent? But such possibilities of subjectivity are avoided, suppressed. We might easily infer that were she to have opinions they would not, in any case, matter – not to God, the man, or the narrator. Men can have opinions about women (the objects of male desire: Genesis 2:24), but women's perceptions of men are not important.

In an explanatory aside, the narrator then maintains that, of all human relationships, the union of man and woman is the primary bond, stronger than the relationship between parents and children: "Therefore, a man shall leave his father and his mother and cleave to his woman and they shall become one flesh" (2:24). Implicit is a claim that the man's desire is the defining norm. He is the one leaving and cleaving. The woman is simply the object to be acquired: she is without desire, without attachments, without a past. She is simply there, waiting to be subsumed. Union with a man is her consummate purpose. *return to orig state? conjugal act?*

Implicit, too, is another claim. Just as relations with parents and children are diminished, so, too, are excluded relations between people of the same sex. The "helper corresponding to [like–opposite]" the human/man is a *no same-sex partnerships.* sexual "opposite." According to this claim, human sexuality is clearly monogamous exogamous heterosexuality: one partner, outside the family, of the opposite sex. Partnership, according to this agenda, demands sexual and familial difference.[5]

Returning to the story line, the narrator introduces a new character, the *serpent* serpent, "shrewder than any other wild animal YHWH God had made" (3:1). The serpent speaks to the woman (3:1–5):

> "Did God really say, 'You shall not eat from any tree in the garden'?" The woman said to the serpent, "We may eat the fruit from the trees in the garden; but the fruit from the tree that is in the midst of the garden, God said, 'you shall not eat it, nor shall you touch it, or you shall die.'" But the serpent said to the woman, "You will not indeed die; for God knows that on the day you eat it your eyes will be opened, and you will be like God, knowing good and evil."

Like the tree in the center of the garden, the serpent's existence and character is both unexplained and deeply intriguing (cf. Landy 1983: 188). Why did God put the serpent in the garden? How does the serpent know so much about the tree of the knowledge of good and evil? Has the serpent eaten of it?

23

Is God in control of this garden or not? If he is, is this all a test? Does God *want* to be defeated by his children? ("God loves to be defeated by his children" – Elie Wiesel.) Landy comments that the serpent "symbolizes a side of God (the tempter; good-and-evil) he refuses to recognize."

The narrator hurries us past such questions to the turning point (3:6).

> And the woman saw that the tree was good for food, and that it was a pleasure to the sight, and the tree was desirable for discernment. She took some of its fruit and ate, and she also gave some to her husband with her, and he ate.

The woman reaches for sustenance, beauty, and wisdom. And for doing so she is blamed, both within the text and by countless generations of biblical interpreters in the text's afterlife. Particularly through the influence of Augustine, she has become known as the authoress of what Christian theology has come to know as "The Fall." Human sin is laid at her door. Why? Because she reaches for sustenance, beauty, and wisdom – and disobeys the divine command to eschew the knowledge of good and evil.

Yet, like God, the woman is an explorer. She seeks the good, fruit that is good for food. She delights in beauty (God took care to create trees that were beautiful) and the fruit is a delight to the eyes. Furthermore, she seeks to learn, to discern. The commentators cry for her blind obedience, her trust. But mature trust grows out of experience. How can the woman discriminate between God's words and the serpent's words until she has the experience of failure or the discrimination she seeks? Why should she believe that one peremptory command is in her best interests and not another? She seeks, reasonably, to be in a position to make a choice. Or, alternatively, she merely responds to her programming: to eat the good food, and to be like God!

Indeed, she desires to be like God! We should not be surprised. God's own breath has transformed the human into a living *nephesh*, "a bundle of appetites/passions/desires" (as W. J. A. Power has pointed out to us; and cf. Landy 1983: 242–43). That is to say, desire is part of the divinely inspired programming of the human. The woman can no more ignore her *nephesh* than she can refuse to breathe.

God had told the human not to eat the fruit for then the human would surely die. Does the woman even know what death is? (She has not even bothered to eat of the tree of life.) Until she has the knowledge she seeks she is unable to do anything but bend to every suggestion. In other words, the command is impossible for her to adhere to as long as God allows the possibility of alternative speech (the serpent's) – which he patently does until it is too late to make any difference. (Its suppression is then gratuitous.) By definition – God's definition – Eve is unable to know the difference between good and evil. How then can she be blamed for her actions? On the contrary, the woman's adventurous spirit, analogous to God's need for discovery, exhibits courage. She is willing to take risks. She is comfortable with lack of closure. She does not know what is going to happen. Obviously, neither does God.

The process by which the Genesis text constructs the character of Eve has been shrewdly tracked recently by Mieke Bal (1987). In the course of her essay she not only shreds "Paul's" careless exegesis of Genesis 3 (in 1 Timothy 2) but also offers a more favorable interpretation of Eve than is usually found in male writing. Eve's decision to eat the fruit is the first act of human independence. This independence forces the human and the divine into a real relationship of give and take rather than an artificial relationship of puppet and puppeteer. Eve does not "sin"; she chooses reality over her naive, paradisiacal existence. Her choice marks the emergence of human character.

Despite her provocative reading of Eve, Bal is, nevertheless, unwilling to see here a "feminist, feminine, or female-oriented text." Rather, she sees a text serving an ideology (patriarchy, the mainstream biblical ideology) that is struggling to be monolithic – struggling, for the text inadvertently encodes some of the *problems* involved in man's priority and domination:

> The burden of domination is hard to bear. Dominators have, first, to establish their position, then to safeguard it. Subsequently, they must make both the dominated *and* themselves believe in it. Insecurity is not a prerogative exclusively of the dominated. The establishing of a justifying "myth of origin," which has to be sufficiently credible and realistic to account for common experience, is not that simple a performance. Traces of the painful process of gaining control can therefore be perceived in those very myths. They serve to limit repression to acceptable, viable proportions.
>
> (Bal 1987: 110)

We find a similar position being taken by David Jobling (1986). Challenging Phyllis Trible's (1978) reading of an ideal equality between the sexes prior to the fall, he doubts that such a "feminist" story would have been composed, and wonders how it could have been received, in the "man's world" which Trible elsewhere sees as the Bible's matrix.

He also argues against Trible's interpretation of the 'adam as first a sexually undifferentiated "earth creature." While that interpretation is logical, since maleness is meaningless before sexual differentiation, the text nevertheless asserts the illogical, namely "the originality of maleness over femaleness" (1986: 41–42).

As Jobling sees the text, the patriarchal tendency of the story is to subordinate the woman in the social order and to blame the woman for the misfortune that has befallen humankind in its struggle to till the earth, which Jobling sees as the main theme of the story. In tension with this

25

agenda, however, are the undeniably positive characteristics of the woman in the text. How has such a conflicting depiction come about?

The incongruities are inevitable. To blame the woman for eating of the tree, continues Jobling (42–43), is to associate her with *knowledge*.

> Part of the price the male mindset pays is the admission that woman is more aware of the complexity of the world, more in touch with "all living." And finally, at the deepest level of the text, ... the possibility is evoked that the human transformation in which the woman took powerful initiative was positive, rather than negative, that the complex human world is to be preferred over any male ideal.

> But these "positive" features are not the direct expression of a feminist consciousness. ... Rather, they are the effects of the patriarchal mindset tying itself in knots trying to account for woman and femaleness in a way which *both* makes sense *and* supports patriarchal assumptions.

Another striking instance of patriarchal knot-tying may be found in the account of the aftermath of eating the fruit from the tree. The man and woman know nakedness and shame (Genesis 3:7, 10–11; cf. 2:25). The knowledge of sexual difference brings shame in its train. Sex and shame. That association, however, primarily serves the interest of the party wanting sexual control – that is, men who want to control women's sexuality. For example, the history of patriarchy is replete with societies where a sexually violated woman is conditioned to be ashamed. As we write, many raped Bosnian Muslim women are unable to return to their homes (if they still have a home) because of the shame that society places upon them. Thus patriarchal sexual mores lend their aid to the horrors of "ethnic cleansing." The double standard in the sex and shame ethic is amply evidenced in the biblical story: rapist Amnon is not described as knowing shame. That is reserved for Tamar, his sister, whom he rapes (2 Samuel 13)! Shame is a mechanism for passing the blame. Amnon does something evil but it is really Tamar's fault. Why else should she be ashamed?

So the story of Genesis 1–3 embodies a splendid contradiction. Sex, it proclaims, is good, part of the divine creative design: procreate (multiply)! Sex, it proclaims, is bad, the result of disobedience: cover yourself, be ashamed! And to reinforce the latter point, sexual relationships are drawn into the sphere of disobedience's consequences, the "punishments" of 2:14–19.

Jobling has suggested that one function of the garden story is (to use Pamela Milne's paraphrase [1989: 30]) to "shift guilt or fault for the fall away from God (since the idea that God is ultimately responsible for evil is intolerable) and away from man (since it is no less intolerable for the male mindset that all the guilt should pass to man)." It seems that man and God are aligned when blame is to be shifted. That is interesting because, at first sight, the blame is all laid, so to speak, at the feet (with apologies to the serpent) of everyone else but God – that is, the man, the woman, and the serpent.

And God said [to the man], "Have you eaten from the tree of which I said not to eat?" The man said, "The woman whom you gave to be with me, she gave me fruit of the tree, and I ate." And YHWH God said to the woman, "What is this that you have done?" And the woman said, "The serpent beguiled me, and I ate." And YHWH God said to the serpent,

> "Because you have done this,
> cursed are you above all cattle,
> and above all wild animals . . . ."

(3:12–14)

Indeed, Gerhard von Rad sees the narrative as being concerned with

> the great disorders of our present life – shame, fear, the dissonances in the life of the woman and the man – and ascribing them to human sin. And this, of course, is the chief concern of the entire narrative . . . For it is concerned to acquit God and his creation of all the suffering and misery that has come into the world.

(von Rad 1972: 101)

If we look again, however, we may decide that God, too, is implicated. The man insinuates as much when he speaks of "The woman whom *you* gave to be with me. . . ." Attention to the rhetoric of blame-shifting can also open up the question of God's involvement. When God asks the man about the eating of the fruit of the forbidden tree, the man blames the woman, and when God asks the woman, "What is this that you have done?" the woman blames the serpent. A reader might notice that though God readily redirects his question from the man to the woman, the serpent's mouth he stops first with words and then with dust.

As cunning as the serpent, God moves to stop the sequence of blame from becoming a cycle. For to the question, "What is this that you have done?" might not the serpent have said, "You didn't tell them the whole truth, so I gave them the chance to choose for themselves"? Or perhaps the serpent might have asked the counter-question, "What is this that *you* have done? Why did you put that tree in the garden?" Or "Why did you allow me, serpent, to have an alternate voice?" Or simply, "Why can you not stand for anyone to be like you?" Instead God moves to stop the cycle of blame from coming to rest on himself. Or, to put it another way, he, like the humans, rushes to shift the blame.

What is at the center of all this blame? Tradition, as we have observed already, blames the woman. The woman reaches for sustenance, beauty, and wisdom – and disregards the divine prohibition. But what is the nature, or better yet, the point, of this prohibition?

27

Does God put this particular tree in the garden in order to <u>test</u> the human? Is it there so that God can see whether the human will recognize God's authority, abide by the prohibition, and accept unquestioning subordination as humankind's ordained place in life? But if so, why would God want to prove that this status pertains? Could God be anxious, or perhaps even insecure, about the docility of his creatures? In the process of challenging that ordained subordination, would the human not become like God? Would this not surely threaten, even provoke from a God, jealous of his power, an anxious response?

jealous God?

"Behold, the human has become like one of us, knowing good and evil; and now, lest he put forth his hand and take also of the tree of life, and live for ever" – and YHWH God put him out from the garden of Eden . . . He drove out the human; and . . . he placed the cherubim and a flaming sword . . . to guard the way to the tree of life.

(3:22–24)

The issue on this reading, then, would be God's need to guard jealously his privileged position, to dominate (or transcend, if you will). Bal words it this way:

It was the likeness to God that the serpent presented to [the woman] as the main charm of the tree. This likeness included the free will to act, which was implied in the interdiction itself. Jealousy about the possible equivalence is alleged [by the serpent] as Yahweh's motive for the interdiction. Yahweh's later reaction proves the serpent was right.

(1987: 125)

Alternatively, is the tree (and accompanying prohibition) there to provoke the human to do just what the human does? That it is a potentially provocative action on God's part (i.e., from the human's point of view) is hard to deny.[6] What would eating from it achieve? Nothing short of a measure of independence (cf. Bal 1987). Why should God want a humankind that is wholly dependent, blandly agreeable, and slavishly conformist? Perhaps that is why God is so conspicuously absent in the crucial central scene, where the serpent is allowed free rein by this otherwise ever-present God.

why God didn't stop them. Wanted their independence

But why, then, the "punishments" of verses 14–19?

But punish—

> To the woman [God] said:
> "I will multiply indeed your toil and your pregnancies;
> with travail you shall bear children,
> but towards your man [husband] shall be your desire
> and he shall rule over you."
> And to Adam [Human] he said:
> "Because you obeyed your woman [wife]
> and ate from the tree about which I commanded you,

punishm

'You shall not eat from it,'
cursed is the ground [*'adamah*] on your account.
With labor you shall eat from it
all the days of your life ...
until you return to the ground,
for out of it you were taken;
you are dust, and to dust you shall return."

The first question to ask is, are they punishments? Some (e.g., Phyllis Trible and Carol Meyers) have argued that they are rather consequences of knowing good and evil. Let us pursue that suggestion. Would not knowing good and evil inevitably have to include the good and bad of what sustains human beings? Procreation involves children to love but also physical and emotional pain, not to mention infant and female mortality (a major risk in the ancient world as in many parts of today's world). Passion allows for love and intimacy, but also the possibility of domination (even violence); it can be the excuse for estrangement and the cause of unwanted pregnancy. In work one may find the satisfaction of accomplishment as well as the weariness of labor and the frustration of failure.

Is this the kind of knowledge of good and evil that God knows? Does God somehow benefit from humans knowing these things too? Yes, we could reply. Just as God claims that it is not good for the human to be alone, neither is it good for God to be alone; and God will always be alone if there is no one to share some part of his experience. Knowledge of good and evil is part of divine experience, and a relationship with humans who know nothing of life's labor, pain and dissonance could only be a facile and impoverished relationship.

At the same time, having pushed the human to open the Pandora's Box of reality and independence, the deity still wants to assert control. So he simply claims control for himself: "I will put enmity . . . I will greatly increase . . ." God's rhetoric turns natural consequences into divinely controlled repercussions. In other words, from the human point of view, they become punishments.

Whether viewed as punishments or predictions, God's words further define the gender roles of the man and the woman who now know good and evil. The woman is defined in relation to the man, as a toiling mother (indeed, the man goes on to reinforce this identity as mother, by naming her Eve, the mother of all living; 2:20), desiring (sexually) her husband but facing the danger of numerous pregnancies (cf. Meyers 1988: 109–117). The man is defined in relation to the ground, with which he must struggle in order to eat. The basic drives of sex and eating are paralleled in these definitions (cf. eating as a common metaphor for sex; e.g., Proverbs 1–9 and Song of Songs), the one ascribed to the woman and the other to the man. But control of her sexuality is denied the woman: the man shall rule over her. Thus both

29

sex and eating end up in the domain of the man. The woman becomes subordinate, the man subjugator.

An air of unreality has descended on the text. It is women's sexual desire for men that is named, not men's for women, and it is this desire that will subordinate women. Because she sexually desires her man so greatly, she will put aside her concern for the risks of childbearing and will be unable to resist her man's (unnamed) sexual advances (Meyers 1988: 116). His (unnamed) desire will predominate because her (named) desire is so predominant! (So when she says "no" she really means "yes"?) Hence, because she really wants him to do so, the man will rightly rule over her. But how curious, in a story where the man is passive and compliant and the woman active and assertive, for such a man to rule over such a woman's sexuality!

Eve's primary characterization in this divine speech carries over to most of the other women in the larger story of Genesis–Kings. Eve's literary daughters are commonly inscribed in the text in the first instance as mothers, mothers of sons who are crucial either to lineage or plot. Yet secondarily they are often inscribed as objects of men's sexual desire, a characterization at odds with the tenor of the speech: only Potiphar's wife (Genesis 39) quite fits that bill. Of course, such discrepancy is to be expected, for the narrative cannot sustain the odd logic of the divine rhetoric. This is again patriarchy tying itself in knots.

Ironically, Adam's sons are not so limited in their vocations. Despite the fact that Adam is charged to work the earth by the sweat of his brow, his successors are hardly confined to farming. The men of Genesis–Kings become herders, musicians, city builders, wealthy landowners, administrators, deliverers, law givers, judges, warriors, kings, sages, prophets, and priests, to name some of the more obvious professions. Men are much more likely than women to be featured in their own stories, whether brief or extended. The few women who do make inroads into these professions may assure us that ability is not at issue, but they also accent the majority who are confined to maternity or who are omitted altogether.

Thus the woman's punishment turns out to be a confirmation of what the man has already claimed and God has already approved, namely, the hierarchical priority of the man. God thus plays to the man. Hierarchies have a way of spawning favorites. God's hierarchies in this story are no exception.[7]

To mediate the "punishment" God extends gracious clemency: "And YHWH God made for Human and for his wife garments of skins, and clothed them" (3:21). On the one hand, the gesture may be seen positively as one of guidance – the deity shows the humans how to care for themselves. After all, from this point on they are responsible for their own (food and) clothing. Clothing becomes a symbol of autonomy and vulnerability, both protecting and revealing that one needs to be protected. Clothing is also a symbol of knowing good and evil. Only humans (who know good and evil) need clothes. This separates them from the other animals and it separates them from each other. On the other hand, one can also read this act as the gesture of the beneficent lord, offering handouts (see Kennedy 1990). The gift creates obligation and is therefore a means of continuing control.

The expulsion, too, slides between consequence and control. We have already observed one obvious dimension of control: expulsion prevents the humans from closing the difference between them and God by eating from the tree of life. Without difference there can be no hierarchy and hierarchy facilitates control. The expulsion is also a natural consequence of knowing good and evil. To know good *and evil* in paradise would hardly be possible. And for the humans to eat from the tree of life and live forever would exclude them from knowing a whole dimension of evil, namely experience related to death. The humans must leave the garden.

But do we not find God exiled as well, following his human creations in their wanderings? The human beings may have chosen their own plot, but God is there to enforce the continuation of the story they have begun. In a sense the humans have led God out of paradise. Why does God follow? Out of a concern for his creatures? Out of his need for relationship? Out of curiosity? Out of a desire to maintain dominion over his creatures and, through them, over his newly created world? However complex the reason, God ventures out and the gate to paradise is closed. The story moves on. There is no return to simplicity, for human beings or for God.

Between human desire and the desire of God in this story there is a creative tension of separation and sameness. Good and evil are not separate elements in simple opposition. They turn out to be shifting, sliding terms, like most of the story's discriminations. Humankind cannot simply "trust" God and vacate its responsibility for its own well-being (even when looking to providence). Women and men need to seek food, beauty, and discernment, and, indeed, be prepared to sweat for them. We can blame the woman for human vulnerability and culpability, yet we then need also to recognize God's vulnerability and culpability. God, too, bears responsibility and God is not capable of simply fixing up the mess.

God's desire for dominion is both creative and corrosive in this story. While it is one of the desires that drives the creation of the world, it is also a desire that complicates and so creates the plot. The complication has an uneasy resolution. The desire to have dominion is coupled with a desire to create meaning through difference, while simultaneously replicating self through likeness. But too much likeness threatens the separation that guarantees dominion. On the one hand: be like me, but not too much like me! On the other hand: why are you so different, when I made you to be like me? YHWH God in the garden wrestles with dilemmas of sameness and difference, power and equity, in creative relationship. These dilemmas readers will meet again and again as the story in which the garden is but a beginning unfolds through Genesis–Kings.

NOTES

1 This chapter, with minor differences, appeared as a chapter in the authors' *Gender, Power, and Promise* (Fewell and Gunn 1993) and we thank Abingdon Press for generously allowing us to reprint it here. It grew out of conversations between the authors over several years and revision and expansion (and complication) of a paper by David Gunn delivered to the Society of Biblical Literature at the Central States Regional Meeting in 1990 and to the Annual Meeting in San Francisco in 1992. It owes much to the invitation, encouragement, and criticisms of colleagues from Central States and the SBL's Reading, Rhetoric, and the Hebrew Bible Section; to students of the Authors, Texts, and Readers seminar at Columbia Theological Seminary and the Ancient Texts and Modern Readers class at Perkins School of Theology; to the anonymous readers of *Christianity and Literature* who panned its predecessor and the one who didn't; and not least to Tim Beal and Tod Linafelt who stuck by it even in its darkest hour.

   We cite work of some of the critics who have engaged us; there is much else for the reader interested in exploring further, including Nehama Aschkenasy (1986), Harold Bloom (1986 and 1990), Athalya Brenner, ed. (1993), David Clines (1990), Sam Dragga (1990), Susan Lanser (1988), Paul Morris and Deborah Sawyer, eds (1992), Ilana Pardes (1992), George Ramsey (1988), Ilona Rashkow (1990), Joel Rosenberg (1986), Graham Ward (1995), and Hugh White (1991).

2 Some scholars argue, with little immediate contextual evidence, that the plural reflects the god speaking on behalf of the "divine court."

3 Critics seeking to uncover the sources from which Genesis 1–3 was composed usually find a "priestly" source (P) in Genesis 1:1–2:4a which has been editorially connected to a "Yahwist" source (J) in the rest of Genesis 2–3.

4 Francis Landy (1983: 189) comments: "[God's] statement ... ignores the one relationship that has mattered to [the human] up to this point, that with God himself; it may also be an indication of God's own need, his own loneliness, out of which he created the universe."

5 This agenda, which implicitly makes genital difference a *sine qua non* of sexuality, has implications for any understanding of God and/or sexuality based on this text (see Eilberg-Schwartz, in this volume, or 1992: 32–33). Given that the human creature is made in God's image, the logic of the text suggests that sexuality is also a dimension of God and, like human sexuality, it must be specifically marked – in other words (since the narrator has consistently spoken of him in the masculine), that God has a penis. But if so, what does that imply for women? Are they not, then, made in the image of God? Or is sexuality not, after all, part of the image of God? Moreover, if sexuality is confined to reproduction, as has often (repressively) been claimed with reference to this text, the same issue arises. Since the monotheistic male God has no use for a reproductive organ, neither should male humans, if they are to be truly like God. "If God has no sex, then the reproductive organs of both males and females are rendered problematic. And if God does have a sex, whether male or female, God's reproductive organs are useless" (Eilberg-Schwartz, in this volume, or 1992: 33). In other words, in constructing heterosexuality as normative the narrator deconstructs the asexual masculine God of monotheism. This passage is another case of "the patriarchal mindset tying itself in knots" (Jobling 1986: 43) – see below.

6 Francis Landy (1983: 215) sees prohibition introducing the idea of rebellion and trespass into an otherwise harmonious world, because arbitrary or incomprehensible regulation "infallibly" ensures infringement. Even to eat from the other trees turns out to be a concession by God. The human suddenly discovers that "[he] has

no independence, no rights, and that his harmonious enterprise in the garden, where he fulfils his purpose in creation by changing it, is part of a rigorous divine order."

7 Later in Genesis–Kings, God, perhaps beginning to learn, will struggle to disturb assumptions of priority and hierarchy (e.g., regarding privileges of birth or occupation). In the very next episode, Cain, first-born and follower in his father's footsteps as tiller of the soil, finds his sacrifice rejected. But God's peremptory rejection and ambiguous words prove stunningly disastrous. His provocation ends with Abel's blood. Does God, once more, tell only part of the story? Does Abel's blood cry out from the ground against both his brother and God? Does God, once more, shift the blame?

2

THE PROBLEM OF THE BODY FOR THE PEOPLE OF THE BOOK

Howard Eilberg-Schwartz

> Perhaps all social systems are built on contradiction, in some sense at war with themselves.
>
> (Douglas 1966: 140)

While many cultures are preoccupied with the body, there are specific, local reasons why the body emerges as problematic in any given cultural formation.[1] This chapter explores factors indigenous to ancient Judaism that turned the human body into a problem. To anticipate, I shall argue that the human body was the object around which conflicting cultural representations met and clashed. Like other religious cultures, ancient Judaism was not a tidy entity. Tidiness is a characteristic of philosophic systems, not cultures. Each culture has its own set of conflicting impulses that struggle against one another for hegemony. In the case of ancient Judaism, at least in one of its formations, it was the human body that was caught between contradictory impulses. To cite two of the more important examples: (1) humans are understood as created in the image of God, yet God has "no-body" – neither others with whom to interact nor a fully conceptualized body with which to do it, and (2) procreation is enjoined as a mandate from God, yet semen is considered polluting, even when discharged during intercourse. These contradictions, which first surface in one form of Israelite religion, are inherited by the rabbis (200–600 C.E.), who continue to find the body a source of conflict.

In relying on the idea of cultural contradictions, I depart from the general tendency to think of Judaism as "a system" or series of systems, a metaphor that implicitly and often explicitly guides research on Judaism. This metaphor induces interpreters to produce a coherence that does not always exist; the result is that one impulse of the culture is selected as exemplary at the expense of others. The idea of cultural contradictions allows interpreters to explore the full "dispersion" of cultural assertions (Foucault 1972).

The idea of cultural contradictions has intrigued many theorists of society and culture, including Marx, Freud, Lévi-Strauss, Gluckman, Spiro, B. Turner, V. Turner, Girard and others. Contradictions operate at various

levels and in various ways. For Marx, they are part of a complex social process such as capitalism that produces conflict between the technological level
and social condition of technological progress (Kolakowski 1978: 299).
Contradictions are also a phenomenon of culture. The *Mythologies* of Lévi-
Strauss (1969; 1975; 1978) show how myths are generated by and attempt to
solve or hide logical contradictions that trouble the mind. Other theorists
have examined how individuals are caught between competing demands
emanating from various sources. Freud and his followers are particularly
interested in the ways in which conflicts between physiological drives and
cultural demands are handled. Spiro (1987: 59–60), for example, notes the
intolerable contradiction in which pubescent boys and girls were placed in
the early years of the Israeli kibbutz movement. In their attempt to create a
sexual equality, in which sexual differences would assume little more importance than other anatomical differences, the kibbutz pioneers established a
practice in which boys and girls would be routinely exposed to each other's
bodies in lavatories, showers, and sleeping quarters. But at the age of
puberty, the kibbutz severely prohibited any sexual contact between the
sexes. "Here," writes Spiro (1987: 80–81), "is a classic example of incompatible demands. Such a contradiction can only result in intolerable conflict
and unbearable frustration." In this case, Spiro argues, the contradiction
seems to be generated by an attempt of culture to override biological
impulses. Other theorists, such as Max Gluckman (1955), Mary Douglas
(1966: 140–158) and Victor Turner (1967: 1–92), have noted how such conflicts may arise from competing social commitments or competing claims of
the social system. For example, Ndembu women experience a conflict
between patrilocal marriage and matrilineal descent. Women live with their
husband's family yet feel the pulls of their matrilineal kin. Fathers want
their sons to remain with them. But the mother's kin want her and her child
to return to them. This culturally produced conflict manifests itself in a
variety of physical ailments that are attributed to the attacks of deceased
matrilineal ancestors. A similar sort of cultural conflict explains the disorder
of anorexia nervosa. Young women afflicted with this disorder experience
psychic conflict generated by irreconcilable cultural expectations (B. Turner
1984: 192–97). On this point, I find myself in agreement with Girard (1977:
147) who writes that, "far from being restricted to a limited number of
pathological cases . . . the double bind – a contradictory double imperative,
or rather a whole network of contradictory imperatives – is an extremely
common phenomenon."

Expanding on the ideas of these theorists, I suggest that the idea of cultural conflicts explains why certain objects arrest more attention than
others. Vast cultural and symbolic resources are invested in those objects
around which conflicting representations revolve. The symbolic elaboration
that occurs around such "conflicted objects" is both a consequence of and
strategy for dealing with the conflict in question. Objects that are caught

35

between incompatible impulses are evocative, puzzling, and dangerous. The multiplication of rules that often occurs around such objects has the effect both of mastering a threatening object and of glossing the generative conflict. Under the sheer weight of legal minutiae, the original contradiction is lost from view. These conflicted objects make valuable symbolic resources. Caught between conflicting cultural processes, these objects are volatile; their power or energy can be transferred by association to other more stable cultural meanings. Consequently, these charged objects are often used to symbolize and hence empower a variety of cultural messages.[2] In turn, the established cultural messages, now associated with a potential source of conflict, help to control an otherwise unruly object.

In ancient Judaism, cultural conflicts of this sort developed around the human body, generating an intense preoccupation with the body and its processes. Ancient Jews multiplied rules that both regulated the body and turned the body into a symbol of other significant religious concerns. It is to the conflicted Jewish body that our attention now turns.

THE PROBLEM OF THE BODY FOR THE PEOPLE OF THE BOOK

To some it may come as a surprise that Judaism is a tradition that is preoccupied with the body. Judaism is often depicted as having a predominantly favorable attitude toward the body. As evidence of this positive tendency, interpreters point out that Jews are enjoined to procreate, with the result that sexuality has a positive regard within the tradition (e.g., Feldman 1968: 21–71; Brown 1988: 63; Gordis 1978: 98–109; Pagels 1988: 12–13). Consequently, one generally does not find the tendency toward sexual asceticism within Judaism as in other traditions such as Christianity. Nor does the Hebrew Bible or subsequent rabbinic tradition treat sexuality as a consequence of "a fall" (Sapp 1977; Anderson 1992). Sexuality is regarded as a natural human act that is part of what it means to be human; the sexual asceticism evidenced among the Jews at Qumran is thus regarded as a deviation. In addition, the sharp dualism of body and soul, characteristic of Greek philosophical traditions, is absent in the Hebrew Scriptures and is resisted in classic rabbinic sources (Urbach 1987: 241; Rubin 1988).

While these characterizations are true, they are also misleading.[3] They ignore the way in which the government of the body has always been a central preoccupation within Judaism.[4] Despite any sharp antithesis between body and soul, and despite the importance of procreation, certain bodily processes are regarded as problematic.

The problem of the body in Judaism is already evident in those very writings that made the Jews a "People of the Book." It is in the Hebrew Scriptures, particularly that strand contributed by the Israelite priests, that the body first appears as a central issue of control. This part of Scripture, which is generally designated as "P" (after its priestly origin), includes narratives and laws, which were generally thought to be written sometime in the sixth to fifth centuries B.C.E.[5] It is in the writings of the priests, especially the book of Leviticus, but also in the writings of the prophet Ezekiel (who was also of priestly descent), that the boundaries and integrity of the body arouse sustained interest.[6] Leviticus pays particular attention to what passes in and out of the orifices, particularly the mouth and the genitals. Certain kinds of food may not be taken into the body (Leviticus 11). Various genital emissions, such as menstrual blood, semen, and other irregular discharges, create pollution (Leviticus 12; 15). Concern with the body's integrity expresses itself in elaborate rules concerning skin diseases that are contaminating (Leviticus 13–14) as well as interest in congenital or accidental disfigurations of the body (Leviticus 21:16–23), which disqualify a priest from serving in the Temple. Leviticus also proscribes intentional disfigurations of the body such as shaving the corners of the face or acts of mutilation associated with mourning (Leviticus 19:27; 21:5). In addition to these concerns about bodily boundaries and integrity, Leviticus strictly regulates the use to which persons put their bodies in sexual alliances (Leviticus 18; 20:10–21).

This government of the body has both prophylactic and moral motivations. Many of the bodily regulations are intended to protect the sacrificial cult from contamination (Milgrom 1976: 390–99). A priest with a disfiguration or with a discharge cannot perform the sacrifices that must be done in a state of purity and wholeness. Furthermore, contamination that occurs among Israelites who are not priests can jeopardize the purity of the cult. "You shall put the Israelites on guard against their uncleanness, lest they die through their uncleanness by defiling My Tabernacle which is among them" (Leviticus 15:30).[7]

But the concern with purity is not exclusively a cultic matter. Israel is enjoined to be holy, just as God is holy. Being holy includes observing the regulations governing what goes in and out of the body (Douglas 1966: 51–52; Wenham 1979). "You shall not eat, among all things that swarm upon the earth, anything that crawls on its belly . . . you shall not make yourselves unclean therewith and thus become unclean. For I the Lord am your God: you shall sanctify yourselves and be holy for I am holy" (Leviticus 11:42–44). While being impure is not considered a sin, the state of uncleanness does signify an alienation from God. Furthermore, the violation of certain rules governing the body, particularly those related to sexuality, does constitute an offense against God (Leviticus 20:10–26).

It is from the priestly writings that the concern with the government of the body first enters Judaism. Subsequent groups of Jews, including those at Qumran (second and first centuries B.C.E.) and the rabbis (200–600 C.E.) take up and elaborate upon the levitical rules governing the body. The Dead Sea Scrolls and the rabbinic writings both reflect a preoccupation with many of the concerns established in Leviticus. To be sure, this is not a passive acquiescence to tradition, since these groups transform the rules in sometimes radical ways. I have explored some of these transformations in another context (Eilberg-Schwartz 1990: 195–216). Nonetheless, had it not been for Leviticus, the problem of governing the body would not have had the prominence it does within subsequent forms of Judaism. What follows, then, is an attempt to understand why the government of the body so preoccupied the priestly community.

THE CONFLICTED BODY

Mary Douglas has already speculated about why the body so preoccupied ancient Jews. The body, she argues, is frequently a symbol of society and thus the dangers and concerns of the social structure are reproduced on the human body

> The Israelites were always in their history a hard-pressed minority. In their beliefs all the bodily issues were polluting, blood, pus, excrete, semen, etc. The threatened boundaries of their body politics would be well mirrored in their care for the integrity, unity and purity of the physical body.

> (Douglas 1966: 124)

Douglas also suggests that the levitical restrictions on the body stem from a concern with wholeness. Body emissions, skin-disease, and defects are threats to the integrity of the body and, like other things that violate notions of wholeness, they are deemed impure (Douglas 1966: 51–52). Douglas's argument has now been canonized in commentaries to Leviticus (e.g. Wenham 1979: 222–23).

But Douglas's arguments are not entirely satisfying. To begin with, Douglas fails to explain why the body became particularly problematic to one specific group of ancient Jews, namely the Israelite priests. If the external pressures on Israel induced a preoccupation with the body, why are the same sorts of concerns not visible in all genres of Israelite literature? Why is this preoccupation located principally in the writings of the priests? Furthermore, Douglas fails to explain why body emissions would be considered a threat to notions of wholeness. Why was wholeness defined in this and not some other way? The answer to these questions emerges when we consider the distinctive religious formation of the Israelite priests.

Within this religious culture, conflicting and to some extent incompatible representations crystallized around the human body. On the one hand, the priests celebrated procreation. They not only believed that God commanded humans to be fruitful and multiply (Genesis 1:27), but regarded reproduction as a central dimension of the covenant between God and Abraham (Genesis 17). This impulse, however, which sprang from the social organization and self-understanding of the priestly community, came into conflict with an

38

important religious conception, namely, that humans are made in the image of God (Genesis 1:26–27). There is a fundamental tension between being made in God's image and being obliged to reproduce. The dilemma arises because Israelite religion places certain limitations on the representation of God. To oversimplify for a moment, God has "nobody," neither others with whom to interact nor a body, or at least a fully conceptualized body, with which to do it. Thus the dual expectations of being like God and being obliged to reproduce pulled in opposite directions. There was no escape for the body. Pressed between these conflicting impulses, the body became an object of cultural elaboration. Let me unravel this conflict in more detail.

BE FRUITFUL AND MULTIPLY

Of all the Israelites who contributed to the Hebrew Bible, the priestly community is by far the most concerned with human reproduction. Procreation is regarded as a central human quality and responsibility. In the priestly myth of creation, for example, the command to reproduce immediately follows the creation of man and woman (Genesis 1:28). In fact, "be fruitful and multiply" are the first words that God addresses directly to humanity. According to the priestly writings, God twice reiterates this instruction to the survivors of the flood (Genesis 9:1, 7). The importance of human fertility is underscored by its close and frequent association with divine blessing (Bird 1981: 157; Sapp 1977: 10; Cohen 1989: 13–24). In both the myths of creation and the flood, the command to procreate is immediately preceded by the statement that God conferred a blessing (Genesis 9:1).

It is not surprising then that the priestly writings regard this blessing as central to the covenant that God makes with Abraham and his descendants.

> As for Me, this is My covenant with you: You shall be the father of a multitude of nations. And you shall no longer be called Abram, but your name shall be Abraham, for I make you the father of a multitude of nations. I will make you exceedingly fertile and make nations of you and kings shall come forth from you.
>
> (Genesis 17:4–6)

As I have argued elsewhere (Eilberg-Schwartz 1990: 141–77), the priests regard the rite of circumcision as the physical inscription of God's promise of genealogical proliferation on the body of all Abraham's male descendants. In the priestly understanding, circumcision is not an arbitrary sign of the covenant, as many interpreters construe it, but a symbol that alludes directly to the substance of God's promise to Abraham, namely to multiply Abraham's seed. It is no accident that the symbol of the covenant is impressed on the penis. The penis is the male organ through which the genealogy of Israel is perpetuated. The removal of the foreskin has the effect of giving the penis the appearance it has when erect, thus symbolizing great things to come.

39

Furthermore, the priestly writings suggest an analogy between an uncircumcised male organ and an immature fruit tree. They thus associate the circumcision of the male with pruning juvenile fruit trees; like the latter, circumcision symbolically readies the stem for producing fruit.

The priestly writings trace the fate of this blessing. When Isaac gives Jacob his final blessing, he prays that God "bless you, make you fertile and numerous, so that you become an assembly of peoples. May God grant the blessing of Abraham to you and your offspring, that you may possess the land where you are sojourning, which God gave to Abraham" (Genesis 28:3). This wish is subsequently fulfilled upon Jacob's return to Canaan when God blesses him with fertility (Genesis 35:11). As his death approaches, Jacob recalls this blessing when he adopts Joseph's sons, Jacob's grandchildren, into his patrilineage (Genesis 48:3–5). The book of Exodus begins by noting that this blessing has been fulfilled: "The Israelites were fertile and prolific; they multiplied and increased very greatly, so that the land was filled with them" (Exodus 1:6).

As is now evident, the preoccupation with procreation is intimately tied to the issue of descent. The priestly writings are interested in reproduction as the means through which the genealogy of Abraham and then Jacob (Israel) is perpetuated and expanded (Eilberg-Schwartz 1990: 163–76; Sapp 1977: 12). In particular it is the patriline, that is, the line of male descendants, that evokes interest within the priestly writings. This interest is evident by the fact that the priestly genealogies generally list only male names; the names of wives and daughters are absent (Bird 1981: 134–37; Eilberg-Schwartz 1990: 171–73; Jay 1985: 283–309; 1988: 52–70). The rite of circumcision also serves as a token of this symbolic link between masculinity, genealogy, and reproduction. Impressing a symbol of fertility on the male organ of reproduction establishes a connection between procreation and masculinity and creates a community of men who are linked to one another through a similar mark on their male members. By contrast, the potential connection between women and procreation is symbolically undermined: menstrual blood and blood of birth, which could easily symbolize procreative capacities, are instead associated with death.[8] There is a tension, therefore, between genealogy and reproduction. For the purposes of genealogical reckoning, wives and hence sexual intercourse cannot exist. But the presence of women is always necessary because men cannot reproduce alone.

The preoccupation with these twin themes of procreation and genealogy makes sense given the historical situation and social organization of the priestly community. Israelite priests were an elite community who presided over the sacrificial cult during the Israelite monarchy (tenth to sixth centuries B.C.E.). During this time, they regulated the sacrificial system in the Jerusalem Temple as well as in local sanctuaries outside Jerusalem. In the late seventh century, the cult was centralized in Jerusalem and priests continued to preside over the animal sacrifices in the Jerusalem Temple.

Scholars frequently date the priestly writings to the period during or shortly after the Babylonian exile, when pressures to increase the population may have been particularly acute. But there are other reasons, springing from the self-understanding and organization of priestly community, that would also explain the concern with procreation. The priesthood was inherited patrilineally, from father to son. All priests were purportedly descended from Levi or one of his descendants, such as Aaron. The priesthood, therefore, legitimated itself with a kinship idiom. This idiom shaped the larger interests of the priestly community and accounts for the obsessive interest in detailing genealogies. The "begats" of the Genesis narratives are primarily the work of the priests. The interest in genealogy and reproduction are obviously linked. Since lineages are replenished through the reproduction of its members, societies that define themselves through a kinship idiom frequently focus intense interest on human fecundity and clear lines of descent.[9] To put it another way, without procreation there would be no genealogy and thus no priestly community.

It is for these reasons that the priestly community could not have produced a myth of creation such as Genesis 2 in which the first person is initially created alone (Genesis 2:7).[10] It is true that in this other myth God eventually creates a human partner for Adam, authorizes marriage and apparently sexuality (von Rad 1976: 84–85; Sapp 1977: 12–16). But here God's original intention does not explicitly include sexuality or human companionship. The decision to create a human partner is the result of a process. After creating the first person, God unilaterally decides that it is not good for the first person to be alone and decides to make a fitting partner for the earthling (Genesis 2:18). It is at this point that God creates the animals, as if they might be a fitting partner for the first person. It is only when the animals turn out to be inadequate companions that God fashions a second person from part of the first person. In this myth, then, the first act of reproduction is a kind of fission: a second person is split off from the body of the first. The first act of reproduction thus does not involve sexuality. With the creation of the second person emerges the difference between man and woman, and this provides the basis for the institution of marriage, and presumably sexual intercourse and reproduction. While the authorization of marriage is regarded as the climax of the story by some interpreters (Trible 1978: 102; Sapp 1977: 12–16), another reading is also possible, namely, that sexual intercourse and reproduction are not part of the human essence. After all, God originally created the first person alone; human companionship, intercourse, and reproduction were divine afterthoughts. Thus it is possible to construe this myth as suggesting that the human is most like God when sexual relations are renounced.

It is with these sorts of conclusions, if not this particular myth, that the priestly story of creation takes exception.[11] By synchronizing the creation of man and woman, the priestly myth avoids the otherwise possible conclusion

41

that the sexual division of humanity and hence sexual intercourse and reproduction are not part of God's original intention in creating humanity. By
locating authority for procreation not only in the creation account, but at
the very moment of human origins, the priestly myth makes reproduction an
essential human trait (see Otwell 1977: 16; Sapp 1977: 10).

But the synchronization of man's and woman's creation, while solving
one problem, generates another in its wake. Specifically, this notion of creation creates a strain with another important conviction of the priestly
writer, namely, that God created humanity in the divine image. In what
sense can a sexually divided humanity, one that is expected to reproduce, be
made in the image of a monotheistic God, who has no partners? It is to this
problem that we now turn.

IN THE IMAGE OF GOD

> And God said, "Let us make Man ['adam] in our image, after our like-
> ness . . . They shall rule the fish of the sea, the birds of the sky, the
> cattle, the whole earth, and all the creeping things that creep on earth."
> And God created Man in His image, in the image of God He created
> him; male and female He created them. God blessed them and God
> said to them, "Be fertile and increase, fill the earth and master it; and
> rule the fish of the sea, the birds of the sky, and all the living things
> that creep on earth.
>
> (Genesis 1:26–28)

There are a number of conflicting interpretations of what it means to say
God made humanity in the divine image. It is not my intention to decide
which of these interpretations is correct (a hopeless task for reasons I shall
suggest). Rather, I explore the implications of each interpretation *on the
presumption* that it is correct. In other words, assuming that each interpretation is valid, what implications does it have for human embodiment and
sexuality? To anticipate, I shall argue that no matter how the priestly community may originally have construed this passage, if indeed there ever was
an original meaning, it must have experienced tension around the human
body.

The conflict in question springs from certain limitations that Israelite
culture imposed on the representation and conceptualization of God. These
limitations made it difficult, if not impossible, to reconcile aspects of human
embodiment, particularly human sexual relations, with the idea of being
made in the divine image. If these religious convictions had gained the upper
hand, they might have generated a renunciation of either the body in general
or sexuality in particular. But these impulses in Israelite religion came in
conflict with the priests' equally strong commitment to the importance of
human sexuality as the vehicle for reproduction. I will sometimes refer to

42

these tensions as the "contradictions of monotheism." But it is important to bear in mind that these tensions appear most forcefully in one particular formation of monotheism, that of the Israelite priests. It is when the conviction that humans are made in the image of God appears in the same cultural formation that exalts human reproduction and sexuality that these tensions emerge most powerfully.

Despite the voluminous literature on the "image of God" passage, the interpretations can be categorized into three major groupings (see below). There are a variety of technical historical and linguistic arguments that support or discount each of these interpretations. These do not bear on the present argument which attempts to show that the body is rendered problematic regardless of which of these interpretations is correct.

A bodiless God

Certain strands within Israelite literature suggest that God has no form, at least no form that humans can see or imagine:

> The Lord spoke to you out of the fire; you heard the sound of words but perceived no shape – nothing but a voice. . . . For your own sake, therefore, be most careful – since you saw no shape when the Lord your God spoke to you at Horeb out of the fire – not to act wickedly and make for yourselves a sculptured image in any likeness whatever: the form of a man or a woman, the form of any beast on the earth. . . . Take care, then, not to forget the covenant that the Lord your God concluded with you and not to make for yourselves a sculptured image in any likeness, against which the Lord your God has enjoined you. For the Lord your God is a consuming fire, an impassioned God.
>
> (Deuteronomy 4:12–24)

This passage, dating to the late seventh century B.C.E., asserts that Israelites heard a voice but did not see any divine form during the revelation on Horeb. This is given as the reason for the prohibitions on depicting the deity in plastic art, a prohibition with roots in a much older tradition (Exodus 20:4, 23; 34:17; Deuteronomy 5:8; 27:15; see von Rad 1966: 49; Childs 1974: 405–406).[12] The original motivation for this prohibition is debatable.[13] Archaeological evidence confirms that Israelite art did not represent God sitting on the divine throne (Hendel 1988), a proscription that may originally have stemmed from an Israelite ambivalence toward the institution of kingship. The representation of a god on the throne was one means through which ancient Near Eastern cultures legitimated royal authority. The prohibitions of such depictions in Israelite religion may reflect a desire to delegitimize the institution of kingship, a desire that developed during the Israelite tribal league when there were no kings in Israel (Hendel 1988). Below, I will suggest another possible reason for this prohibition. But whatever its prime motivation, the effect of the proscription is clearly to place restrictions on the visualization of God.

Many interpreters reasonably assume that these Israelite impulses to "de-form" God provide the background for the priestly claim that humans are made in the image of God (e.g., Barr 1968/69; Bird 1981; Cassuto 1978: 34–35).[14] In other words, humans resemble God in some qualitative sense only. Being made in God's image implies no resemblance between the human and divine forms. Interpreters disagree as to the particular qualities humans and God share.[15] But generally they include the "spiritual" or "higher" human functions. Nahum Sarna (1970: 15–16) is representative of this trend when he writes

> the idea of man "in the image of God" must inevitably include within the scope of its meaning all those faculties and gifts of character that distinguish man from the beast and that are needed for the fulfillment of his task on earth, namely, intellect, free will, self-awareness, consciousness of the existence of others, conscience, responsibility and self-control.

Other interpreters suggest that humans are like God in ruling over creation. Indeed, the idea that humanity is made in the image of God who is king of the universe slides easily into the idea that humans rule the earth: "They shall rule the fish of the sea, the birds of the sky, the cattle, the whole earth, and all the creeping things that creep on earth" (Genesis 1:26). This line of interpretation is supported by ancient Near Eastern parallels in which the King is said to be the image of God (Bird 1981: 140; Cohen 1989: 16; Miller 1972: 289–304; von Rad 1976: 59; Westermann 1984: 150ff).[16] In addition, the priests considered God's activity at creation paradigmatic in establishing an order that Israelites were responsible for maintaining. Israelites were expected to preserve those classifications that God had implanted at creation (Douglas 1966: 29–57; Eilberg-Schwartz 1990: 217–25).

According to these qualitative interpretations, the priests understood humans to be made in the image of a disembodied and sexless God. "The Creator in Genesis is uniquely without any female counterpart and the very association of sex with God is utterly alien to the religion of the Bible" (Sarna 1970: 13). Embodiment and sexuality are thus traits that humans share with animals. "*Unlike* God, but *like* the other creatures, *adam* is characterized by sexual differentiation" (Bird 1981: 148).[17] On this reading, the image of God does not parallel the human differentiation into male and female. It is "generic Man" that is the image of God, but not humankind as sexually differentiated. The "image of God refers to neither Adam alone nor to Eve, but only to the two of them together" (Sapp 1977: 10). "Man's pro-creative ability is not here understood as an emanation or manifestation of his creation in God's image" (von Rad 1976: 60).

44

We must be careful not to assume that because biblical writers associated reproduction with animals they therefore regarded sexual intercourse as a "beastly" activity. On the contrary, the command to be fruitful and multiply is considered a blessing that humans share with animals (Genesis 1:21–22; see Bird 1981: 157; Sapp 1977: 10). Indeed, Israel is metaphorically identified with the herds and flocks (Eilberg-Schwartz 1990: 115–40), and multiplying like animals is regarded as a positive image. "I will increase Israel with men as a flock of sheep," says God (Ezekiel 34:31).

Nonetheless, these interpretations leave the human body caught between contradictory expectations. On the one hand, human embodiment and sexuality are considered good; but they are good because God said so (Genesis 1:31), and because they are products of God's creative activity. Yet at the same time they are the very symbols of human difference from God. That is, it is the non-sexual and non-embodied part of the human person that is made in God's image. For this reason, there is a tension between obeying God and being like God. A person who wishes to obey God should be fruitful and multiply. But in doing so, one engages precisely that dimension of human experience that denies one's similarity to God. In fact, sexual intercourse contaminates a couple, alienating them from the sacred and hence from God. These dilemmas arise on any of the strictly qualitative or spiritual interpretations.

God "re-formed"

But not all strands of Israelite religion deny that God has a form or body, as many interpreters have observed (Barr 1959; Kaufmann 1972: 236–37; von Rad 1976: 58; Westermann 1984: 149ff; Mopsik 1989; Boyarin 1990). Indeed, several sources make it clear that some Israelites imagined that God has or at least assumes a human appearance (e.g., Exodus 24:9–11; 33:17; 1 Kings 22:19; Amos 9:1; Isaiah 6:1; Ezekiel 1:26–28; Daniel 7:9).

> Then Moses and Aaron, Nadab and Abihu, and seventy elders of Israel ascended and they saw the God of Israel: under His feet there was a likeness of a pavement of sapphire, like the very sky of purity. Yet He did not raise His hand against the leaders of the Israelites; they beheld God and they ate and drank.
>
> (Exodus 24:9)

> And the Lord said [to Moses], "See, there is a place near Me. Station yourself on the rock and, as My presence passes by, I will put you in a cleft of the rock and shield you with My hand until I have passed by. Then I will take My hand away and you will see My back; but My face must not be seen."
>
> (Exodus 33:23)

45

HOWARD EILBERG-SCHWARTZ

The most detailed description of God is given in the book of Ezekiel. Ezekiel sees "a semblance of a human form. From what appeared as his loins up, I saw a gleam as of amber ... and from what appeared as his loins down, I saw what looked like fire. There was a radiance all about him. . . . That was the appearance of the semblance of the Presence of the Lord" (Ezekiel 1:26–28). Since Ezekiel is a priest, it is possible that Ezekiel's image of God was shared by the priestly author of Genesis 1.

There is, then, an important impulse in Israelite religion that does ascribe a human form to God and assumes that, under certain conditions, the divine form is visible. Given this impulse within Israelite religion, an alternative understanding emerges of what it means to be made in God's image, namely, that the human body resembles the divine form.[18] Support for this view comes from the use of the word "image" (*tselem*), which most interpreters construe to mean a physical likeness.[19] Furthermore, in Genesis 5:1–3, the terms "image" and "likeness" are used to describe the resemblance between Adam and his son Seth. The repetition of the same terminology here suggests that humanity resembles God in the same way that Seth resembles Adam, which includes a physical resemblance (Sapp 1977: 8; Mopsik 1989: 52).[20] This latter interpretation of the "image of God" passage is compatible with the qualitative interpretations given above. Humans can be like God both in their appearance and qualities (Westermann 1984: 151ff; von Rad 1976: 58; Sapp 1977: 7).

Advocates of the second interpretation, which "re-forms" God, believe this reading rehabilitates the human body in important ways. And to some extent they are right. Since the human form mirrors the divine appearance, having a body is part of what it means for humans to be made in the image of God. The form of the body ceases to be a sign of human and divine differ-ence. But on further reflection, it becomes clear that even the ascription of a human form to God does not completely solve the problem of human embodiment, since having the form of a body does not mean that God is materially embodied. From those sources that depict God's body it is impos-sible to determine whether it is substantive. Indeed, one can make the argu-ment that God's materialization takes other forms, such as fire (Exodus 3:2; Deuteronomy 4:11–12). If God's body is immaterial, one that does not die, have emissions, require sexual intercourse, and so forth, then it is only the form of the human body that is legitimated but not the experience of embodiment itself.

Furthermore, Israelite sources are extremely reticent about describing the divine body. Indeed, seeing God is considered dangerous and consequently appears to be the privilege of certain qualified leaders (Barr 1959; Boyarin 1990). According to one passage, God tells Moses you "cannot see My face, for no person may see Me and live" (Exodus 33:17–23). Even those sources that suggest that the full body of God is visible avoid any descriptions. When Moses, Aaron, and the elders reportedly see God, the text describes only

46

what is under God's feet. Even Ezekiel is careful to qualify his description of God in fundamental ways. He sees only "the appearance of the semblance of the Presence of the Lord." This circumspection about God's body – about describing and representing it – is also evident in the way Israelite literature avoids certain kinds of anthropomorphisms. While God does a variety of humanlike things, including speaking, walking, and laughing, God does not perform "baser" human functions, such as eating, digesting, urinating, or defecating.[21]

In the official conceptions of Israelite religion, then, God's body is only partially conceptualized. This reticence has the effect and may indeed be partially motivated by the desire to veil the divine sex.[22] Ezekiel's description of God, for example, does not make clear whether God's lower regions are human in form: "from what appeared as his loins down, I saw what looked like fire."[23]

A similar concern may be present in the story in which God allows Moses to see only the divine back. Indeed, this incident (which is from the J source) is reminiscent of another story recounted by the same author (Genesis 9:20–27): when Noah is drunk, his son Ham (which means "hot"), sees his father's nakedness. This is purportedly the sin for which Canaan, Ham's son, is subsequently cursed. When Ham tells his brothers, Shem and Japheth, what he has seen, they take a cloth, place it against both their backs and, walking backward, cover their father's nakedness; "their faces were turned the other way, so that they did not see their father's nakedness." The similarities between these two accounts are too striking to be passed over. Noah's sons walk backward and divert their gaze so they cannot see their father's nakedness, while God turns away so that Moses can only see the divine behind.[24] It is as if God is being modest about disclosing the divine sex.

Does God have genitals and, if so, of which sex? It is interesting that interpreters have generally avoided this question. This seems a particularly important lacuna for interpreters who understand Genesis 1:26–27 to mean that the human body is made in the image of deity. By avoiding the question of God's sex, they skirt a fundamental question: how can male and female bodies both resemble the divine form? Since God's sex is veiled, however, any conclusions have to be inferred indirectly from statements about God's gender. But however this question is answered poses a problem for human embodiment generally and sexuality in particular. If God is asexual, as many interpreters would have it, then only part of the human body is made in the image of God.

But suppose Israelites did imagine that God had a sex. Given the preponderance of masculine imagery for God (e.g., as man of war, king, father), Israelites would presumably have assumed that God had a penis, if they had bothered to think about it.[25] The story about the sons of God taking wives from daughters of men (Genesis 6:1–4, by the J writer) gives support to the assumption that the divine is considered male. And the parallel between the story of Noah's nakedness and the story of Moses seeing God's back might also suggest that what God is hiding is a phallus.

While the assumption of a divine phallus may legitimate the male body, it nonetheless leaves human sexuality problematic. To put it bluntly, what would a monotheistic God do with a reproductive organ? In official Israelite monotheism, God had no divine partners with whom to consort. Thus, in contrast to other ancient Near Eastern creation myths in which the gods copulate, Israelite creation stories depict God as creating the world alone (Sarna 1970: 12–13; Sapp 1977: 2–3; von Rad 1976: 58–60). And in the priestly story, God creates the world by speaking (Sapp 1977: 1; Scarry 1985: 181–210).[26] Feminists have emphasized the way that an image of a male God creates a problem for being a woman. If God has the physical likeness of a male, the female body is by definition problematic. But what is emphasized much less frequently is how a monotheistic, male God also leaves males in conflict with their own bodies. If males are to be like God, then their penises are only for show; they should not be used for reproduction. The form of reproduction that can most easily be reconciled with a monotheistic God is fission, as in the second story of creation. Thus even on the interpretation that treats the human form as made in the image of God, the body remains a problem in certain fundamental ways. If God has no sex, then the reproductive organs of both males and females are rendered problematic. And if God does have a sex, whether male or female, God's reproductive organs are useless.[27]

These religious convictions, of course, could easily generate a sexual asceticism. But it is important to remember that the priests could not entertain this option. The theme of reproduction was so deeply embedded in their self-understanding and organization as a patrilineally defined community that to reject these themes would have been tantamount to dismantling their community. So even if the priests had imagined an embodied God, the human body would have been left facing fundamental and irresolvable tensions. But these tensions are generally not visible. And they are not visible because the debate about the image of God passage generally revolves around the question of whether that passage implies a similarity between the human body and the divine form. That debate draws attention away from the deepest contradiction of all: namely, the purpose of reproductive organs on the body of a monotheistic God. And it is perhaps this dilemma that contributes to the prohibition on representing God in material form, which is another way of hiding the problem of God's sex.

The sexuality of God

If the attempt to embody God does so at the expense of God's sexuality (a monotheistic God can have no sexual experience), the obverse is also true:

sexuality can only be predicated of God at the cost of divine embodiment. In other words, a monotheistic God cannot have both a body and a sexual experience. This second form of incompatibility is evident in the attempt by some interpreters to reconcile the sexual division of humanity with the image of God. After all, it is reasonable to read Genesis 1:26–28 as suggesting that men and women are both made in the image of God. Phyllis Trible's *God and the Rhetoric of Sexuality* is one of the most articulate expositions of this argument.[28] In Trible's view, the division into male and female is what distinguishes humans from animals. "Procreation is shared by humankind with the animal world . . . sexuality is not" (Trible 1978: 15). That is, although Genesis 1 says that both animals and humans reproduce, the attributes of male and female are exclusively human characteristics, at least in Genesis 1.[29] Animals, by contrast, are divided "according to their kinds," a form of categorization that does not apply to humans. Through a literary analysis, Trible goes on to suggest that "male" and "female" correspond structurally to "the image of God." That is not to say that sexual differentiation can be applied to God (Trible 1978: 21). But sexuality is one of the human experiences that points toward an understanding of Israel's transcendent deity. Trible develops her argument by exploring the metaphors used to depict God. God is metaphorically not only a father, husband, king, and warrior but also a woman who conceives, gets pregnant, gives birth, nurses, and mothers children.

Trible's interpretation is self-consciously an attempt to recover female imagery and motifs within the Hebrew Scriptures. As suggested by the title of her book, her project includes the attempt to redeem human embodiment and sexuality. Her interpretation thus goes a long way toward reconciling human sexuality with the conviction that humans are made in the image of God.

But in crucial ways this interpretation also leaves the experience of embodiment and sexuality problematic. It is striking that Trible completely ignores the interpretation that ascribes a form or body to God. This omission is interesting in a book that seeks to redeem sexuality. Upon reflection, however, it is clear that this omission is a necessary precondition for any interpretation that seeks a reconciliation between the sexual division of humanity and the image of God. Since there are no other gods, God's act of copulation *can only be metaphoric*. Ezekiel, for example, invokes the metaphor of sexual intercourse to depict the covenant between God and Israel (Ezekiel 16:8). While these metaphors do validate human sexuality in important ways, they still leave something to be desired. God cannot have an embodied sexual experience. If God has a penis, it plays no role in the divine relationship with Israel. From this perspective, the metaphor of God having intercourse with Israel actually devalues human copulation in one significant way. If the relation of God to Israel is analogous to that of husband and wife, then what parallels the human act of intercourse is revelation, the

49

insemination of Israel with God's will. Divine intercourse with Israel is mediated through speech. This substitution of speech for sexual intercourse is evident in Ezekiel's depiction of God's intercourse with Israel. Thus God says, "I spread My robe over you and covered your nakedness and I entered into a covenant with you *by oath*" (Ezekiel 16:8). Israel is inseminated with the divine will. It is even less clear how the analogy works when God is metaphorically a woman who is impregnated and conceives. Who is Israel's metaphorical father? So when the metaphor of human copulation is projected onto the relationship between God and Israel, it effects only a partial reconciliation between human sexuality and the conviction that humans are made in the divine image. The rehabilitation of human sexuality must take place at the expense of God's body. It is impossible to simultaneously embrace the idea that God has a body with a sex and is a sexual being. As soon as one of these ideas is grasped, the other slides into obscurity. In order for God to have sex, God must not have a body, and to have a body, God can have no sex.

MYTH, CONTRADICTION AND AMBIGUITY

I have consciously avoided favoring any interpretation of "the image of God" passage in order to show that on any of the interpretations, the priests are left with their bodies caught in a morass of fundamental tensions. It is impossible to affirm both the conviction that human sexuality and reproduction are divinely authorized aspects of human experience and the assertion that humans are made in God's image without at the same time rendering the human body or sexuality problematic in some aspect or another. To push this line of thinking further, it is possible that the "image of God" passage never had a single meaning. James Barr (1968/69: 13) anticipates me in writing that "there is no reason to believe that this writer had in his mind any definite idea about the content or the location of the image of God." But according to Barr, this hesitation stemmed from a "delicacy and questionability . . . of any idea of analogies to God." But another possible explanation is now obvious. The ambiguity of "the image of God" passage may attempt to hide the fundamental dilemmas implicit in the religious formation of the priests. If so, then none of the contemporary interpretations of Genesis 1:26–28 can be construed as the original meaning of this passage. Rather, the wide range of interpretations testifies to the power of this myth to simultaneously hold together what are radically different possibilities and thus gloss irresolvable tensions in the priestly religious culture. Indeed, it seems that the passage is carefully formulated so as to obscure, as much as is possible, these various problems.

The shift between plural and singular nouns and verb tenses is one means by which this myth negotiates the conflict between a monotheistic God and a humanity that is sexually divided. The plural "Let us create" has always been puzzling to interpreters. Is the plural referring to other divine beings (von Rad 1976: 58; Sawyer 1974: 423–24) or is it a royal "we" (Speiser 1964: 7)? However this question is answered, it is clear that this construction glosses the problematic fact that there is only one God but two sexes of human beings. Phyllis Bird (1981: 148) writes that "'Let us' cannot be a slip . . . it appears also to have been selected by P as a means of breaking the direct identification between *adam* and God suggested by the metaphor of image, a way of blurring or obscuring the referent of [*tselem*]." A similar obfuscation is accomplished by the shift from singular to plural in speaking of humanity (He created *him*, male and female he created *them*). The use of two nouns "image" (*tselem*) and "likeness" (*demut*), the former of which seems to imply a plastic representation and the latter a more abstract, qualitative similarity (Miller 1972: 291), also contributes to the confusion.[30] Furthermore, interpretations of the "image of God" passages differ depending on which of these terms is taken as primary and which secondary. For example, most interpreters argue that the priestly writer introduced the more abstract term "likeness" to qualify the more graphic term "image" so as to avoid any suggestion that the human appearance resembles the divine form (Sawyer 1974: 420).[31] Miller, by contrast, argues that the term "likeness" (*demut*), which has linguistic affinity with the word for "blood" (*dam*), was original and goes back to Mesopotamian myths that conceive of humans as made from the blood of the gods. The introduction of the term "image" was intended to rule out this sort of interpretation by substituting a word for resemblance that did not have associations to blood.

The second "image of God" passage only adds to the confusion. This passage employs the term "likeness" to describe the similarity between God and humanity: "This is the record of Adam's line. When God created man, He made him in the likeness of God; male and female He created them." But the passage then goes on to use the terms "likeness" and "image" to describe the similarity of Adam and his son Seth: "When Adam had lived 130 years, he begot a son in his likeness after his image, and he named him Seth" (Genesis 5:13). If Genesis 5:1–3 is read by itself, it seems to suggest that the likeness between God and humanity is of a different order than the likeness between a father and son. The resemblance between God and humanity is described by the word "likeness" only. But Adam begets a son who is in both his likeness and his image. But if Genesis 5:1–3 is read as a supplement to Genesis 1:26–28, the opposite is the case: the same terms are used to describe the resemblance between Seth and Adam (Genesis 5:3) and between God and humanity (Genesis 1:26–27). The point of these myths, then, may be to hide the basic tensions through a screen of confusion. To be sure, these maneuvers do not entirely hide the problem. But given an impossible task, these myths rise to the occasion.

It is important to realize that the tensions that I am describing were not characteristic of all Israelite writers. As long as humans were understood as

51

different from God, the impulse toward monotheism and the impoverished conceptualization of God's body need not have rendered human embodiment or sexuality problematic. The asexual or formless nature of God would pose less of a problem to the human body on the assumption that humans are made from the dust of the earth (Genesis 2:7). As an earthly substance, humans would be expected to have functions and needs that God does not. Neither the impulse toward monotheism nor toward a disembodied God by themselves necessarily creates a problem for the human body. It is only when these tendencies are coupled with the conviction that humans are created in the likeness and image of God, as the priests suggest (Genesis 1:26–27), that human bodies become problematic.

For these reasons, it is in the priestly writings in particular, and not in Israelite religion as a whole, that the boundaries and integrity of the body become such an intense preoccupation. This cultural obsession, I have suggested, springs from the fact that the human body is caught between contending cultural impulses. This higher order contradiction is reproduced at a lower level in rules governing sexuality. While the priests regard reproduction as one of the most important religious injunctions, semen is contaminating, even if ejaculated during a legitimate act of intercourse (Leviticus 15:16–18). One might say that for the priests, therefore, one is "damned if one does and damned if one doesn't." In the very act of carrying out God's will, one alienates oneself from God by becoming contaminated.

These tensions help explain the obsessive interest in the human body in priestly culture. The elaboration of the rules around the body was in part an attempt to control a puzzling object. But these rules did more than control a "foreign body." The absorption in legal regulations also diverted attention from the fundamental conflicts that surrounded the body. Absorbed by the legal particularities surrounding ejaculation, menstruation, and skin disease, those inside and outside the priestly community would have lost sight of the larger dilemmas that inhered in the priests' religious culture. It is for this reason too that the body became one of the richest sources of symbols in the priestly community. As I have shown elsewhere, the circumcised penis is a symbol of the covenant, procreation, and patrilineal descent. In addition, distinctions among body fluids are associated with other symbolic meanings, such as that between life and death, control and lack of control, themes embedded in the larger cultural system of ancient Israel (Eilberg-Schwartz 1990: 141–94). The superimposing of such themes on bodily processes and organs effects a transfer of energy from the conflicted object to the theme symbolized and thus heightens the power of the latter. The human body, then, was the site at which conflicting cultural impulses met and clashed. It was that conflict that made the Jews more than just a People of the Book. They also became a People of the Body.

NOTES

1 I would like to thank Robert Cohn, Ronald Hendel, Martin Jaffee, Louis Newman, and Riv-Ellen Prell, who all made helpful suggestions on an earlier draft. I also profited greatly from conversations with Tikvah Frymer-Kensky.

2 This idea has an affinity with Victor Turner's (1967: 54–55) insight that physiological processes are often symbolic of more abstract cultural messages because they lend those messages a power that they otherwise would not have. The present argument differs from Turner's in seeing that power as deriving, not from physiological processes, but from contradictions in a cultural formation.

3 See also Biale (1994) who is attempting to correct this overly apologetic presentation of Judaism.

4 I am indebted to B. Turner for the concept and term "government of the body."

5 Some scholars following Kaufman defend a pre-exilic date for P. A review of this issue can be found in Wenham (1979: 9–13). See also Friedman (1987: 16lff). This debate is not crucial for the present argument, which does not depend on pinpointing the historical context in which the priestly writings were produced.

6 I am not making any claims about any specific literary relationship between the book of Ezekiel and the P source in the Hebrew Bible, a problem that has exercised a great deal of biblical scholarship. Rather, I am suggesting that Ezekiel's priestly origin may have contributed to his concern with the government of the body.

7 All quotations of the Hebrew Bible are taken from the translations of the Jewish Publication Society (1962; 1978; 1982).

8 See my discussion of circumcision, menstruation, and the issues of genealogy (Eilberg-Schwartz 1990: 141–95).

9 See my survey of ethnographic studies of circumcision in Africa, which show a recurring linkage between issues of genealogy, virility, and reproduction (Eilberg-Schwartz 1990: 141–77).

10 Most interpreters regard Adam in this story as male and Eve as being separated from a male body. See, however, Trible (1978: 72–105) and Bal (1987: 104–31), who argue that the original Adam is neuter and that sexual differentiation occurs only when a split is introduced. To avoid attributing a sex to the first human creation, I refer to Adam as "the first person."

11 See Frank Moore Cross (1973: 293–325), who argues that the priestly writer did not write a complete narrative paralleling the JE narrative, but rather expanded and supplemented it. If so, then the priestly writer felt compelled to supplement the creation story as told in Genesis 2.

12 See von Rad and Childs for the possible connection between the prohibition on images of God and the deuteronomic idea that Israel only heard but did not see God at Horeb. The latter idea is very likely a later interpretation of the already existing prohibition.

13 Childs (1974: 407–408) summarizes various attempts to explain this prohibition. Von Rad, for example, argues that images were prohibited because they failed to deal adequately with the nature of God. Similarly, Zimmerli argues that the prohibition reflects the idea that God has chosen to be revealed not in a static image, but in ambiguity of dynamic history. Below, I will suggest an additional reason for the prohibition: the representation of God would require defining the sex of God, which would force to the surface the complex tensions surrounding gender and sexuality that are implicit in Israelite monotheism.

14 James Barr (1959: 31–38) originally suggested that the "image of God" passage presupposes the resemblance between the human and divine forms. But he subsequently (1968/69: 11–26) retracted that view, based on historical and linguistic analysis.

53

15 Westermann (1984: 147) provides a review of interpreters who hold this position.

16 For a review of the relevant arguments and the ancient Near Eastern evidence, see especially Westermann (1984: 150ff).

17 It is interesting to compare Bird and Trible on this issue. Bird notes that in other contexts the priestly writer treats the categories of "male" and "female" as applicable to animals. Trible, for her part, argues that in Genesis 1 the division into "male" and "female" is unique to humankind since the animals are divided "according to their kinds," a type of categorization that does not apply to humans. According to Trible (1978: 15), "Procreation is shared by humankind with the animal world . . . sexuality is not."

18 Barr (1959) originally suggests this possibility and then changes his mind (see the previous note). For a history of this interpretation see Miller (1972: 292) and Westermann (1984: 149ff).

19 Not all interpreters agree with this interpretation of *tselem*. For a different reading, see Barr (1968/69). Furthermore, most interpreters argue that the other term, "likeness" (*demut*), qualifies the term "image" and is intended to rule out the idea that the human and divine forms are similar.

20 This is not the only reading of the relation between Genesis 1:28 and 5:1–3. I discuss an alternative below.

21 Sexual intercourse is one exception that I shall take up below.

22 In a subsequent context, I hope to consider this whole issue from the vantage point of Lacan's argument that the phallus must be veiled (Lacan 1977: 281–91). [See Eilberg-Schwartz 1994: 27–29]

23 I would like to thank my colleague Tikvah Frymer-Kensky for pointing this out to me.

24 The text suggests that God's modesty is motivated by a desire to hide the divine face "for man may not see my face and live" (Exodus 33:20). In another context, I hope to explore how God's face, or more specifically the divine mouth, is treated as a genital organ because of its generative role in creation.

25 Some feminist writers have assumed that God's sex is male on this basis. For example, in *Beyond God the Father*, Mary Daly (1973), in a section entitled "Castrating 'God,'" writes that "I have already suggested that if God is male, then the male is God. . . . The process of cutting away the Supreme Phallus can hardly be a merely 'rational' affair."

Trible and others have noted the feminine images of God. But none of these writers has argued that Israelites would have imagined God as being female, that is, as having a body with breasts, vagina, and womb. For a possible interesting exception, see Biale (1982). Biale argues that the priests thought of God as a "God of Breasts." This is reflected in the priests use of the term "El Shaddai" to describe God, a term that traditionally has been interpreted as "God Almighty." But the word *shaddai* also refers to "breasts," enabling the expression "El Shaddai" to be read as "God of Breasts." To strengthen his interpretation, Biale shows that this association is explicit in one early biblical passage and that the priestly writings use the term "El Shaddai" precisely in those contexts dealing with promises of fertility.

26 Scarry offers a provocative reading of biblical texts in the context of her larger argument about the relationship of voice, body, and pain. She sees a dialectic set in play by the fact that God is imagined as disembodied, as only a voice, whereas humans are embodied. This distance is frequently transversed by a weapon, which mirrors the relationship between a torturer, who magnifies a regime's voice through torture, and the victim, who loses his or her voice through the magnification of bodily pain. Scarry's reading is illuminating in many ways, but her theory

needs to be nuanced since it does not deal with those texts that imagine God in human form, an idea that confounds the sharp dichotomies with which she is working.

27 The only remaining possibility is that God is androgynous, an idea that does develop in late antique religions. On this view, male and female bodies are both partially made in God's image. Moreover, it is in the act of sexual intercourse, in the joining of male and female bodies together, that the human achieves the most complete reflection of the androgynous deity. This interpretation comes the closest to reconciling the division of the sexes with the image of God. But there does not seem to be any biblical evidence to support it. Moreover, a hermaphroditic God is a kind of hybrid, and the priestly writers generally find hybrids and other anomalies abhorrent. Finally, an androgynous deity does not procreate or have a sexual experience, thus still leaving an important difference between humans and the deity.

28 Trible's interpretation has been dismissed by some as a feminist reading that does not pay sufficient attention to the place of Genesis 1 in the larger context of the priestly writings (see, e.g., Bird). To a certain extent, this criticism is valid. To read Genesis 1 as an example of incipient egalitarianism ignores the fact that the priestly writings generally privilege the male over the female. As noted previously, the priestly genealogies do not even mention the presence of wives. But Trible's reading cannot be dismissed out of hand. As I have suggested, the simultaneous creation of male and female is motivated by a desire to legitimate procreation. But in order to do so, the priests had to tolerate the seeming implication that both male and female are made in the image of God. To reformulate Trible's question, then, it is interesting to ask how and why the priests managed to tolerate the association of "the female" with the image of God.

29 As noted earlier, Bird points out that the categorization of male and female is used elsewhere in the priestly writings to talk about animals.

30 See, however, Barr (1968/69), who argues that *tselem* was the term most apt for avoiding the suggestion of resemblance of the human body and divine form.

31 See Miller (1972: 293) for other references to this argument.

3

THE HEBREW GOD AND HIS FEMALE COMPLEMENTS

Athalya Brenner

THE HEBREW GOD'S GENDER

Was God a woman at the dawn of Religion (Stone 1977: 17)? The Hebrew god, as described in the Hebrew Bible (Old Testament), was not. The Hebrew god's gender, from the very beginning as documented in the Bible, was almost invariably referred to as M (male/masculine).

It would be an error to attribute this gender definition of the Hebrew divine being to the restrictive usage of the Hebrew language alone. Indeed, Hebrew has no N (grammatical neuter) class, no equivalent of the English "it." Thus every animate as well as inanimate entity, abstract concept or concrete phenomenon, has to be grammatically gendered in the language as either M or F (female/feminine). The linguistic practice of relating to the divine through M terminology seems like a matter of deliberate choice and world view. YHWH is, of course, not simply a male. How can "he" be, given "his" lack of physical characteristics beyond metaphor, a lack reinforced by the severe — albeit also transgressed — command not to supply "him" with plastic representation? He is male nevertheless, and a specific kind of male at that. He is rational and intellectual. Hence, he creates the cosmos and its contents by speech acts, that is, through language (Genesis 1:1–2:4a). At least according to the mainstreams of the biblical canon, that male god is omniscient, omnipotent, immanent. The question of his morality and justice, the so-called "theodicy," is not easily settled (Crenshaw 1983). Sometimes, as in the book of Job or in Ecclesiastes (Qohelet), his moral constitution seems questionable. He undoubtedly has a dark side, as well as a graceful and loving side (Exodus 20:5–6; 34:6–7; Jonah 4:2).[2] But, first and foremost, he is a paternal figure.

God is primarily depicted as a single M parent, cast and stereotyped from the outset as the Great Father. In the Garden of Eden narrative (Genesis 2:4b–3:24) he is a father who exiles Adam and Eve, his rebellious children, from the original homestead after they have eaten from the forbidden tree of knowledge. He makes explicit his fear that, if not expelled, the humans

56

might act to resemble him in divinity (3:22), that is, knowledge and unlimited life. Throughout the Eden story he maintains an authoritative if benevolent stance. His commands are inexplicable and unexplained but to be obeyed. All humanity, but particularly the Hebrews (Amos 9:7; Hosea 11:2), and especially King David and his dynasty are depicted as his "sons."

Humankind, M and F together in that order, is created in god's image (Genesis 1:26–8).[3] Does that actually mean that the Hebrew god embodies both M and F principles and that he is genderless, beyond gender or bi-gender? We shall see that this is perhaps so in places, but infrequently.[4] At any rate, humankind's destiny is set immediately at the time of its inception: to control the world, much the same as males are to control females (Genesis 3:16) and fathers their inferiors – women, minors, slaves, foreigners, everyone. The model for this societal image is obvious. Biblical law[5] and narratives imply that a patriarch of the premonarchical period was like a god: his was the right to judge and even condemn to death; see the Tamar and Judah story, where Judah condemns Tamar to death by burning for alleged "fornication" and her pregnancy, of which he is the unwitting agent (Genesis 38). In short, thus man creates his god in his father's image through the statement that god created man in his own divine image.

From a psychological perspective, god-as-father corresponds to Freud's analysis of the beginning of religion in the eventual deification of ancestral (mainly M) spirits, and to Rudolf Otto's attribution of religious sentiments primarily to horror/fear of the holy. The identification of the father idea with intellect, rational behavior, justice and control – considered self-evident by orthodox religious and theological systems, and by twentieth-century M psychology and psychotherapy – seems to inform the biblical texts.

A sociological perspective should also be considered. Literature is often reflexive of social attitudes, mores and norms. It is not too far-fetched to expect the social realities of the patriarchal order to be reflected in the design of the biblical construction known as the Hebrew god. *Contra* the revisionist feminists, Christian and Jewish alike (e.g., Trible 1973; 1978), who attempt to salvage the Hebrew god for their faith, it can be said emphatically that this god was never a "woman," was never even fully or largely metaphorized as a woman (but see below). Nor was he ever, on the whole, a womanly male. Therefore, it is difficult to relate to him – a common feminist practice – as "s/he," or as anything more than incorporating some features of femaleness or female symbols or deities.

To what extent does the assigning of an M gender to a communal god illustrate the social and legal inferiority of women in that same community? This is a separate issue which, strictly speaking, lies outside the scope of the present inquiry. We shall, however, briefly return to it later. Let us also note in passing that, even in cultures that partly admit goddess influence, women's status is not automatically superior.

YHWH IS THE SUPREME FATHER: HOW A LACK IS CONCEALED

Genesis

One way of evaluating the M-parent–child relationship between YHWH and his children (his sons, really) is to pronounce this relationship a continuous failure and increase disillusion in biblical myth (Clines 1990: 49–66, 85–105). In the origin myth (Genesis 1–11), the relationship deteriorates rapidly and steadily. The newly created woman initiates the eating of the fruit from the forbidden tree, and the human couple is driven out of the Garden. The first murder, a fratricide (4:1–16), soon follows the birth of Cain and Hebel, or Abel (Pardes 1992: 39–59). A brief erotic encounter between the sons of god (who are they anyhow?) and the daughters of man (6:1–4) threatens to bring together heaven and earth, reported earlier (chap. 1) to have been drawn asunder by god himself (cf. Davies 1993: 194–201). Humanity's morals have become so corrupt that god decides to destroy his children by a flood (chaps 6–8). And what happens to the family chosen to survive? No sooner is Noah saved than he starts a vine culture and gets drunk; then two of his sons either show disrespect by looking at his nakedness or, as some Jewish sages interpret the passage in their commentaries, castrate him or have homosexual intercourse with him (chap. 9). Humanity now attempts to consolidate by building a city and a tower so as to stay together and speak one language. This, once more, is a threat to the divine plan. God frustrates it and scatters his children further afield (11:1–9).

God now concentrates on Abraham's family (chap. 12 onwards), calling to Abraham to leave his homestead and go to a new, divinely appointed land: this is of course a replay in reverse of the expulsion from the primeval Garden. But does the new beginning, so promising since Abraham obeys god without hesitation, signify an end to the chain of disappointments? Not so. Soon after the entry to the land, Abraham has to leave it because of a famine. His wife is in danger of being violated by a foreign king (12:10–13:2; and cf. the two other versions of the same story, chaps 20 and 26). He has no son to inherit the extravagant divine promises liberally bestowed upon him. When he has two sons, Yitzhak and Yishmael, Sarah makes him send the firstborn away (chap. 21). Two generations later, Jacob steals the inheritance rights from his older brother Esau, and has to leave the country for many years (chap. 25 onwards). Then his son Joseph is sold to Egypt by his brothers, who eventually follow him there (chap. 37 onwards). Through strife, trickery and dishonesty, the promised land is evacuated by its presumed inheritors for many years.

After a prolonged sojourn in Egypt, YHWH sends Moses to deliver the Hebrews back to their land. He saves them from bondage by inflicting plagues upon the Egyptians and by parting the Sea of Reeds for them (Exodus 1–15). He reveals himself at Sinai and gives them the Ten Commandments and the Law, formalized as a political treaty binding both sides to one another (chaps 19-24). He protects, feeds, and guides his children, the Children of Israel. What does YHWH get in return? Crises. Complaints. A golden calf (chap. 32). Rebellions. Incidents of fear, skepticism, distrust, and disobedience recur throughout Numbers and Deuteronomy too. The corrective measure required yet again is, as in the case of the Primeval flood, extinction. The people are sentenced to roam the desert for a formulaic period of forty years. The desert generation – including Moses – has to die before a new beginning, the re-entry to the land, is embarked upon.

The remaining biblical books, which narrate the "history" of Israel and Judah until the destruction of the first temple and Jerusalem and the first exile in 586 B.C.E. (Joshua, Judges, Samuel, Kings: the so-called first biblical historiography), are informed by the same vision of failure and disappointment. It is claimed again and again that the Israelites keep turning away from their god, to whom they are supposedly bound orthogenetically as well as by legal covenant. He tries to save them from the consequences of their own follies by sending intermediaries – judges, leaders, prophets (see the prophetic books), kings – but to no avail. Finally, and against his will, he has to punish them by taking away both political organization and territory. They have to go into exile.

The second "historiographical" cycle – Chronicles, Ezra, and Nehemiah – takes us again to the very beginning of the world through to the restoration of Jerusalem and the temple into the fifth century B.C.E. In it, as well as in prophetic works which relate to the same period (Isaiah 40–66, for instance), the exile is understood as a period of re-education for the erring children. Here the general tone is more optimistic. Nonetheless, is the rehabilitation program considered wholly successful? Only partially so, as the various transgressions of the Law reported in Ezra and Nehemiah show. The Book of Daniel, the last and latest chapters of which refer to the very last years of the Hashmonaean revolt against Hellenized Syria (at the beginning of the second century B.C.E.), ends with a message similar to its predecessors. Only a few, the chosen ones, will survive the forthcoming political and religious tribulations. Thus the biblical story concludes with a message of hope but, once more, the hope is underlined by human anxiety of divine disappointment.

I have here summarized the story of Israelite/Judahite history, as narrated in the Hebrew Bible. Many details, especially of the earlier "history," cannot be verified by external (archaeological and other) evidence, thus their historicality – in the modern sense of the term – must remain questionable. However, the cultural/ideological thrust of the biblical macro-story is quite clear. It seems that the father-and-child model which informs the origin myth continues to operate in "history." This, by and large, is the societal model operative in the Bible as a literary configuration. While individual passages or story-lines may advance a different message, it seems that the overall framing ideology is conditioned by the pressing need to exonerate YHWH of his *justify parental abandonment.*

apparent periodic abandonments of his children. Rather than destroy the father image (as sons do, either metaphorically and symbolically or figuratively, in many non-monotheistic myths), biblical authors and editors opted for an ethos of *human* responsibility. The sons are blamed for their own bad fortunes, whereas the fatherhead's theodicy remains intact.

In Lacan's terms, the psychological and cultural construct "Father" is perceived by his children as the supreme phallic symbol. It is easier, perhaps, to plead recurrent instances of collective non-integrity than to demolish an ideal. However, three observations seem to be in order at this point.

First, it is difficult if not impossible, within the process of education and socialization, to draw a clear demarcation line between the failure of a child and that of a parent or to distinguish their respective burdens of responsibility. The process is one of mutuality, as is the outcome.

Second, one cannot help but wonder whether the singularity of the divine parent, and the insistence on his M attributes (justice and morality as prerequisites for gaining love, in so many instances) in his dealings with his children, is not at least one of the reasons for the continuous mutual failure of both partners throughout myth and "history."

Third, other solutions in the Hebrew Bible present the Hebrew god in images other than the ultimately fair Father with errant sons. Broadly speaking, these images fall into two main categories. The first supplies YHWH with various types of F consorts; the second supplies him with F attributes. It remains to be seen to what extent each of these categories is successful in removing the blame from YHWH. Both categories, though, illustrate an admission of the problematics involved in the divine lack of an overt F element and, also, the need to fill this lack.

HUMAN SEXUALITY AND DIVINE SEXUALITY: MATTERS OF FERTILITY AND F PRINCIPLES

The Bible establishes that the Israelites, whatever exactly their origins and history, were familiar with various cults practiced in the land that they eventually came to regard as theirs. Moreover and dialectically, in spite of zealous disparagement of those cults, they assimilated elements of them into their own cult. Deuteronomy and the related editorial framework of the books of Kings make it abundantly clear, through their heated and frequent polemics, that the fertility aspects of the so-called "Canaanite" rites were too attractive for the Israelites and Judahites to ignore. In the reigns of Jezebel and Athaliah, the Bible tells us (1 Kings 17 to 2 Kings 11), the cult of Baal and his female consort Asherah became official state cult in the northern kingdom ("Israel") as well as in the southern kingdom ("Judah"), alongside the cult of YHWH. A passage in Jeremiah (7:17–18) reports of such cults in Jerusalem itself, just before its destruction.

> Do you not see what they are doing in the cities of Judah and in the streets of Jerusalem? The children gather wood, the fathers kindle fire, and the women need dough, to make cakes for the queen of heaven;[6] and they pour drink offerings to other gods, to make me angry.

In other words Jeremiah the prophet (if he is a historical person), or whoever wrote under that name, is able to narrate the worship of the "queen of heaven" as an eyewitness. He disapproves of what he knows: the cult is a widely practiced family cult, in which the women are dominant, and this is considered one of the reasons for YHWH's wrath (cf. Jeremiah 44:15–30). As Carroll writes (1986: 212–13; see also 734–43),

> An idyllic picture of egalitarian religion with a strong emphasis on the family worshipping together! The cakes have impressed on them the image of the queen of heaven, the mother goddess of the ancient world . . . or they may be cakes in the shape of a star . . .

Who is this "queen of heaven"? Carroll rightly maintains that her precise name – the Babylonian Ishtar, the Canaanite Anat or Astarte, the Egyptian Isis – is less than important. All the names point to the same cultural manifestation of great mother goddess. Significantly, the people claim that her worship brings peace and economic prosperity (44:16–19). Jeremiah, of course, is indignant: YHWH's anger is provoked by this cult. In his view, that of YHWH's messenger, the goddess cult ultimately helped bring about the destruction of temple, city, and land.

A few points are worth noting here. It appears that as late as the sixth century B.C.E. cults of a/the mother goddess were popular even in Jerusalem, the supposed stronghold of YHWH's exclusive worship. Therefore, although it constituted an unwanted subculture for the author of the relevant biblical passages, the modern reader is under no obligation to label it as such. Furthermore, it seems that the goddess cult or cults flourished – and, significantly, as family cult – in times of political and economic stress. In such times people, especially women, seem to have turned back from the cult of the disappointing Hebrew Father to a divine Mother in a quest for maternal love and assistance. It follows that the accusations expressed by the literary "Jeremiah" have a sound basis in the reality of "his" day. The Father's disappointment in his children appears to be mirrored by his daughters' disappointment in him! Ironically, the information concerning this muted (minority?) view of the "daughters" is preserved by the patriarchal YHWH opposition to it.

Most narrators of the Hebrew Bible were probably males narrating for M consumption. They often accuse women of turning to non-monotheistic religious practices. And when the women are of foreign descent, the accusation becomes stereotypic. Such an approach is a useful ideological device, since it makes women the chief culprits in the drama of divine disappointment. For example, the religious influence of Solomon's many foreign wives is cited as a factor justifying the division of his kingdom into two kinglets immediately upon his death (1 Kings 11:1–13). In the age of Ezra and Nehemiah (mid-fifth century B.C.E.), foreign wives and mothers are divorced for their cultural and religious influence on the newly organized Jewish community. In other words, the usual societal, political, and economic rationale for exogamy and endogamy (Lévi-Strauss 1966; 1985) becomes secondary to the ideology of the Father. This ideology must be safeguarded against F religiosity and devotion to alternative cults.

Goddess cults were celebrated all over the ancient Near East, including the southern Levant or ancient "Israel." These cults had hallmarks. In them, the F divine element was dominant and often symbolized by the earth. The female deity stood for both fertility and sexuality: she was a lover and mother combined, but almost never enacted the socially inferior role of a daughter. She often had an M consort. He started his career by being her son, lover, and husband rolled into one. He died, sometimes because of her wrath, while she reigned eternal. She would in places rescue him from death back into divine life, only for the script to be repeated periodically. Later on, who knows when, the tables were turned: the M consort became the chief symbol for fertility/sexuality – perhaps through his recurrent resurrection, perhaps as an imitation of the seasonal fertility cycle. The goddess then became *his* demoted consort (Neumann 1955).

It is important to realize that, whatever the internal gender dominance might be, so-called pagan pantheons from the third millennium B.C.E. onwards were organized mostly in F/M couples. Imitative fertility rites of the *hieros gamos* (sacred marriage) type – a dramatically enacted "marriage" of a priestess and a priest, a king and the goddess's priestess, an F commoner and an M priest – were an integral part of Mediterranean culture and known as such to the "Hebrews," who finally defined themselves as Israelites and Judahites. Sexual intercourse indulged in under the auspices of a religious sanctuary or custom, which looks like – at least in part – "white" magic for encouraging fertility in the biological and human cosmos, could not fail to be attractive. The prophetic books, as well as Numbers and Deuteronomy, acknowledge this attraction indignantly. They demote the practice to no more than fornication, adultery, and prostitution. However, surprisingly, they put the non-monotheistic reality which surrounded them and which, by their own testimony, was practiced by their compatriots to a fresh literary use. They incorporated it into their own metaphorical/symbolical world, thus providing YHWH with his lack: the missing F consort. To use Jungian terminology, YHWH's animus side is provided with its complementary anima.

GOD THE HUSBAND: LOVE, MARRIAGE, AND COVENANT IN THE PROPHETIC BOOKS

The beginning of the book of Hosea (chaps 1–3), which refers to political events of the end of the eighth century B.C.E., might be the earliest passages to contain the new metaphor. The relationship between YHWH and his people, formalized in the Torah (Pentateuch) in terms of a binding covenant, is metaphorized in terms of a marriage situation. God is depicted as a steadfast, supportive, responsible, and loving husband. The Israelites are his adulterous, promiscuous, immature wife. There is no doubt that the scenario is a takeoff of sexuality/fertility rites. The metaphorical woman's illicit "lovers" – in the plural! – are named *ba'alim* after Baal, the Canaanite male god of storm and rain and hence the fertilizer of the earth. In Hosea, the speaker himself (the prophet?) reports an illustration of this marriage principle: "he" takes a "woman of harlotry" for a wife (chap. 1), and accuses women of participating in that cult freely, with the knowledge of their male kin (4:13).

In chapters 2 and 3 of Hosea we learn how a change can be effected. The woman-nation is clearly in need of re-education. First, a divorce by the divine husband; a period of isolation and training will follow. Then, and only then, will the woman-nation be worthy again of the divine husband's honorable intentions, and he will remarry her.

The same metaphor is employed in the Book of Jeremiah, which refers to a later period (beginning of the sixth century). The roles have not changed. On the contrary, they have become further polarized through the exaggerated imaging of the "wife." The woman-nation (Judah, in fact, since the northern kingdom was destroyed by the Assyrians in 722 B.C.E.), once more in danger of being divorced (Jeremiah 3), is even likened to a she-ass in heat (Brenner 1993a: chap. 2). In the book of Ezekiel, referring roughly to the same period or a little later, YHWH is both foster father and husband to the woman-Jerusalem; once grown, she becomes a common whore who commits religious and political adultery (chap. 16). This description, as well as that of the twin sisters Jerusalem and Samaria in chapter 23, is extremely pornographic (Setel 1985; van Dijk-Hemmes 1993).

Only in prophetic literature relating to the period after the destruction of Jerusalem and the exile do we get different versions of the same metaphor. Now, after the punishment (the exile) has been carried out, YHWH promises to reinstate his "wife" as mother and spouse in his/her land (Isaiah 49:14–23; 50:17–23, 54; 62:4–5; 66:7–13). Within the context of Isaiah 49–66, the image of god-as-husband is as frequent as that of god-as-father.

What can be gleaned from the continuing literary life of the divine husband/human spouse convention? The attribution of [metaphorical] matrimony to YHWH was probably facilitated not only by his exclusivity but also by his pronounced maleness. In stereotypic thinking, this maleness implies both a lack of and need for an F complement. The tendency to preserve YHWH's reputation of justice and fairness operates here as in the metaphor of the divine father. And last but not least, this religious-literary convention reflects societies in which the androcentric ethos, world view and vision are the norms. The negative F imagery consistently applied to the "erring" people becomes progressively more extravagant until, with Ezekiel, it achieves vulgar misogynistic proportions. It is designed to humble and intimidate the recipients. It must reflect, to a high degree, a reality of gender relations in an M world in which F sexuality is the Other, fatally attractive to males and because of that degraded and deemed in need of M control. To come back to Jungian terminology, YHWH is provided with an animal rather than an anima to complement his maleness.

THE THEOLOGICAL QUEST FOR A DIVINE FEMALE CONSORT: THE SONG OF SONGS

Within the Hebrew Bible, the Song of Songs is unique. It is an anthology of secular, non-matrimonial love lyrics, erotic and outspoken. Although the poetic material incorporated in it varies and has no clear plot line (in spite of many readers' attempts to find one), it has a well-organized structure (Exum 1973) which is probably due – like other features of the book – to the editor's or editors' efforts. One of the outstanding other features of the collection is the predominance of F voice(s) in it. Most of the lyrics assume the form of monologues and dialogues, and most of these are spoken by an F "I." Furthermore, those F voices compare favorably with their M counterparts. They are direct, articulate, loving, loyal, steadfast, imaginative, enterprising. The M lovers are weaker by comparison. No jealousy, no treachery, no accusations are admitted into the lovers' garden. There is no mention of a "father's house" or a father figure, as against references to a "mother's house" and mothers. The imagery employed by the M voices in regard to the F love object is strong, positive, beautiful. In short, egalitarian mutuality and gender equality – with a bias in favor of the F partner(s) – underlie the literary picture.

There may be many reasons for this unusual picture of gender roles in love and sexuality. One feasible explanation is the attribution of the Song of Songs, as a literary collection, to F authorship or editorship (Brenner 1989). This is probably less far-fetched than it seems at first, since love poetry is culturally tolerated for women even in patriarchal societies. What is most relevant to our agenda here, though, is not the biblical Song of Songs *per se* but, rather, the theological-allegorical exegesis attached to it by the orthodox Jewish and then Christian establishments from ancient times on.

Post-biblical Jewish interpretation coped with the uniquely secular nature of the Song of Songs and its apparent incompatibility with the rest of the Hebrew canon by promoting its allegorical interpretation as the only legitimate one. In the allegory, first hinted at in a text of the first century C.E., the

M lover is once more the Hebrew god and the F lover is his nation. In contradistinction to the previous love stories and disappointments, this allegorized "story" is a happy affair in which mood, traditional role, and outcome are inverted. The nation-woman now actively and loyally seeks her master; other partners are out of the question. This allegory was taken over by the Christian church as well: here the partners are Jesus and the soul/church/community (the Christological approach) or Mary and the soul/community (the Mariological approach). Such traditional interpretations of the Song of Songs, which persist until our times, claim to decipher its original meaning through the negation of its profane erotic meaning, and by attributing the active role to the male [divine] partner rather than to the female [human] one.

The religious and theological advantages of such allegorical interpretations are evident. To begin with, it chastises an unusual text and truly canonizes it. It also supplies god, finally, with a worthy loving partner. The allegory's therapeutic value almost cancels out the harsh harangues of the earlier prophetic books.

In passing, I would like to note that modern feminist critics share this ancient notion of the therapeutic import of the Song of Songs. Thus, for instance, Trible reads it as a counterfoil to the Garden of Eden story, a rectification of the gender relations and F social inferiority condoned there (Trible 1978).

YHWH AND HIS CONSORT: CONTEMPORANEOUS EXTRA-BIBLICAL EVIDENCE

At the beginning of the twentieth century, documents written on papyrus in Aramaic were found at Elephantine, a settlement on the small island in the Nile opposite Aswan. The documents discovered – legal, literary, religious – disclosed the existence of an organized colony of Jewish soldiers who populated the site from the beginning of the Persian rule in Egypt (525 B.C.E.) to the beginning of the common era. The Jewish settlers had a local temple and were conscious of their religious identity: their priests even attempted to correspond with the Jerusalem priests on religious and cultic matters (Cowley 1923; Kraeling 1953).

Whom did the Jews of Elephantine worship? The Hebrew god, of course, whom they called Yhw (a shorter form of YHWH?). And alongside him, in the same temple, two goddesses: Asham (probably the Ashmat of Samaria named in Amos 8:14) of Beit El (a chief city in the northern, Israelite kingdom according to biblical historiography) and Anat of Beit El.

Scholars have found it relatively easy to affirm that Yhw of Elephantine is YHWH of the Hebrew Bible, even though Yhw has two (!) female consorts. They regarded the religious practice of Elephantine as Jewish, albeit not normative, and excused it on various grounds. The first excuse cites populist culture:

> The Elephantine Jews brought with them to Egypt the popular religion combatted by the early prophets and by Jeremiah shortly before the destruction of the First Temple. It is true that this religion placed the God of Judah, Yahu . . . in the centre of the faith and worship.
>
> (Schalit 1971: 608)

Other scholars cite geographical distance and lack of communication with the prescriptive, normative Judaism of Second Temple Jerusalem, and/or assimilation to the foreign (non-monotheistic) environment. However, more recent archeological finds, earlier in date and closer to the Jerusalem centre, invalidate such apologies.

A Hebrew inscription in the old Hebrew script on a broken pythos, found in Kuntillet ʿAjrud in north-eastern Sinai (on the road from Gaza to the Red Sea) and dated to the beginning of the eighth century B.C.E., has three primitive figures drawn on it (fig. 1).

While the interpretation of these figures is still hotly debated by scholars (Dever 1984; Margalit 1989), I side with those who read it thus. The bigger figure in the foreground, on the left, is a crowned male figure; a smaller female figure, with breasts and a smaller crown, stands just behind him to

Pirhiya Beck, Tel Aviv University.

66

the right.[8] Their arms are locked, spouse-like. A third figure, probably a female (note the breasts again!) is seated to the far right, holding a musical instrument. The Hebrew inscription above the drawing reads: "I bless you by YHWH of Samariah and his Asherah" (Dever 1984; King 1989). Furthermore, a tomb inscription from el-Qom in Judea, dated approximately to the same period, also concludes with the words, "to YHWH and his Asherah" (Margalit 1990).

Asherah, like Anat, is a well-documented goddess of the north-west Semitic pantheon. We remember that, according to the Bible itself, at times Asherah was officially worshipped in Israel; her cult was matronized by Jezebel who, supposedly, imported it from her native Phoenician homeland. Other traces in the Bible either angrily acknowledge her worship as goddess − 2 Kings 14:13, for instance, where another royal lady is involved − or else demote her from goddess to a sacred tree or pole set next to an altar (2 Kings 13:6; 17:16; Deuteronomy 16:21; and many more). The apparent need for the hostile and widely distributed polemics against Asherah worship constitutes evidence for its continued popularity. Margalit (1989) claims that, linguistically, "Asherah" signifies "[she who] walks behind," displaying a stereotypic if divine attitude that befits a wife (and is reflected in the Kuntillet 'Ajrud drawing). Thus both the partially suppressed and distorted biblical evidence and the archeological evidence combine to suggest one conclusion. The cult of a goddess, who was considered YHWH's spouse, was celebrated in more than one place during the first temple era; and, beyond this period and the land, also by the Jewish settlement in Elephantine.

Readers and critics of the Hebrew Bible tend to balk at the idea that YHWH, the traces of canonical testimony notwithstanding, in fact had a divine consort in biblical times and well into the Persian period. They explain away the husband-wife imagery as "mere metaphor," as if metaphors are unproblematic figures of poetic expression.[9] But this is not so. The polemics of prophetic books appears to have been based on first-hand knowledge of the religious practice prevalent at the time. As hard as some elements fought to promote pure [M] monotheism, popular F cults continued to flourish. And in those cults, the unnatural deficiency of the Father god was supplemented by coupling him with a borrowed goddess figure. The archeological finds bear the most valuable witness to this phenomenon since, unlike the biblical texts, they are not overtly tendentious.

Finally, scholarly attempts to dismiss a consort status for Asherah in the Kuntillet 'Ajrud and el-Qom inscriptions, attempts motivated by the same purist ideologies found in the Bible itself, have been repudiated by many scholars. The need for an F complement was felt, the gap filled. Traditionalist protestations can no more obliterate YHWH's divine consort from the history of biblical religion, even if the Bible itself promotes her rejection with tell-tale vehemence. Patai's much criticized book, *The Hebrew Goddess* (1967), should therefore be revalued in the light of recent discoveries.

ATHALYA BRENNER

There are perhaps other and more traces in the Hebrew Bible for a divine F consort.[10] At this point, however, we shall turn to ancient Bible exegesis of another kind.

BEYOND THE HEBREW BIBLE: THE FEMALE PRINCIPLES OF THE SHEKINAH AND THE SHABBAT

Jewish mysticism does, of course, relate to the Hebrew Bible as to a canon and prooftext. Since Jewish mystical texts date from the first century C.E. on, they constitute another type of testimony for ancient Bible interpretation. And lest we think that mysticism is esoteric only, let us remember that esoteric it may be but it is theosophical too. At any rate, it has pervaded Jewish life and customs more and more over the ages.

The language of Jewish mysticism is erotic. The mystic's attempts to come closer to divine phenomena through the *Sefirot* ("stages") are depicted in sexual terminology (as well as in terms of light/darkness, letters and number combinations). It is therefore not too startling to find among the imaginative literature of the Qabbalah (mysticism) some fresh variations on YHWH's F complements. These hark back to biblical notions which are further developed, but with a twist. We shall name two such cases by way of illustrating this point.

According to the Bible, god's immanence (Hebrew *kabod*) "dwells" (Hebrew *shakan*) in certain parts of the world and among his people. Postbiblical Judaism developed the concept of immanence, and alongside it, that of god's *Shekinah*, "dwelling." In the Qabbalah, the *Shekinah* is the F element of the *Sefirot*, the first of the ten "stages." The mystic's ultimate purpose is to recover god's oneness through the reunification of his F and M elements – the oneness damaged by Israel's sins and other factors.

Another divine spouse is the Shabbat. In sixteenth-century Safed, a great Qabbalic centre, the Shabbat was hailed as the "queen": let us remember that one of the biblical god's appellations would translate as "the king of the royal kings." That the divine king is paired with the royal Shabbat becomes more explicit with the spreading of the custom to recite the Song of Songs for the Shabbat. Another poem recited for it was the biblical passage praising the woman or wife of valor (Proverbs 31:10-31). In time, the view of the Shabbat's divine matrimonial status spread beyond mystical circles.

YHWH AS MOTHER

God the father (as distinct from mother) is the norm in the Hebrew Bible. An additional partial list of passages referring to his paternal attributes includes the following: Deuteronomy 32:6; 2 Samuel 7:14; Isaiah 63:16; 64:7; Jeremiah 3:4, 19; 31:8; Malachi 1:6; Psalms 103:13; and three occurrences in Chronicles. Nevertheless, in some instances he is likened to a woman and, specifically, to woman-as-mother. The F images attributed to YHWH are infrequent but distributed throughout the Hebrew Bible. They occur in the Torah (Numbers 11:12), the Psalms (123:2), and Hosea 11, but mainly in Isaiah 40–66.[11] These chapters in Isaiah are, by scholarly consent, poems written and delivered not earlier than the middle of the sixth century B.C.E., from the time of the return from the Babylonian exile. In some passages (e.g., 42:13–14; 45:9–10; 49:14–15; and 66:13), YHWH is compared to a mother and a woman in labor. Gruber rightly states that, within these same poetic collections, the image of god-as-father features too (in 42:13; 63:16; 64:7). Gruber explains the sudden proliferation of positive F imagery applied to god, in addition to the more traditional M imagery, as perhaps a deliberate response on the part of the exilic author to other earlier prophetic traditions which had intimated "that in the religion of Israel maleness is a positive value with which divinity chooses to identify itself. Perhaps, as a result of this realization our prophet deliberately made use of both masculine and feminine similes for God" (Gruber 1983: 358). Perhaps. But, on the whole, the literary situation remains unambiguous. References to the motherhood of god, even if they are more frequent in Isaiah 40–66 than elsewhere in the Hebrew Bible, are still rare. Although their existence cannot be denied, it should be neither overstated nor magnified out of proportion. Accrediting YHWH with motherhood is but another stratagem for filling his F lack.

A more traditional formulation of the problematics involved in a one-gender representation of the divine is offered by Gruber in his conclusion: ". . . a religion that seeks to convey the Teaching of God who is above and beyond both sexes cannot succeed to do so in a manner which implies that a positive-divine value is attached to one of the two sexes" (Gruber 1983: 359).

Indeed. The biblical god is not a bi-gender god. His predominant image is that of a male single parent. His lack of F components is filled by various means. In some passages he is provided with F consorts, human or divine, a line attested by external drawings and inscriptions and continued in Jewish mysticism; in yet others he displays stereotypic F attributes. (Is not being a mother a biblical ideal for women?) The former solution has damaging consequences for YHWH's credibility as an exclusive god. The latter solution is too infrequent to be influential. The implications of this state of affairs for the women and men of the biblical communities, and for our Jewish and Christian cultures today, are the subject of intense debates among feminist critics of the Bible, and between them and non-feminists.

A PERSONAL POSTSCRIPT

I readily admit that my reading of the Hebrew Bible is motivated by what I am: Jewish, Israeli by birth and choice, middle class, an academic, a female, a feminist, a mother, divorced, non-religious, politically minded – in that or any other order. My emotional and intellectual sensibilities are the prisms through which I perceive and critique. My reader location motivates me to ask the biblical text certain questions. The questions I ask condition, to a very large extent, the answers I attempt to glean.

From my perspective, gender issues in the Hebrew Bible can hardly be redeemed for many feminists. Small consolations can indeed be gleaned from one specific text or another; but, on the whole, the so-called Good Book is a predominantly M document which reflects a deeply rooted conviction in regard to woman's otherness and social inferiority. Its M god is made to pretend, most of the time and against all odds, that he does not really need F company or F properties. Paradoxically, the fight itself is testimony to its futility. In spite of this small victory, the post-reading sensation I experience focuses on the bitter taste in my mouth.

This is my heritage. I am stuck with it. I cannot shake it off. And it hurts.

NOTES

1 Cf., for instance, the command opening the Decalogue, Exodus 20:2–4, and the parallel passage in Deuteronomy 5:8–9.
2 Numerous feminists believe that YHWH's loving and caring traits should be equated with the female/feminine maternal principle, somehow incorporated/taken over/ motivating this obviously male deity. The equation of F and emotion/caring, as against M and discipline, constitutes in itself compliance with stereotypic gender norms. More on this below.
3 I use a lower-case "g" for "god" instead of the customary upper case, since the god we are discussing here is a literary figure like others in the biblical story. As such, I do not want to give him the privileged status of a privileged spelling.
4 For a sample of feminist discussions of and additional bibliography for the two creation stories – the creation of both humans together (Genesis 1) and the creation of each separately in the Garden story (Genesis 2) – cf. articles by various scholars in Brenner (1993b: 24–172).
5 See Pressler (1993: 113–14), who writes in her conclusion,

> Several recent scholars have argued that the Deuteronomic laws exhibit a "peculiarly humanistic" view of women or a non-hierarchical view of gender relationships within the family. An examination of the presuppositions and purposes of the Deuteronomic family legislation calls into question this assessment. . . . [The laws] do aim at protecting dependent family members, including women. . . . Nonetheless, none of these protective laws challenges that hierarchical, male-defined structure of the family in any fundamental way. Moreover, they presuppose the authority of the male head of the household even as they set limits on that authority.

6 The vowel signs for the word translated "queen" here actually obscure the word. However, ancient bible translations are reliable witnesses that "queen of heaven" – that is, the goddess of heaven – is the original sense of the (initially vowel-less) text.
7 In the Hebrew Bible the option of terminating a marriage is not given to the wife. Only the husband can initiate a divorce or legally accuse a wife of adultery.
8 In this interpretation, the overhang between both figures' legs is *not* defined as penises (it is situated too much to the back which, even in the lack of perspective,

can be seen clearly). Rather, that overhang is a tail, probably an Egyptian influence, signifying the divine status of both figures.

9 For the relations of metaphor, desire, and subconscious, and much more, see Lakoff and Turner (1989).

10 In the first collection of the Book of Proverbs, chapters 1–9, a personified figure of Woman Wisdom appears again and again. She is often described, in erotic terms, as the right "consort" for a human male. In chapter 8 she is depicted as YHWH's daughter; in chapter 9, a woman with her own household. Many scholars have noted that, in both cases, the Woman Wisdom cuts a goddess figure. Hence, they ask whether these descriptions of her do not point to her status as YHWH's divine consort. I think that the main source for this goddess description (Proverbs 9) is too isolated to provide any firm basis for conclusion. The imagery appears to be derived from a human rather than divine context. See Camp (1985: 23–147); see also Camp's chapter (5) in the present book.

11 On Numbers 11, see Trible (1978: 32), and against her interpretation see Gruber (1985: 77); on Hosea, see Schüngel-Straumann (1986: 119–34); on Isaiah 40–66, see Gruber (1983; 1985) and Darr (1994).

4

OEDIPUS WRECKS
Moses and God's Rod
Ilona N. Rashkow

A significant link between psychoanalytic literary theory and biblical scholarship lies in the privilege both accord the language of images and symbols.[1] One image that seems to connect the two disciplines is God's rod, mentioned first in Exodus 4:1–5 and later in 7:8–12 as an object that changes its form into a serpent and then back again into a rod. Since the language of images and symbols is equally important in mythology,[2] a discipline that bridges psychoanalytic literary theory and biblical scholarship, I would like to *return to* Egypt, instead of *leaving* it as Moses did, and read the Egyptian myth of Isis and Osiris as a lens through which I view the symbolism, and hence significance, of Moses and God's rod.[3] First, however, I would like to clarify some presuppositions, primarily in terms of "who" or "what" I mean by Moses and in what sense the text is "historical."

Narratives are concerned with temporal events and incidents as well as with characters and their personalities. Aristotle stressed the centrality of action and incident and, until fairly recently, literary criticism has tended to emphasize the importance of plot over character. Within the last several years, however, "characterization" has become a focus of critical inquiry. As Henry James asks, "What is [narrative] incident but the illustration of character?" Indeed, in James's view, the very purpose of literary narrative is to provide and elucidate the *varieties* of human characters and their eccentricities.[4] But who "is" the literary character? Is the literary character a "real" or "historical" being?

My premise is that literary characters are both more and less than real persons (contra Edmond Cross [1988: 107], for example, who rejects "the referential illusion that would make a character something other than a product of writing and . . . would . . . presuppose the hypostatization of a real person").[5] Literary characters (and Moses is no exception) resemble "real people" in that they represent human action and motivation. At the same time, literary characters are "textual." Pertinent information about a character is narratively presented and/or withheld in order to further the action, and a character's behavior is determined by the writer's manipulation rather than by divine, natural, or social causes. From this perspective, Moses is part of the story-line and nothing else.

Back to Isis and Osiris. Briefly summarized,[6] Osiris, the great-grandson of Re, grandson of Shu, and first son of Geb and Nut, succeeding his father as king in Egypt, married his sister, Isis. Osiris, widely regarded as a just and wise king, organized the agricultural, religious, and secular life of his people and, assisted by Isis, acquired additional territory through many peaceful foreign conquests. This happy state of affairs was soon destroyed, however, by Seth, the younger brother of Osiris. Jealous of Osiris's power and prestige, he wanted the throne and accolades for himself. When Osiris returned to Egypt from travels abroad, Seth invited him to a banquet at which seventy-two accomplices were also present. During the festivities a beautifully decorated casket specifically built to the measurements of Osiris was brought into the hall. Seth promised that the much-admired casket would be given to the person who fitted inside it perfectly. Of course, when it was Osiris's turn to try it out for size, it was . . . just right! Seizing the opportunity to usurp his brother's position, Seth and his followers closed the lid, fastened it securely, and threw the casket into the river Nile in the hope that it would be carried out to the Mediterranean Sea and lost forever. Unfortunately for Seth, the casket washed ashore near the city of Byblos on the Syrian coast, close to the base of a young tamarisk tree, which quickly grew to enclose the casket inside its trunk. The King of Byblos noticed the tree, ordered it to be cut down, and had it made into a column to support the hall roof in his palace.

Meanwhile, back in Egypt, Isis had heard what Seth had done to Osiris and in great distress she set out to find her husband/brother. Eventually she came to Byblos, succeeded in having the palace column removed, retrieved the casket, and took it back to Egypt where she hid it in the marshes of the Delta. Although Osiris was dead, Isis at least had the body of her late husband/brother.

One night Isis left the casket unattended and Seth discovered it. Determined to destroy his brother's body permanently, he cut it up into fourteen pieces and distributed them over all of Egypt. When Isis became aware of this outrage, she travelled throughout the country searching for the various body parts, assisted by her sister Nephthys (who also happened to be the wife of Seth). Gradually, they found thirteen of the fourteen pieces, reassembled them and reanimated them. The only part of Osiris's body she could not find was his penis, which had been eaten by a Nile fish. To replace this irretrievably lost member, Isis created a simulacrum — the Phallus. The resurrected Osiris had no further part to play on earth. Thus, he became the ruler of the dead and Isis superseded Osiris as the fertility deity in Egypt. The simulacrum of Osiris's penis was now an object of veneration, and in honor of this Phallus, according to Plutarch, "the Egyptians even at the present day celebrate a fertility festival."[7] Herodotus, in Book 2 of *The Histories*, graphically describes the celebration:

> [T]he Egyptians . . . have . . . eighteen-inch-high images, controlled by strings, which the women carry round the villages; these images have a penis that nods and in size is not much less than all the rest of the body. Ahead there goes a flute-player, and the women follow, singing in honor of Osiris. Now why the penis is so much bigger and is the only movable thing in the body – about this there is a sacred story told.
>
> (Herodotus 1987: 152)

Neither Plutarch nor Herodotus say anything further about the excessive dimensions of the Phallus or its movement. Indeed, Herodotus seems bound to silence. Apparently, it is a secret that had to be guarded – religiously. Indeed, Isis is depicted time and again in Egyptian monumental art hovering over the dead, penisless body of her late husband/brother while holding a large simulacrum, and the "religious" aspects of this cult apparently included hymns of praise dedicated to Isis as the new fertility goddess.[8] In more modern times, the religious practices of this cult so astonished Voltaire that he used it as an illustration of relativism:

> The Egyptians were so far from attaching any disgrace to what we are desirous as much as possible to conceal and avoid the mention of, that they bore in procession a large and characteristic image, called Phallus, in order to thank the gods for making the human frame so instrumental in the perpetuation of the human species.
>
> (Voltaire 1906: 309)

A long and tedious commentary would be necessary to give all of the details of this myth's wealth. In political terms, for example, the myth has been described as preserving dim historical elements of a time during the Predynastic Period when Egypt was divided into the two kingdoms of Upper and Lower Egypt, each with its own ruler. According to Parkinson (1991), Osiris represents an early king whose death led to war between the two kingdoms. In agricultural terms, the death and resurrection of Osiris as a very early nature god apparently were celebrated each year in ceremonies at the time of the Nile flood when the crop was sown and when the harvest was gathered (Sarna 1991: 39). In ritual terms, the old agricultural ceremonies were joined with the cult of the dead to form the official Osirian rites and festivals, performed at the places where parts of the body of Osiris were reputed to be found, such as Athribis (heart), Busiris (backbone), Memphis (head) and so on. The festivals included "mysteries," dramatic performances of episodes relating to the life, death, and resurrection of Osiris, and often involved the planting of seed in Osiris-shaped molds to germinate and grow by the end of the festival (Griffiths 1980). But what is particularly striking from a psychoanalytic literary perspective is that the myth of Isis and Osiris interprets the dramatic relationship between the castrated "real penis" of Osiris, the one-time fertility *god*, and the oversized "Phallus" – now a fertility symbol – carried by the female devotees of the new fertility *goddess*.

What is the relationship between the spectacular simulacrum of the displayed, fully erect, sacred Phallus of Osiris carried in procession during religious ceremonies and God's rod? While "Phallus" is interchangeable with "penis" in ordinary usage, in psychoanalytic literary theory "Phallus" does not denote the anatomical organ; rather, Lacan (1977) associates "Phallus" with the concept of "power." The Phallus is emblematic of that which we want but cannot or do not have (that is, what we desire but lack), irrespective of which sex we happen to be. Rose (1982: 43), for example, attributes a sexual neutrality to the Phallus by characterizing it as "a term which, having no value itself . . . can represent that to which value accrues." Similarly, Ragland-Sullivan (1986: 271) asserts that "the phallic signifier does not denote any sexual gender [or] superiority." For the cult of Osiris, the Phallus comes "in place of" Osiris's penis. It is a fabrication, a constructed model, an artifact that simulates what is missing and, simultaneously, renders it sacred and larger than life to make it a goddess cult fertility object. Indeed, Lacan uses this very myth when he distinguishes between the penis as *organ* and the Phallus as "the simulacrum that it represented for the Ancients" (1977: 285). I read the Exodus narrative in a similar way: like Osiris's simulacrum, God's rod represents the ultimate power of a sacred Phallus.

When God first identifies himself to Moses, it is as "the God of your *father*, the God of Abraham, the God of Isaac, and the God of Jacob," reminding Moses (who had been reared by Pharaoh's daughter) of the covenant made with the patriarchs (his biological father's ancestors) – a covenant that in no way includes the fertility goddess, Isis! Moses, perhaps remembering the parades of women carrying the immense Phallus so graphically described by Herodotus, or perhaps anticipating skepticism by his fellow Israelites still in Egypt (who, for 430 years have been witnessing these fertility rites of Isis), says in effect, "Okay. I'll tell them 'the God of your *fathers* has sent me,' but what good will that do? They're going to need proof." Thereupon, God gives Moses instructions. First, Moses is to tell all the "*sons* of Israel" that "the Lord God of your *fathers*, the God of Abraham, the God of Isaac, and the God of Jacob has sent me." This simple statement establishes opposition between "the *sons* of Israel" and the *women* of the Egyptian villages, women who "religiously" parade with an oversized fertility symbol and worship a *female* fertility deity. God reinforces this schism linguistically by saying "this is my memorial [*zikri*]," a word etymologically related to the word for male (*zakar*). Next, Moses is told to gather the elders of Israel and, using the same formulaic language ("the God of your *fathers*, the God of Abraham, of Isaac, and of Jacob"), to remind *them* of the covenant, a covenant made only with the *male* members of the community. The centerpiece of this covenant is God's promise that Abraham will have vast numbers of descendants, but only because of the intervention of the Israelite deity:

> I shall establish my covenant between me and you, and *I* shall make you exceedingly numerous . . . this is my covenant with you: You shall be the father of a multitude of nations . . . *I* shall make you the father of a multitude of nations. *I* shall make you exceedingly fertile, and make nations of you; and kings shall come forth from you.
>
> (Genesis 17:2; 17:4–6; emphasis added)

By these two acts, Moses subliminally associates *God* (the Israelite *male* deity) with Abraham's fertility, thus diminishing the role of Isis (the Egyptian *female* fertility deity) in procreation. Moses, however, is still not completely convinced. As a result, God draws upon the authority of his "rod."

In the Hebrew Bible, there are four words that are commonly translated as "rod," all of which refer to an elongated object. While the distinctions in English are not particularly pronounced, in Hebrew the words are used for quite different purposes. The *maqqel*, for example, is a "rod" in the sense of a "walking stick" or "hand-staff"; the *shevet* is a "rod" used for punishing; and the *ḥoter* is generally used to denote a "twig." A *matteh*, the term used in reference to God's rod, denotes a leader's staff and carries the Lacanian weight of power in both positive and negative contexts. (In Psalm 110:2, for example, the psalmist sings that "YHWH will send your strong rod [*matteh 'uzka*] out of Zion," while Ezekiel uses the term negatively: "violence has risen to a wicked rod [*matteh resha'*, 7:11]). Indeed, the only place where *matteh* is used to refer to a shepherd's "rod" is here in the Exodus narrative, where the deity proves his might to Moses (the hesitating future leader) by changing his *matteh* into a . . . snake (*naḥash*)! Snakes and rods, two time-honored phallic symbols, represent both Freudian sexual symbolism (the two phases of the male organ in its active and quiescent states) and Lacanian phallic/power symbolism. By juxtaposing a snake and his rod, God establishes *his matteh* as *the* signifier of ultimate authority, a simulacrum of even greater proportions than those the devotees of Isis carried, a signification that continues throughout the confrontation with Pharaoh.[9] That is, like Sarna (1991: 38–39), I see the interactions between God, Moses, Pharaoh, and the magicians as attempts to discredit Egyptian polytheism in general, and worship of the Egyptian fertility goddess Isis in particular.

When Moses returns to Egypt, he presents himself before Pharaoh, but wields God's rod, and this time it turns into a . . . serpent (*tannin*)! Pharaoh's magicians, wielding their *own* rods, apparently possess the same power. Thus, at first it seems that the emissaries of the Egyptian fertility goddess[10] carry phallic symbols as potent as God's rod: both sides can transform their elongated objects into *serpents*. However, the change in reptile from *naḥash* to *tannin*, snake to serpent, is significant from the perspective of traditional biblical scholarship *and* psychoanalytic literary theory since both disciplines rely on the same strategy: being open to the sudden switches and rearrangements that reveal alternate messages and expose the dynamic play of meaning behind what may seem to be a simple statement. In the case of specific word choice, repetitions *and* shifts represent the basis for a wealth of scholarly material among biblical scholars and psychoanalytic literary critics alike. The study of lexical similarities and differences is a mainstay, since words can mean more than they seem to mean and do more than they seem to do. Among biblical scholars, Berlin (1989), for example, explores how "lexical cohesion" (the ways in which words are linguistically connected within a sequence) plays a role in interpretation, and how awareness of this relationship can lead to better readings. In a very different kind of criticism, Bloom (1976) examines "poetic crossings," the ways in which a text can destroy its own integrity if examined within the framework of lexical similarities and differences. This particular change in word choice (from *naḥash* to *tannin* – snake to serpent) has been commented upon by biblical scholars. Cassuto (1983: 95), for example, attributes the change to geographical factors: the snake, he claims, is more suited to the desert, where the sign was given to Moses, than the serpent of the Egyptian setting. Sarna (1991: 21), in a more literary vein, notes the "special relevance to Pharaoh, who is addressed as follows in Ezekiel 29:3: 'Thus says the Lord God: I am going to deal with you, O Pharaoh, king of Egypt, Mighty Serpent [*hattannin haggadol*].'"

I prefer to examine the change from snake to serpent from the perspective of both traditional biblical exegesis *and* psychoanalytic literary theory. In biblical Hebrew, *naḥash* ("snake") derives from the verb "to hiss." It is used *literally* to signify the actual creature, and *figuratively* for enemies or oppressors (see, for example, Jeremiah 8:17; Isaiah 14:29). The term *tannin* (or *tannim* [Ezekiel 29:3]), "serpent," is an *intensive* noun which derives from the root *tan*, "to elongate." It is used in more dramatic and dangerous circumstances, for example, a *"venomous* serpent," *"devouring* dragon," "sea-(or river) *monster*" (see, for example, Deuteronomy 32:33; Jeremiah 51:34; Genesis 1:21). When *tannin* is used in the figurative sense, it refers to enemies, and again, the metaphoric usage is intensified, that is, it refers to *particularly* dangerous enemies such as the Egyptians (Psalm 74:13) or, more commonly, to the personification of chaos (Isaiah 27:1; 51:9). Here in the Exodus narrative, Moses is first introduced to God's power by a *naḥash*, a "hiss." When Moses does the wand-into-serpent trick before Pharaoh, God's rod becomes the more dramatic *tannin* (serpent), intensifying the strength of his authority in the eyes of Moses who, faced with the magicians of Isis, may still need encouragement. When the magicians of the fertility goddess, Isis, perform the same act, it appears that God's rod, in the hand of

Moses, is no greater than that of Isis in the hands of her magicians. However, the more God's rod is wielded, the greater the significance of *tannin* and its derivation from the root "to elongate." As God's rod becomes longer, it becomes more potent, more able to wreak destruction upon the Egyptians. Finally, God's rod swallows up the sorcerers' rods. Most important, since by metathesis *bala'* ("swallow") suggests *ba'al* ("possess"), by "swallowing" the rods of Pharaoh's magicians, God's rod now "possesses" the symbolic procreative power and authority of Isis. At this point, God's rod, *the* most elongated, and thus ultimate Lacanian Phallus, becomes the simulacrum that firmly identifies *this* deity as *the most* powerful. In the Lacanian sense, the symbolic and functional value of God's rod highlights God's desire – and ability – to vanquish Pharaoh's magicians, and stands for the ultimate symbolic authority *it* carries and that Pharaoh and the magicians of Isis lack. Due to God's "elongated" rod, Pharaoh and his magicians symbolically have been castrated. Equally significant, the fertility goddess, Isis, has been dethroned. The Israelites' fertility deity, God, is one and he is Male. Parenthetically, it should be noted that metathesis allows a more Freudian interpretation as well – *bala'* also suggests *be'ilah* ("sexual intercourse"). Perhaps it is in this context that Sarna describes the book of Exodus as "the greatest *seminal* text of biblical literature" (1991: xii; emphasis added).

As the myth of Isis and Osiris highlights, although the Phallus *is* a symbol and not an organ, it undeniably derives a part of its signifying attributes from what the real penis can evoke. Indeed, Freud proposed that symbolization works by pictorial analogy. Long, thin objects regularly represent the phallus, and concave objects, vessels, and containers represent the vagina.[11] As a result, it may not always be easy or even productive to differentiate sharply between penis and Phallus. Indeed, although psychoanalytic literary theory has benefitted enormously from Lacan's distinction between the two, the metaphors of veiling and unveiling deployed by Lacan himself emphasize the difficulty of differentiating between them (1977: 281–91). As Lacan writes (1977: 287), the Phallus, "by virtue of its turgidity . . . is the image of the vital flow as it is transmitted in generation," emphasizing its irreducible anchorage in the function of reproduction. Thus, Silverman (1992b: 89) notes that "to veil the Phallus in this way is to permit it to function as a privileged signifier, as Lacan himself acknowledges. It is also to conceal the part that gender plays within many important Lacanian texts." In the Exodus narrative, the association of penis and Phallus is particularly strong. As if to highlight this relationship, the narrator reports an otherwise irrelevant episode: on the trip back to Egypt, Zipporah, Moses's wife, *circumcises* their first-born son while Moses carries – the rod of God![12]

How do snakes, serpents, penis, Phallus, and Isis relate to "Oedipus Wrecks: Moses and God's Rod"? When Moses threatened Pharaoh with the eighth plague, locusts, he warned that it would be "something that neither your *fathers* nor *fathers' fathers* have seen." Later, in the desert, God explains to Moses that the purpose for the entire conflict with Pharaoh is "that you may recount in the hearing of your *sons* and of your *sons' sons* how *I* made a mockery of the Egyptians and how I displayed my . . . *signs* among them." I see these two simple statements linking the snakes, serpents, penis, Phallus, and Isis to form a construct that locks God and Moses into a classic, Oedipal conflict. Let me explain.

According to Freud's famous Oedipal theory, the male child first loves his mother and his attachment to her becomes charged with sexual overtones. In the world of the son's unconscious fantasy, Mother is the object of incestuous desire. At this stage, the son's ego identity focuses on the active, "masculine" genital organ – the penis. Father, who also possesses a penis, becomes a model. Simultaneously, however, the boy views his father as a rival for his mother's love, an adversary who must be destroyed or removed for gratification to be achieved. But the boy recognizes that Father is the *legitimate* owner of Mother, and as a result, the son views his desire as a transgression that produces anxiety, guilt, and renunciation. Fearing retaliation (specifically, castration) by his father for his incestuous wishes, the boy experiences a conflict: love for his mother and fear of his father's power. In effect, Father's penis, the anatomical organ, becomes Father's Phallus – the symbol of Father's power. The only way the male child can keep his penis and masculine identity is by transcending the familial Oedipal triangle, and replacing it with the father-dominated superego, a process that for Freud (1931: 229) is "designed to make the individual find a place in the cultural community." "The father is the oldest, first, and . . . only authority" (1900: 293).

According to Freud, the Oedipal conflict, although universal in structure, undergoes transformations and is subject to cross-cultural variability. As Spiro (1961: 486–87) notes, this is particularly true in societies in which the conflict is not successfully resolved and thus necessitates constant repression. With Freud and Lacan as the basis, I read this narrative from a psychoanalytic literary perspective: God is the father-image, Moses is the son, and the entire panoply of Egyptian gods and goddesses (the fertility cult of Isis in particular) is a *composite* mother-image.

Moses (the male-child figure) first loves his "mother" (Isis) and has the unconscious desires Freud describes.[13] Consistent with Freud's theory, the son's ego identity (in this narrative, Moses) focuses on his active, "masculine" genital organ (remember Zipporah and the strange circumcision scene?). When Moses sees God's rod symbolically rendering the simulacrum wielded by Isis's magicians impotent, in effect he hears the father's voice, what Freud calls the "superego" and what Lacan calls "the Name of the Father" (in French, *le Nom du Père*, which sounds like *le Non du Père*, "the No of the Father," the verbal expression of the father's function as a disciplinarian). Thus, as in Freud's paradigm, Moses, fearing retaliation for his wishes, experiences a conflict: love for his mother (polytheism in general and Isis in particular) and fear of his father's power (if Osiris's *oversized* Phallus can be destroyed, what about Moses's penis?). Consequently, Moses sublimates his desire for the Egyptian goddess/Mother whose fertility rites he had observed for most of his life, identifies with his father-image, Israel's *male* deity, and renounces his affinity with and worship of Isis. By accepting YHWH as *the* supreme Law – the will of the Father – Moses and his offspring, the "sons of Israel", become a "kingdom of priests" (Exodus 19:6). By reminding Moses of the covenant made with the *fathers*, the power of God's rod is thereby linked to the male organ, as male sexuality replaces and sublimates the procreative power of Isis; and for Moses and the "sons of Israel," the penis, and not the simulacrum of Osiris, is the focus of the holy covenant.

Once in the wilderness, however, God reminds Moses that this link with power, the penis, is to be circumcised. In fact, only those who *are* circumcised can commemorate their deliverance from Egypt. While biblical scholars have discussed the political and religious implications of this covenant,[14] they have not paid much attention to the "token" that seals the arrangement. Why the penis? Certainly, if the purpose was to distinguish this band of wanderers from all other people, a more obvious part of the body might have been chosen, for example, piercing the ear or the nose. Indeed, there are some interesting resonances in the terms of a relationship that stipulates that those who do not "cut" will be "cut off." As Sarna notes:

> This punishment . . . is peculiar to ritual texts and is largely confined to offenses of a . . . sexual nature. . . . [T]he impersonal, passive form of the verb is used . . . so that . . . the executive authority is uncertain. In Lev 20:3 the active first person is used with God as the subject of the verb: "I shall set my face against that man and will cut him off from among his people." This reasonably presupposes that [*karat*] is not a penalty enforced by the courts but a punishment left to divine execution. . . . Certainly the general idea is that one who deliberately excludes himself from the religious community of Israel cannot be a beneficiary of the covenantal blessings and therefore dooms himself and his line to extinction.
>
> (Sarna 1991: 58)

Significant for the purposes of this chapter, Freud sees circumcision as the "symbolic substitute" for castration, for what is no longer there, since the circumcised penis both asserts the possible threat of castration (the foreskin has been removed) and denies it (the head of the penis is prominent as in an erection; 1916–17: 165; 1937: 122). Thus, the sexual symbolism in the relationship between Moses and God is powerful in its reverberations. The original covenant was with *males* only, and the essence of the arrangement was the multiplication of *men*. However, offspring are possible only with the assistance of *this* male god ("*I* shall make you exceedingly numerous . . . *I* shall make you the father of a multitude of nations . . . *I* shall make you exceedingly fertile, and make nations of you").[15] (Of course, not only psychoanalytic literary theorists have reached this conclusion. Indeed, relying heavily on ethnographic literature, Eilberg-Schwartz argues that "the practice of circumcision, despite its role in symbolizing the covenant . . . nonetheless symbolized the fertility of the initiate . . . and ability to perpetuate a lineage of *male* descendants" [1990: 142; emphasis added; cf. Eilberg-Schwartz, chap. 2 in this volume]).

Repeating the terms of the covenant to Moses has two results: first, God implicitly erases the female fertility rites of Isis's followers. Since the covenant of circumcision signifies that procreativity now lodges in the relationship between God and human *males*, Isis, the Egyptian fertility goddess/Mother, is displaced by the fertility God/Father. Male sexuality forms the nucleus of filiation, a common bonding (Eilberg-Schwartz), and the Israelite penis, rather than the Egyptian god Osiris's simulacrum, is once again the focus of the holy covenant. The male organ is linked with power (in the sense of both Eilberg-Schwartz's comparative fertility thesis and the one I am developing here), and goddess/Mother-worship is rechanneled.

Since the covenant endows the male with the ability to engender life, and then extends this ability from father to son, by implication Moses would *seem* to possess both God's procreative powers and the authority to wield God's rod, a paradigmatic representation of the Freudian male child's Oedipus construct. However, the second consequence of reminding Moses of the terms of the covenant is that God immediately establishes the vulnerability of the human anatomical organ, the penis. Although once again God promises to bless Israel's "seed," Moses must depend upon *this deity* for fertility. Certainly, no other part of the body would emphasize as effectively the connection between male reproductive capacity and the deity's ultimate potency. The lure for Moses is affiliation with the father/God and the power inherent in his rod, the superiority of masculine identification and masculine prerogatives over the feminine influence of Isis. (Freud, as one recalls, writes that "whosoever accepted this symbol [circumcision] showed by so doing that he was ready to submit to the father's will, although it was at the cost of a painful sacrifice" [1939: 156].) However, as in Freud's Oedipal construct, the potential threat of castration is always there and struggle is inevitable. Oedipus wrecks!

Curiously, the Freudian account of the Oedipus story reveals a peculiarly selective reading of Sophocles's text: Laius, who is rife with anxieties, is absolved by Freud of his crime, and his sins and fears have been displaced by the guilt of his son, Oedipus. In the biblical narrative, the relationship between Moses and God exposes similar displacements. Circumcision, seen as a partial castration, is the price God-as-father exacts from Moses-as-son to be in a somewhat, but not quite, analogous paternal position *vis-à-vis* the "sons of Israel." That is, only the deity has a thoroughly intact organ, and thus only the deity can provide offspring.

Further, circumcision symbolically feminizes. As the Zohar asks concerning God's actions in Egypt: "Why is it written, 'And the Lord will pass over the door' [Exodus 12:23]? . . . Read it [door] literally as 'opening'! . . . the opening of the body. And what is the opening of the body? That is the circumcision" (*Zohar* 2:36a). In Freudian analysis, of course, the "door/gate" is a symbol of the female genital orifice (Freud 1916–17: 156). From a psychoanalytic perspective, by reminding Moses that he and his offspring, the "sons of Israel" are to be circumcised, God displaces his own anxieties and views Moses, as well as the "sons of Israel" as female. Hence, there is no threat to his power.[16]

From this perspective, Moses's relationship to God's rod reads almost like a Freudian case-study! Moses-as-son emulates the father; in place of the women of Egypt dedicating their sexuality to the goddess Isis by engaging in a ritual parade while carrying Osiris's oversized phallic simulacrum, Moses will now celebrate the fertility (and virility) of a *male* deity and *male* procreativity. Implied within this construct, however, is a warning by the father/God: "if you worship women, and specifically, Egyptian goddesses (that is, if you continue to desire Mama/Isis), I'll finish the job started by circumcision, and *fully* castrate you to *make* you a woman." This implied threat symbolically ensures that the son can never be as powerful as the father.

As many commentators have noted, the stories about Moses in Exodus through Deuteronomy are not really about the *man*, but rather the God who stands behind the man. Despite Moses's seeming power, he does nothing except in response to the deity's commands. Indeed, Schnutenhaus describes Moses as a "Jahvemarionette" (quoted in Coats 1988: 33). In Lacanian terms, Moses may possess the penis, but never the Phallus, the ultimate symbol of paternal authority and the privilege it signifies.

The relationship of Moses and God's rod lasts beyond Egypt.[17] In Numbers 21:4–9, for example, "venomous snakes" attack the Israelites because of their rebellion against both God and Moses, their bites causing the death of many of the people. The remaining population confess their sins, and Moses, interceding for them, receives instruction for the remedy: a bronze *snake* on a *pole* that will reverse the fatal quality of the bites. Those stricken need only see this double phallic symbol in order to survive the fate inflicted by the snakes. Although there is no explicit connection between God's rod and the bronze snake, in Exodus *and* Numbers, serpents, rods, and God's power merge. As in the myth of Isis and Osiris, a sacred Phallus has been invested with power.

The fundamental themes of the Oedipal conflict – desire, the meaning of the father figure, law, and guilt – characterize the relationship of Moses and God's rod. Isis has been displaced by God's rod; the Egyptian sacralization of *female* sexuality has been displaced by Israelite *male* sexuality; and Egyptian women carrying eighteen-inch-high images with eighteen-inch-long nodding Phalluses have been displaced by the *circumcised* penises of the Israelites, *the* manifest symbol of the relationship of Moses and God's rod. That is, Moses may wield God's rod, but never its power. For Freud, Oedipus wrecks. So too for Moses.

NOTES

1 An earlier version of this chapter was read at the Society of Biblical Literature Annual Meeting, Washington, D.C., 1993.

2 As Freud wrote (1926: 211), "mythology may give you the courage to believe in psychoanalysis."

3 Of course, I am not the first to return Moses to Egypt. See, for example, Freud's *Moses and Monotheism* for a different reading of the Moses/Egyptian connection.

4 For a more in-depth analysis of the import of character for James, see his "Preface to The Portrait of a Lady" in James 1934.

5 See also Robert Alter (1992: 22), who takes Harold Bloom to task for anthropomorphizing the biblical deity.

6 Unfortunately, no complete account of the myth of Isis and Osiris has been preserved in an Egyptian text, although several references and additional and varying details are found in Egyptian religious writings and monumental inscriptions. The only extant text of the whole legend is Plutarch's *De Iside et Osiride*, a late form of the myth with several Greek influences. However, Plutarch does provide a very useful story outline. In depicting this myth I have relied on Griffiths, Parkinson, and Ochshorn.

7 "Of the parts of Osiris's body the only one which Isis did not find was the male member ... but Isis made a replica [*mimema*] of the member to take its place, and constructed the Phallus, in honor of which the Egyptians even at the present day celebrate a fertility festival" (Plutarch 1936: 47).

8 See Lichtheim (1976) for a compilation of hymns dedicated to the cults of Isis and Osiris, and Downing for examples of Egyptian art devoted to the enormous dimensions of the wooden Phallus.

9 Danna Nolan Fewell has reminded me that *matteh* also includes the meaning "tribe," lending further weight to its procreative connotation: God's "rod" produces the "tribes" of Israel.

10 The Hebrew *ḥartummím* (magicians) derives from an Egyptian title meaning "chief priest" (Sarna 1991: 37); since the cults of Osiris and Isis were the most popular, it is likely that these "magicians" were part of the cult of Isis and Osiris.

11 Both Freud and his follower Ernest Jones insisted that although there are vast numbers of symbols, the objects or ideas symbolized are limited in number. Psychoanalytic symbols are restricted to the body and its functions (particularly the sexual ones), family members, birth, and death.

12 Pardes (1992) also sees interesting (but different) echoes of the Isis and Osiris myth in this incident with Zipporah, viewing the brief passage as an example of monotheistic censorship and a "repressed cultural past." According to Pardes (1992: 93), the well-known story of Osiris and Isis is retold in the circumcision scene, and Isis (as a character) is "wrenched apart as her role of midwife-mother-sister-wife is divided among Shiprah, Puah, Yocheved, Miriam, Pharaoh's daughter, and Zipporah."

13 It is important to remember that for Freud, the "reality" reference of the Oedipus story is to the inner psychic reality of latent desire (1914b: 16–18). That is, the "events" of the story constitute unrecognized wishes; they are products of fantasy

rather than actual reproductions of memory. In fact, in the historical formation of psychoanalysis, Freud replaced the "fairy tale" of infantile parental seduction, in which the reality reference of the story was to *actual*, external, objective events (1896: 203), with the Oedipus myth.

14 See, for example, Graves and Patai (1983: 240); Fox (1967: 557–96); Sarna (1970: 131–33); De Vaux (1961: 46–48).

15 See Rashkow (1993) for an elaboration, particularly with reference to Genesis narratives.

16 Contra Boyarin who posits that "circumcision is a male erasure of the female role in procreation" (1992: 476).

17 Rabbinic legends relate the history of God's *matteh* (how it was handed down from Adam, generation by generation, until it came into the possession of Moses), and tell of the Tetragrammaton which was inscribed thereon, the mnemonics of the Ten Plagues which were also engraved on it, and other similar details (Exodus Rabba, viii, 2).

5

WOMAN WISDOM AND THE STRANGE WOMAN

Where is Power to be Found?

Claudia V. Camp

But where is wisdom to be found?
And where is the place of understanding?

(Job 28:12)

It is no doubt a mark of our time and situation that for me the quest for wisdom, the object of Job's longing, has become a question about power – a question of finding it, to be sure, but also a question of defining it and our relationship to it. I choose two figures from the book of Proverbs, the female personifications of Wisdom and Strangeness, as guides for the quest, partly because of my long scholarly acquaintance with them, partly because of the current controversy about Sophia in the Protestant churches. As female images constructed by men, they are in one sense inherently disempowering for women; they inhibit our ability to name and shape ourselves by telling us in advance who we are and may become. On the other hand, as *powerful* female images they tantalize the female questor/questioner of power. Could there be an imagistic surplus of power available here that is not under the control of the fashioners?

In its broadest sense, this is an essay on *language as power*.[1] I am interested in how language works: how it is manipulated and by whom, and how it shapes our situation beyond any conscious intent. To speak of language and power means, inherently, to speak of specific social-historical contexts. Thus, this chapter begins and ends with reflection on such contexts: first, the postexilic situation in which the book of Proverbs, with its female imagery, approached canonical status; finally, the contemporary firestorm provoked by the purported worship of the "goddess" Sophia at the Re-imagining Conference, held in Minneapolis, Minnesota, in November, 1993 to celebrate the midpoint of the World Council of Churches' ecumenical decade of women. In each case, I ask the questions of who uses the female imagery, and to what ends, with particular attention to its effect on women's power. In each case, we shall find that power is a multi-faceted force, that the power and powerlessness mediated through female imagery cannot be seen as simple opposites, but must be sorted out in varying degrees and kinds.

The middle two sections of the chapter deal with metaphor and (metaphorical) theology. They provide transition between the ancient and modern contexts, in several ways. First, metaphor's attention to similarity and difference generates a constructive play, and thereby a hermeneutical bridge, between the expectations and associations of the two historical eras. Metaphor theory thus helps us articulate and address the challenges of theologically appropriating an ancient text – whose original power lines may have been quite different – in the modern context. Second, and relatedly, because metaphor is a way of speaking theologically, it bridges the enterprise of understanding the Bible's theology, which is often metaphorically expressed, and that of constructing theology from the Bible, a task in which the appropriators of Sophia are actively engaged. Finally, analysis of metaphors in terms of their sublimation of meaning allows us to dis-cover the (also powerful) "unsaid" suppressed by powerful manipulations of language. Such discovery is crucial to understanding how language works as power – and as theology. In particular, attention to the unsaid may illuminate the vicissitudes of power – its shifting margins and centers – in the days of the life of Sophia and her traditioners.

WOMEN AND WISDOM IN PROVERBS: A CASE-STUDY ON POWER AND POWERLESSNESS IN ANCIENT THEOLOGICAL DISCOURSE

One way to approach the question of power in these texts is to think historically. What, in heaven's name, are they doing in the Bible? Who wrote them, read them, preserved them? And, in particular, what do they tell us about women's power in that society?

Female imagery and the structure of Proverbs

Scholars often think of the book of Proverbs in three parts. The central section (chapters 10–30) comprises collections of short sayings that modern readers usually connect with the term "proverb." Chapters 1–9, however, are longer poems, either instructional in nature or reflective on the idea of wisdom. It is here that the figures of Woman Wisdom and Woman Stranger are developed in quasi-mythical terms. Chapter 31, the book's final chapter, is made up of two poems, one an instruction to an unknown "King Lemuel" by his mother, and the other an acrostic paean to the "woman of worth." Female imagery thus dominates the beginning and ending of the book of Proverbs, serving in effect as the main structural supports for the book as a whole. Whereas Wisdom and the Strange Woman are almost mythic figures, however, the women in chapter 31 appear more "real-to-life," however idealized they may be. Nonetheless, abundant similarities in vocabulary establish a relationship, especially between Wisdom and the worthy woman.

Female imagery for Wisdom in Proverbs 1–9

Proverbs 1–9 uses a multiplicity of images to develop the Wisdom figure. In Proverbs 1:20–33, the image of the prophet, who calls out in public places to chastise a sinful people, is woven together with vocabulary ("reproof," "simple," "scoffers," "fools," "counsel") typically identified with the wise sage or teacher.

> Wisdom cries out in the street;
>> in the squares she raises her voice.
>
> At the busiest corner she cries out;
>> at the entrance of the city gates she speaks:
>
> "How long, O simple ones, will you love being simple?
>> How long will scoffers delight in their scoffing
>> and fools hate knowledge?
>
> Give heed to my reproof;
>> I will pour out my thoughts to you;
>> I will make my words known to you.
>
> Because I have called and you refused,
>> have stretched out my hand and no one heeded,
>
> and because you have ignored all my counsel
>> and would have none of my reproof,
>
> I also will laugh at your calamity;
>> I will mock when panic strikes you,
>
> when panic strikes you like a storm,
>> and your calamity comes like a whirlwind,
>> when distress and anguish come upon you."
>
> (1:20–27)

Importantly, although Woman Wisdom uses the stock phrase "fear of the LORD" (1:29) as the object of her teaching, she also speaks very much on her own authority. Actions elsewhere identified with God she here takes herself, pouring out *her* thoughts, calling and stretching out *her* hand. One seeks and finds *her*; listening to *her* assures security and ease (1:33). There are a number of associations to human women implicit in the poem: to the mother as teacher, regularly referred to in Proverbs (e.g., 1:8; 31:1, 26); to female prophets like Huldah (2 Kings 22:14–20); to the lover who "seeks and finds" her beloved in the Song of Songs. Nonetheless, the Woman Wisdom of chapter 1 is also a transcendent figure.

Proverbs 4:1–9 and 7:1–5 are both instructional poems in which wisdom is first identified with the father's teaching and then personified as an independent entity.

> Listen, sons, to a father's instruction,
>> and be attentive, that you may gain insight.
>
> . . .

Get wisdom; get insight:
do not forget, nor turn away from the words of my mouth.
Do not forsake her, and she will keep you;
love her, and she will guard you.

. . .

Prize her highly, and she will exalt you;
she will honor you if you embrace her.
She will place on your head a fair garland;
she will bestow on you a beautiful crown.

(4:1, 5–6, 8–9)

My son, keep my words
and store up my commandments with you;
keep my commandments and live,
keep my teachings as the apple of your eye;
bind them on your fingers,
write them on the tablet of your heart.
Say to Wisdom, "You are my sister,"
and call Insight your intimate friend.

(7:1–4)

In these passages, Wisdom is depicted as lover and wife: "sister" is a term of endearment, as we learn from the Song of Songs, and Proverbs 12:4 tells us that "a good wife is the crown [cf. 4:9] of her husband." These ideas are reminscent of Proverbs' expectation of the sexual enjoyment (5:15–19) and the economic bounty (31:10–31) a man can expect from his wife. This wife is one "given," furthermore, under the father's authority, and she has a protective function. The ensuing verses in chapter 4 (10–27) show the young man's need of protection from "evildoers," while 7:5–27 identifies the "strange woman" as the danger from which Wisdom will shield her lover. Similarly, the love poem in 5:15–19, which refers to a real-life wife, becomes a warding against this strange woman in verses 20–23.[2]

Chapter 9 also presents images of wifely provisioning and protection against the strange woman (here Woman Folly, 9:13), but adds to them a transcendent strength. Wisdom has not only "slaughtered her animals, . . . mixed her wine, . . . [and] set her table," but "Wisdom has built her house, she has hewn her seven pillars" (9:1). While the reference to "her house" is thrice echoed in the poem on the good wife (31:15, 21 [twice]), the reference to "seven pillars" (not to mention her "hewing" them!) sounds as much like a deity building a temple, perhaps even the cosmic temple, the earth supported by seven mountains.

Chapter 8's wisdom poem contains the most dramatically transcendent imagery in Proverbs.[3] It begins similarly to the poem in chapter 1, with Woman Wisdom crying out in public places, offering words of truth worth more than earthly treasure (see also 3:15). Then, however, she asserts herself as the power (not so very far!) behind the throne:

> By me kings reign
>   and rulers decree what is just;
> by me rulers rule,
>   and nobles, all who govern rightly.
>
> (8:15–16)

Although the context may alter the connotation here, it is interesting to note that these verses are followed immediately by a return to the "wifely" images of love and prosperity:

> I love those who love me,
>   and those who seek me diligently find me.
> Riches and honor are with me,
>   enduring wealth and prosperity.
>
> (8:17–18)

Verses 22–31 provide the biggest surprise of all. Although certain vocabulary is curiously ambiguous in meaning, Woman Wisdom is depicted as present with God before and during creation, and then deciding to take her place on earth with the human race.

> YHWH conceived [or: acquired] me at [or: as] the beginning of his way,
>   the first of his acts long ago.
> Ages ago I was installed [in office; or: woven in the womb],
>   at the first, before the beginning of the earth.
> When there were no depths I was labored forth,
>   when there were no springs abounding with water.
> Before the mountains had been shaped,
>   before the hills, I was labored forth.
>   . . .
> When he assigned to the sea its limit,
>   so that the waters might not transgress his command,
>   when he marked out the foundations of the earth,
> then I was beside him like a master artisan [or: darling child];
>   and I was daily a delight,
>   rejoicing before him always,
> rejoicing in his inhabited world,
>   and my delight was in human beings.
>
> (8:22–25, 29–31)

Wisdom then offers life and favor from YHWH to those who watch at her gates, and wait beside her doors (verses 32–36). In these last few verses, however, the voice of Woman Wisdom once again blends with the voice of the teacher (perhaps a mother here?) in the address to "my sons." If female imagery in the preceding poems has served to make the quest for wisdom an attractive one to the young male student, chapter 8's dramatic elevation of this imagery adds as well a ringing note of authority to the teacher's instruction.

Female imagery for Wisdom and women's power in the post-exilic period

What does this overview of the wisdom poems tell us in terms of our questions about women's power? Two considerations operate in tension with each other around this question.

First, I see little doubt that a certain kind of woman was empowered by these texts. The wise, hardworking wife who could counsel her husband astutely and teach her children well is given enormous pride of place. She is not celebrated for meek obedience, moreover, but for energetic industriousness and management skills that take her into public places as well as the home. It is even possible that a mother's teaching rather than the father's lies behind certain texts (Brenner [1993a] and van Dijk-Hemmes [1993] propose chapter 7; I would perhaps also add at least the last few verses of chapter 8).

Although Israelite household stability and prosperity always relied on the wise wife and mother, this need was particularly keen during the period after the Babylonian exile (from about 538 B.C.E. on), as the returned exiles attempted to re-establish a society whose basic form of political organization – the monarchy – had been shattered (Camp 1985; 1991). This context may have provided the impetus for binding the more predictable adulations of the wise wife managing "her house" together with the striking depictions of Woman Wisdom as source of all government and builder of the ritual or cosmic "house." Powerful, divinely authorized Woman Wisdom functions in part as a symbolic replacement for the lost king, becoming one of the first of the idealized mediator figures that would populate Jewish religious thought in ensuing centuries.

There is another symbolic issue at stake as well, related to the structuring of the book of Proverbs by means of female images, as noted above. The book was edited during a time when written texts were rapidly becoming a definitive part of the religious tradition, although that tradition was still heavily influenced by orality. The enclosing female images seem not only to give structure to a largely unstructured collection of proverbs, but also to provide an authorizing *voice*, not simply to wisdom teaching in general but to this book, *qua* book. Indeed, Skehan (1971: 9–45) provides a convincing structural argument that at least one metaphorical referent of Wisdom's house in chapter 9 is the book of Proverbs itself, "built" by her.

The question of why a *woman's* voice was chosen for this authorizing function then becomes important. I would suggest, first, that men's experience both of their mothers' instruction and the good wife's love, counsel, and support created the possibilty of a female voice. Their experience supplied, in other words, the affective grounding that is necessary for a symbol to be embraced as constitutive of reality. But what makes this possibility achieve realization? One answer lies, I believe, in the contingencies of the social situation described above, and which will receive further elaboration below: in the post-exilic period conditions were right for women's on-going contributions to society to be noticed consciously and even found desirable of further authorization. At one and the same time, this recognized status lent authority in turn to the concept of wisdom it embodied.

A second reason may lie in another of Israel's symbol traditions, namely, the tendency to personify the community (usually, though paradoxically, defined as the *male* members of that community) as female. This typical prophetic device (but see also Numbers 25:1) usually works itself out in the marriage metaphor, with Israel as the adulterous wife who "plays the harlot" with other gods and YHWH as the betrayed husband who punishes (and sometimes forgives and restores) her. Female personification is also at work in Proverbs, but with two key differences. First, Proverbs' Woman Wisdom combines transcendent qualities with her earthly ones; second, she is powerful and righteous rather than ripe for punishment.

What can we make of this similarity and difference? I turn again to the relationship of the book of Proverbs to the wisdom tradition, of which it is both product and paradigm. The wisdom tradition in Israel was essentially a human tradition. Although never conceived antithetically to Yahwistic faith, it was nonetheless basically composed of the teachings of the mothers and fathers of Israel. In an era when books were beginning to be perceived as loci of divine revelation, however, the editors of Proverbs clearly sought a higher level of authorization for the tradition it represented. They achieved this through the use of the female Wisdom figure, a figure present with God during the most crucial acts of ordering creation, yet not quite identical with God. Not identical in part because she is female to Yahweh's male. On analogy with the prophetic personification of the human community of Israel as female, this gendering of Wisdom suggests her on-going identification with the wisdom tradition as product of that community. I propose, then, that the sages, perhaps hesitant to fully equate a human tradition with the voice of the male God, did the next best thing in imagining Wisdom's persona as transcendent, but female. If so, they drew on the tradition of female personification of the community, but also shattered it with their previously unimagined characterization of a woman both powerful and righteous.

With respect to women's power, however, there is a second consideration, with a contradictory force. It is clear that, precisely as products of a patriarchal society, part of the very purpose of these powerful female images was to define and control female identity. We must therefore consider the inherent limitations in the symbol of Woman Wisdom with respect to real women's power. First, Brenner and van Dijk-Hemmes (1993) have argued that at least chapters 7 and 31 of Proverbs represent female traditions of instruction. If this is true, the point certainly reinforces what I have said above about the power of a certain kind – the "right kind" – of woman. But it also shows the over-reaching power of patriarchy: the women who speak with the fathers' voice are the women who have a place, and they are divided off from other women who refuse this allegiance. Second, Carol Newsom has argued that these texts represent not only gender struggle, but generational struggle; that is, the fathers are attempting to control their sons, as well as their wives (1989: 142–60). This argument would explain the unusual (for the Hebrew Bible) expression of concern for husbands remaining sexually faithful to their wives, as well as vice versa, while also illuminating the patriarchal manipulation of the Woman Wisdom image.

These observations come into focus when we attempt to account not only for the presence of exalted Woman Wisdom in these texts but also for her opposite, the Strange Woman. The presence of female personified evil along-side woman as the perfect embodiment of righteousness is a sure tip-off to the gender reality of the ultimate purveyors of power in Proverbs. Examples abound in history of this imagistic either/or, one of patriarchy's favorite symbolic games. Yet there is still, I believe, something to be learned from studying the particulars of the figures in Proverbs. Let us, then, consider the Strange Woman in terms of imagery and socio-historical context.

The Strange Woman

We have already noted the oppositional conjunction between Woman Wisdom (along with the beloved wife) and the Strange Woman: one of the major functions of the ideal female is to protect her lover from this particular danger. But what is the exact nature of the danger? Much hinges on how one understands the two terms, typically used in parallel structure, that designate the negative female. Although the word pair most often comes into English as something like "loose woman/adulteress" (still so even in the NRSV), the Hebrew terms *zara* and *nokriyya* represent most literally the feminine forms of "stranger," "foreigner," "outsider to the family," or "other."[4] Thus, while the ensuing characterization of this figure is one of sexual looseness – she is indeed the "other" woman in our modern collo-quial sense – the terms themselves are broader in meaning.

From a literary point of view, there are two features of Proverbs's Strange Woman important to our purposes here. First, like Woman Wisdom, her portrait is multi-dimensional and thus difficult to channel into a single meaning. Second, in spite of the apparent opposition between Woman Wisdom and the Strange Woman, there are in fact many fascinating literary linkages between them.

The multi-dimensionality of the Strange Woman derives in part from attempting to articulate an answer to the question: in what sense is she strange?[5] The first inclination is to assume that she is a foreigner, a non-Israelite. Closer analysis reveals that her ethnic status is not the first consideration.[6] Rather, strangeness of a sexual sort looms large, though this is metonymically paired with religious "infidelity" of some sort. Thus, the young man who finds wisdom

> ... will be saved from the strange woman,
>> from the outsider with her smooth words,
> who forsakes the partner of her youth,
>> and forgets her sacred covenant.
>>> (2:16–17)

In a curious layering of sexual perversions, the adulteress – whose husband is away from the marital bed on a long journey – dresses and acts like a prostitute, seeking and boldly propositioning her customer out on the streets (7:10–12). What's more, this prostitute-adulteress also manages to choose a time for her activities during the days of peace-offering sacrifice (7:14), when sex is ritually forbidden (Leviticus 7:11–21). Thus, improbably, yet a third layer is added to her sexual offenses. The punishment for this ritual offense is, moreover, precisely that threatened by the Strange Woman: Leviticus 7:20 prescribes that offenders shall be "cut off from their people," while those who dally with the Strange Woman will be "cut off from the land" (Proverbs 2:22) and "in utter ruin amidst the assembly" (Proverbs 5:14).

Based on the preceding observations, I would suggest that the Strange Woman does not represent any particular real women or class of women. Rather, the layering of different kinds of sexual misbehavior, as well as ritual offense, generates a portrait of idealized evil in its multiple dimensions. With this in mind, we can reconsider the notion of ethnic foreignness that is a primary connotation of the terms *zar* and *nokri*. I do not believe that this connotation can ever be removed from the force of these terms. Whether or not the authors of Proverbs are concerned with foreign women in a literal sense, it lurks always as a powerful part of the system of commonplaces associated with the metaphor of strangeness, and adds yet another horrendous dimension to the portrait of Evil inscribed in the Strange Woman.

From a social-historical perspective, the characterization of this female figure as "strange" to the point of death takes on special power in the context of Israel's on-going struggle to define itself over against those foreigners in their midst, the Canaanites with whom they had so much in common. At least by the time of the late seventh-century Deuteronomist, the danger of marriage to foreign women, who contaminate Israel with worship of foreign gods, had become part of the cultural polemic.[7] Even beyond this, biblical rhetoric often so mixes the language of female sexual impropriety with that of foreign worship that the two components are inseparable. At least echoes of this metaphorical convention are at work in Proverbs.

Consideration of the post-exilic context may nuance this picture further. Women were important in this period not only in their on-going roles as household managers and educators of children, but also, through advantageous marriages, as a means for gaining and sealing land claims among Jews returning from Exile. "Foreign" women were dangerous not only as potential conduits of foreign worship into Israelite families, but also as representatives and mediators of the claims that non-Jews – or the "wrong kind" of Jews – might make on the land. This last qualification is an important one for, in this period, Jews were divided in a contentious struggle to define the nature and control of the community itself, and especially the norms of right worship. They faced, in other words, a most devastating psycho-social reality: the "foreigner" could be another Jew. In this context, the layering of many sorts of "strangeness" – ethnic and sexual, moral and cultic – onto a single figure produced a powerful symbolic touchstone against which to assert one's own claims to orthodoxy. The fact that this figure was female is hardly an accident. Woman, the quintessential Other, was the perfect embodiment of the full-orbed Strangeness that tormented post-exilic Jews in Palestine. What we have in the end is a quasi-mythic figure, whose dangers are conceived not merely in the material terms of separation from land and people, but in terms of death itself. Thus, the young man is warned that

> ... many are those she has laid low,
> and numerous are her victims.
> Her house is the way to Sheol,
> going down to the chambers of death.
>
> (7:26–27)

To bring this consideration of the Strange Woman to a close, we must return once more to her alleged opposite, Woman Wisdom. There can be no doubt that, on one level, the text presents an absolute dichotomy here, one that confronts the reader with a forced choice between good and evil, life and death. Yet there are numerous items of vocabulary and imagery in Proverbs 1–9 that connect the two figures as well. Encounters with each involve "embracing" and "grasping." Both are found "in the street" and "in the marketplace." Both invite followers to their respective houses; both offer bread and beverage. With either the Strange Woman or his wife, a man can "fill himself" with "love" or "her breasts" (the latter two words are quite similar in Hebrew: *dodim/dadeyha*). Aletti (1977: 129–44) suggests that the editor of Proverbs, through this ambiguous use of vocabulary, has created a deliberate confusion between Woman Wisdom and the Strange Woman in order to stress the difficulty and importance of discerning true speech. The effect of this ambiguity within a contemporary discussion of power and powerlessness will be taken up in subsequent portions of this chapter.

A METAPHORICAL PERSPECTIVE

The concept of metaphor

These historical observations on the use of a female image, however right-eous and powerful, by men for their own ends confronts modern readers with a hermeneutical dilemma: will reference to Woman Wisdom empower women today, or will it not? What are the advantages and dangers of appeal to this biblical figure?

I have argued elsewhere (Camp 1987: 45–76) that there are a number of advantages for the reader who, in effect, disavows the image's ideological history, its patriarchal source and manipulation, and thinks, instead, in terms of metaphor. One way to theorize this intellectual process is to distin-guish between the functions of metaphor and those of symbol, the term I have up to now been (loosely) using to refer to Woman Wisdom. McFague (1982: 10–18) argues that a symbolic view of the world tends to be static, by virtue of its stress on the similarities and harmonies between things. It also tends to be hierarchical: the substance of the symbol is valued primarily in terms of its divine referent. Thus, according to various interpreters, Woman Wisdom may symbolize the wisdom of God, the wisdom tradition, the order of the world, the book of Proverbs, etc. We notice two things here. First, the significance of the symbol seems to pale beside what it symbolizes. Second, in every case, the *female* element in the symbol – its unconventional element – is thoroughly suppressed in favor of the male-determined referent. This is certainly one way to view Woman Wisdom, but it is not the only option.

To personify as female an abstract concept like wisdom is, in effect, to create a metaphor, "Wisdom is a woman." Now the second term is not only noticed; it is also highlighted as crucial to understanding. While it is possible to create such a personification and leave it at that (think, for example of the Statue of Liberty), the Proverbs poems go on to carry through the metaphor-ization process with their varied allusions to different roles of human women. Certain relevant historical associations of "woman" have been dis-cussed above: in Israel, woman was wife, lover, provider, prophet, counsel-lor, etc. Such images constitute what Max Black (1962: 38–44) calls the "system of associated commonplaces" evoked by a metaphor.

A metaphor with a wide and powerful range of such associations falls into the category of "root metaphor," one that goes beyond mere symbolic repre-sentation or condensation of ideas and actually carves out the conceptual and affective space in which we live. Root metaphors create reality. I believe that the metaphor of Woman Wisdom in fact functioned as a root metaphor historically and has the potential to so function again in current Christian religiosity.

A metaphorical perspective has at least two advantages for a theological discourse centered in biblical texts. The first is related to the notion of meta-phor as expressive of a system of associated commonplaces, or, perhaps better, the interaction of the systems of commonplaces associated with each of its terms. If a historical understanding of "Wisdom is a woman" requires elucidation of those systems entailed by "wisdom" and "woman" in post-exilic Israel, it is equally true that the contemporary reader can hardly approach these terms without what is commonly denigrated as "our own cultural baggage," but which here might be more usefully framed as our own systems of commonplaces. A hermeneutical bridge between past and present is constructed as we play with – and meet the challenges of – the similarities and differences not just between the terms of the metaphor, but also between the eras. The role of the reader in generating meaning from texts is thereby acknowledged, but not at the cost of repudiating all possibility of historical meanings.

Second, a metaphorical approach is advantageous insofar as metaphor functions by means of sublimation (Bal 1993: 205–206). That is to say, metaphors operate as much by suppressing and concealing meaning as by overtly creating it. With Bal, one must ask "the question of what the metaphor makes unspeakable." Let us consider, then, the spaces carved out and concealed by Woman Wisdom.

Wisdom and Language as metaphor

Wisdom thought is deeply concerned with language, a concern that Proverbs clothes in female garb. Based on the number of proverbs that address proper and improper speech, we can assume that the traditional sages were much interested in both the efficacious and truth-telling aspects (not always identical!) of language. Language itself, with both its positive and negative aspects, is personified in Proverbs 18:21:

> Death and life are in the power [lit: hand] of the tongue,
>   and her lovers will eat of her fruit.

Woman Wisdom, of course, represents the claim to truth and life, and makes these available to her lover:

> Hear, for I will speak noble things,
>   and from my lips will come what is right;
> for my mouth will utter truth;
>   wickedness is an abomination to my lips.
> All the words of my mouth are righteous;
>   there is nothing twisted or crooked in them.
> They are straight to the one who understands,
>   and right to those who find knowledge.
>   (8:6–9)

Death, however, also embodied in female form, is the end to the devious user of language, and to one who is taken in by it. Nowhere is this point clearer than in Proverbs 9, where the Woman of Folly echoes, but subverts, the words of Woman Wisdom. Wisdom says,

> "You that are simple, turn in here!"
>   To those without sense she says,
> "Come, eat of my bread
>   and drink of the wine I have mixed.
> Lay aside immaturity, and live,
>   and walk in the way of insight."
>
>   (9:4–6)

Folly parodies:

> "You who are simple, turn in here!"
>   And to those without sense she says,
> "Stolen water is sweet,
>   and bread eaten in secret is pleasant."
> But they do not know that the dead are there,
>   that her guests are in the depths of Sheol.
>
>   (9:16–18)

Three features of the space of language may be discerned in Proverbs' assertion that Wisdom is a woman. First, by locating truth in human speech, Woman Wisdom locates a divine immanence within this essential human attribute. God's presence is found in the world and, particularly, in women's world: the world of relationships in both home and marketplace, in the private and the public domains. Second, by embodying Language itself, as well as Wisdom, in female form, this essential human attribute is identified as female. Third, the embodiment of Language's deception, as well as its truth, in female form gives rise to a double vision. On the one hand, this dualistic linguistic embodying represents the (male) need to divide and conquer both women and language by distinguishing Wisdom from Folly, *the* truth in the midst of lies. Thus also, however, an appropriate reservation is articulated against all assertions of absolute truth; attention is called to the ease with which language becomes deformed. The possibility of a critical approach to these texts is embedded in the material itself.

Rereading women's roles

Analysis of Woman Wisdom as a metaphor allows for more empowering readings of the Bible with respect to women's roles, readings that move beyond some of the more detrimental possibilities of the text. Disconnected from the first nine chapters of Proverbs, for example, the closing poem on the woman of worth can easily be read as a license for slavery: the good wife is one who works her fingers to the bone night and day so her husband can parade around like a prince at the city gates. Alternatively, but relatedly, we have already noted how the opposition of Woman Wisdom and the Strange Woman may appear as the woman-negating "virgin/whore" dichotomy. While it is important for the sake of honesty not to deny these spaces in the texts, there are also others.

The closing poem by itself presents a "dead metaphor," the terms of which are taken literally and for granted: the good wife is wise. This is a space in which we live, but one that we no longer see as such.[8] The good wife has "mastered" her wisdom, just as her *ba'al* (= husband, master, verse 11) has mastered her. The book's opening chapters, however, turn the metaphor around. Now Wisdom is the good wife. And mastery she has! She does not simply "keep" her house; rather she builds it. And her house is not simply the family dwelling; it is the community, the cosmos, the written revelation of God. She is not mastered but sought and embraced.

If we could go no further than to say that this portrayal of Woman Wisdom valorizes traditional women's work, we would have said something important, but not sufficient. Hitler used a similar ploy. We must rather extend our analysis of the roles of women and wisdom to the mode of relationship involved. Wisdom as woman and the wise woman stand together at the nexus of at least two relational polarities. The first is that of the public and private spheres of social existence. Social-historical study alone would show us that these two spheres were not divided in ancient times in the same way or extent that they are today. The family household was the basis of societal formation both materially and symbolically. Thus it should not be at all surprising that the woman of worth operates in the domain of public economic activity, bringing food "from far away," buying and financing the cultivation of a vineyard, selling to merchants the garments and sashes she produces (31:14, 16, 24). If she, with her transcendent counterpart, is not merely "home-maker" but also "house-builder," then she is responsible for the interface between these two arenas. Her power is public as well as private, while at the same time investing the public realm with the relational values of the household.

As builder of the cosmic house, as well as of the family household, Woman Wisdom stands at the juncture of the divine and human realms as well. This is a location we shall explore further below. Here I shall simply note the wonderful immanance of the divine expressed through this figure, now in body as well as in language. And in choice as well as in body. The woman who originates with God, who plays with God, decides of her own volition to reside and play with human beings (8:30–31).

Rereading sexuality

Before considering Wisdom as goddess, there is one further observation to be made in regard to the metaphor "Wisdom is a woman." We highlight here the association of woman to sexuality: Woman Wisdom is a lover. As with other dimensions of this figure, this one is both problematic and salutary. In all probability, the sexually embodied aspect of Wisdom as woman is more surprising to a modern sensibility conditioned by later Greek influence than it was to the ancient Israelites. Let us accept our surprise gladly. Whatever negative opposition is constructed in these texts between the good woman and the bad, it is *not* an oppostion based on sexual experience versus its negation. If some version of the "whore" is in a sense on one side of Proverbs's polarity, it is curiously not the "virgin" on the other. Proverbs 1–9 is remarkable for bringing the vocabulary and forms of the Song of Songs into its portrayal both of Woman Wisdom and of the beloved wife. The former is to be sought, grasped, loved, prized, spoken to with terms of endearment, waited for at her gates and doors. Similarly, the latter should be faithfully attended to and rejoiced in as the source of emotional and physical pleasure:

> May her breasts satisfy you at all times;
>> may you be intoxicated always by her love.
>
> (5:19)

The liberative potential of this valorization of sexuality in a religious context comes under the double-barreled fire of patriarchy and heterosexism. Although the "good" female here is not a virgin, she *is* a wife. Her job is to protect her husband from the Strange Woman, while at the same time avoiding "going strange" herself, a possibility imagined in 2:16–19:

> You will be saved from the strange woman,
>> from the outsider with her smooth words,
> who forsakes the partner of youth
>> and forgets her sacred covenant . . .
>
> (2:16–17; see also 7:10–20)

Sexuality is celebrated, but only if it is properly controlled.

Sexuality is also assumed to be heterosexuality. Indeed, nowhere in the entire Bible is it more obvious not only that a man is writing[9] but that a male audience is intended. Who else would say to Woman Wisdom, "You are my sister" and call Insight "intimate friend" (7:4)? Who else indeed? But this literary display of the audience pushes the readers of every new generation to the foreground as well. Can we identify? What will we do if we cannot? How delightfully shocking to insist that women today should read this text literally, to insist on our right to be the audience of the text, to feel its call to intimacy with Woman Wisdom, to speak to her words of love, to identify each other with her, and be intoxicated always with that love. The text's unmitigatedly male discourse provides the implement for its own un-manning.

A THEOLOGICAL PERSPECTIVE

As we turn to consider the explicitly theological dimensions of this material, we will leave behind neither the historical nor the metaphorical perspectives introduced above. To assert that "Wisdom is a goddess" is to make the same sort of epistemological claim – one of metaphorical naming – that was made with "Wisdom is a woman." And the "ess" suffix assures that considerations of femaleness cannot be outside the picture, even as its absence subverts rather than supports claims of gender neutrality. The two metaphors are metonymically linked. Reflection on the metaphor "Wisdom is a goddess" entails again both recurrence to historical-literary considerations and reference to contemporary usage. The latter has been dramatically limned as a power issue since the Re-imagining Conference in November of 1993. The possibility of owning Wisdom as goddess has generated a crisis, a term rendered (so I've been told) in Chinese script with the characters for "dangerous opportunity."

Wisdom: God and Goddess

The goddess elements in the figure of personified Wisdom have always been a matter of dangerous opportunity. The creation of this figure in the first place depended in part on language and imagery drawn from Egyptian, Canaanite, and Mesopotamian goddesses.[10] This coopting of foreign traditions was commonplace in the development of Israelite religiosity, but always entailed a risk. These elements had to be integrated into the orthodox tradition in such a way that they were ultimately marked as "us," not "them." In the case of Woman Wisdom, I have argued that it was precisely the concomitant reliance on human female imagery and the experience of real women that mediated in this process. Thus the Woman Wisdom of Proverbs is, as demonstrated above, an amalgamation of the traits and roles of real women with a transcendent aura.

But was she, or should she be, regarded as a goddess? Historically, in Proverbs, my sense has been that she was understood as essentially what she appears to be: an act of theopoetic imagination that reflects claims about and for the wisdom tradition in its social context as much or more than claims about the nature of divinity.[11] This way of thinking about the figure begins a trajectory that culminates in Ben Sira's identification of Wisdom with Torah, about 180 B.C.E. Only a poetic image whose meaning was open and polyvalent could support such a fresh moment of inspiration.

On the other hand, "life and death are in the hand of the tongue": the rich fruit of poetic language can easily take on a life of its own. In hindsight, who can gainsay the fact that Proverbs 8 seems to portray a living being with divine powers, whether or not we choose to use the loaded term "goddess"? Thus the tradition seems to have noticed. As Cady, Ronan and Taussig argue in their book, *Wisdom's Feast* (1989), by the time the Wisdom of Solomon was written (either first century B.C.E. or C.E.), the ambiguously divine Woman Wisdom of Proverbs had become a more fully-fledged divine figure, not an independent goddess, but rather a way of talking about, of relating to, Yahweh and "his" works. This particular naming of divinity (not only of God but also, in the New Testament, of Jesus as well) has more recently been taken up in the feminist context, for example, in the worship elements introduced by Cady, Ronan and Taussig in their pastorates and study groups; in the more academic theology of Elizabeth A. Johnson's *She Who Is* (1992); and by the liturgists of the Re-imagining Conference.

While I can only affirm this liberating use of long-neglected Scripture, there are some underlying issues that need attention, spaces hidden, if you will, by the metaphor "Wisdom is a goddess." If we begin from Bal's perspective that metaphor works by sublimation, by making certain things unspeakable through its "cover-up" language, we might notice that the most important thing that "Wisdom is a goddess" makes unspeakable is itself. That is, none of the scholars and churchpeople just mentioned actually wants to *say* "Wisdom is a goddess." In the current denominational political climate, none of them *can* say it even if they want to. Thus, the only people saying "Wisdom is a goddess" are those who construe that statement as a heresy charge against those who cannot or do not wish to say it.[12] What's at stake here?

Feminist theologians deny the practice of "goddess worship" insofar as this suggests an entity over against the biblical God rather than simply a renaming of him. Ah, yes, but there you have it or, rather, there you have "him." In a language that distinguishes gods from goddesses, if you cannot use the latter word, have you not merely folded the female into the male, allowing him to coopt her? It is certainly accurate to say that these feminist theologians are not calling for "goddess worship" in the sense of imagining a divine figure apart from the biblical god. However, to say, in a way truthful both to the biblical tradition and to the impulses of feminist theology, that *Woman* Wisdom (or "Sophia," as many prefer) names God, we must be also able to say that God is Goddess. In this sense, the self-styled orthodox have called the results of the game correctly, though using the wrong rules.

Wisdom: truly Woman and truly God/dess[13]

Now, this proposal that Sophia-God names God as Goddess has a problem of its own, namely that goddesses don't always help real women. History is replete with societies that acknowledge strong female deities and yet are also politically male dominated. This is very obvious in the ancient Near East, and should give the lie to any attempt to blame Israel for patriarchy. What became orthodox Yahwism may have made an unprecedented attempt to kill the goddess, but women's lives did not much change, at least at the political level.[14] The role of the Virgin Mary in Catholicism is similar: the Queen of Heaven may be a comfort to women, but is hardly a standard-bearer for women's power.

Even more to the point is the case of Woman Wisdom herself, and I think there's a multiplex paradox here yet to be accounted for by Sophia-logians. I have suggested above a development in the portrayal of Woman Wisdom from the more earth-bound characterization of Proverbs to the divine being of the Wisdom of Solomon (Camp 1990: 194–203). This development co-incides, however, with an apparent de-valuation of human women in the texts and, to the extent we can tell, of real-life women in society. Proverbs not only casts Woman Wisdom in human female images, but also sings a hymn to the woman of worth. Ben Sira, perhaps a couple of centuries later, continues to use female imagery for wisdom, but the language becomes more formal and abstract. His Wisdom is a rigid disciplinarian, a role more like a male teacher than a woman, and he ultimately identifies "her" abstractly with the Torah. This author has much to say about human women, but virtually all of it is negative, and virulently so. Wives and daughters are a constant threat to male sexual and economic honor; indeed, in Ben Sira's view,

> From a woman sin had its beginning,
> and because of her we all die.
> (25:24)

The Wisdom of Solomon gives us divine Wisdom, but no human women at all. Instead of the intoxicating love and breasts of his wife, here the sage's fantasy is uncoupled from living flesh and real relationship:

> When I go home I shall take my ease with [Wisdom].
>   for nothing is bitter in her company,
> when life is shared with her there is no pain,
>   gladness only, and joy.
> (8:16)

Well, if a man had a wife like Ben Sira's this would be quite a relief. But does this goddess empower women?

We encounter, then, what I would submit is a crucial thealogical proble-matic. We know that control of language, especially the key metaphors that name ultimate reality, can be a powerful force for change, as it has been a powerful supporter of the status quo. Feminists have long assented to Mary Daly's dictum that a male god in effect makes men gods. Yet, we know his-torically that the mere presence of female deities does not make women god-desses. Specifically, we see that the presence of Woman Wisdom may or may not do much for women. The question, then, is: when does the metaphor God is Goddess or, specifically, Wisdom is God/dess, make a difference and when does it not? My reflections thus far suggest at least a tentative part of an answer. This metaphor holds power when it is not allowed to conceal another metaphor, namely, that "Wisdom is woman," with its entailment that "God/dess is human."

Now, this proposal is either extremely radical or highly orthodox. If I say that "God is known through the humanity of Jesus Christ," I have said at least part of what I mean, and few Christians would argue. If I say "Goddess is known through the femaleness of human women," I would have said another part of what I mean and opened myself to heresy charges. What is the real difference between these two statements? The male vs. female difference of course leaps out, but it is matched by another of equal importance, namely the particularity of the singular Jesus vs. the universality of human women. It is not just that Jesus is male, it is that Jesus is *the* (one and only and therefore) *perfect* male. Human women are never that. It is precisely at this point that I return to Proverbs to highlight another element of paradox that illuminates both its patriarchal conservatism and its openness to radical rereading.

Wisdom: good God or Strange Woman?

Imperfection is the issue here. Yes, even evil. We have noted Proverbs's good-woman/bad-woman dichotomizing. Already this would seem to be a problem for a Sophia-based theology. It would seem to raise a particular problem for precisely that element of Proverbs's theology that I praised a moment ago: the book that highlights and supports "real" women also uses female imagery to create a symbol of deadly evil in the Strange Woman, which is absent in both Ben Sira and the Wisdom of Solomon.

We have a couple options here. We can, on the one hand, ignore and suppress the Strange Woman texts, as most contemporary Sophia-logians have done. Why deal with her when we have the Wisdom of Solomon's goddess to worship? Just let one metaphor erase the other, as the tradition itself did. If "Wisdom is God/dess," why bother with "Woman is the Stranger"? We must bother because, of course, the tradition did not erase the latter metaphor at all. It persists in the canonical state of Proverbs and it persists, poisonously unspoken, in social practice. What happens if we take another option, and bring "Woman is the Stranger" to speech?

One thing we notice is that "Woman is the Stranger" conceals another metaphor under the surface of the tradition, namely, "the Stranger is God/dess." As it does with the transcendent Woman Wisdom, Proverbs endows this negative figure not only with attributes of human women, but also with divine ones. And, as with Woman Wisdom, the result is the creation of a dramatically new theological motif with long-lasting implications. My point of reference here is a comparison of language used for the Strange Woman with that used for God, specifically in Isaiah 28.

Outstanding among the numerous items of vocabulary and imagery connecting Proverbs 1–9 to the Isaiah text[15] is the reference to YHWH's works with the same word pair that repeatedly limns Woman Stranger. YHWH will rise up

> to do his deed – strange [*zar*] is his deed!
> to work his work – alien [*nokriyya*] is his work!
>
> (28:21)

In this same chapter, Isaiah also ascribes to God several terms used by Proverbs of Woman Wisdom. In Proverbs, Woman Wisdom offers her follower a fair wreath and beautiful crown (*'ateret tiph'eret*, 4:9); in Isaiah, YHWH will be to his people a "glorious crown" and a "beautiful diadem" (*'ateret-tsebi/tsephirat-tiph'arah*, 28:5). Similarly, just as Wisdom gives strength (*geburah*) to give to those who judge rightly (*shophte tsedeq*, 8:14–16), YHWH is a spirit of justice to the one who sits in judgment (*yosheb 'al hammishpat*) and strength (*geburah*) to warriors (28:6).

Remarkably, the positive and negative attributes that are *combined* in the prophetic depiction of YHWH are *divided* in the sage's rendition of the two female characters. But both sets of attributes remain fundamentally *divine* attributes. The Strange Woman is shaded no less with this transcendent aura than is the Wisdom Woman. The enduring import of the Strange Woman lies in its personification, for the first time in Israelite religious thought as far as I can tell, of a divine power of evil over against a God who is now unstained by death-dealing qualities. If God is Goddess, Devil is also Woman. It's not just that women are not perfect, it's that Woman is Death. Now, there's an enormous amount of power at stake here, but what do we want to do with it?

POWER, POWERLESSNESS AND THE DIVINE: A CASE-STUDY ON THE BIBLE IN CONTEMPORARY THEOLOGICAL DISCOURSE

Let me turn first to what it seems *has* been done with it in the context of the feminist theology conference known as the Re-imagining Conference, which produced considerable conservative reaction within the mainline denominations that supported it.[16] It may first be worth noting that the conflict aroused by this conference was anticipated by several years in a similar reaction of conservative Methodists to Cady, Ronan and Taussig's book, *Wisdom's Feast* (1989). Cady and Taussig, both Methodist pastors, were threatened with a heresy trial for this work. What was the problem? The book is a fine piece of both historical scholarship and liturgical creativity. It is actually composed of two parts. The first part is a historical look at the figure of Sophia in Jewish and Christian scriptures, which had in fact appeared three years earlier as an independent monograph (entitled *Sophia: The Future of Feminist Spirituality*). To the best of my knowledge, no one raised any particular issue with the earlier publication. It was the second half of *Wisdom's Feast* that generated the heat. Here the authors offer Bible studies and liturgical elements that were actually used in churches and that were intended for others to so use. Quite an example of how little scholarship matters until it involves praxis! By the same token, I would argue that the Re-imagining Conference would not have created a blip on the conservative radar screen if it had just been theologians reading papers to each other; surely nothing was said there that has not been said at academic professional meetings or in many published feminist works for years. The difference at the conference was that there were not just scholars in attendance and that what was said intellectually was also ritualized.[17]

I believe that understanding the prior Methodist uproar over *Wisdom's Feast* is one crucial element in understanding the fall-out of the Re-imagining Conference. If all one had was the record of the conference, one would have to ask why so much attention has been paid in the conservative denominational presses to Sophia. This figure actually received little reflective time in the overall conference, though she was invoked at certain ritual moments: in a brief litany that preceded each speaker's presentation, although *no* speaker actually talked on Sophia, and in a liturgy that celebrated Sophia as creator alongside aspects of women's embodiment in the context of a "milk and honey" meal that closed the gathering. The latter usage was anticipated by, if not directly drawn from, *Wisdom's Feast*. But, more than this, *Wisdom's Feast* and the worship experiences that generated this book created the conservative awareness of Sophia that, in spite of the infrequent conference references, led to headlines like *Christianity Today*'s "Fallout Escalates Over 'Goddess' Sophia Worship" (4/4/94). One of the most-quoted blasts against Sophia — retired Methodist Bishop Earl Hunt's statement that "no comparable heresy has appeared in the church in the last 15 centuries" — was, by his own account in the *United Methodist Reporter*, prepared *before* the conference took place. I can only assume that its impetus was *Wisdom's Feast*.

The larger point to be taken here is that Sophia becomes a problem when the church is forced to notice her, specifically, in a worship context. Left to her own devices in the Bible, she can be safely ignored. So ignored, in fact, that Susan Cyre, in the *Christianity Today* article just cited, credits the Bible's statements about Sophia to the conference organizers: "Organizers *claimed* Sophia is the embodiment of wisdom, found in the first nine chapters of Proverbs. Sophia, *they said*, was with God at the Creation, and she is 'the tree of life to those who lay hold of her'" (emphasis mine). The quotation in the last phrase (from Proverbs 3:18) provides an ironic comment on Cyre's attempt to blame contemporary feminists for these ideas!

There is another point as well that requires attention, one that is articulated clearly in a paper by Catherine Keller.[18] As part of the system of commonplaces contemporary Christianity associates with female deities, Keller points to the conference critics' conflation of "heretical" worship with "feminist-womanist-lesbians," terminology that appeared on a tear-out postcard provided by the conservative Methodist magazine *Good News* for the convenience of those who wished to mail in their protest to the United Methodist Church Women's Division of the Board of Global Ministries. This conflation reveals a metonymic link between the notion of religious apostasy and what is regarded as aberrant female sexuality. "Aberrant," we might note, applies any time women have control over their own sexuality.

This figuration has, again, a paradoxical quality when it comes to feminist theologizing with respect to the Bible. On the one hand, Sophia is *there*, and it may well be regarded as miraculous that she is. The attempt to implicitly deny Sophia's biblical basis by those who rant about heresy shows how deep the cover-up has been. On the other hand, it is problematic for those who wish to claim the Bible's Sophia tradition as authoritative, for the tendency to metaphorize apostasy as female sexual aberration is also precisely a biblical one. The Bible can hardly speak of non-monotheistic worship without the language of non-monogamous behavior. Metonym becomes metaphor as aberrant female sexuality comes to name the heresy: false worship *is* adultery and fornication. As we have seen, moreover, Proverbs takes a step beyond even this languaging to constitute Evil itself as the woman who is sexually strange. What kind of authority, then, is the Bible for us here? When we go to the Sophia image for power, what exactly are we doing? How can feminists claim Sophia without automatically authorizing that other element in the tradition that spearheads the attack? Or, to frame the question as I shall take it up here: on what basis can feminists claim authority for and from Woman Wisdom, while ignoring the Other Woman – the Strange Woman – beside her?

It would be remiss to imply that these questions have gone unnoticed in general, even though they have not been applied to Sophia in particular. Christian feminists have long struggled over the question of biblical authority, and appeal could easily be made in this instance to ideas like "usable tradition" (see, e.g., Letty Russell) or to the authority of the biblical people to proclaim the life-giving elements of the tradition, while refusing to acknowledge the revelatory nature of the rest (see E. Schüssler Fiorenza). What makes such hermeneutical moves difficult in the case of Sophia is the profound rhetorical linkage that Proverbs creates between what feminists would regard as positive and negative imagery for women. I would like to conclude by pressing further on the paradox of this linkage.

What Proverbs has joined subtley, by means of common vocabulary and imagery, the critics of "Sophia worship" have joined perversely, by reconfiguring the Bible's own valuations. Keller appropriately describes this move as "the hereticizing of Sophia," but I would suggest that the biblical imagery lets us sharpen the point even further. Rather amazingly, by making Sophia the object of the contemporary equation of aberrant sexuality and false worship, *the Sophia-critics have in fact turned Woman Wisdom into the Strange Woman*.

As I have stressed, what the defenders of Sophia have to contend with is the fact that the possibility for this move is implicit in the linkage created by the text. Keller has pungently noted how "[t]he lurid accounts of the *Good News* writers rip image after image [from the Re-imagining liturgies] out of context, yoking together the most sensuous metaphors in order to create an aura of pornography." The hands-down winner of the Most-Quoted Line Award in the conservative denominational press is extracted from the Conference's liturgy celebrating women's embodiment: "We are women in your [= Sophia's] image. With nectar between our thighs, we invite a lover, we birth a child." Keller notes that similar sentiments are celebrated in the Song of Songs, but I would also recall the Strange Woman's invitation to her prospective lover:

> I have come out to meet you,
> > to seek you eagerly, and I have found you!
> I have decked my couch with coverings,
> > colored spreads of Egyptian linen;
> I have perfumed my bed with myrrh, aloes and cinnamon.
> Come, let us take our fill of love until morning;
> > let us delight ourselves with love.
>
> (Proverbs 7:15–18)

This, precisely, is the sensibility with which the conservatives calumniate Sophia and her "worshippers." And, to an extent, bibilically speaking, they are right: to the extent that Woman Wisdom and the Strange Woman share a female embodiment, to the extent that they share the language of seeking and finding, and, through the beloved wife, of sexual delight, there is latent in this common imagery an understanding that *all* women, even Woman Wisdom, are Other.

But in Proverbs this understanding is ambiguated by the contradictory willingness to affirm a powerful and empowering goodness in women, a goodness that in some sense represented the very core identity of "Us" as well. Such redemptive ambiguity is lost to the Sophia-critics, at least in part, because they do not realize how they have twisted the text to produce their invectives or, more precisely, how the text's own rhetoric turns its surface message on end.

For feminists who are conscious of the powerful work of metonym and metaphor, another shaping of the linkage of Wise and Strange is possible. Regarding the two Women of Proverbs as unified, rather than opposed, has generated for me the beginnings of a fruitful meditation on the relationship of the power of the center to the power of the margin (Camp 1987: 14–36). Here we read against the surface grain of the text, with its power to pit one woman against another. We read, rather, to use an image from folklore, as tricksters, those two-sided characters who appear both as creators and disruptors of social order, whose flaunting of the boundaries of social convention is embraced as part of the life-giving fabric, whose strangeness is acknowledged as part and parcel of their wisdom. We read as Strange Women.

The textual dialectic of wise and strange, surely intended by its authors to remain a polarity, creates its own semantic energy, forcing itself beyond the bounds of its original historical context into a hermeneutics of power. The power manifests as deadly venom when anti-Sophia polemicists channel all its dialectical energy into strangeness, laying patriarchal claim to the center and consigning all dissenters to the Sheol outside the community's circle. Keller has powerfully analyzed the ideological force at work here as one of racism and sexism, framed in ancient rhetoric.

> The rhetoric of heresy and apostasy armors [the ecclesial right] in the battle against the new abomination they have now managed to name feminist/womanist/lesbian goddess worship. Only by achieving this particular configuration could they hope to sidestep charges of racism regarding actual womanists, charges of gender competition in relation to white women, and the disinclination of half the [Methodist] denomination to bash gays and lesbians. By erecting the goddess Sophia as the idol of their opponents, they have constructed a "heresy" which . . . functions to disqualify every feminist/womanist experiment in God-language, and therefore to de-legitimate the "subordinated knowledges" whose insurrection in the churches has begun . . . to gain institutional power.
>
> (Keller 1994: 340–42)

The hermeneutics of power generated by Proverbs's dialectic of wise and strange also manifests as the rush of the Spirit for Christians who reimagine the biblical deity as Sophia, and I have tried to argue that there is nothing to be gained in pulling our theological punches as we name God Sophia. Granted that all attempts to speak of the holy are partial and metaphorical, there are metaphors and there are metaphors. To call God Sophia is *not* on the same level as calling God a mother hen.[19] Sophia is a powerful naming, a root metaphor, that names God with the same fullness as the name Jesus Christ. Indeed, though we have not pursued the New Testament data here, it is clear that many early Christians – *orthodox* Christians, I hasten to add – named Jesus Sophia as well.

But this latter move is also one that channels a dialectical energy into a single course, albeit one of powerful goodness. It empowers us; it affirms our identity at the center. But it also shapes God/dess in our image; it disallows the existence of evil in our midst. The paradox of divinity and humanity, of the goodness and evil that infuses both, is denied; something of reality slips away. Again, Keller's analysis is most helpful. She contrasts "the language of heresy-charges [that] always sought to enclose a domain of orthodoxy pure of mistakes" (p. 23) with the reality of power as "something intrinsically amoral [that] fuels both sin and grace." "Power," she says, "is first of all life-force, energy, circulating freely through networks of relationship" (p. 27). Power, I would say, is both wise and strange, and the deification of Woman Wisdom without attention to her Strange companion risks the denial, the sublimation, of those aspects of power we have difficulty seeing or do not care to see, whether the unconscious striving toward a claim to orthodoxy in ourselves, or the various forms that resistance to oppression might take.

Again we take up the struggle to stay inside the space of paradox, to live the tensive relationship of the liminal to the center. Woman is One: patriarchy has made of each and all the Stranger. Woman is not One: we have not all been equally on the outside and Sophia does not move us all equally to the center. As we live inside the paradox, the whole notion of center and margin shifts and shifts again. The center of what and of whom?

Through Sophia, the power of female liminality is drawn into and reinvigorates the center. There is a danger of patriarchal cooptation in this move, however. The dynamic is effective for women only if Sophia remembers her connection to the Stranger. In Proverbs, Sophia lent power to the good wife, but that power was controlled and channeled to the support of a patriarchy that divided woman from woman. We are no doubt more sophisticated now, more resistant to being manipulated by the existing power structure. Perhaps the fact that women are using the Sophia metaphor for themselves will liberate it, and us, from the trap of cooptation.

Yet all naming entails a kind of reification. Making Deity female, making Deity Other, will fall into the same absolutizing traps as all other theologizing unless we remember that Otherness itself is multiple, unless Otherness itself remains at some level yet Strange, even to us strange women. The memory of Strangeness inhibits Wisdom's turn to imagining herself One, "centered," perfect.

Who owns the center, who the margin, and where is power to be found? The center has long been held by men, but never without the help of their good wives. In small circles over recent years, and in a large circle last November, the center was claimed by those long regarded as strange. Yes, call us by our proper name: feminist, womanist, lesbian, Goddess worshiper. Yes, call us by our proper name: Christian. But where is the margin now? Does it fall along the pew where the good wife sits each Sunday? Is it marked by a strand of rosary beads that comforts an abused woman? Is it stepped out in the notes of a spiritual sung in a blighted city or in the hymns of a dying prairie church? How will the wise and powerful women with the bold imagination to call forth blessing on the nectar between our thighs continue to speak to strangers like these? The memory of the Strange Woman forbids a claim to the center, even by Sophia. The mistake made by the men who wrote Proverbs was to see this denial as the source of death. To the contrary, precisely through her representation of the ever-shifting margin of power, the Strange Woman – like Wisdom and with Wisdom – promises life and favor from the unnamable I AM.

CONCLUSION

In what is surely one of the world-class examples of academic overkill, I have been writing on the female imagery in Proverbs for 15 years. My own powerful attraction to this material has for most of that time seemed one of those scholarly idiosyncracies. Repeatedly I have asked myself whether this language, these metaphors with their curious and tensive twists and turns, would ever make any difference to anyone, empower anyone, but a few lonely souls in their ivory towers. The current Sophia controversy, beginning with the publication of *Wisdom's Feast* and coming to wide public attention with the Re-imagining Conference, has begun to answer that question loudly! Where a few women have caught a vision of Sophia, a rampaging right wing, gathering momentum from a well-meaning but uninformed middle,[20] have made her a cause. Most strangely of all, they have done so by making Woman Wisdom out to be a Strange Woman.

This inversion points to another underlying issue as well, namely the power of the Bible itself. It is curious that the Bible suddenly makes such a difference in this particular way. I expect lines to be drawn over whether to "believe" the Bible or not; over whether to take it "literally" or not; over what to do with its problematic stances on issues like homosexuality. I do not expect to see bombs bursting over people just accepting what it says about God. It must be hard to be one of "them" right now, desperately trying to recover (the contradictions of) the Bible's metaphorical power.

NOTES

1 This chapter was originally prepared for a working group on the relationship of the Bible and theology, funded by the Lilly Foundation. I thank Lilly and the members of this group for providing a stimulating context for discussion on power, powerlessness, and the divine.
2 Carole Fontaine (1988: 502–503) notes the coincidence of many of these features with the folklore type of the "sought-for person," or princess-bride, bestowed by her father on the hero after a set of trials, who provides both good counsel and material blessings, and who must be discerned from the "false bride."
3 This imagery is anticipated in Proverbs 3:13–18 and 19–20. Although these two brief units in chapter 3 were no doubt originally independent, their contiguity in the book of Proverbs is telling, and surely related to the chain of associations made in chapter 8. In 3:13–18, Wisdom is better than earthly treasure, though she offers that, too, as well as life (cf. 8:10–11, 18–21, 35–36). She is to be laid hold of (*hzq*), a

verb used elsewhere of intimate embrace (7:13). Verses 19–20 shift suddenly to YHWH's wisdom by which he founded the earth (cf. 8:22–31).

4 The two terms overlap in this range of meanings, though they are not absolutely identical. *Zar*, for example, has two connotations apparently not available in *nokri*: it can mean, specifically, an outsider to the Aaronid priestly family; more generally, it can also simply mean "not oneself, another."

5 See Camp (1991) for a detailed discussion of the dimensions of strangeness in Proverbs.

6 This point is arguable, and has indeed been much argued. Even if I am wrong in my judgement, the multiplicity of meaning in this figure does not allow a limitation of the Strange Woman's significance to this connotation.

7 This polemic against foreign wives may, in fact, be no older than the Deuteronomist. Biblical scholars, observing that there are no differences at the material level between so-called Israelites and Canaanites, increasingly tend to view intermixing as the norm until relatively late in the biblical period, citing Josiah's nationalistic reforms as the likely origin of the Bible's polemic.

8 Compare the analysis of "metaphors we live by" by Lakoff and Johnson in their book by that title (1980).

9 It may be, as Brenner and van Dijk-Hemmes argue, that a mother actually delivers some of these teachings, but even they do not attempt to dispute the fact that it is a patriarchal voice we hear.

10 See Fontaine (1988: 502–503) for an overview of the data.

11 A new dissertation by Judith McKinlay (1994; soon to be published by Sheffield Academic Press) will likely lead to further nuancing of this assessment. McKinlay not only proposes Asherah as a meaningful element in Wisdom's ancestry, but also argues that the Proverbs poets systematically suppressed the goddess through increasingly domesticated images of Wisdom.

12 I allude here to the controversy surrounding so-called "Sophia worship." See below for further discussion of this debate.

13 For want of other options, I shall resort to Rosemary Radford Ruether's writable if not readable designation for divinity that both incorporates and transcends all aspects of human sexuality (1983: 46).

14 In response to the conference presentation of this chapter, Carole Fontaine appropriately called for a nuancing of my implication that the presence of goddess worship makes no difference to women if the society is socially and politically male dominated. In fact, women can be profoundly empowered at the spiritual level, with all the attendant ramifications thereof, by goddess-piety. Fontaine's own historical research (1987: 96–126) gives a fine example of this in the case of the Hittite queen Puduhepa's worship of the Sun-goddess Arinna. Carol Christ (1979: 273–87) makes a similar argument for contemporary goddess-worship.

15 See Camp (1991) for further examples and discussion.

16 Readers wishing to track the debate are referred to several denominational publications, dating from just before the conference and for close to a year after it. The *United Methodist Reporter* and the *News of the Presbyterian Church* are the official organs of their respective denominations. The *Presbyterian Layman*, *reNews* (a publication of Presbyterians for Renewal) and the Methodist *Good News* are conservative publications that published virulent attacks on the conference. More recently, the ecumenical periodical *Christian Century* has published critical (though not negative) assessments of both the conference and of Sophia-centered theology (Small and Burgess 1994; Lefebure 1994).

17 There was, of course, denominational money involved in putting on the conference and sending delegates to it. Particularly in the United Methodist and Presbyterian

(USA) churches, some outcry has overtly centered on how such funding decisions are made. I would argue, however, that the funding issue is a smoke screen. Denominations spend infinitely more money year after year supporting colleges and seminaries where these theologians teach and write. Although there are a few seminary professors (notably Tom Oden of Drew [Oden 1994: 10–13]) attacking the issue at this level, there is generally little hue and cry about money, as long as those feminist theologians are off doing their thing in the ivory tower. The problem arises when church people are confronted with the possibility of putting the ideas into practice. Although I formulated this analysis independently, I thank Cynthia Rigby for sharing a paper that supports it, though from the other side! "An Open Letter to Presbyterians: Theological Analysis of Issues Raised by the Re-imagining Conference," (Allen, *et al.* 1994) states:

> Had the Re-imagining Conference been nothing more than an exercise in theological experimentation, there would be less cause for complaint. Little was said there which had not already been said many times over in books written by the Conference speakers. . . . But the Re-imagining Conference was much more than an exercise in theological brain-storming. It was a worship event – indeed, an event in which the deities worshipped can only be judged (in light of the New Testament and the Confessions of our church) to be idols.

18 "Power and the Politics of Heresy: A Case Study." Quotations are from their unpublished paper. A portion of this paper was published in *The Christian Century* as "Inventing the Goddess" (Keller 1994).

19 The latter metaphor, used by Jesus in Matt 23:37 and Luke 13:34, has sometimes been cited as an example of the Bible's gender inclusive imagery for God.

20 As I prepared this chapter, I learned that Chung Hyun Kyung, one of the theologians who did not speak about Sophia at the Re-imagining Conference, had been engaged to speak at the Women's Quadrenniel of my denomination, the Christian Church (Disciples of Christ). Publication by the conservative Methodist and Presbyterian presses of a radical snippet or two from one of her earlier addresses provoked one of my fellow Disciples in Fort Worth – an older gentleman with a long-established liberal reputation on most matters – to write a protest letter to the Department of Church Women, and send copies to many associates at least around this city, if not further afield as well. The letter was an excellent example of the hysterical linkage of references to foreign goddesses (in this case Korean), Canaanite fertility worship and Sophia which Catherine Keller analyzes so well. After actually seeing a video tape of Chung's address, the letter-writer had the good grace to send another, recanting of his worst objections to her appearance before Disciples women. Still, the ability of the right wing to whip a relative liberal to action by appealing to these fears was a mighty evidence of their power.

PART II

GLEANINGS

For the reader who does not take up the subject position offered by the text, Proverbs 1–9 ceases to be a simple text of initiation and becomes a text about the problematic nature of discourse itself.

Carol A. Newsom

The movement from killing "Others" to killing each other appears to be symptomatic of the same trauma of identity. *Israel cannot rewrite the face of the Other without rewriting its own face.*

Danna Nolan Fewell

As long as people of the land remain faceless, they may be killed with little remorse. Joshua, however, reveals the real danger involved in contact with the people of the land: Israel may see its own image reflected in the other.

L. Daniel Hawk

With the monarchy, however, the theological issue of succession becomes precisely that, the issues of the "issue". . . . The lament betrays a certain cultural anxiety over the "issue," revealing what is at stake for monotheism when the issue of an heir for the king arises.

Mark K. George

Pornography as a path to utopia? Violence as a harbinger of the world restored? Ezekiel forces its present day readers to confront everything that is most difficult and disturbing about how human desire shapes our spiritual and political worlds.

Jan William Tarlin

HUMAN BODIES

Questions concerning divine identity are leading into questions concerning strangeness, otherness. The line between self and not-self, identity and the other, begins to blur even as some try desperately to sharpen it. In this part the focus on Scripture and the politics of identity becomes much more explicit. How are the body politic and individual political bodies constructed or deconstructed, shored up or shattered, in or by biblical literature and its divine speaking subject? How by its readers – whether a sixth-century B.C.E. Ezra or an early twentieth-century C.E. Freud? What possible relationships are there between nationalism, sexism, racism, xenophobia, and Scripture? Of course, these discussions continually harken back to the previous discussions, because in biblical literature the political corpus is a theological corpus, and vice versa. At the same time, Scripture is not univocal (does not simply say one thing) when it comes to either body of concerns, and so the relation between the two is anything but simple or unproblematic.

6

WOMAN AND THE DISCOURSE OF PATRIARCHAL WISDOM

Carol A. Newsom

A casual reader asked to describe Proverbs 1–9 might reply that it was the words of a father talking to his son, mostly about women. While that might be a naive reading, its very naivete brings into focus some of the features of Proverbs 1–9 that have not always been sufficiently attended to in scholarly discussions. First, these chapters are virtually all talk. They are, to use a currently fashionable word, discourse. But even more importantly, discourse, the dialogic, social dimension of language, becomes a central topic of these chapters. Second, the cast of characters is severely limited, and the privileged axis of communication is that from father to son. The reader's locus of self-identification, that is, the subject position established by the reader, is that of the son, the character who never speaks. Third, discourse embodies and generates a symbolic world. Consequently, it is significant that although woman is not the sole topic of the chapters, talk about women and women's speech occupies an astonishing amount of the text: men, preoccupied with speech, talking out women and women's speech. What role, then, does sexual difference play in this symbolic world both in making men's speech possible but at the same time rendering it problematic?

PROVERBS 1:2–9

Although it is widely recognized that the father/son address of Proverbs 1–9 is not to be taken literally, very little attention is generally given to the significance of the fictional level established by these terms. It is a rather minimal fiction, but nonetheless important. The father, who speaks, is the "I" of the discourse. The son, addressed in the vocative and with imperative verbs, is the "you." Though other types of speech are occasionally embedded within it, the fiction never moves beyond this repeated moment of address. The linguist Emile Benveniste has drawn attention to the peculiar nature of the pronouns "I" and "you." What is unique to them becomes evident when one asks what they refer to. They don't refer either to a concept (the way that nouns like "tree" do), nor do they refer to unique individuals (the way

116

that proper names do). Instead "I" and "you" are linguistic blanks or empty signs filled only when individual speakers and addressees appropriate them in specific instances of discourse. Their oddity among linguistic signs is related to the problem they serve to solve, which is none other than that of intersubjective communication (Benveniste 1971: 219). In fact Benveniste claims that it is through language that our subjectivity, our ability to constitute ourselves as subjects, is made possible. "Consciousness of self is only possible if it is experienced by contrast. I use *I* only when I am speaking to someone who will be a *you* in my address. It is this condition of dialogue that is constitutive of person" (1971: 224–25). The striking prominence of the pronouns "I" and "you" and the repeated use of vocative and imperative address in Proverbs 1–9 are clear indicators of what is at stake in these chapters: the formation of the subjectivity of the reader.[1] Because of the social nature of discourse in which subjectivity is established, it can never be ideologically neutral. There is no Cartesian self that can be established apart from all else, but always a self in relation. The emergence of subjectivity is always in the context of ideology. In a well-known analogy the Marxist theoretician Louis Althusser speaks of the way in which ideology "recruits" subjects, "hails" them as a policeman might: "Hey, you there!" The individual, recognizing himself or herself as the one addressed, turns around in response to the hailing. And with that gesture he or she becomes a subject, takes up a particular subject position in a particular ideology. Althusser uses the term *interpellation* for this process (1971: 174–75). The actual hailing by ideology is seldom as direct as one finds in the instruction literature of Proverbs 1–9. But here the intent is explicit and self-conscious. The reader of this text is called upon to take up the subject position of son in relation to an authoritative father. Now that would be a rather banal statement if this were a piece of children's literature, used exclusively in a school setting and then outgrown. But clearly it is not. The intended readers identified by the text include not only the naive youth (verse 4) but also the mature sage (verse 5). All readers of this text, whatever their actual identities, are called upon to take up the subject position of son in relation to an authoritative father. Through its imitation of a familiar scene of interpellation the text continually reinterpellates its readers.

The familiar scene, a father advising his son, is important. Proverbs 1–9 takes a moment from the history of the patriarchal family and gives it a privileged status as a continuing social norm.[2] The choice of the patriarchal family as the symbol of the authority structure of wisdom has important implications. Since it is in the family that one's subjectivity is first formed, the malleability called for in the text is made to seem innocent, natural, inevitable. In addition the symbol of the family causes the discourse to appear to stand outside of specific class interests. This is not a landed aristocrat speaking, not a senior bureaucrat, not a member of the urban middle class or a disenfranchised intellectual, but "your father." Families are not ideologically innocent places, but because everyone has one, they give the appearance of being so.

The specific social dimensions of Proverbs 1–9 are also cloaked by the preference for abstract terms, such as "righteousness, justice, and equity" (1:3). The pragmatic meaning of these terms is seldom clear from the text. And yet it is precisely in the struggle to control the meaning of such terms that one finds evidence of ideological conflict between social groups. Occasionally, one can catch a hint as to the social location of wisdom discourse, but the type of speech used in Proverbs 1–9 largely serves to deflect that inquiry. What is important for Proverbs 1–9 is the issue of interpellation and the need for continual reinterpellation.

PROVERBS 1:10–19

The first speech that is addressed to the son is precisely about how to resist interpellation by a rival discourse ("My son, if sinners try to persuade you, do not consent," verse 10). Because the discourse of the "sinners" is presented by the father, their alleged speech is really completely controlled by the father. In fact the sinners' speech is crowded with negative markers: they are made to describe their own victims as "innocent" (verse 12a). Their metaphor for themselves is that of death itself, Sheol swallowing up life (verse 12b). They act gratuitously, "for the hell of it" (Heb. *hinnam*, verse 11). Assuming, with many commentators, that verse 16 is a late marginal comment drawn from Isaiah 59:7, the father follows an interesting rhetorical strategy in soliciting the son's agreement to his point of view. He first reiterates his admonition (verse 15) and then poses a challenge: "in vain is the net spread in full view of the bird" (verse 17). The wise son, the reader who can "deconstruct" the discourse of the sinners, won't be trapped in their net of words. Since the self-incriminating elements of the hypothetical speech are hard to miss, the reader enjoys a moment of self-congratulation, a moment that bonds the reader closer to the father. The father then confirms the reader's judgment in verse 18, making explicit the self-destructive quality of the sinners.

But what else is going on here? Who and what is the son really being warned against? It seems scarcely credible that the advice should be taken at face value as career counseling. It is much more likely that this depiction of brigands is a metaphor for something else. Indeed, verse 19 confirms it. The summary statement of the address explains that "such are the ways of all who cut a big profit." Here at least is one clue to the social location of the text, though we still do not know precisely what economic activity is identified by the pejorative phrase. A closer look at the sinners' speech offers a different avenue of approach. The structure of authority embodied there is strikingly different from that of the overall discourse of Proverbs 1–9. The persuaders are not fathers hierarchically related to the son, but peers. Their speech uses the cohortative rather than the direct imperative. Featured pronouns are not the counterposed "I–you" pair but the often repeated "us," "we." The egalitarian subtext is made explicit in verse 14b, "we will all share a common purse." The rival discourse against which the father argues can be made visible in its general outlines: it is one with a horizontal rather than a vertical structure of authority, based not on patriarchal family affiliation but on common enterprise, and one that offers young men immediate access to wealth rather than the deferred wealth of inheritance. What lurks under the surface is the generational chasm, the division of power between older and younger men in patriarchal society. The genuine appeal to younger men of the set of values just described is cleverly defused by associating them with what is clearly outside the law.

PROVERBS 1:20–33

Here and in chapter 8 the father's discourse is interrupted by speeches of personified Wisdom (*Hokmot*). These speeches serve to buttress what the father has said, however, and belong to the same cultural voice that speaks through the father. Although the pronouns and inflected verb forms identify Wisdom as female, the significance of her gender emerges more clearly in the later part of Proverbs 1–9. Here I want to focus on the relative positions of speaker and addressee established in the speech. That Wisdom is an extension of the cultural voice that speaks through the father can be seen in the complementary authoritative position she occupies. Where the father is the authoritative voice in the family, *Hokmot* is the corresponding public voice ("in the streets," "in the public squares," verse 20) who occupies the places that are physically symbolic of collective authority and power ("at the entrance of the gates," verse 21). She also has the power to save from disaster (verses 26–33). Although she addresses a plurality of listeners, the frequent second-person forms identify the reader as directly addressed. Perhaps the most interesting feature of the text is that it posits a past to the relationship between Wisdom and the reader. Her first words are "How long will you . . ." (verse 22). The reader's subjectivity is furnished not only with a past but with a guilty one. As one who is "naive," "cocky," and "complacent" (verse 22), he has refused advice and correction. The reader discovers himself in the text as always, already at fault. And the fault is recalcitrance before legitimate authority.

The two paired speeches of chapter 1 have attempted to construct a subject who is extremely submissive: perennially a son, willing to forgo the attractions of non-hierarchical order, and yet despite it all, somehow never quite submissive enough. But one may sense, lurking behind this nearly supine persona, a shadow figure of significant power. A world made of discourse, a symbolic order, an ideology exists only by consensus. If it cannot recruit new adherents and if those whom it reinterpellates do not recognize themselves in its hailing, it ceases to have reality. Wisdom may threaten the recalcitrant with destruction, but the inverse is also true: enough recalcitrance and Wisdom ceases to exist (see Crenshaw 1981: 16).

PROVERBS 2

The problematic aspects of discourse already present in chapter 1 are given a sharper focus in the carefully constructed composition of Proverbs 2. One can summarize the argument as follows: accept my words and internalize them with the help of God (verses 1–11), and they will protect you from the man who speaks perversely (verses 12–15) and from the Strange, smooth-talking Woman (verses 16–20). The world is presented as a place of competing and conflicting discourses: the words of the father, the words of the crooked man, the words of the Strange Woman. One is hailed from many directions, offered subject positions in discourses that construe the world very differently. Far from valuing the plurality of discourses that intersect a culture, Proverbs 1–9 seeks the hegemony of its own discourse. If one has internalized a discourse, one is insulated from, or as the text more polemically puts it, protected from other voices. But how is this to occur? How is one's subjectivity formed in that definitive way? Verses 1–11 make the astute observation that allegiance precedes understanding, not the other way around. We should not be surprised that these wisdom discourses do not closely define the pragmatic content of wisdom and contrast it with the competing discourses, seeking to convince the hearer of its superiority. Rather it repeatedly asks first for allegiance ("accept my words," "treasure up my strictures," "incline your ear," "extend your heart," verses 1–2). Nor is the allegiance passive. It must involve active participation ("call out," "seek," verses 3–4). Only then does understanding follow ("then you will understand fear of Yahweh," verse 5; "then you will understand righteousness and justice and equity, every good path," verse 9), for at that point habituation to the assumptions, values, and cultural practices of the group will make them seem one's own ("for wisdom will come into your heart and your soul will delight in knowledge," verse 10). As Althusser pungently paraphrases Pascal, "Kneel down, move your lips in prayer, and you will believe" (1971: 168).

For this reason it isn't surprising that the metaphors of "way," "path," and "track," which occur throughout Proverbs 1–9, appear in this chapter with particular density (twelve occurrences in verses 8–20). "Way" or "path" may be a hackneyed metaphor for customary behavior, but its connotations are worth some reflection. A path is a social product, made by many feet over a period of time. But its purely physical record of customary social behavior is often transposed in terms of a teleology and a will ("Where does that path lead?"). A path does not, in fact, exclude movement in any direction. It only makes its own direction the easiest, most natural, most logical way of proceeding. As each individual "freely" chooses to walk the path, that act incises the path more deeply. Finally, a path orders the world in a particular way as it establishes relations between place and place, relations that are not necessarily the shortest distance between two points. It is understandable why, in a chapter that construes the world as a place of conflicting discourses, the metaphor of the path figures so prominently. Customary social behavior, represented by the image of the path, is a type of non-verbal discourse. Manners, dress, food, orientation to time, divisions of labor, and so forth, are all elements of a social group's discourse, alongside its explicit words. Words and ways are related, as the parallelism of verse 12 suggests.

But against whom is the father arguing so strenuously? Who are the man and woman whose speech the son is warned about? Of the man all we learn is that he is associated with inversion of values (he delights in what is bad, verse 14a; his words are all "turned about," verse 12) and with perversion of values ("twisted," "crooked," verse 15), the opposite of the quality of "uprightness" and "perfection" associated with the father's advice (verse 21). His function is definitional. He simply serves to signify whatever stands over against "us," the group of the father's discourse.

It is with the symbol of the Strange Woman, however, that the text discovers its primary image of otherness. For a patriarchal discourse in which the self is defined as male, woman qua woman is the quintessential other. Much ink has been spilled in attempting to clarify why she is identified as a "strange" or "foreign" woman, whether the terms refer to an ethnic, legal, or social status. But it may not be an either/or question. Whether the terms were originally ambiguous or have only become so after the passage of years, any and all of the possible interpretations underscore the quality of otherness that she already possesses as woman in male discourse. As a foreigner, she would recall the strong Israelite cultural preference for endogamy over exogamy, the choice of same over other. If, as seems to be clearly the case in chapter 7, she is an adulteress, then she may be called strange/foreign because she is legally "off limits."[3] Or, if 2:17 is meant to suggest that she has left her husband ("one who has abandoned the companion of her youth"), then she is strange/foreign because she is an anomaly who no longer has a place in the system of socially regulated sexuality and now belongs on the side of the chaotic. In any case her otherness serves to identify the boundary and what must be repressed or excluded.

Woman is a much more serviceable symbol for this definitionally important "other" than was the man of verses 12–15 because she can be posited as a figure of ambivalence, both frightening and attractive. Her words are described as "smooth," a term that suggests both pleasure and danger (= slippery). Once experienced, the ambivalence has to be tilted in the proper direction, and so she is identified with the ultimate boundary, death.

A textual problem in verse 18 provides a clue to the psychological basis for the equation. Judging from the parallelism and the meaning of the verb, one expects the text to read "her path sinks down to death, her tracks are toward the shades." As it stands, it reads "her house sinks down to death. . . ." If the Masoretic Text is a textual corruption, it is in truth a Freudian slip, for "house" is a common symbolic representation of woman or womb. The ambivalence is the attraction and fear of a return to the womb.[4] The Strange Woman is the devouring woman, for "none who go in to her will return" (verse 19).

With this text one can begin to see the significance of sexual difference for the existence of patriarchal discourse. Invoking the Strange Woman as a threat provides a basis for solidarity between father and son. Her difference makes available a shared sameness for father and son that bridges the generational divisions of patriarchy that were visible in Proverbs 1. But, more importantly, the woman and her discourse exist as a persistent irritant located, to borrow Julia Kristeva's phrase, at the margin.[5] In the following chapters she continues to preoccupy the father's advice. He can never quite be finished with her. The competition she represents is the cause of the father's speech, the incentive for its very existence. The Strange Woman figures the irreducible difference that prevents any discourse from establishing itself unproblematically. That is to say, she is not simply the speech of actual women, but she is the symbolic figure of a variety of marginal discourses. She is the contradiction, the dissonance that forces a dominant discourse to articulate itself and at the same time threatens to subvert it. Those dissonances can no more be eliminated than can sexual difference itself. And their existence is a source of slow but profound change in symbolic orders.

PROVERBS 3

In giving discourse a privileged position and in representing the world as a place of conflicting discourses, Proverbs 1–9 appears to acknowledge the socially constructed nature of reality and the problematic status of truth. Such reflections were part of the broader wisdom tradition, as the saying in Proverbs 18:17 illustrates: "The one who argues his case first seems right, until someone else is brought forward and cross-examines him." The implications are disturbing for the representatives of authority. What can ensure that the content given to the terms "righteousness, justice, and equity" or "wisdom, knowledge, and discernment" can be stabilized according to the values of the tradents of Proverbs 1–9 and not captured by rival discourses? The text has attempted to buttress its authoritative position by claiming the symbol of the patriarchal father and by discrediting other voices as alien and criminal. Thus the signifiers point to the father and to the law. Though powerful, that is not sufficient. What is needed is an anchorage beyond the contestable social world, in short, a transcendental signified to which all terms point and from which they derive their stable meanings.[6] In a provisional way the parallel between the speech of the father and the speech of Wisdom in chapter 1 provided this anchorage. But that strategy is not fully developed until chapter 8. In chapter 3 we encounter the first sustained effort to provide the transcendental signified that stops the threatening slippage of meaning.

The first indication is in the initial call for hearing: "My son, don't forget my teaching [Heb. *torati*] and let your heart guard my commands [Heb. *mitswotay*]." Various paired terms refer to the father's instruction throughout the chapters. But this particular pair has resonances of God's *torah* and *mitswot* to Israel and so subtly positions the father in association with divine authority. The benefits of long life and peace that are promised (verse 2) also suggest that the father's teaching and commands derive from transcendent power. In verse 4 it is made explicit. The father's advice will be validated both in the social and in the transcendent realms ("before the eyes of God and humankind"). For several further verses the father actually speaks on behalf of God, urging the son to obedience to God and promising rewards. The appeal parallels in structure and motivation the father's call for obedience to himself in verses 1–4. It comes as no surprise that in the Masoretic Text the passage concludes in verse 12 with the metaphor of God as a father reproving his son. It is not enough to ground the authority structure of Proverbs 1–9 in the patriarchal father. The authority of the transcendent Father of fathers is needed.

Having claimed access to the transcendent realm through the alignment of the father and God, the chapter next turns to secure the stability of its comprehensive terms of value, "wisdom," and "understanding" (verses 13–21). A variety of linked images carries the argument. First wisdom is compared with riches. Then it is personified as a woman holding riches and honor in one hand, long life in the other. The tableau may well be an evocation of the Egyptian goddess Maat, but the meaning of the image does not require knowledge of the allusion. A figure who holds life in her hand belongs to the transcendent. References to her pleasant ways and safe paths recall the paths of the Strange Woman of chapter 2 and establish this figure as her opposite. As death belongs to one, life belongs to the other. The chain of association completes itself with another mythic image, wisdom as the tree of life. Such a phrase sets up an intertextual play with Genesis 2–3. Here the two trees of Genesis are condensed into one knowledge that gives life. In the Genesis narrative the quest for knowledge was marked as rebellion and resulted in exclusion from the source of life. Here it is submissive obedience that is correlated with wisdom and with life. In Genesis the desire "to be like God" with respect to wisdom ("knowing good and evil") was a mark of hybris. Here the one who finds wisdom (verse 13) is blessed precisely because he is like God, having found that by which God created the world (verses 19–20). Wisdom is not one discourse among others but the stuff of reality itself. The values of the father are built into the structures of the world.

PROVERBS 4

In Proverbs 4:3–4 the father speaks and says "I was a son to my father; a precious only son to my mother. And he taught me and said to me. . . ." In part this is a strengthening of the claim to authority, as fathers quote earlier fathers. But there is another function. I made the point earlier that the subject position of the reader in Proverbs 1–9 is that of the son, established through the fiction of direct address by the father. But the situation is somewhat more complex than that. There is always a measure of identification between father and son, so that a son understands and thinks "when I grow up, that's what I will be." The father status already exists as potentiality in the son. That identification is, of course, vital in negotiating the intergenerational divide of patriarchal society. For the young male deferral is not endless. So, in Proverbs 1–9, where the reader is continually reinterpellated in the subject position of the son, chapter 4 speaks of the transformation of sons into fathers in the chain of tradition. The male subject is to a certain degree apportioned between father and son. One is always a subordinate son to the collective authority of the symbolic order. But its transcending father status is what underwrites the father status of those who occupy positions of authority within it.

Each of the following poetic sections of Proverbs 4 is built up by a playful use of one or more metaphoric conceits that employ various cultural codes. Despite the apparent heterogeneity, the various sections all relate to the familiar issues of subjectivity, discourse, and allegiance. In verses 5–9 what appears to be an economic code ("acquire wisdom," "with all of your acquisition, acquire understanding") is combined with an erotic code ("don't abandon," "love," "embrace"). What seems to connect the two is the notion of the relationship as a transaction between the son and Wisdom, an exchange of value. Verses 10–19 develop a code of movement: way, lead, walk, paths, steps, run, stumble, go, come, road, go straight, avoid, cross over, etc. At least some of the possible connotations have been discussed above in connection with chapter 2. The most curious of the codes is the rewriting of the self as a series of body parts in verses 20–27: ear, eyes, heart, flesh, mouth, lips, eyes, pupils, feet. Intertwined with this inventory of the body are terms from a code of physical orientation (incline, extend, twist away, turn aside, twistedness, crookedness, make distant, straight, in front, straight before, swerve to right or left). The values associated with straightness and twistedness were made explicit in chapter 2. What is of more

interest is the subdivision of the body. There are two other similar poems in
6:12–15 and 6:16–19. In the first of these we are introduced to the man "who
goes about with a twisted mouth." What is wrong with his speech is made
evident in verse 13. He allows other body parts to act, improperly, as speaking mouths, setting up commentaries or other discourses that invert the
words of the mouth. "He winks with his eyes, communicates with his feet,
instructs with his fingers." No wonder his speech is duplicitous. In the
numerical poem that follows there is a catalog of the crucial body parts and
their characteristic misuses: arrogant eyes, a lying tongue, hands shedding
innocent blood, a scheming heart, feet that speed to whatever is bad. The self
is not presented as a simple entity. Or perhaps it is better to say that various
parts of the body can represent the whole by synecdoche. The individual's
subjectivity can be seen as invested in each of these parts, any of which has
the power to work his ruin. But it seems odd that one part of the body, that
part that males traditionally have considered to be the privileged representation of their subjectivity, is not mentioned. Although the phallus is never
referred to explicitly, the problems of that important but unruly member are
taken up in chapters 5–6.

PROVERBS 5–6

If the image of the woman has figured importantly in the first chapters of
Proverbs 1–9, it utterly dominates the second half of the text. The most
vivid and extensive representations are those of the Strange Woman. As in
chapter 2, her sexuality is repeatedly associated with speech. She has "a
smooth tongue" (6:24), "smooth words" (7:5), "smooth lips" (7:21). In the
most explicitly erotic description it is said that "her lips drip with honey"
and the inside of her mouth is "smoother than oil" (5:3). That she figures as
the father's chief rival for the allegiance of the son would be clear simply
from the length and intensity of the attack on her, but in 7:21 it is even said
that she misleads the naive youth with her "teaching," a term used of the
father's instruction as well (4:2). The fear that the father has of her is
revealed in one of the images used to describe her deceptiveness. In patriarchal thinking it is woman's lack of the phallus and the privilege that the
male associates with its possession that grounds woman's inferiority. In the
father's phantasm the danger is that behind that reassuring smoothness, that
visible absence of the phallus, there lurks something "sharp as a two edged
sword" (5:4). The fantasy is that she not only possesses a hidden super
potency but that it is a castrating potency as well. She threatens to reverse
the body symbolism on which the father's authority is established.

The simple opposition between male and female is fundamental to the
symbolic order of patriarchy, but it does not exhaust the role of woman in
the symbolic economy. The triple association of sexuality, speech, and

authority needs to be followed a bit further. The association of authority with speech is clear. In Proverbs 1–9 the father speaks, the son is spoken to. The father's control of speech is further indicated in that the speech of the sinners and of the Strange Woman does not reach the son directly but only as filtered through the father's speech. And in general, the silencing of women in patriarchal society is both symbol and result of the inferior status based on their perceived sexual "lack." On the other hand, sexuality is by its nature dialogical, as the term "intercourse" well suggests. Culturally, it is closely associated with speech: courting speech, seductive speech, love songs, whispered sweet nothings. The point at which the horizontal speech of the woman's sexuality comes into conflict with the vertical speech of the father's authority is precisely at the point of generational transition, when the boy becomes a man. In her provocative study of the Samson story, Mieke Bal makes reference to the moment of sexual maturity as the point at which "the trinity of the nuclear family is sacrificed to the alienating relationship with the other, the fourth person" (1987: 57). The sexual maturation of the son is a critical moment not only in psychoanalytic terms but also a critical moment for the social and symbolic order. It is the moment at which the patriarchal family will be successfully replicated or threatened. The system of approved and disapproved sexual relations forms a language through which men define their relations with one another. Proverbs 5:7–14, 15–20 and 6:20–35 set up three parallel situations: the woman outside the group/ the proper wife/the wife of another man inside the group.[7]

It is interesting to see how the benefits and consequences of each are described. Sexual relations with the first woman ("approaching the door to her house," 5:8) are described in terms of depletion:

lest you give to others your wealth and your years to the merciless; lest strangers batten on your strength and your labors in the house of a foreigner. You will be sorry afterwards when your flesh and body are consumed.

(5:9–11)[8]

Although there is an obvious element of psychosexual fantasy here, it is overwritten by social references. The others/the merciless/the strangers/the foreigner who are the devourers here are all masculine nouns and imply the community of males to whom the woman belongs. Exogamy is deplorable because it results in the alienation of wealth. The communal context is further indicated by the concluding lament: "I was quickly brought to ruin in the midst of the congregation and the assembly." Going outside deprives a man of standing in his own group as well.

By contrast, appropriate sexual relations have a centripetal direction. In 5:15–20 sexual connections are described under the figure of water contained and dispersed.

Drink water from your own cistern and running water from your own well. [Don't] let your springs overflow outside, streams of water in the public squares. Let them be for yourself alone, not for strangers with you.

Because there is a considerable subjective investment in one's own proper wife ("your cistern, your well, for yourself alone"), the selfhood of individual males and the solidarity of the community is severely threatened by adultery. The "foreign" woman of 6:20–35 is not ethnically foreign but off limits because she is "the wife of one's neighbor." As in the first example, the code of property crops up, here in a comparison between theft and adultery (verses 30–31). The point of comparison is not between the rights of the male to the woman or property but to the social rather than the merely private dimensions of the offense. The criminal is in each case the object of contempt or scorn, though much more so in the case of the adulterer.[9] Not only will the wronged husband refuse an offered settlement; the entire community is implacable in its judgment of "his reproach which can never be effaced" (verse 33). The code of behavior between men and women is raised up in these passages as an important code of signifying behavior among groups of men. Metaphorically, in the social fabric of patriarchy woman is the essential thread that joins the pieces. But equally she indicates the seams where the fabric is subject to tears.

Although much of the advice offered in Proverbs 5–6 about relations with women appears to be strictly pragmatic, one often has a sense of a curious slippage between the literal and the symbolic. When one understands from Proverbs 5:15–20 that a good marriage will protect a man from foreign women and "thy neighbor's wife," one also remembers the themes of protection associated with Wisdom in 4:6–9. When the ruined son recollects in Proverbs 5:12–13 how he "hated discipline," "despised criticism," and never listened to his teachers, his regrets seem to refer to more than just the lesson on sex. Is the Strange Woman not a problem in sexual mores after all, but an allegory of folly? The final pairing in chapter 9 of the allegorical women *Hokmot* and *Kesilut* (Wisdom and Folly) would seem to point in that direction. But it would be a mistake to pose the pragmatic and the allegorical as either/or alternatives. When symbolic thinking is carried forward by means of concrete objects or persons, statements and actions pertaining to these concrete entities can never be merely pragmatic on the one hand or simply metaphorical on the other. All customary praxis involving women is nonverbal symbolic construction. All use of the feminine in symbolic representation implicates behavior. So long as a society's discourse is carried on by males alone, that fact is scarcely noticeable. But as women enter into public discourse as speaking subjects, the habit of patriarchy to think symbolically by means of woman is thrown into confusion. Woman cannot occupy the same symbolic relation to herself that she does to man. With that change the long, slow crisis of the symbolic order is at hand.

PROVERBS 7–9

Something of the both/and, pragmatic/symbolic totality of woman in the discourse of Proverbs 1–9 can be seen in the two great paired poems of Proverbs 7 and 8. Although very different in style and content, these poems of the Strange Woman and of Wisdom form a diptych. Chapter 8, with its strong mythic overtones, is written largely in the symbolic register; chapter 7 largely in the realistic. But in the framing of chapter 7 there are certain elements that establish its relationship to chapter 8 and disclose its mythic dimensions. In the father's account of the meeting between the vapid youth and the Strange Woman the words are ominous and negative. The woman is associated with many of the wisdom tradition's bad values, yet appears to be an ordinary, mundane character. The setting is twilight, so that the woman arrives with the onset of "night and darkness" (verse 9). She is associated with concealment and with the appearance of what is illicit (verse 10). Where wisdom tradition values quietness, she is "noisy" (verse 11), and her movement is characterized as restless, vagrant, and flitting. When she is still, she is "lying in wait" (verse 12), a predatory quality that is made explicit in verses 22–23. Her smooth speech "turns" the young man (verse 21). The symbolic register is more explicitly evoked in the introductory and concluding remarks of the father. Calling Wisdom "sister" and "kinswoman" (verse 4) introduces explicit personification. Those words also set up a relation of equivalence between Wisdom and "the wife of your youth" from chapter 5, instilling actual marriage with the protective values of wisdom. Similarly, the father's concluding words in verses 24–27 expose the monstrous, mythic dimension of the Strange Woman. She is not just a woman who has seduced a simpleminded young man. She is a predator who has slain multitudes. Indeed, her vagina is the gate of Sheol. Her womb, death itself.

Chapter 8 is radically different in style. Where the Strange Woman's speech is passed through the father's admonitory speech, Wisdom speaks autonomously. Although there are traces of the erotic associated with her ("love" in verse 17, perhaps the reference to "delighting" in verses 30–31, and the allusion to the man waiting and watching at her gate in verse 34), her speech and self-presentation are thoroughly unlike the Strange Woman's. Her movement is public, direct, and authoritative. Unlike the smooth, seductive, but deceptive speech of the Strange Woman, Wisdom's is like that of the father: "straight," "right," and "true," not "twisted," or "crooked." Her voice, of course, is the cultural voice that speaks through the father, the voice that grounds the social fathers: the kings, rulers, princes, nobles of verses 15–16. Hers is the voice that mediates between the transcendent father and his earthly sons.

But how can it be, when so much energy has been invested in disclosing the terrifying dangerousness of woman as represented in the Strange Woman, that Proverbs 1–9 turns to woman also for its ideal representation of the central term of value, wisdom itself? In fact it is not surprising at all. Thinking in terms of sexual difference, of woman as man's other, difference serves to articulate both what is inferior and what is superior. Toril Moi develops Julia Kristeva's understanding of women's position of marginality in patriarchal thinking in a way that precisely explains the symbolic projection of Proverbs 7–8:

> If patriarchy sees women as occupying a marginal position within the symbolic order, then it can construe them as the limit or borderline of that order. From a phallocentric point of view, women will then come to represent the necessary frontier between man and chaos; but because of their very marginality they will also always seem to recede into and merge with the chaos of the outside. Women seen as the limit of the symbolic order will in other words share in the disconcerting properties of all frontiers: they will be neither inside nor outside, neither known nor unknown. It is this position that has enabled male culture sometimes to vilify women as representing darkness and chaos, to view them as Lilith or the Whore of Babylon, and sometimes to elevate them as the representatives of a higher and purer nature, to venerate them as Virgins and Mothers of God. In the first instance the borderline is seen as part of the chaotic wilderness outside, and in the second it is seen as an inherent part of the inside: the part that protects and shields the symbolic order from the imaginary chaos.
>
> (Moi 1985: 167)

Wisdom's self-presentation as a divine figure in chapter 8 not only serves to anchor wisdom discourse in the transcendent realm. It also positions her as the counterpart of the Strange Woman. One is the gate of Sheol, the other the gate of Heaven. Together they define and secure the boundaries of the symbolic order of patriarchal wisdom. Chapter 9 draws the conclusion self-consciously with its explicit parallel of personified wisdom and folly.

CONCLUSION

Analyzing the symbolic structure of Proverbs 1–9 is not merely an anti-quarian exercise. Phallocentric constructions of the world continue to be deeply dependent on such uses of sexual difference for their articulation. A good illustration of the profound psychic attachment to this mode of thinking as well as the symbolic dimensions of apparently "realistic" speech is the recent film *Fatal Attraction*. Its subtitle could easily have been "cling to the wife of your youth, and she will save you from the Strange Woman." In the film the viewer's subjectivity is rigorously identified with that of the male character, Dan. He is consistently depicted as a good but naive and occasionally impulsive man, an object of seduction. The "Strange Woman," Alex, is portrayed as belonging to the margin in many ways. Her family background is obscure, her employment with the company recent. She has no husband or recognized lover. She stands outside the realm of socially ordered sexuality. Her apartment is located in an ambiguous commercial/ residential neighborhood, where workers ominously carry about large pieces of butchered animals ("like an ox to the slaughter," 7:22). Like the Strange Woman of Proverbs 7 she has a brilliant power of speech, always more than a match for her male victim. But also like the Strange Woman of Proverbs, it is only an illusion that we encounter her and her speech directly. She is not a speaking subject but rather is an effect of someone else's speech, the paternal speech of the film itself.[10]

When the predatory seduction has been accomplished, the chaotic, monstrous dimensions of Alex become evident: madness, violence, an uncanny unstoppable will. In an allusion to the tradition of horror films, Alex is drowned (we see her staring eyes and parted lips) and yet comes back from the dead. Against the inbreaking of chaos, the male character proves himself to be finally helpless. It is "the wife of his youth" who must rescue him. The wife has been presented, as is the wife of Proverbs 5, as herself a deeply erotic, desirable woman. Equally, she is the center of the domesticity of the patriarchal family. Her symbol is the house, where, more than once, we see the brightly burning kitchen hearth. It is in her climactic appearance, however, that we glimpse her mythic status. In contrast to the frantic, ineffectual, and messy struggle of the husband, her single shot is decisive. But it is her bearing when the camera turns to view her that has such an effect on the viewer. She stands framed in the doorway, quiet, impassive, erect, authoritative. She is a *dea ex machina* and, for one familiar with Proverbs 1–9, a figure evocative of *Hokmot*.

As is well known, the original end of the film was changed by the director in response to the reaction of the audience in test screenings (Forsberg 1988: 21). He had originally filmed an ending that was a twist on the Madam Butterfly theme, in which Alex's suicide would implicate Dan as her murderer. Preview audiences, however, disliked the ending. They recognized the mythic structure of the film and insisted on its "proper" conclusion. The version of the film as we have it is thus the result of a collective writing. The extraordinary emotional reaction from subsequent audiences, especially among men, confirms how deep is the investment in the patriarchal positioning of women as the inner and outer linings of its symbolic order.

Although the similarity of the symbolic positioning of woman in *Fatal Attraction* and Proverbs 1–9 is unmistakable, it is the difference in their manner of presentation that makes Proverbs 1–9 of particular interest to feminist analysis. Where the film skillfully attempts to naturalize its discourse, to conceal its speaking subject, and mask its interpellation of the viewer, Proverbs 1–9 emphasizes precisely these features. Certainly Proverbs 1–9 also makes its own claims to universality and transcendent authority, but its explicit self-consciousness about the central role of discourses in competition provides an internal basis for questioning its own claims. Having learned from the father how to resist interpellation by hearing the internal contradictions in discourse, one is prepared to resist the patriarchal interpellation of the father as well. For the reader who does not take up the subject position offered by the text, Proverbs 1–9 ceases to be a simple text of initiation and becomes a text about the problematic nature of discourse itself. Not only the dazzling (and defensive) rhetoric of the father but also the pregnant silence of the son and the dissidence that speaks from the margin in the person of the Strange Woman become matters of significance. Israel's wisdom tradition never examined its patriarchal assumptions. But its commitment to the centrality of discourse as such and its fascination with the dissident voice in Job and Qohelet made it the locus within Israel for radical challenges to the complacency of the dominant symbolic order.

NOTES

1 Because of the masculine subject position offered to the reader, I will refer to the reader as "he."
2 I say "family" because the mother's authority as well as the father's is invoked (1:8; 4:3; 6:20). In no way is she seen as constituting an independent voice, however, but serves as a confirmer of what is presented as essentially patriarchal authority.
3 Mieke Bal observes that "there is a verb in Dutch for 'to commit adultery,' which is literally 'to go strange,' to go with a stranger (*vreemd gaam*)" (Bal 1987: 43).
4 We can be certain that the error is not a meaningless one since the image of the house recurs in chapters 5, 7, and 9. For a discussion of the house/female body symbolism in the Samson story see Bal (1987: 49–58).
5 See Kristeva (1986b: 187–213 and 1986c: 292–300). Ironically, Roland Barthes entitled an early review of Kristeva's work "L'étrangère," the strange or foreign woman, referring to her Bulgarian nationality and the unsettling quality of her work. See Moi (1985: 150).
6 The illusory nature of the transcendental signified is argued by Derrida (1978: 278–80).
7 Not all commentators understand 5:7–14 to refer to social or ethnic outsiders. Some argue that adultery is at issue. The language is probably intentionally ambiguous and polyvalent. But the contrast between "others, strangers, foreigners" in 5:9–10 and "your neighbor" in 6:29 (where adultery is explicitly at issue) suggests that the connotation of social or ethnic alienness is to the fore in 5:7–14. There is also a sharp contrast in the relation between improper sex and money in 5:9–10 and 6:35, implying different social situations.
8 Reading *wenihamta* in verse 11. Cf. the Septuagint. The Greek text also suggests that "your wealth" in verse 9 may be an error for "your life," which would fit the parallelism better.
9 I read verse 30 as an implied question.
10 For an excellent discussion of the problem of enunciation and subjectivity in film see Silverman (1983: chap. 5).

131

7

IMAGINATION, METHOD, AND MURDER

Un/Framing the Face of Post-Exilic Israel[1]

Danna Nolan Fewell

Across the ages, sacred literature may never have done anything but use various forms of sacrifice to enunciate murder *as a condition of Meaning.*

(Kristeva 1995)

It is a violence within that protects us from a violence without. It is the imagination pressing back against the pressure of reality. It seems, in the last analysis, to have something to do with our self-preservation; and that, no doubt, is why the expression of it, the sound of its words, helps us live our lives.

(Stevens 1951)

We should read the Bible one more time. To interpret it, of course, but also to let it carve out a space for our own fantasies and interpretive delirium.

(Kristeva 1995)

Her uncle had a heart attack when she was seventeen and it did not look as though he would live. He was a testy hard-edged fellow. Had never darkened the door of a church. For as long as she could remember his speech had been salted with curse words she didn't even know. He drank too much. He smoked too much. And he was known to announce from time to time that black people didn't have souls (only he didn't use the term "black people"). She knew that he was going to hell. Everything in her Southern Baptist upbringing assured her this was true. Later, as she listened to her aunt desperately voicing the only thing a loving wife could possibly believe in this moment of fear and grief – that her husband was a good man at heart, that God couldn't possibly relegate him to an eternity of torment – she said nothing. She simply sat there sickened by her privileged truth.

That night she had a dream. A Flannery O'Conner kind of dream. This great big Jesus was standing with his feet on the earth and his head reaching the sky. He was pulling on cords that were lifting giant elevators up to heaven. What astounded her was that everybody she knew was on those elevators. Everybody who had ever lived on God's green earth. Even her salty old bigot of an uncle. And all her obnoxious cousins.

The Bible is a conflicted book about religious identity. The Bible is a book about conflicted religious identity. It can't make up its mind about who's in and who's out of the chosen circle. And it attracts many readers eager to place themselves inside or outside of various chosen circles. Who are the people of God? asks the Bible and its readers. What do they look like? How do they behave? How can they be distinguished from other people? (*The questions readers rarely ask, though the Bible's own ambivalence may raise them, are, Why should such distinctions be important? In whose interests are such distinctions made?*)

"Oh, no," the faculty colleague said. "I do nothing to dissuade students from taking your courses. I merely tell them that it is more important to be part of the trunk than one of the branches."

Whoever does not abide in me is thrown away like a branch and withers; such branches are gathered, thrown into the fire, and burned.

(John 15:6; NRSV)

Family systems therapists tell us that it is common for a group facing a transition or a threat to experience a crisis of identity. The group often undergoes a process of deciding who is "in" and who is "out." Many religious and academic groups now find themselves in such a situation as they struggle with what it means to live in a postmodern world.[2] Local ways of knowing now question the notion of "absolute truth." We live in a world of competing discourses and contested spaces, where power determines who and what gets heard. Academic and religious readers of the Bible are confronted now more intensely than ever with the "politics" of truth, that is, how issues of meaning are merged with issues of power and representation.

Many Jewish and Christian readers for whom the Bible has had (some sort of) religious authority now encounter disturbing questions about the nature of that authority: *In whose interests are these texts written? In whose interests are these texts read? Who determines what these texts mean?* Academic readers of the Bible now must ask the same questions, not only of the Bible, but of the critical writing in their respective fields. *Who chooses the texts to be studied? Who has the power to determine what these texts mean? Who controls how scholarship is done? Who controls whether or not or how it gets read? How is truth to be represented?* Claims to objectivity can no longer stand undisputed: methods and ways of reading are not inevitable, but are culturally and institutionally constructed and supported. Many would argue that even readers themselves are culturally and institutionally constituted subjects, defined both positively and negatively in relation to the norms privileged by the structures within which they live and operate. Scholarly inquiry is in crisis, out of (institutional?) control some would say, because there is no longer consensus about what "scholarly inquiry" is or what it should it be or what it is supposed to do or who can do it.

"What makes you think you can do that kind of work here?" he said. "Why aren't you in an English Department somewhere? This is not critical method. What are your controls?"

"What are yours?" she asked.

"Well, at least I can count and classify potsherds."

"On the other hand," says Kristeva, "one could delight in a strict, 'mathematical' reading of the biblical text, a reading that avoids all ambiguities. . . ." (1995)

As boundaries and definitions are being breached and questioned by some readers, they are being reinstituted and reinforced by others. In the cases of both academic and religious readers, there seems to be a preoccupation with who belongs and who does not, a scurry to defend institutional parameters lest our life's work or our beliefs be somehow rendered meaningless in the face of other legitimate alternatives. *Lest we discover we are not so specially elected after all.* We eagerly define who is a "real" Christian, a "real" Jew, a "real" scholar. If we can just delineate our borders, then we can be safe inside. We can rest assured of who we are. And who we are not. *And we forget the violence that is the condition of our self-preservation. We forget to ask ourselves what it means to be part of a particular kind of community that values [knowledge of] the world and its inhabitants. We forget to ask, what difference should our reading and our writing be making? We forget to ask, How then should we be living?[3] In short, we forget all about transcendence.[4]*

134

For ancient Israel, the critical moment of threat and transition was much less nebulous, much less philosophical, but I dare say much more traumatic. The transition that colors the whole of the Hebrew Scriptures is the Babylonian Exile. It is presupposed. It is narrated. It is forecasted. It is remembered. It is re-enacted. It is the grief, the trauma, that Israel works through again and again in its literature.[5]

Babylonian culture, like its own mythic monster of chaos, opened its jaws to consume Israel, but many in Israel, the (male) elite we must presume, pushed back against the great gullet threatening to digest them. They pushed with their pens. With their pens they told their stories and inscribed their identities. They drew their faces over and over again. In the words of Hélène Cixous, they "discovered that the Face was mortal" and that they "would have to snatch it back at every moment from Nothingness" (Cixous 1991).

The drive to write is always complicated. It is the desire to preserve. To explain. To order. To reorder. To remember. To create. To revise. To reveal. To reveil. To legitimate. To delegitimate. To recover. To discover. To cover over. To include. To exclude. To occlude. The essential desire to write is a life giving, life supporting impulse. "Writing:" says Cixous, "a way of leaving no space for death, of pushing back forgetfulness, of never letting oneself be surprised by the abyss." People in exile know this. They become survivors by inscribing themselves as *survivors.*

They know, too, that in living, we kill.[6] They have been the food to satiate the Babylonian appetite. They know, too painfully, that our very existence depends upon the murder of something or someone else. (*Murder, a condition of Meaning.*) Only in our imagination (*the imagination pressing back against the pressure of reality*) can we envision a world where there are no such things as predator and prey, where the wolf dwells with the lamb, where children have nothing to fear, where nothing evil or vile will ever be done again (Isaiah 11). Otherwise, we negotiate our way between life and death, recognizing (*if we can at all see beyond ourselves*) that to live is to be guilty. To live is to be guilty, but we choose life over death nonetheless. To live is to be guilty. To write is to be guilty. For in taming our texts we violate them and perhaps, too, those destined to read them. (*Isn't that the way of scholarship? Our writing: always killing someone else's? always reducing the subject to something manageable and coherent?*)

Exile is Israel's crisis. It is the pivotal event that overshadows everything that comes before and after. The one event that must be made manageable and coherent. Why did this happen? Israel's sin. What was Israel's sin? Not following YHWH. How did they not follow YHWH? They worshipped other gods. Why did they do that? They were influenced by foreigners. Specifically foreign women. If only they had not associated with foreign women, they would not have lost their land. As the postexilic community seeks to restore and reconstitute itself in the homeland, the question of the community's identity becomes primary. How can the community reconstitute itself as followers of YHWH? Ezra and Nehemiah respond by moving to define more rigidly who is "in" and who is "out" of Israel.[7] The experience of survival has its privilege. The elite returning can look with disdain upon the "people of the land," the descendants of poor Israelites who had been left behind and of other peoples brought in by the Assyrians centuries before. Despite the declaration of the people of the land that they, too, worship YHWH, they are excluded from the rebuilding of the House of God by those returning (see Ezra 4:1–3). Order in the community comes by way of definition. The people of the land are quickly labeled "adversaries of Judah and Benjamin" (Ezra 4:1) while the returnees become the "people of Judah" (4:4) and the "heads of families in Israel" (4:3).[8] *There's nothing quite like the power to name!* Indeed, we might see in the rebuilding of Jerusalem's walls the very attempt to shore up the boundaries of Israel's ethnic and cultural identity. People who do not fit neatly within the established boundaries are oppressed (Nehemiah 13:23–30) or done away with (Ezra 10): the foreign element (wives taken from among the "peoples of the land") are forced to bear the stigma of Israel's past sin. They become the scapegoat for the Exile itself. They and their "mixed" children threaten Israel's future.[9] Association with them is labeled "treachery" (Nehemiah 13:27; NRSV). *Nothing like the power to name.* Consequently, they are expelled from the community (*Where do they go? How do they survive? We kill in order to live: a condition of Meaning*) and the complicated past becomes a palimpsest, a text erased and written over and over again in order to justify the action now taken.[10]

The shadow the Exile casts backward comes in the form of rereading and rewriting the past. Genesis through Kings is a document that embodies the reconstruction of the family story, a story that paints the face of the family over and over again. The prominent face is one without variation. It is a family tree without deviation, a trunk without knots, a multitude without individuals, a nation that speaks and acts as one man.[11] And it is a face that has failed to focus on YHWH alone. A face that has, to its detriment, associated with foreigners. It has tolerated them. It has loved them. It has refused to kill them in order to live. Because of this, Israel was led astray to worship other gods and was subsequently punished with the Exile.

But something strange happens when you paint the same face again and again. So says British painter Frank Auerbach, "To paint the same head over and over leads you to its unfamiliarity; eventually you get near the raw truth about it, *just as people only blurt out the raw truth in the middle of a family quarrel.*"[12]

The family portrait begins, of course, in Genesis with the "toldoth," the family stories, of Israel's origins. Families make interesting choices about what they choose to tell or not to tell about themselves. The main story

Israel tells about itself is one of special election. Abraham is singled out for a special promise. Much of Genesis deals with the pruning (*a circumcision?*)[13] of Abraham's family tree to a singular trunk. (*A rather desperate and futile exercise since family trees, if they are to thrive, must be allowed to send out branches and roots. A rather desperate and futile excision since the scars remain. The knottiness [naughtiness?] of this tree cannot be carved away completely.*) In the guise of domestic strife, certain family members are disassociated. They are cast as foreigners, fathers of different nations that must be distinguished from Israel. *And the rhetoric of Abraham's promise shifts as well: from being a blessing to all the families of the earth (Genesis 12:3) to possessing the gates of his enemies (Genesis 22:17; cf. 24:60).*

Whoever does not abide in me is thrown away like a branch and withers; such branches are gathered, thrown into the fire, and burned.

(John 15:6; NRSV).

First the nephew Lot is severed from his uncle. His sons become the nations Moab and Ammon. Their faces are painted very differently. They are the children of a man who chose to live among the most wicked of the wicked. They are the children of incest, the children of nameless mothers who rape their father. *The "yo mamma" story par excellence.* We are children of a miraculous conception. You are children of incest. Despite the family connection, there is no resemblance. *Not yet, anyway. (This is not the face, by the way, that the Moabites or the Ammonites would have painted for themselves.)*

Then there is Ishmael, Abraham's firstborn by Hagar the Egyptian, the first Other Woman in the family portrait. She is foreign and she is a slave and she and her son must soon be painted out of the picture to make way for Isaac, the son of Sarah and Abraham's old age. The son promised (and delivered) by God. Ishmael, destined to be "a wild ass of a man" (*so say the descendants of Isaac*), leaves with his mother who takes for him an Egyptian wife, an event that further underscores his foreignness. Ishmael fathers the Ishmaelites while Isaac grows up to be a pale clone of his father.

Isaac and his cousin Rebekah have twin sons, Jacob and Esau. But while they are twins, they certainly do not bear the same face. Jacob is smooth. Esau is hairy and is repeatedly compared to an animal. Jacob is a man of tents. Esau is a man of the wild. Jacob is shrewd and conniving. Esau is easily duped. Jacob plans for the future. Esau lives for the moment. Jacob marries family women. Esau marries foreign. The portrait makes clear why Esau

137

could never inherit the promise. Esau becomes Edom while Jacob becomes Israel.

But identity definitions are not yet complete. Jacob, the favorite of his mother Rebekah, has also to distinguish himself, Israel, from his matrilineal kin, the Arameans. The family trait of trickery is strong here, but eventually there must be a parting of the ways. How can he become the patriarch of a nation as long as he serves as a bondsman in his father-in-law's house? Jacob must take his family away, with Laban contending all the while that he has no right to do so: "The daughters are my daughters, the children are my children, the flocks are my flocks, and all that you see is mine. But what can I do today about these daughters of mine, or about their children whom they have borne?" (Genesis 31:43; NRSV). A boundary marker is erected to symbolize both geographical and identity boundaries between the families of Laban and Jacob (Genesis 31:43–54). People once considered as "bone of bone and flesh of flesh" (Genesis 29:14) now diverge into separate nations.

The Philistines are another group that figures prominently in the stories of Genesis, but their position *vis-à-vis* Israel is much more ambiguous. There is no claim that the Israelites and the Philistines came from the same family tree (in fact, just the opposite, Genesis 10 claims that the Philistines are descendants of Ham), probably because the Philistines' origins as sea-faring immigrants were well known. Nevertheless, Israel and Philistia have some very "close encounters" and the text makes every effort to keep the two groups separate. Abraham gives Sarah to the Philistine king Abimelek who takes her into his harem (Genesis 20). The narrator, however, adamantly defends Isaac (who is born in the very next chapter) against possible Philistine paternity. Twice we are told that Sarah is never the object of Abimelek's embrace (20:4, 6) and, as if these notices are not sufficient, we are informed that God "closed fast every womb of the household of Abimelek" (20:18; TANAKH). Isaac, like his father before him, is also willing to give his woman to the Philistines in order to ensure his own security and prosperity, but the Abimelek of Isaac's generation does not take the bait (Genesis 26). Nevertheless, Isaac prospers so vigorously that the Philistines insist on geographical boundaries. "Go away from us," says Abimelek, "for you have become far too mighty for us" (Genesis 26:16).

The gist of the story is that Israel was once kin (or in the case of the Philistines, near[ly] kin) to the peoples in the midst of whom it lives, but now Israel is different, set apart. While Israel admits to this much affinity to the surrounding peoples, it still resists openly admitting that its line cannot be pure. And so the story proceeds with marked ambivalence. On the one hand there is much protest that Isaac, then Jacob, not be allowed to marry one of "the women of the land." The story of Dinah and Shechem insists that intermarriage with the "uncircumcised" cannot be tolerated. "We cannot do this thing, to give our sister to a man who is uncircumcised, for that is a disgrace among us" (Genesis 34:14; TANAKH). And yet, we are told (*a blurting out of the truth in the midst of a family quarrel?*) that, in their revenge against Shechem's rape of their sister, the sons of Jacob think nothing of capturing the women and children of Shechem as their booty. Are we to believe that Jacob's sons treated these captives any differently than Shechem treated Dinah? Are we to believe these women were never taken/used as mates? (*In other words, are the faces of Jacob's sons looking suspiciously like those of the men of Shechem?*) For the most part, the text is silent about who the children of Jacob/Israel actually marry. Judah takes a Canaanite woman, but is tricked (deservedly so) into siring offspring through his Canaanite daughter-in-law Tamar. (*Is Judah's face looking a lot like Lot's?*) Joseph, we're told, marries an Egyptian (*Is Joseph's face looking like Ishmael's?*), an inevitable choice under the circumstances. But what of the rest of Jacob's sons? They would have had to marry, by the text's own logic, Canaanite women, just as Judah did (and of course, the next generations would have married Egyptians), but Israel cannot bring itself to include that part of the story. *It will tell of desperate measures taken by the mothers of the Moabites and Ammonites, but it will not tell such a tale about the men of Israel. Not yet, anyway.* The text doesn't deny outright the foreign matriarchy. It merely keeps a family secret. Consequently, we are left with the impression that the majority of Jacob's sons procreated all by themselves.[14] (*An impression that leads scholars like Meir Sternberg to mimic the text and praise the endogamy of Jacob's sons despite its textual and historical impossibility!*)[15]

She hid in a box waiting for her siblings to come home from school. (Their coming home was always the high point of her day.) She was sure they would ask where she was and would instigate a great search at which point she would jump out and surprise them.

Her brothers and sister came home. She waited and waited. They never even noticed she was missing. Only when her mother chided them, did they realize she had not been there to greet them as usual.

Buried in Israel's history is the memory that at least some of its ancestry was indigenous to Canaan and the surrounding areas. This is the family secret the story seeks to repress and yet it is dying to tell (*even to savor its scandal if the story of Judah and Tamar is any indication*). The story proceeds, negotiating its ambivalence: allowing Moses to marry a Midianite (and then a Cushite), but in all probability inscribing Moses's Egyptian face as that of a Hebrew.[16] Finessing the identities of the midwives in Exodus 1: are they Hebrew midwives or (Egyptian) midwives to the Hebrews? Admitting, but then quickly ignoring the heterogeneity of the slaves coming out of Egypt.

After all, it is important that the Egyptians be painted as villains – how else can you get away with murdering their firstborn? Treating with special care the Edomites, the Moabites, and the Ammonites upon Israel's attempted entry into the promised land but then insisting that no Moabites or Ammonites can enter the sanctuary of God up to the tenth generation (*a law Nehemiah is quick to light upon – if not write himself – when his Ammonite adversary is found living in Temple quarters*). Insisting that Israel is to take care of strangers because they were once strangers in the land of Egypt while simultaneously ordering the annihilation of the inhabitants of the promised land.

But when the narrative reaches the point where Israel must actually take the land, the event that mirrors the return of the exilic elite, the conflict inherent in Israel's telling comes to a head. The Divine Mandate (but Kristeva asks, *Who is speaking in the Bible? For whom?*) is that, in order to take the land, Israel must dispossess its inhabitants (*read "the peoples of the land"? Ezra and Nehemiah and those like them liked to draw the face of God in just this light. "It is the imagination pressing back against the pressure of reality."*) But in reality, the inhabitants are Israel's "kinfolk," a crucial part of its heritage. (*But the only way to keep the secret is to kill [or at the very least, silence] Others who know it. That is why the spies would have liked to have killed Rahab [Joshua 2]. She was the one who knew their secret. She was the one who saved their lives. And she was the one who believed in the power of their God. She complicated completely the simple Difference of Canaanite. If only we had never seen her face! She made killing the Others much harder.*) The conquest and settlement is the domestic strife of Genesis writ large: in order to define itself, Israel must systematically dispossess the Others – the Lots, the Ishmaels, the Esaus, the Labans – and deny its Canaanite matriliny. Wipe out the faces of the Others. Draw the family face with firmer, more definitive, strokes. And yet, the features still emerge nuanced, bearing remarked resemblance to the inhabitants of the land. The face is drawn again. And again. Bigger. More pronounced. More intractable. It is engraved by word and by s/word.[17] (*You shall not make for yourself a graven image...*). Yet the hard edges keep crumbling and the subtle features remain.

To paint the same head over and over leads you to its unfamiliarity; eventually you get near the raw truth about it, just as people only blurt out the raw truth in the middle of a family quarrel.

The book of Judges marks the middle of the family quarrel. Here Israel's ambivalence about its origins and its zeal to suppress those origins meet head to head (*or face to face as the metaphor so dictates*). Markers of Israel's ambivalence are concentrated in Judges 1 where we see the text vigorously deconstructing Israel's face as quickly as it constructs it. Israel sets out to take the land according to Divine Mandate (*Who is speaking in the Bible? For whom?*), but instead of wholesale conquest, we see Israel's decreasing resolve to eradicate the Canaanites. Judah, the first tribe to make an incursion, starts with much zeal – defeating, capturing, proscribing – but finishes with the qualification "but they were not able to dispossess the inhabitants of the valley for they had iron chariots" (1:19). As the catalogue of tribes progresses, the successes mutate into notices of compromise, multiple instances where the Israelites choose to live among the Canaanites. Finally there is complete failure on the part of Dan to make any inroads at all into its allotted territory. The juxtaposition of Judah's execution of Adoni-bezek with the House of Joseph's negotiation with the man from Luz is symbolic of the dwindling resolve to destroy the Canaanites.[18] While Judah dismembers and destroys Adoni-Bezek, Joseph "deals hesed" with the citizen of Luz who, with his family, relocates and builds another city named Luz. The citizens and the cities slip out of Israelite control.

We also see in Judges 1 obvious traces of rewriting manifesting themselves in chronological ambiguity. We are told in temporally vague terms that, "when Israel grew strong, they subjected the Canaanites to forced labor" (1:28). Historians are quick to point out that the labor corvée was a monarchical institution (that is here being rewritten back into an earlier point in history). The king most notorious for his conscripted labor is, of course, Solomon. Despite the claim that he made a fastidious distinction between Israelite and Canaanite in the matter of forced labor (1 Kings 9:15–23), the larger story cancels out such discrimination: indeed, his undue burden on the northern tribes brought about the downfall of the united monarchy (see 1 Kings 4:1–19; 5:13–18; 9:15–23; 11:26–12:17).[19] Consequently, the text sneaks us a glimpse of the blurred faces of the Canaanite and Israelite peasantry in political reality. And the traces of rewriting expose the strategy of designating the lower class as the "foreigner" and so justifying their exploitation. (*Not unlike the depiction of the "peoples of the land" in the Ezra-Nehemiah literature! Only for Ezra and Nehemiah, who had no authority to conscript a labor force from among the peoples of the land, labor on the house of God and the city walls became issue of privilege and elitism. And Nehemiah is quick to cite Solomon's failure to preserve difference (Nehemiah 13:26). But, according to Nehemiah, it is not the work corvée that is Solomon's downfall, but his association with foreign women!*)

"Look, Mom," said the 4-year-old playing with her toy horses, "they're fighting."

"Why are they fighting?" asked Mom.

"Because they're not the same."

"What do you mean, they're not the same? They're both horses."

"Oh, no, they're different. This one's white and this one is purple. And they live in different cities. Cities with walls around them. That's why they are fighting."

Perhaps the most curious mark of Israel's ambivalence is the story of Achsah, Othniel, and Caleb. The first problem that presents itself is the city Kiriath-sepher, the "city of writing." Can any *reader* sympathize with those who would destroy a city of *writing*? The text clearly accentuates Judah's enthusiasm and success in contrast to the other tribes, but does not the designation of this particular city subvert the story's triumphalism? Have they not in fact attacked a center of learning rather than face the iron chariots? Instead of attacking a military base, have they not taken a (relatively defenseless?) university town? Instead of a citadel, a library? Judah can't face the trained soldiers and heavy artillery, so they gang up on the scribes and the scrolls!

How does one "capture" a city of writing? Does Othniel destroy the city? Total destruction in biblical texts usually requires more than just "capture." (Cf. notice about Jerusalem in Judges 1:8: "they fought against Jerusalem and captured it and struck it with the edge of the sword and set the city on fire.")[20] Does Othniel "capture" Kiriath-sepher like David "captures" Jerusalem (2 Samuel 5:6–8)? Could it be the case that the city and its inhabitants (and its books) are preserved just as was the case when David "captured" Jerusalem? Are the city and its writings merely renamed? (*Marked on? Is Israel engraving its face on the walls of this city?*) Do the inhabitants simply answer to a different political authority? Indeed doesn't this pairing of the capture of Kiriath-sepher with the David's capture of Jerusalem underscore the ambiguity of Israel's identity? Is it not David who has the most stubborn face of all? The face that refuses to be purified by the post-exilic priesthood. *Despite the Chronicler's portrait of the "unadulterated" David!* Is it not David who is surrounded by mercenaries of every cultural background imaginable? Is it not David who adopts the Zadokite priesthood already in place in Jerusalem? Is it not David who marries a woman from Geshur, another group that should have been eradicated by the Israelites (see Joshua 13:13)? Is it not David who is purported to have a Moabite grandmother? (*Is it not ironic that Ezra and Nehemiah will claim Zadok in their genealogies, but will banish Moabite women from the community? Were they too busy re/writing the history ever to read it?*)[21]

The capture and renaming of the city of writing becomes a kind of allegory for Israel's rewriting of its identity conflict: as they attempt to capture and control "someone else's" history, they also (re)adopt that writing, culture, history as their own. They are now masters in the city of writing, trying to master their own story, trying to determine what will be written and not written, but perhaps all they succeed in doing is renaming (Debir) what cannot be finally erased (Kiriath-sepher)[22] and claiming in their naming that the place is their special sanctuary. [23]*"Why aren't you in another department? This is not critical method. What are your controls?"*

The episode presents a more striking problem, however. Just as Judah, under the leadership of Othniel, captures the city of writing for its own, so Judah/Israel has captured and held the story of Caleb, Achsah, and Othniel. Though the episode is embedded in Judah's "toldoth," so to speak, in fact, Caleb, Othniel, and Achsah are not from the tribe of Judah at all. They are Kenizzites, not Israelites. And Kenizzites, according to Genesis 15:19, are among those to be dispossessed from the land. Here is the conflict: how can we dispossess those who are heroic, who are more worthy to be "Israelite" than Israelites? Obviously we can't. So we redraw their faces to look more like ours. And we put them in Judah's family portrait. Othniel the Kenizzite (*the Kenizzite: the label that got blurted out in the midst of the family quarrel?*) will go on to become Israel's first and most ideal judge, setting a literary precedent in the book for other "foreign" heroes (whose ethnic identities are diplomatically hedged), such as Shamgar son of Anath and Jael the wife of Heber the Kenite.

So it seems that, in Judges 1, Israel cannot completely kill or even erase its kinfolk after all. Indeed Israel seems to stop trying. After YHWH pronounces that he will leave the inhabitants in place so that "they shall become like (after the manner of) sides *[identity boundaries?]* to you" (2:3) and in order to "teach war" to the subsequent generations of Israel (3:2), the story deflects attention away from the inhabitants of the land among whom Israel now lives. In fact, the inhabitants of the land seem to disappear. (*Does anyone notice that they are missing? Are their faces simply absorbed, as Achsah's and Caleb's and Othniel's are, into the multitude of Israel? Are they, like Kiriath-sepher, simply renamed?*) Any war learned by Israel comes not from struggle with the inhabitants of the land,[24] but from struggles against outside oppression. (*Forget about Mother. We'll hide her between the lines. We'll simply avoid drawing her face at all. Well, except for Achsah. But people will forget who she really was.[25] It's the brothers we have to worry about — always surrounding the house, always trying to steal our inheritance.*) In the rewriting of the story, this is where Israel's zeal to reinscribe its face takes over.

The brothers surrounding the house are: first, the Mesopotamians (from Aram-naharaim) or the Arameans, the people of Laban (cf. Genesis 29), then the Moabites, the children of Lot (cf. Genesis 19:37), then the Canaanites (from whom the children of Jacob must have taken their mates), then the

Midianites, who are also in passing identified as Ishmaelites (Judges 8:24, an identification also made in Genesis 37; cf. the stories of Ishmael in Genesis 16 and 21), then the Ammonites, also children of Lot (cf. Genesis 19:38) – all people who were, according to Genesis, once Israel's kin. Faces once familial are now painted foreign – foreign and hostile (*adversaries so says Ezra*).

Furthermore, the Philistines, who also had a prominent place in Israel's story of origins, make their appearance as well. But as far as the Philistines are concerned, Judges reverses the situation found in Genesis. While Israelite patriarchs had given or been willing to give their women to the Philistines for the sake of their own security and prosperity, here the Israelite judge Samson takes Philistine women, much to the detriment of his own security and prosperity. His violence against Philistine men is viewed dimly by his Israelite compatriots. "Do you not know that the Philistines rule over us? What is this you have done to us?" (Judges 15:11; cf. Abimelek's question to Isaac in Genesis 26:10) The Israelites hand Samson over to the Philistine men, just as the patriarchs handed over their women to Philistine men, in order to protect themselves.

The book of Judges rewrites Genesis. But why? It is as though, having reached the point in the story where they (the Israelites inside the text as well as the returning exiles outside the text) must justify their divinely appointed place in the land, the conflictual nature of Israel's identity has now surfaced again. Symbolically, the Arameans, the Moabites, the Canaanites, the Midianites/Ishmaelites, the Ammonites, and the Philistines threaten to "take over" Israel. Through territorial encroachment, the exacting of Israelite resources and allegiance, these "foreign elements" move in too close.[26] They are the brothers/foreigners who surround the house of Israel threatening to take what belongs to Israel, threatening to rape the late comer. (*And so Israel turns the narrative table with rapacious imagery against their enemies: Ehud's sword thrust into Eglon's belly; Jael's tent stake driven through Sisera's parted lips.*)[27] The (exilic/postexilic) threat to Israel's constructed identity is encoded as a story of Israel's determined survival of/ self-defense against physical, political, economic oppression. In order to deal with the conflict, the separations narrated in Genesis must be re-enacted. *Israel must save its (manly) face.* Only this time the re-enactments are more hostile, more definitively categorical. In Genesis we watched family members become foreigners through scenarios of domestic strife. In Judges we watch those foreigners become enemies who must be militarily defeated. *In the case of Sisera, the face is literally raped and killed. In order to save its own face, Israel rapes and kills by word and by s/word the face of the Other.* Indeed Israel defeats them all except for the Philistines, the only group who are not, in Israel's story, "kin."[28] *Israel calls the Philistines "the uncircumcised,"*

a term that associates them with women.[29] *And Israel can no more eradi-*
cate the Philistines ("Do you not know that they rule over us?") than they
can erase women from their story. Do "the uncircumcised" so define "the
circumcised"?

She was asked to preach in chapel during Rape Crisis Week. She had never
heard a sermon about rape and she had no idea how to preach one. So she
simply stood in the pulpit and read stories from the Bible, stories about
sexual violence. There were too many to read them all.

When the service was over one of her colleagues said, "I don't like getting
hit over the head with this kind of stuff. You're preaching to the wrong
crowd. That kind of thing doesn't happen here."

All week long students, women and men, came by her office to tell their
stories of violation. (*That kind of thing doesn't happen here, he had said.*)

"My father's business partner raped me when I was twelve," one woman
said, "several times. I think my father knew, but he never did anything
about it."

In Judges, Israel re-enacts its aggressions against those with whom it was
once too closely associated. But Israel, it seems, doesn't know when to stop.
Their hostilities get turned on their own people. Not only are there the
repeated instances of Israelite violence against Israelite cities and tribes
(Judges 8 and 12),[30] but Israelites wreak violence on their own family mem-
bers (Judges 9; 11:1–2, 30–40). These events, too, have their precursors in
Genesis. The fights with the Ephraimites rewrite the abuse of Joseph
(Ephraim's father) at the hand of his brothers. Both Joseph and Ephraim are
portrayed as provoking the violence and they are the ones who pay the physical price. *The voice of your brother's blood cries to me from the ground. . . .*
The abuse and ostracization of Jephthah at the hands of his brothers replays
Joseph's story as well as Ishmael's: the son denied inheritance because of
who his mother was. Jephthah's sacrifice of his daughter echoes Abraham's
attempt to sacrifice Isaac, but we find in this story as in others that females
are always more dispensable than males. *The voice of your daughter's blood*
cries to me from the ground. . . . A chosen patriarch with impeccable lineage
intact and his miraculously conceived son cannot be displaced from the
center of the story, while the son of a prostitute from across the river[31] and
his nameless, motherless daughter are completely expendable in the larger
scheme of things. *Ezra and Nehemiah would have never approved of*
Jephthah and daughter, would they?

Violence against kin reaches its most painful crescendo, however, in Judges 19–21 where the abandonment, rape, and murder of the Levite's wife leads to the near eradication of Benjamin by the other tribes of Israel. The men of Benjaminite Gibeah treat the Levite and his wife as if they were foreigners. The Benjaminite men behave like the foreign Sodomites.[32] Sexual assault justifies textual assault: the rest of Israel turns on Benjamin as though they were foreigners rather than Israelites. *To paint the same head over and over leads you to its unfamiliarity; eventually you get near the raw truth about it. . . .* As several scholars have noted, many of the images used to describe Israel's fight against the inhabitants of the land in Judges 1 now make their way into this story. We are again engaged in warfare. Judah is told to "go up" first to fight. There is a ritual dismemberment. There is a woman on a donkey. The images suggest we have come full circle, that the killing of the Benjaminites is somehow connected to the killing of the inhabitants of the land, or that the murder and dismemberment of the woman is somehow connected to the carving up of the land and the murder of its inhabitants. The movement from killing "Others" to killing each other appears to be symptomatic of the same trauma of identity. *Israel cannot rewrite the face of the Other without rewriting its own face.*

On the one hand, Israel, in an effort to defend a singular identity, moves to kill those, that is the Benjaminites, who can't distinguish between "family" and "foreign." *Ezra and Nehemiah punishing the men with "foreign" wives and "mixed" children?* But by killing their own "kin," the Israelites show themselves to be no better than the Benjaminites. In fact, the Israelites paint themselves with the features of the Philistines who, in their vengeance against Samson, also kill their own people. *Eventually you get near the raw truth of it. . . .*

On the other hand, the Israelites' revulsion against killing their own kin ("Why has this happened in Israel, that one tribe must now be missing?" Judges 21:3) is strangely reminiscent of their initial zeal but then their gradual unwillingness to wipe out the inhabitants of the land (their maternal kinfolk) in chapter 1. Furthermore, their willingness to lay the blame at YHWH's door ("The people relented toward Benjamin for YHWH had made a breach among the tribes of Israel" Judges 21:15) echoes the narrator's earlier insistence that the extermination of the inhabitants of the land is YHWH's design. It is YHWH, say the people, who insists we must kill in order to live. *The guilty face. The blameless face. The unique face. The same face. All gathered as one man. Standing before one God (whose face is well-hidden).* One text. One story.

You will displace your hatred into thought; you will devise a logic that defends you from murder and madness, a logic whose arbitrary nature shall be your coronation. The Bible offers the best description of this transformation of sacrifice into language, this displacement of murder into a system of meanings. In this way, this system, which counterbalances murder, becomes the place where all our crises can be exploded and assimilated.

(Kristeva 1995)

The story of Benjamin also does something else. It encodes the problem Israel feels about its Canaanite matriliny. Here the text is clearly at odds with itself. On the one hand, the story systematically kills women. It rapes them, murders them, and cuts them in little pieces so that they are unrecognizable.[33] *The ultimate engraving by word and by s/word.* As Israel kills its own women, it re-enacts with violence its earlier disavowal of its Canaanite mothers, thus underscoring the dispensability of women. It is no accident that the woman on the donkey reappears – it is Achsah and all the indigenous women she stands for who must be done away with. (*And so, too, Ezra and Nehemiah can throw "foreign" women and their children out of the house to whatever dangers await them, unmoved by defenseless cries, knuckles rapping at the door, or fingers clinging to the threshold. Murder, a condition of Meaning.*)

"Where does the twelfth piece go?" she asked.

"What do you mean, the twelfth piece?"

"Well, the text says that the Levite cut the woman into twelve pieces and sent a piece to each of the tribes. Would he have sent one to the tribe of Benjamin?"

"I wouldn't think so."

"Neither would I," she said. "I think the twelfth piece has come to us. What are we to do with it?"

We are confronting, therefore, a set of events, not only beyond our power to tranquilize them in the mind, beyond our power to reduce them and metamorphose them, but events that stir the emotions to violence, that engage us in what is direct and immediate and real, and events that involve the concepts and sanctions that are the order of our lives and may involve our very lives. . . ."

(Stevens 1951)

Rewrite her face (and in so doing, rewrite our own?)
with the blood that cries out to us from the ground
and the ink that cries out to us from the page?

On the other hand, in the very inscription of its violence, the story of Benjamin rewrites a justification for the Canaanite matriliny so deftly suppressed in Genesis. (*"You will devise a logic that defends you from murder and madness, a logic whose arbitrary nature shall be your coronation."*) Practically speaking, women are not so dispensable after all. They are required for survival. And some of them know more about survival than do the men. *"You've set me in the Negev-land,"* says Achsah to her father, *"give me also springs of water" (Judges 1:15). "She is more righteous than I," says Judah of Tamar (Genesis 38: 26).* Some of them secure not only their own survival but the survival of others. *"The midwives feared (the) God(s) and they did not do as the king of Egypt said to them – they kept the male children alive" (Exodus 1:17). "Swear to me by* YHWH*," says Rahab to the spies, "since I have dealt hesed with you, that you will also deal hesed with my father's house . . . and shall keep alive my father and my mother and my brothers and my sisters . . . and shall deliver our souls from death" (Joshua 2:12–13).* By the end of Judges, the Benjaminites are in the same situation as the sons of Jacob and, ironically, the daughters of Lot. Without prospective mates who belong to their own tribe, the Benjaminites take Other women, just as the sons of Jacob would have had to. When only men are left, the taking of Other women, while not ideal, is necessary. So the Benjaminites, and by extension the sons of Jacob, are excused because of their circumstances. The Canaanite matriliny, all but ignored by Genesis, could not have been helped. And so, too, the incest of the daughters of Lot? The propaganda designed to paint their faces inferior now casts them in a different light: victims? survivors? heroes? of circumstance. *The faces of Israelite men. The faces of foreign women (the stubborn stain on Israel's palimpsest). All inscribed as survivors. Survivors without innocence.*
Inscribing their writers
and their readers
all without innocence.

The Bible is a text that thrusts its words into my losses. By enabling me to speak about my disappointments, though, it lets me stand in full awareness of them.
  This awareness is unconscious – so be it. Nevertheless, it causes me, as a reader of the Bible, to resemble someone who lives on the fringe, on the lines of

demarcation within which my security and fragility are separated and merged. *Perhaps that is where we might discover what is known as the sacred value of the text: a place that gives meaning to these crises of subjectivity, during which meaning . . . eludes me.*

(Kristeva 1995)

"Mom," said the 4-year-old, "Can I play on the computer now?"
"Just a minute, honey. Mom's trying to think about something."
"What are you thinking about?"
"Mom's trying to figure out the ending of this."
"The ending to a story?"
"Yeah, sort of."
"Don't they live happily ever after?"
"No, honey, not exactly. But some of them do live."

NOTES

1 I would like to thank the following people for their comments upon and contributions to various versions of this piece: Tim Beal, Pat Davis, David Gunn, David Jobling, Roy Melugin, Mary Anne Reed, Janice Virtue, Patricia Zaiontz-Newcomer. Special thanks go to Claudia Camp (for encouragement, enthusiasm, and numerous connections) and Gary Phillips (who heard what the piece wanted to become and said "Just do it").

2 "Postmodernism puts into question some of the most basic assumptions and beliefs which have, up until now, been fundamental to cultural politics both in the West and in 'socialist' countries such as the G[erman] D[emocratic] R[epublic]. These assumptions include the belief in automatic progress based on rational planning, education and legislation, the existence of universal standards and values, and the possibility of 'true' knowledge of the world" (Jordan and Weedon 1995: 18). "The postmodern has to do with transformation in the local ways we understand ourselves in relation to modernity and to contemporary culture and history, the social and personal dimensions of that awareness, and the ethical and political responses that it generates. The postmodern as unruly, nebulous, elusive, decentered, and decentering . . . needs to be engaged creatively and critically rather than summarily dismissed or fetishized as the latest intellectual fashion" (Bible and Culture Collective 1995: 9).

3 "The overwhelming *cultural* character of the postmodern transformation means questioning the 'given' organization of the [biblical] discipline and the nature of its ethical responsibilities and accountability to the field, community and culture" (Phillips 1994: 407–408).

4 "If a general feature of the modern crisis could be said to be the loss of transcendence, reading religiously will mean something like finding strategies and resources to promote and signify encounter with the Other. Biblical critics will have to develop unexplored resources beyond the biblical narrative and traditional modern reading strategies in order to re-envision what is Other about the Bible and one another" (Phillips 1994: 405–406).

149

5 I resonate with David Jobling's idea that, for the most part, the Hebrew Bible is a document of grief in which Israel is dealing with its failure to live up to an ideal vision. (Private communication, April 12, 1995.)

6 "In society such as it functions one cannot live without killing, or at least without taking the preliminary steps for the death of someone. Consequently, the important question of the meaning of being is not: why is there something rather than nothing ... but: do I not kill by being?" (Levinas 1994: 120)

7 In theory, the more flexible a group's system is with regard to insiders and outsiders, the more likely it is to survive the transition and to continue to function.

8 For an interesting analysis of how this community labeled itself and others, see Weinberg (1992: 62–74).

9 It is not clear exactly who these women are. Historically, there may have been less difference in their ethnicity than in their affiliation with particular theological communities. See Eskenazi and Judd (1994) who make a provocative comparison between the situation in postexilic Israel and the situation pertaining in the modern state of Israel.

10 A palimpsest, however, leaves traces of what has been written before. Like the "mystic writing-pad," Freud's famous metaphor of the unconscious (see Freud 1925a), inscriptions remain (in the case of Freud's writing pad, in the wax beneath the cover paper) long after the surface marks have been erased. Derrida's reading of Freud critiques Freud's mechanistic approach to the unconscious by twisting Freud's own metaphor. The question, suggests Derrida (1978: 199), is not so much whether the human psyche can be thought of as a "text," but rather, "what is a text, and what must the psyche be if it can be represented by a text?" Texts are governed, says Derrida, by repression and censorship (226), metaphors taken from the political arena which point to the political potential of texts. Consequently, "there is no question of affirming some delusive realm of 'pure' textuality beyond the claims of political or ethical life" (Norris 1987: 208).

11 This is symbolized again and again by collective characterization.

12 Quoted in Robert Hughes, "The Art of Frank Auerbach," *New York Review of Books*, October 11, 1990, 28 (italics in the text). Cited in Susan Rubin Suleiman's introduction ("Writing Past the Wall") to the work of Cixous (1991).

13 Eilberg-Schwartz (in this volume) observes that the priestly writings suggest an analogy between circumcision and the pruning of a fruit tree.

14 Cf. Eilberg-Schwartz (in this volume): "There is a tension, therefore, between genealogy and reproduction. For the purposes of genealogical reckoning, wives and hence sexual intercourse cannot exist. But the presence of women is always necessary because men cannot reproduce alone." Kunin (1995) offers a structuralist analysis of these problems: the myth of the separated families in Genesis mediates the reality of exogamy and the distinctive identity of Israel that can be preserved only through endogamy. Furthermore, the pressure to have divine seed located in one person is set over against the development of Israel as a nation. Supposedly by the fourth generation of Jacob's children, the family is no longer of a divided nature. They should have been all one family, but the myth cannot seem to stop. There is still, according to Kunin, the attempt to locate the divine seed in Joseph.

15 Sternberg on Levi and Simeon in the story of the rape of Dinah: "Their concern has been selfless and single-minded: to redress the wrong done to their sister and the whole family, which includes *the prevention of an exogamous marriage, by hook or by crook*" (1985: 472; emphasis mine). On Jacob: "[H]is inaction amounts to an acquiescence in what a patriarch, whatever his paternal instincts, must fight tooth and nail: *exogamous marriage*" (1985: 474; emphasis mine). Who, pray tell, is

Dinah, or her brothers, supposed to marry? See the response of Fewell and Gunn (1991).

16 This view, while toyed with by the rabbis, gained prominence in Freud's *Moses and Monotheism* (1939). Freud argued that Moses, an Egyptian, was murdered by the Israelites. There has been an attempt in the biblical text, according to Freud, to cover over the murder as well as the ethnic identity of Moses. Set over against this cover-up, however, is also an opposite impulse in the very same text: the attempt to preserve the story of murder. "The distortion of a text is not unlike a murder," writes Freud. "The difficulty lies not in the execution of the deed but in the doing away with the traces." According to some scholars, Freud's own writing of *Moses and Monotheism* is itself making a gesture analogous to that of the biblical text. In arguing for the murder of Moses and for the reinscribing of Moses's identity, Freud, a Jew, is attempting to rewrite his own story of origins. The killing of the father (Moses) represents Freud's desire to break with his own father's Jewish tradition as well as his desire to depose the paternal authority of the biblical text. See Robert (1976); Handelman (1982: 129–52); Bible and Culture Collective (1995: 187–95); also Boyarin in the present volume.

17 In psychoanalytic terms, in order for the conflict to be resolved it must be re-enacted.

18 Younger (1995: 79). This failure of resolve is matched in the book of Joshua by the Israelites' negotiations with Rahab (Joshua 2 and 6) and the Gibeonites (Joshua 9).

19 Historians seek to harmonize the apparent conflict between 1 Kings 9:15–23 and 5:13–18 by arguing that the conscription of Israelites (*mas*, "forced levy," corvée, 5:13) was temporary and that of the Canaanites (*mas obed*, "forced levy of servitude/slavery," 9:21) permanent. But the extent of the king's massive building program and the burden of the Israelites' complaint against Solomon in the account of the dissolution of the united monarchy (1 Kings 11–12) effectively makes moot the notion of temporary.

20 In general, "capture" (*lkd*), when occurring by itself, is used when something or someone is being siezed without being destroyed. "Capture" basically means to take possession. See, e.g., Numbers 21:32; 32:39–42; 1 Samuel 14:47; 2 Samuel 12:27; 2 Kings 17:6. In order to communicate destruction, other verbs are needed. See, e.g., Joshua 8:21; 10:1, 28, 31–39; 11:10, 17; Jeremiah 34:22.

21 "The Hebrew Bible is the product of the Second Temple period. . . . While I can see that there *may* be something to be said for the view that the Bible contains fragments of material from before the collapse of the temple in the sixth century, the claim that the Bible *as we know it* (i.e. the fully redacted final form of the various books constituting it) comes from the Second Temple period seems to me to be quite ungainsayable" (Carroll 1991: 108).

22 On connotation and word play involved in the renaming see Fewell (1995).

23 *Debir* is the name used to describe the Holy of Holies (1 Kings 6:5; 2 Chronicles 4:20; 5:9). See Meyers (1987) for a discussion of the logic of this title.

24 With the possible exception of the "Canaanites" in chapters 4–5, but even here this group is depicted as living far to the north of Israel, in the area of Hazor, rather than interspersed among Israelites.

25 So writes Kristeva (1995: 118): "We notice, among other things, that separating oneself from the mother, rejecting her, and 'abjecting' her; as well as using this negation to resume contact with her, to define oneself according to her, and to 'rebuild' her, constitutes an essential movement in the biblical text's struggles against the maternal cults of previous and current forms of paganism."

26 As for the postexilic analogue, the conflict between the returning Israelites and the people of the land was also most likely fueled by issues of land ownership and

political control. Carroll (1991) offers a provocative discussion on how this conflict centering on land and power works itself out in other texts (provocative despite the retreat he makes at the end regarding the Bible's use as sociological evidence! On this retreat, see Jobling's response [1991a] to Carroll in the same volume).

27 The word usually translated "temple" (*raqqah*; cf. *rqq*, "to spit," and *roq*, "spittle") is better translated as "mouth" or "parted lips." See Fewell and Gunn (1990: 393–94 n. 11).

28 Jobling and Rose (forthcoming) offer an exceptional reading of Israel's (and subsequent Western culture's) ambivalence toward Philistines and "Philistines."

29 "Circumcision is the mark of participation in the covenant community of Israel. . . . Religious difference is inscribed in the penis as a physical difference setting Israelite men apart from Philistine men. The Philistines as a people, which includes both men and women, are referred to as 'the uncircumcised.' Women, who are uncircumcised, are by nature on the Philistine side of this opposition. And Philistine men, who do not bear the distinct mark of covenant relationship on the male organ, are strongly identitfied with the female . . ." (Exum 1993: 72–73).

30 See Jobling (1986) for a structural analysis for how this violence replays itself.

31 As Jobling (1986) shows, the river is already creating a sense of Otherness within Israel.

32 It should come as no surprise then that Ezra has such difficulty deciding how to identify Benjamin in relation to Judah. Benjamin is sometimes associated with Judah and sometimes not.

33 On violence against the bodies of biblical women, see also Fewell and Gunn (1993: 164–86).

8

THE PROBLEM WITH PAGANS

L. Daniel Hawk

The book of Joshua relates the execution of an ancient program of ethnic cleansing, initiated and legitimized by divine decree, and narrated with little expression of remorse save that Israel did not finish the job. The program is accomplished through a war of conquest, in which difference of religion and ethnicity constitute just cause for extermination. For many readers in an age haunted by violence – often sponsored, sanctioned, and sanctified by religious ideologies – this is an ugly, repugnant story that scarcely deserves retelling. John Bright no doubt expresses a common sentiment when he writes, "the smoke of burning towns and the stench of rotting flesh hangs over its pages" (1967: 243).

But Joshua is a text configured by contradiction. Exaggerated claims of conquest are juxtaposed with reports of failure and neglect. Episodes depicting Israel's careful adherence to the commandments of YHWH are subverted by others that seem to show Israel asleep at the switch. And dispensations of mercy counter the wholesale destruction of cities.[1]

These incongruities intimate a profound tension. Portions of the text make grandiose claims for Israel in the idiom of Deuteronomy, enunciating an intense concern for group survival and the maintenance of internal boundaries. These claims are opposed by a narrated reality represented by episodes and reports that argue for moderation as Israel takes its place among other peoples who inhabit the land. Narrated reality thus resists the imposition of inflexible idealism, engendering a pronounced ambivalence regarding Israel's identity, status, and relationship to other peoples of Canaan.

The battle stories in Joshua 2–11 focus this conflict of perspectives by exploring the conflict of peoples. The first three campaigns reported in Joshua, those against Jericho, Ai, and the five kings at Gibeon, are each expanded in ways that challenge Deuteronomic exclusivism. In the stories of Rahab and the Gibeonites, Israel incorporates outsiders who resemble itself, while in the case of Achan, Israel excises an insider who has appropriated Canaanite plunder. The transformations that occur in these stories effectively blur the boundaries articulated by the Deuteronomic code and resolve contrary perspectives by affirming them; the stories of Rahab and the Gibeonites argue for flexibility in the determination of Israel's internal boundaries, while the story of Achan emphatically argues that the boundaries must nevertheless be preserved intact.

The Deuteronomic Code, in various ways, establishes and enjoins the preservation of the boundaries which distinguish Israel from the other peoples of Canaan. Deuteronomy refers to Israel as "a holy people," a people which YHWH has chosen out of all the peoples on the earth to be God's "cherished possession" (Deuteronomy 7:6). It repeatedly and emphatically urges obedience to the ordinances which define Israel, mandating severe punishment for those who stray outside the prescribed limits. Louis Stulman has recently demonstrated that these concerns articulate a "focal concern for group survival," what he terms an "ethos of encroachment" (1990: 613).

> The social environment encoded in D [the Deuteronomic Code] reflects a great deal of *internal* anxiety and a marked sense of vulnerability. The world of D is fragile and fraught with danger, and Israel's survival is perceived to be in jeopardy.
>
> (Stulman 1990: 626)

Articulating its perspective through the words of Moses, Deuteronomy identifies the risk faced by Israel as it prepares to invade Canaan. The Israelites will enter a land inhabited by others more numerous and powerful than themselves (7:1–2; 9:1–2). The aboriginal inhabitants threaten Israel, not by their imposing cities or great stature (which will be neutralized by the might of YHWH), but through their *difference*. Israel's perceived vulnerability to the power of difference finds expression in Moses' directives concerning the peoples of Canaan: the Israelites must exterminate the "seven nations," seeing to it that they do not associate or intermarry with them in the process. The rationale behind the commandments is telling. Any contact with the peoples of Canaan will inevitably compromise Israel's identity, causing the community to turn to "other gods" and away from the God who has constituted the nation through law and covenant. As a consequence, Israel will no longer enjoy an existence uniquely its own (life in the land given by YHWH), but will suffer the fate reserved for the aboriginal inhabitants. Difference is so virulent that not even a trace of the aboriginal inhabitants must be allowed to remain in proximity to Israel (7:1–26; cf. 8:19–20; 12:29–32).

Israel perceives an even greater threat from within: "indigenous outsiders" who refuse to abide by communal norms, challenging the social structures or those who enforce them. These "bad insiders" constitute an even more pressing danger: their practices (idolatry, sexual misconduct, homicide, dishonoring parents, kidnapping) compromise communal integrity and blur the boundaries between Israel and the other nations (Stulman 1990: 628).

The laws addressing their conduct mandate a response that links them with the other peoples of Canaan; indigenous outsiders must also be exterminated. Difference, whether geographical, ethnic, or internal, constitutes for Deuteronomy a pernicious threat to the survival of the nation.

The book of Joshua depicts Israel's confrontation with difference. The story of Rahab and Jericho (2:1–24; 6:1–25) parallels the story of the Gibeonites and the battle at Gibeon (9:1–10:15). In each case, a great Israelite victory is preceded by an incident in which Israel encounters the people of the land. The plots of the two stories proceed along similar lines: inhabitants of Canaan approach Israelites and succeed in wangling an exemption from destruction. The encounters culminate in agreements appropriating covenantal language, validation of the agreements by oath, and reports of Israel's implementation of the agreements (2:12, 17, 20; 9:19, 20).[2]

Both stories begin with undercover operations and appropriate themes of concealment and disclosure. In preparation for the destruction of Jericho, Israelite spies secretly enter the city on a reconnaissance mission and take refuge in the house of a prostitute (2:1). The spies' attempt to conceal their identity (unsuccessfully) contrasts with Rahab's efforts to hide them (successfully) under stalks of flax (verses 3–6). Rahab, it seems, is far more adept at trickery.[3] When the king's men arrive at her house and interrogate her about her guests, she denies knowing them and throws her interrogators off the scent by sending them into the hills. She returns to the spies when the danger of discovery has passed and only then reveals her motives for hiding them: she seeks a *quid pro quo* for the kindness rendered.

> Now swear an oath to me by YHWH. Because I have been loyal to you, you should be loyal to my father's house.
>
> (2:12)

The encounter with the Gibeonites reverses certain aspects of the scheme. Gibeonite "wayfarers," seeking to *save* their city from destruction, enter the *Israelite* camp at Gilgal disguised as emissaries dispatched from a far-off country. They conceal both their motives and identities, packing stale provisions in worn-out bags in an attempt to avert the suspicions of the Israelite elders. They too are interrogated, and suspense increases when the Israelite elders begin to prod too close to home: "Perhaps you live among us" (9:7). But, like Rahab, the Gibeonites successfully distract their interrogators, in this case by inviting them to investigate their provisions rather than their identities (9:11–14). Their motives and identities remain hidden until they have been able to secure their deliverance.

The discovery of the Gibeonites' identity leads to protest, negotiation, and a modification of the initial agreement. After the Israelites learn that their new covenant partners are in fact new neighbors, they grumble against their leaders (9:18). The leaders respond by confirming the covenant.

We have sworn to them by YHWH the God of Israel and now we can't touch them.

(9:19)

Then they suggest a compromise. The Gibeonites will be spared but will be consigned to cut wood and bear water for the Israelite nation. The compromise bodes ill, because in sparing the inhabitants of the land the Israelites disobey Moses's commandment to slaughter the Canaanites without exception. Honoring the covenant with Gibeon will mean failure to abide by a component of the covenant with YHWH. The situation requires an intervention by Joshua, Moses's successor, who ratifies the decision of the elders by ruling that Israel will honor the covenant with Gibeon (9:22–27).

A corresponding pattern configures Rahab's conversation with the spies. The spies also protest their oath, intimating that it was made under duress. Three times they protest their innocence, while placing additional restrictions on Rahab.

We are innocent of this oath which you made us swear. . . . Anyone who exits the door of your house will have their own blood to account for. We will be innocent. . . . And if you divulge any of this business we will be innocent of this oath which you made us swear.

(2:17, 19, 20)

Later, when the city of Jericho falls to the Israelites, Joshua ratifies the oath to Rahab by instructing the erstwhile spies to transport her and her family to safety outside the encampment.

The episodes conclude on a note of considerable ambiguity regarding the status of Canaanites. On the one hand, the Deuteronomic pronouncement that they are cursed is decisively affirmed. After Rahab and her family are spared and assigned a place on the periphery of the camp, Joshua pronounces a curse against Jericho and against anyone who attempts to rebuild it (6:26). The Gibeonites, too, are cursed by Joshua, but paradoxically are assigned a place at the center of Israel's life – at "the house of my God" (9:23). On the other hand, the text notes the incorporation of the former outsiders, reporting the implementation of the agreements (6:25; 9:26–27) and remarking on the continuing presence of the survivors, who live in the midst of Israel "to the present day" (6:25; 9:27).

The episodes also confuse the attributes conventionally applied to the inhabitants of Canaan. Rahab offers unsolicited glory to Israel's God, while the spies remain silent on the subject.

I know that YHWH has given you the land and that the dread of you has fallen on us; all the inhabitants of the land have despaired because of you. We have heard how YHWH dried up the waters of the Red Sea before you when you came out of Egypt and what you did to the two kings of the Amorites on the other side of the Jordan – Sihon and Og, whom you devoted to destruction. We heard and our hearts melted, and everyone lost their nerve because of you, for YHWH your god is God in the sky above and the earth below.

(2:9–11)

The Gibeonites acclaim the deeds of YHWH in similar terms (9:9–10), again presenting a contrast to Israelite silence on the topic of God.[4]

In contrast to the energy and savvy of the Canaanites, the Israelites appear passive and inept. The spies enter Jericho, go to the house of a prostitute and "lie down" (2:1).[5] Their negotiations with Rahab take place when they are again lying down (2:8), and they attempt disclaimers while they dangle from a rope she holds (2:15). In a similar fashion, the Israelites evince an inordinate gullibility when confronted with the Gibeonites' ruse. Strangely susceptible to their rhetoric, the Israelite leaders approve a covenant with them without consulting YHWH.

The Israelites thus exhibit less of their ancestor Jacob's cunning than those they have come to destroy, and the oaths they swear raise troubling questions about their commitment to abide by the law of Moses. Given Moses's stern warnings that the people will forfeit YHWH's blessing and presence if they disobey YHWH's commandments, one might expect dire consequences. Yet in both cases great victories follow, and YHWH's presence with Israel is explicitly affirmed. As Joshua gives the command to raise the war cry against Jericho, he announces that YHWH is with the people: "Shout! For YHWH has given you the city" (6:16b). A similar assurance is given directly by YHWH as Joshua marches from Gilgal to defend the Gibeonites from the five kings: "Don't be afraid of them, because I have given them into your hands" (10:8).

Both battles are fought by the whole of Israel, which acts as a unit under the direction of Joshua, and victories are achieved by the might of YHWH rather than force of arms. YHWH fights for Israel, causing the walls of Jericho to fall upon its inhabitants (6:20) and causing the sky to fall on the terrorized troops of the five kings (10:11). In both cases, Israel is called upon to complete a slaughter that YHWH initiates by supernatural means. YHWH even stops the sun at Gibeon so that the slaughter can be fully executed, leading the narrator to reiterate the assertion that YHWH indeed was fighting for Israel (10:14). Reports then confirm that Israel fulfills its task: Jericho is devoted to destruction (6:21), as are the forces of the five kings and a sequence of southern cities (10:16–39).

YHWH participates conspicuously in the battles against Jericho and the five kings but is conspicuously absent as the Israelites negotiate with Rahab and the Gibeonites.[6] This absence is accentuated by the Canaanites' unexpected courage, cunning, and acclamations of faith – unexpected because YHWH had promised to reduce all the inhabitants of the land into quivering weaklings who would offer no significant resistance (Deuteronomy 7:23–24; 9:3; cf. Joshua 1:5). Why have these particular inhabitants proven immune to the divine terror directed against their peers?[7] Has YHWH neglected his duty? Why does YHWH have nothing to say about Israel's blatant contravention of the commandment to devote all the inhabitants of Canaan to destruction? YHWH's seeming inconsistency in the cases of Rahab and the Gibeonites elevates the textual ambivalence regarding outsiders to the realm of the divine, further obfuscating the demarcation of Israel's internal boundaries.

The features of these stories are reversed in the case of Achan and the campaign against Ai (7:1–8:29). The account begins with a battle instead of an encounter, and the result is a humiliating defeat rather than a remarkable victory. The defeat is linked to the theft of plunder devoted to YHWH. YHWH is angry that an Israelite (Achan) has kept Canaanite booty for himself. In the course of the story, Achan becomes the negative image of Rahab and suffers the fate that should have been hers. In a reversal of the other accounts, YHWH is conspicuous by his presence as Israel encounters Canaan (the story itself opens in 7:1 with the comment that YHWH's anger burned against Israel) but is conspicuously absent during the battles themselves.

In a departure from its practice in the previous and following campaigns, Israel – not YHWH – takes the initiative in prosecuting the opening battle. Instead of moving as one, Israel (now overly confident and aggressive) assaults the city with a few thousand troops (7:3–5). The results are disastrous, and as a consequence Israel takes on the attributes of the Canaanites: *Israelite* hearts melt and turn to water (7:5b; cf. 2:9; 10:2), and the elders put dust on their heads, thus assuming the appearance of pulverized Jericho.

The city is finally taken through conventional means rather than supernatural ones. YHWH takes no direct part in the battle other than to dictate a strategy for the conquest of the city and to assure Joshua that he has given it into Israelite hands (8:1–2, 18). The city is taken through a stratagem that employs a bit of irony: *Israelites* now do the concealing and revealing. Half the force conceals itself to the west of Ai, while the other half camps in full view of the king. When the king sallies forth to engage the troops, the hidden force falls upon the city, causing the soldiers of Ai to panic (8:3–22). The victory is thus accomplished by tactical ingenuity rather than supernatural intervention, although the outcome is the same: Ai is destroyed and its people are devoted to destruction (8:21–28).

The associated story of Achan corresponds to those of Rahab and the Gibeonites. But like the battle account, the common elements appear in the obverse. Achan's story, too, is about concealment and disclosure, but Achan's deception is motivated by a less noble motive than securing the safety of himself and others; he has taken plunder devoted to YHWH and has hidden it under his tent. The theft and concealment elicit anger from the deity (7:1), who responds with some chicanery of his own. Hiding his outrage as Israel sallies forth against Ai, YHWH reveals it only when the routed warriors return to camp.

In contrast to the other stories, there are no negotiations – although Joshua tries. Adopting a tactic from Moses, who had successfully diverted YHWH's anger in a similar situation (Numbers 14:13–35), Joshua appeals to YHWH to rescue Israel for the sake of his great name (7:9).[8] YHWH, however, is not so easily taken in and responds with a barrage of accusations.

> Israel has sinned! They have transgressed the covenant I decreed to them. They have taken from that which is devoted; they have stolen; they have concealed; they have put it with their own possessions.
>
> (7:11)

The indictments are followed by instructions for identifying and eliminating the transgressor, as well as repeated warnings that YHWH will no longer continue to be with Israel unless the offender is executed.

In stark contrast to his absence from the other stories, YHWH here dictates the course of events and defines their meaning. Although he remains silent as Israel disobeys the words of Moses and exempts Canaanites from being "devoted," he reacts intensely when an Israelite takes for himself "devoted things."[9] YHWH also indicts the people as a whole for the transgression, making it clear that he holds the entire nation responsible for the actions of individual members.

In response to YHWH's demands, the people assemble to identify and excise the offender. Achan is named by the lot, and Joshua commands him to confess. The words he speaks are a wry echo of his counterparts'. While Rahab and the Gibeonites utter paeans to YHWH, Achan confesses his sin. And although the Canaanites' praise is unsolicited, Achan's words come only when Joshua commands him to "give glory to YHWH God of Israel and confess to him" (7:19).[10] Rahab and the Gibeonites succeed in deceiving other human beings and use their words effectively to protect themselves. Achan, however, attempts unsuccessfully to hide something from God, and the only words he speaks effectively seal his doom. His confession is effusive. He not only confesses to the deed but also reveals the location of the booty, thus providing the proof of his guilt.[11]

When the stolen plunder is presented in plain view of assembled Israel, Joshua again issues a ruling, pronouncing a sentence in language reminiscent of his curses on Jericho and the Gibeonites: "Why have you brought disaster on us? May YHWH bring disaster on you this day" (7:25). Israel then acts on YHWH's behalf to fulfill the curse; Achan and his family are stoned, burned, and buried under a pile of rocks. The story thus concludes with a unified Israel directing at one of their own a measure of violence previously reserved for the people of Canaan.

The episode ends with a note that again injects a note of ambiguity regarding the blessing and curse.

> They piled a big heap of rocks over him that remains to the present day. YHWH then turned from the heat of his anger. Therefore, that place is called the Valley of Disaster to the present day.
>
> (7:26)

The pile of rocks both differentiates Achan from the Canaanites who are incorporated into Israel and identifies him with the accursed inhabitants of Canaan. The manner of his interment associates him with the king of Ai, who embodies the curse by being hung from a tree (8:29; cf. Deuteronomy 21:23) and whose pile of rocks also remains "to the present day." Furthermore, the repeated phrase "to the present day," which occurs both with reference to Achan's pile and to the place of his execution, ironically sets his fate against those of Rahab's house and the Gibeonites, who survive and remain "in the midst" of Israel to the present day (6:25; 9:27).

In the course of the story Achan is transformed into one of the accursed inhabitants of the land, just as Rahab and the Gibeonites are transformed from accursed outsiders to marginalized insiders. Achan's line ends under a pile of rubble, while Rahab and the Gibeonites survive to claim a place within the promised land. The transformations effected by the stories blur and challenge the boundaries between Israel and Canaan, which are rendered in stark and strident terms by the Deuteronomic code.

The expanded accounts of the first three campaigns in Canaan, with their appended stories of transformations, are no doubt presented as paradigms for the conquest as a whole. But what do they signify? Marked symmetry of plot, theme, and characterization between the stories of Rahab, Achan, and the Gibeonites indicate that they are to be taken together. A story of Israelite disobedience and destruction is framed by accounts of Canaanite resolve and deliverance; Canaanites who give praise to YHWH and receive mercy surround the story of an Israelite who intrudes on YHWH's domain and rouses YHWH to anger.

The stories reveal an acute ambivalence regarding notions of Israelite identity. That this ambivalence occurs at the deepest level of the stories can be discerned by a number of allusions to the constitutive and definitive events of Israel's charter story. The stories of Rahab, the Gibeonites, and Achan allude, respectively, to the deliverance from Egypt, the making of the covenant, and the possession of the land. In the stories, Canaanites are incorporated by experiences which recall Israel's constitutive events, while Israelites (Achan and his family) are put to death in a manner that makes similar allusions.

The spies' instructions to Rahab reverberate with eerie echoes of Moses's instructions to Israel on the night of the Passover.

Your father, mother, siblings, and all your father's household you shall
gather to yourself at your house. Those who exit the doors of your
house will be responsible for their own blood.

(2:19)

Like Israel in Egypt, Rahab is told to gather her family within her home and
to mark a portal with red (a scarlet cord here, the lamb's blood in Egypt). In
so doing, she and her family are spared when destruction comes to Jericho.
Rahab and her house experience their own passover and thereby share a constitutive experience with the Israelites.

The circumstances surrounding the Gibeonites' covenant allude to the
ratification of Israel's covenant with YHWH. Joshua's odd ruling that the
Gibeonites will be spared, albeit to cut wood and carry water, recalls
the covenant renewal ceremony in Moab (Deuteronomy 29:1ff). In that ceremony, Moses addresses all those who stand before YHWH to make the covenant — including the "foreigners in your camp, both those who cut your
wood and carry your water" (29:11).[12] Joshua's ruling thus affirms that the
Gibeonites had been prolepticly and potentially present in Moab as Israel
ratified its covenant with YHWH.

In the opposite sense, Achan's story alludes to the third constitutive event
in Israel's story, the possession of the land. Achan's execution is facilitated
by the casting of lots. He is therefore excluded from life in the land through
the same means that will later be employed to demarcate the areas in which
the various tribes will settle (Joshua 18:9ff). Like the tribes of Israel, Achan
and his family are identified and assigned a place in the land. But theirs is a
place of death, not life.

So rendered, these stories manifest an ambivalence about the Deuteronomic perspective which ostensibly configures the narrative. The stories of
Rahab and the Gibeonites make a strong case for extending Israel's internal
boundaries. Although condemned by the rhetoric of Moses (Deuteronomy
9:5), the inhabitants of the land are here accorded humanity. In the course of
Israel's encounters with them the reader discovers a people of remarkable
vitality, ingenuity, and fidelity: they acclaim the works of God, succeed in
securing their survival in the land, and escape the curse to dwell among
Israel "to the present day." The transformation of Canaanites from others
into marginal Israelites thereby issues an implicit challenge to the exclusi-
vistic boundaries set out in Deuteronomy and validates the expansion of
those boundaries.[13]

The story of Achan counters this perspective with an insistence that
expansion of the boundaries must not be mistaken for their dissolution.
Outsiders may become insiders, but transit in the opposite direction will not
be tolerated: *Israelites* may not cross the boundaries that differentiate Israel
from Canaan. Canaanites may find a space among the people of YHWH, but

the people of YHWH must not take to themselves anything of Canaan. Thus, while the boundaries may be *extended* they must nevertheless be preserved.

The stories' ambivalence about internal boundaries also calls into question the ethic of extermination decreed by Deuteronomy. The commands to exterminate the nations work in complicity with admonitions that Israel keep its distance from the inhabitants of the land (Deuteronomy 7:1–6). As long as the people of the land remain faceless, they may be killed with little remorse. Joshua, however, reveals the real danger involved in contact with the people of the land: Israel may see its own image reflected in the other. And recognizing the humanity of others makes killing them a far more unsettling enterprise.

NOTES

1 These tensions have been recently explored from a number of perspectives. See the studies by Polzin (1980), Gunn (1987), Eslinger (1989), Hawk (1991), and Stone (1991).
2 In the case of the Gibeonites, the agreement is actually termed a covenant (9:15). While the agreement with Rahab is not so specified, her negotiations with the Israelite spies are heavy with covenant language. See Campbell (1972: 242-43).
3 Trickery and deceit, prominent attributes of the prostitute in folklore, are here expressed in unexpected ways; see Phyllis Bird's fine discussion of Rahab (1989).
4 The narrator in fact comments on this silence by reporting that the Israelite leaders failed to consult YHWH on the important business of treaty-making (verse 14b).
5 The Hebrew verb (*shakab*) here means "to lie." To "lie with" is a common idiom for sexual intercourse (e.g. Genesis 34:7; 39:7, 10, 12; Exodus 22:16; Numbers 5:13; Deuteronomy 22:23; 28:30; 2 Samuel 12:11).
6 The use of masculine pronouns for YHWH in the translation is intentional. In this book, at least, YHWH takes on male attributes and aligns himself with the concerns of patriarchy: defining boundaries, possessing land, establishing legitimate lines of and structures for inheritance.
7 Eslinger asserts that YHWH's failure to proclaim and explain his neglect of the promised preparation brings him into complicity with the making of the forbidden covenants (1989: 25–54).
8 Joshua's prayer paradoxically echoes the grumbling of the Israelites at Kadesh rather than the intercession of Moses (7:7-9; cf. Numbers 14:2–4); see Hawk (1991: 76-77).
9 The same Hebrew root, *ḥ-r-m*, is used in each of these instances.
10 The second clause carries a double meaning. The phrase *ten lo todah* can mean "give him praise" or "confess to him." Thus, Joshua's command that Achan confess alludes ironically to the unsolicited ascriptions offered by Rahab and the Gibeonites.
11 Achan's words hint that he may not understand the gravity of his offense and expects some measure of leniency. He uses the more general term *ḥatṭa'* (7:20), whereas both YHWH and the narrator utilize the more specific term *ma'al* which denotes transgression against holy things (7:1, 11).
12 The phrase "those who carry water and cut wood" occurs only in these two texts.
13 The precedent for expansion of Deuteronomy's prescribed boundaries has already been set in geographical terms by the concessions granted to the tribes of Reuben,

Gad, and half-Manasseh. Although they are reckoned as Israelites, they have been allowed to settle outside the boundaries of the land as originally specified (Numbers 32:1–33; 34:1-12; Deuteronomy 1:6–8; Joshua 1:12–18; 22:1–34). Their story conveys all the ambiguity characteristic of the stories of Israel's contact with Canaan; see David Jobling (1986: 88–147).

Robert Polzin (1980: 80–91, 115–23) has commented on these stories' power to challenge Deuteronomic dogmatism and to present a case for flexibility. He remarks: "The situation of the Canaanites viz-à-viz the justice and mercy of God is amazingly close to that of the Israelites" (89). Through the stories of Rahab and the Gibeonites, a voice of "critical traditionalism" comments on key Deuteronomic texts by suggesting connections between Israel's situation and that of the peoples of the land.

ASSUMING THE BODY OF THE HEIR APPARENT

David's Lament

Mark K. George

What does the Old Testament mean when it refers to "Israel" or the "Israelites"? It strikes me that the Old Testament is quite unsettled about how these terms are to be constructed or defined. Indeed, the Old Testament seems to be a series of attempts to define these terms.

In the text, "Israel" traces its origins back to Abraham, who is promised in Genesis 12:1–2 that he will have land, that he will be made into a great nation, and that he will be a blessing. Another definition is constructed when the actual name "Israel" is given to Jacob, Abraham's grandson, by God, who comments that Jacob/Israel has "striven with God and with humans" (Genesis 32:28; NRSV; cf. 35:10). The Passover celebration and the Exodus from Egypt construct yet another definition for "Israel" and "Israelites." The Passover lamb is to be slaughtered by every Israelite household on the fourteenth day of the first month of the year, and then the blood of the lamb is to be sprinkled on Israelite door-posts (Exodus 12:1–13). This act of cutting creates and defines the community – this is the nation whose children God did not slay, because of the blood on their door-posts.

THE KING'S TWO BODIES

The monarchy is another attempt at constructing definitions for "Israel" and "Israelite." Kingship in Israel is thought in terms of, or thought through, the body of the king. Kingship *is* bodies, the bodies of those who have become king, because the body of the king created a particular set of issues and concerns for Israel. In Israel's ideology of kingship, the king is the embodiment of both the deity and the nation.

To construct the identity of the king is, at least in part, to simultaneously construct the identity of the nation. The king is the embodiment of the nation (its "head"; 1 Samuel 15:17). Who the king was, what family and tribe he was from, what he looked like, his relationships with others – these and other discourses provided a model for how "Israel" and "Israelite" were to be defined.[1]

For Israel there is also a theological dimension to the identity of the king, and this raises particular problems and concerns for the biblical discourse on kingship. The king, as the representative of the deity, acts as the earthly embodiment of God in whatever he does. The problem this creates, and the anxiety it produces, concerns the theological injunctions against making any images of God. The second commandment expressly forbids such images ("You shall not make for yourself an idol, whether in the form of anything that is in heaven above, or that is on the earth beneath, or that is in the water under the earth"; Exodus 20:4; cf. also Deuteronomy 5:8). This injunction is related to a claim in Deuteronomy that, since YHWH had no form when YHWH spoke to the people at Horeb, the people should not make any idol or image of YHWH (Deuteronomy 4:15–20).[2] Constructing the body of the king in theological terms stands in tension with, if not outright violation of, these injunctions.

There is another concern and anxiety created by the body of the king: fertility and procreation. Kingship brought with it changes, including the expectation of hereditary succession.[3] The king's *son* was to rule after his death. But if the actions of the earthly king mirror and represent those of the deity, how does one theologically explain hereditary succession in a monotheistic community? How can the deity have a son when the deity has no consort with whom to procreate?[4]

For the community that most likely produced the discourse on kingship, namely those returning from exile in Babylon, hereditary succession may have been a prominent concern, as they attempted to determine who did or did not have rights within the community – who was, or was not, an "Israelite," part of "Israel." Only if one could construct oneself as an 'Israelite" could one participate in the community and inherit the promises made to Abraham.

DAVID'S LAMENT

This concern with hereditary succession – how to establish such succession and interpret it theologically – helps to explain the presence of David's lament over Saul and Jonathan in 2 Samuel 1:17–27. This lament comes at a crucial moment in the narrative. In 2 Samuel 1:1–16, the Amalekite messenger informs David of the deaths of Saul and Jonathan, David and his men mourn these deaths, and David kills the Amalekite for claiming to have slain YHWH's anointed. In 2 Samuel 2:1–5, David inquires of YHWH about going up to Judah, receives a positive response, and is crowned king in Hebron. The narrative could have moved directly from 1:16 to 2:1 with no discernible break in its progression. So why, at such an important moment in the story of David's accession to the throne, is this lament included?

The lament appears to address the cultural anxiety regarding fertility. Readers know that David has previously been anointed by YHWH (1 Samuel

16:13), and at this point in the text we might expect David simply to become the new leader after Saul's death. This was the pattern in the period that preceded that of the monarchy (the period of the judges), when YHWH could raise up whomever he desired as the new leader in Israel by sending his spirit upon the chosen person (e.g., Gideon in Judges 6:34; Samson in Judges 13:25; 14:6, 19; 15:14). But Saul was a king, not a judge, and hereditary succession dictated that one of his sons succeed him. Although it is not a new idea in the Genesis–Kings narrative (see Judges 8:22, where the people request Gideon, his son and grandson to rule over them), hereditary succession has not actually taken place up to this point. How could it be explained theologically?

The lament provides one answer. The text is clear that, although David is YHWH's anointed, he is the son of Jesse, not of Saul. If hereditary succession is to be maintained, David must be created as Saul's son. Others have noted the political necessity of David's being viewed as Saul's son, but more than politics are at issue here if hereditary succession is to be taken seriously. David needs, in some sense, to be legitimate – to be Saul's son. Consciously or unconsciously, this appears to be one of the reasons why the lament is included at this point in the text of Samuel.

In the lament, the conspiracy between David and Jonathan to create a son, or more specifically to create David as Saul's son and thus as heir apparent, comes to completion. It is in their relationship that we see the politics of male homosociality, what Eve Kosofsky Sedgwick has termed "male homosocial desire," operating in the text, as Jonathan and David produce what has not been produced before: a "body" created by men alone. No woman or female consort is needed. Human (and divine) fertility is answered via this male homosocial desire, for when the question of succession arises again, regarding who will succeed David, it is YHWH himself who authorizes David's and Jonathan's relationship and conspiracy.

BODY(IES) COUNT

There are many and various bodies, body parts, and extensions of bodies mentioned in 2 Samuel 1:17–27: Saul, Jonathan, the slain, the daughters of the Philistines and Israel, the sons of Judah, eagles, lions, blood, fat, the uncircumcised, a shield, sword, and bow, and clothing. Live and dead, male and female, animal and human, body parts and extensions of those bodies, . . . bodies fill this lament. It is, however, the *absence* of bodies that becomes the issue at this moment in the text. Saul and his three sons have been killed in the battle with the Philistines, and their bodies have been hung on the walls of Beth-shan (1 Samuel 31:8–10, 12). With the deaths of Saul and Jonathan, the heir apparent, the political leadership of the nation has died, and the question of who will become king, what body will take Saul's place as heir and "embody" the nation, comes to the fore. This is one of the concerns, one aspect of Israel's anxiety, which is present in this lament about bodies, and which the lament seeks to address by means of David's claim to the throne as Saul's son.[5]

Eying bodies

The lament focuses our attention on two pairs of (male) individuals: Saul and Jonathan, and Jonathan and David. Saul and Jonathan are easily recognized as the focus of the lament because they are each named in it four times. No others are explicitly named. But Saul and Jonathan are not merely named in the lament; they are intimately bound together, both by the structure and the content of the lament.

Structurally, the names Saul and Jonathan are arranged chiastically in verses 22 and 23. In verse 22 the pattern is Jonathan–Saul: "the bow of Jonathan did not turn back,/the sword of Saul did not return empty." In verse 23, the pattern is Saul–Jonathan: "Saul and Jonathan,/beloved and lovely!" These two men, their lives and their bodies, intersect and cross each other even as the legs of the chiasm do. Saul and Jonathan are, of course, father and son, and have familial and patrilineal bonds. But they are also connected to each other as king and heir apparent, a socio-political bond, a bond created by familial and patrilineal bonds. In addition, in the absence of any knowledge about David's being anointed by Samuel, one might have expected a third bond between Saul and Jonathan to have developed in the future, that of men upon whom the spirit of YHWH rested. But we as readers know that this bond will never develop between them, because the spirit of YHWH now rests on a different man: David.

The naming of Saul and Jonathan, and the structural binding of them together, particularizes them. The lament is not just about any two men, or any father and son, but about specific, individual men, and the content of the lament focuses our attention on their particularity. In verse 22, each man is referred to in terms of a weapon, something possessed by and an extension of the body: a bow for Jonathan, and a sword for Saul. The content of the chiasm focuses our attention even more. In verse 23, it is the bodies of these two men that are celebrated: "Saul and Jonathan,/beloved and lovely!" Beloved for whom and what they were, they were also lovely in appearance. Their bodies – their physical characteristics – are now explicitly the focus of the lament. And, with our attention focused on their bodies, the interrelatedness of these two men suggested by the structure of the chiasm is made explicit: "In life and in death they were not divided." The deaths of these two men, of the father and son, the king and heir apparent, raise the question of who, and what body, will fill their places. It is this question that David seeks to answer in the lament.

David and Jonathan are the other pair that receives our attention in the lament. Again, the structure of the lament focuses our attention. The refrain

"How the mighty are fallen" is used at the beginning and end (verses 19 and 27) to form an inclusion for the entire lament. It is also used in verse 25, and this provides a secondary division of the text, with verse 26 set off from the rest of the lament. This is the verse in which David inserts himself – into the lament as well as into Jonathan's "body" – by stating the importance of his relationship with Jonathan. Recalling his relationship with Jonathan, and its significance to him, is important for David, for it is on the basis of this relationship that he inserts himself into the role of king.

ASSUMING THE "BODY"

There are three ways in which David inserts himself into the lament and into Jonathan's social "body." Two of them have to do with the language of verse 26. First, David assumes Jonathan's body by making this a personal lament. First person pronouns are used here for the first and only time in the lament: "I am distressed . . . my brother Jonathan . . . pleasant to me . . . love for me." Without being named in the lament itself, David is inserted into it, and the lament is no longer only about Saul and Jonathan. Our attention has been fixed on Saul and Jonathan, but with this first person lament the speaker, David, is now present along with them.

Love and politics

Second, David expresses, for the first time, the importance of Jonathan's love to him. The political overtones and nuances present in the "love" language used here have long been commented on by biblical scholars (McCarter 1980: 342; 1984: 77). What has not received much attention is the politics of male homosocial desire which this language and this relationship suggest, for there are both political and sexual overtones present in this language.

Danna Nolan Fewell and David Gunn have noted that David casts his relationship with Jonathan in a particular light:

> The point of comparison is women. Jonathan belongs in the relationship in the position of a woman, even if only to surpass her . . . Jonathan is such a "son of perversity and rebellion" that he puts (even) a woman to shame.
>
> (Fewell and Gunn 1993: 151)

Their comments point out that David's comparison of Jonathan with women explicitly introduces gender and sexuality as issues, both in the text and in their relationship.

Women serve as the means of comparison in the relationship, solidifying this male relationship, and in turn receiving their identity in relation to men and male relationships.[6] In speaking of how very "pleasant" Jonathan was to him (*na'amta*), however, David uses language that one might expect between a man and a woman in love (e.g., Song of Songs 7:7). Fewell and Gunn, in their reading of the lament, suggestively tease out the homosexual overtones present in the relationship between Jonathan and David. They point out that Jonathan's sexuality is in question both in the lament and in Saul's invective – his sexuality is being constructed in terms of a woman. But Fewell and Gunn do not go far enough in following out the implications of their claim that Jonathan is (so to speak) a woman. Jonathan may be feminized – he may be located in the relationship with David in the position of a woman – but he is still a man. To read with Fewell and Gunn, then, we could say that Jonathan is both/and, both a "woman" and a man: he coopts a woman's body with his own body and makes it into a man's body. The sum of male power is maintained in the text, even if one of the males in the relationship is feminized. Women are (again) left without a subject position (or a sexuality or identity) of their own in the text, because men can coopt this position. Yet, while the sum of male power is maintained, ambiguity and instability exist within that power. If the sexuality of Jonathan, the male heir apparent, can be constructed in terms of a woman, then the construction of sexuality for any male body is variable and available (able?) to be constructed differently.

Men loving men, and men promoting the interests of men

Fewell and Gunn conclude from their reading of the lament that David capitalizes on his relationship with Jonathan by defining it in terms favorable to himself (he was the object of Jonathan's affections), and that Jonathan's loveliness and love become political endorsements (Fewell and Gunn 1993: 151). In terms of the continuum of male homosocial desire, Fewell and Gunn's homosexual reading of the lament situates Jonathan's and David's relationship near the homosexual end of the spectrum. But Jonathan and David's relationship is not simply to be characterized as "homosexual." It is also "homosocial," because men promote the interests of men. The "love" between these two men flows into the actions taken to promote the interests of these same men.[7]

From the moment these men first met, when the "soul" (or "life" or "being": *nephesh*) of Jonathan was bound to David's "soul" (*nephesh*), Jonathan and David conspired together to create a body for David. The binding of Jonathan's soul to David's in 1 Samuel 18:1 carries connotations of banding together in a conspiracy.[8] Jonathan loved David "as his own soul" (1 Samuel 18:1). He made a covenant with David "because he loved him as his own soul" (18:3). Jonathan warned David that Saul wanted to kill him, then spoke to his father and convinced him to allow David to return

169

(19:2–7). Jonathan went out to meet with David to inform him that, although Saul sought David, Saul would not find David, and then reaffirmed that David would be king, an action that resulted in the two men making a covenant before YHWH (23:16–18).

Jonathan's continual actions toward David, and the covenants these two men establish and re-establish between themselves (1 Samuel 18:3; 20:16; 23:18) place their relationship on Sedgwick's continuum of homosocial desire. Jonathan's emotional reaction to David at their first meeting ("Jonathan loved him as his own soul"; 1 Samuel 18:1) explicitly situates their relationship near the homosexual end of the spectrum. But the actions he then takes toward David are more homosocial in nature: they further the interests of these men.

Jonathan removes his cloak, armor, sword, bow, and belt, and places them on David (18:4). Others have noted the political significance of this exchange of clothing (McCarter 1980: 305). If we read Jonathan's clothing and weapons as an extension of the body, as an outer layer of skin, we might say that Jonathan steps out of his skin and disembodies himself. Divesting himself of his clothes or "skin," Jonathan divests himself of his social "bodies": the familial (that of the son) and the political (that of the heir apparent). These are the social bodies at stake in Jonathan's relationship with David, the bodies they conspire to create. Or, to put it another way, the characteristics which Jonathan divests himself of, the familial and political, are the same characteristics with which he and David invest David's body. In the lament, these are the two axes of the (literary) chiasm, the two bonds which link Saul and Jonathan. In addition, David is able to establish a third bond with Saul, one that Jonathan could not: that of men upon whom the spirit of YHWH has rested. It is clearly these two bodies, of the son and heir apparent, that "suit" David: he can wear Jonathan's clothing, his "skin," whereas in the battle with Goliath in the immediately preceding chapter, 1 Samuel 17, David cannot wear Saul's armor: it does not "suit" him.

This exchange of clothing comes after the cutting/making of a covenant between David and Jonathan (18:3), and, as McCarter (1980: 305) has argued, this exchange "seems to be a kind of 'sign' or formal gesture that seals the pact." David and Jonathan make a series of covenants in the text (18:3; 20:8, 16; 23:18). The cutting of such covenants echoes the cutting of the covenant between YHWH and Abraham, and the ratification ceremony and sacrifice that accompanied it.[9] These covenants create a new identity for David, as part of Jonathan's patrilineage.

Nancy Jay, in a cross-cultural study of several societies in which blood sacrifice is performed, has argued that sacrifices establish patrilineal descent groups between those men participating in the sacrifice (1992: 30–60). Social and religious lines of descent are established via sacrifice rather than via childbirth, allowing men to transcend their dependence upon women's reproductive powers.[10] This suggests that, in making these covenants with

Jonathan, David becomes a part of Jonathan's (and therefore Saul's) patri-lineage, resulting in David's becoming a legitimate heir of Saul, able to inherit his property (kingship). Jonathan, on the other hand, is able to ensure that what should be his inheritance, the kingship, is passed on to a person of his own choosing.[11]

A good son's lament

The third way in which David inserts himself into Jonathan's "body," and thus into the role of king, is by the lament itself. One of the duties of a good son in the ancient Near East, at least in terms of literary convention (if not actual custom), was to raise up a lament over his dead father. In the Ugaritic tale of Aqht, Dan'il, a righteous chief, had no son. Dan'il was distressed over this, for there were twelve proper duties a son was to perform for his father during his father's life and after his father's death. One of these duties was to free the father's spirit from the earth after death. Dan'il lamented because, with the death of Aqht, Dan'il once again had no son who could perform these duties.

Some understanding of what it means to free a father's spirit from the ground comes from another Ugaritic text, that of the liturgy of Ammurapi III for his dead father Niqmaddu III.[12] Ammurapi acted to assure the legiti-macy of the royal succession by worshiping the ancestors of the new king, and to initiate the cult of his dead father. That is, Ammurapi freed his father's spirit from the earth.

By raising up a lament for Saul and Jonathan, David acts as Saul's son, performing the duties of a son for his dead father. Such actions are appropri-ate for David on the basis of his relationship with Jonathan. Having become part of Jonathan's patrilineage he has become Saul's "son," and as son he carries out the appropriate actions expected of a good son by lamenting for his patrilineal "father" (both Jonathan and Saul). Inserting himself into the lament, David calls to mind the relationship that incorporated him into Saul's patrilineage, and then carries out the appropriate actions for a son within that patrilineage (and it is significant that, at least in the text, it is David, not Ishbosheth, who is recorded as lamenting for his "father").

DIVINE PATRILINEAGE AND NATIONAL IDENTITY

There remains another concern, a more subtle anxiety, that needs to be addressed: that of divine fertility. As I asked earlier, if the king is the earthly representative of the deity, but the culture is monotheistic, how will the issue of succession be resolved? The deaths of Saul and Jonathan left open the question of succession, of who would or could lay claim to the throne. But is this issue a theological issue? Prior to the monarchy, presumably not, for Yʜᴡʜ could simply designate and anoint a new leader. With the monarchy, however, the theological issue of succession becomes precisely that, the issue of the "issue," of fertility, since Yʜᴡʜ does not have "issue." How does a deity who has no consort procreate? To put it another way, how can the king, as representative of a deity for whom procreation is by definition impossible, procreate? How can he have heirs?

This issue has not presented itself to Israel before. In the period of the judges, the issue of the judge was not a concern, for a different judge would be raised up when the need arose, and Yʜᴡʜ could choose whomever Yʜᴡʜ pleased. Things are different in the monarchy; hereditary succession is part of what distinguishes the monarchy from the period of the judges. Saul is Israel's first king; although hereditary succession is presumed for Saul, how was this to be addressed and explained theologically? Matters are complicated even more with the deaths of both Saul and Jonathan. From where is a new king to come if hereditary succession is to work? How does the deity create a new king? The lament betrays a certain cultural anxiety over the "issue," revealing what is at stake for monotheism when the issue of an heir for the king arises.

In David's lament, and in the earlier conspiring of Jonathan and David, this theological problem is negotiated by male homosocial desire to complete a new royal body for David. Jonathan and David create this body across the bodies of men, excluding women's bodies. Jonathan steps out of his skin, and David steps into it: they produce a body for David between themselves. By creating this body without the need for women, the theological concern to preserve monotheism is addressed: no women, and hence no consorts, are required. It is produced in the relationships between men, with one of the men becoming feminized in the relationship.

That this is an accepted solution becomes apparent when the issue of succession arises again in Israel, with David. In the dynastic promise made by Yʜᴡʜ to David in 2 Samuel 7, Yʜᴡʜ tells David in verse 12, "when your days are fulfilled and you lie down with your fathers, I will raise up your seed after you, which shall come forth from your 'body' [or 'belly': mēʿeh]." Male homosocial desire is at work again. Only this time, in this relationship, *David* is feminized, not Jonathan, for it is out of *David's* "body" (or "belly") that his heirs will come. Women are once again excluded in the text – theologically, socially, and even biologically.

POSITIONS

David's lament reflects and addresses the anxiety of a culture in which the king is the embodiment of both the nation and the deity. The answer to this anxiety, both narratively and theologically, is provided by the politics of male homosocial desire and the "body" produced for David in his relationship with Jonathan. David is able to accede to the throne, and thereby maintain Jonathan and Saul's property (i.e., the kingship), as a member of Jonathan and Saul's patrilineal descent system. Theologically, David's relationship with Jonathan provides justification for hereditary succession, because patrilineal descent can be established in the relationships and covenants between men, human and divine. For the community that produced this text, then, David's lament provides a definition of "Israel" and "Israelite" that makes possible, through the relationships and covenants of men, membership in the community of "Israel."

NOTES

1 For a fuller discussion of the ways in which the construction of identity takes place in the discourse on kingship, see my dissertation, "Body Works: Power, the Construction of Identity, and Gender in the Discourse on Kingship" (George 1995).

2 Eilberg-Schwartz (in this volume) provides a helpful discussion of what he views as the three major groupings in Israelite literature concerning the body of God (no body or form, a human form, and an asexual body), views which create tensions within the text, as they undoubtedly did within the community that produced the text.

3 Following Buccellati (1967) and Ishida (1977). Alt (1989) has provided the classic statement of the opposing position, that hereditary succession was not part of the monarchy from its inception.

4 See Eilberg-Schwartz (in this volume) for some of the "contradictions of monotheism" involved in the question of divine sexuality.

5 David is not the only candidate for the throne. Abner makes Ishbosheth king over Israel in 2 Samuel 2:8–9. Ishbosheth is said to be a son of Saul (although his name is absent from those sons cited in 1 Samuel 14:49). The king's body, however, must be legitimately constructed in both human and divine terms (e.g., family, physical characteristics, and theological characteristics, particularly that the king be a man after YHWH's own heart). The text does not inform the reader about how Ishbosheth's body has been constructed; we are told only his age, the length of his reign, and his name ('ish-bōsheth: "man of shame"). Thus, in terms of the social construction of their bodies, it is uncertain whether or not Ishbosheth has the qualifications to be king, while 1 Samuel 16–31 makes clear that David does have the qualifications (his body has been appropriately constructed). The lament makes clear that David is the appropriate candidate for the throne in terms of hereditary succession as well.

6 Of course, by employing women as the standard of comparison, David destabilizes this love. Jonathan's love might be better than the love of women, but the love of women is always already present in Jonathan's love, or at least David's evaluation of it, as the necessary term which is excluded or absent in order to give Jonathan's love meaning.

7 In Sedgwick's terms, David and Jonathan demonstrate the unity of the continuum between "men loving men" and "men promoting the interests of men", and this extends at the very least to the social, familial, economic, and political realms, if not to the erotic as well.

8 In Koehler-Baumgartner (1985: 860); see also Ackroyd (1975: 213–14).

9 Dennis McCarthy (1978: 91) argues that the idiom "cutting a covenant" (kārat berît) is based on the association of symbolic rite and covenant. Mendenhall (1962:

720) notes that the ratification of covenants frequently included the cutting up of an animal (or animals) in a sacrifice to seal it.

10 There are some problems with Jay's theory, as others have noted (Nye 1993: 227–228; Exum 1993: 119), but her work remains useful for its insights into male relationships in the Old Testament.

11 Jonathan was also able to get David's promise not to cut off his love from Jonathan's house after Jonathan's death (1 Samuel 20:15), a promise David fulfilled as king by seeking out Jonathan's son Mephibosheth and bringing him to David's table (2 Samuel 9:1–13). David's actions toward Jonathan's family were part of his responsibility to Jonathan's patrilineal descent system.

12 KTU 1.161. Ammurapi III was the last king of Ugarit, *ca.* 1200 B.C.E. Levine and Tarragon (1984: 654) describe this text as a "canonical liturgy," stating "[t]he text of our liturgy was undoubtedly canonical, to be used whenever succession took place," a comment which is suggestive for this discussion of David's lament.

10

UTOPIA AND PORNOGRAPHY
IN EZEKIEL

Violence, Hope, and the Shattered Male Subject

Jan William Tarlin

Read in its entirety, the book of Ezekiel radiates violence – violence in multiple forms. First there is the violence in the form of war, massacre, and exile that Yahweh has brought on Israel, is bringing on Judah, and will bring against the surrounding nations. Then there is the graphically depicted violence against women that pervades both the parable of Yahweh's people as the unfaithful adopted daughter/bride, in the notorious chapter 16, and the allegory of Jerusalem and Samaria as promiscuous sisters in the equally notorious chapter 23. Finally there is the violence to which Yahweh subjects the prophet himself: exile, seizure-like vision, aphonia, and paralysis.

This aura of violence makes it difficult enough simply to survive a cursory reading of Ezekiel. For readers trying to approach the text at a level of engagement sufficient to produce literary and/or theological interpretations, however, Ezekiel's violence becomes even more insidious. Insidious because the more deeply one becomes involved with this text, the harder it is to avoid the impression that its violence is deeply eroticized.

The reader is repeatedly invited to take up the position of voyeur before spectacles of carnage as Yahweh puts one people after another to fire, sword, or death by drowning; the sufferings of the slaughtered are presented in visual imagery that affords a high degree of scopophilic satisfaction. In passages such as chapters 16 and 23, the prophet, speaking the words of Yahweh, invites the reader to identify with the triumphant pleasures of male sadism as the text gleefully details the assertion of mastery over would-be rebellious women via the infliction of humiliation and pain. In his visionary state, the prophet in turn assumes a masochistic posture with which he invites the reader to identify: experiencing a homoerotic ecstasy through self-debasement in submission to (a decidedly male) Yahweh's violent will. Indeed, if one defines pornography as the imaginative depiction of eroticized violence and/or violent eroticism that exceeds a given culture's permissible norms, it is hard to escape the conclusion that, for contemporary western readers at least, Ezekiel must function as pornography.

Frightening as it may be to encounter a biblical book that invites, indeed seduces, us into an exploration of realms of the erotic in which few of us are

likely to be immediately comfortable, what is probably even more frightening is Ezekiel's implicit suggestion that these realms are somehow intimately
connected to the vision of paradise regained with which the book concludes.
Pornography as a path to utopia? Violence as a harbinger of the world
restored? Ezekiel forces its present-day readers to confront everything that is
most difficult and disturbing about how human desire shapes our spiritual
and political worlds.

I suggest that one possible strategy for engaging in that confrontation can
be developed by following out the implications of some observations offered
by the German film maker Rainer Werner Fassbinder in a remarkable interview given just hours before his untimely death in 1982.[1] Fassbinder had just
completed filming an adaptation of Jean Genet's novel *Querelle from Brest*.
Genet's book, permeated as it is with gay male sado-masochistic eroticism,
had often been condemned as pornographic. The interviewer asked whether
Fassbinder was afraid that his film would meet a similar fate. Fassbinder
replied that he himself thought that *all* his films were pornographic to some
degree because they were all in one way or another utopian. In order to
imagine something that truly goes beyond prevailing social reality, Fassbinder explained, one must shatter that reality and transgress its norms,
thereby entering onto the terrain of the pornographic. "Everything that
reaches the social boundaries, or crosses [them], must necessarily be pornographic in this society" (in Katz 1987: 198).

The equations that Fassbinder makes here between sexual taboo and political repression, between erotic violence and social transformation, between
pornography and utopia, cannot simply be accepted as assertions. These
equations do, however, mark out a territory for theoretical exploration. That
exploration has been undertaken by the feminist theorist Kaja Silverman in
a series of works (1983; 1988; 1992a). The most important of these for the
purposes of this chapter is the most recent, *Male Subjectivity at the Margins*,
a work indebted in equal parts to Fassbinder's cinematic art and to the
psychoanalytic theory of the French analyst Jacques Lacan. In the remainder
of this chapter, I will summarize those aspects of Silverman's work that are
most useful for meeting the unnerving challenges posed by the text of
Ezekiel and then let the theoretical, cinematic, and prophetic texts meet
head on. The result, I hope, will be a sketch of a new strategy for reading
Ezekiel in this time and place.

Following Lacan, Silverman defines the human as "the subject whose
being has been sacrificed to meaning" (1992a: 4). This constitutive sacrifice
sets in motion the process by which eros, gender, violence, and politics
become inextricably interwoven with each other in the making of human
culture. Silverman explains:

> Lack of being is the irreducible condition of subjectivity. In acceding
> to language, the subject forfeits all existential reality and forgoes any

future possibility of "wholeness." If we were in possession of an instrument which would permit us to penetrate deep into the innermost recesses of the human psyche we would find not identity but a void . . . [T]he [human] subject is acephalic . . . headless, or to be more precise, devoid of "self" . . . It speaks but with *"the voice of no one:"* This subject . . . is devoid both of form and object; it can perhaps be defined as pure lack and hence as "desire for nothing."

(Silverman 1992a: 4)

Silverman, still following Lacan, describes this forfeiture of being in exchange for a subject position within the symbolic (i.e., linguistic) order as "symbolic castration" (1992a: 5). By becoming human, by submitting to the mediation of language in its relations with its own body and with both its human and natural environments, the subject has been violently torn from its own being. For the human to take on an identity, for the subject to assume subjectivity, the imagination must attempt to suture the wound inflicted by language through the creation of a fictive "self" that "fills the void at the center of subjectivity with an illusory plenitude" (1992a: 5). Further, for this illusion to be complete, the objectless subject's "desire for nothing" must be "translated" into desire for something by the creation of imaginary objects in relation to which subjectivity is defined and elaborated (1992a: 4). Silverman situates this imaginary effort to transcend symbolic castration along two axes: that of the ego, the fictive self, and that of the fantasmatic, the realm of imaginative scenarios in which the ego articulates itself through its desire for objects (1992a: 7).

The ego, according to Silverman, is built from images offered by the world around us "ranging from the subject's mirror image and the parental imagoes to the whole plethora of textually based representations which each of us imbibes daily" (1992a: 3). For example, "in the case of children: dolls, picture books, trains, or toy guns" (Silverman 1983: 160). These examples (the toy gun as much as the picture book), along with others such as the identification of the mirror image as "self" or the construction of specific others as "parents," are all here understood as being "textually based representations." The "ego" or "self" is thus the shape that the shapeless subject assumes through the incorporation of pieces of its symbolic environment magnetized by desire.[2]

The ego, then, is the precondition for a human identity that can articulate itself by desiring objects, the fiction that facilitates the shaping of the subject that speaks with "the voice of no one" into a subjectivity that speaks as someone; but it is also something more. The ego is also the first concretization of the subject's desire. As such, the ego serves both as a model for its own objects and as the entity that opens the space within the subject where objects can be organized into scenarios of desire. Through these scenarios, the "someone" the subject has become articulates itself ever more elaborately by playing out its desire for objects modeled on the object that brought it into being: its own ego.

These scenarios, which Silverman calls collectively the subject's fantasmatic, are constructed, like the ego and its objects, from representations that come to the subject from the outside. Fantasmatic scenarios derive first of all from the dramas of adult desire being played out in the subject's nuclear and extended families (1992a:7), but grow to encompass, as we shall see, the exemplary stories of the subject's community, nation, and culture (1992a: 15–51). What is most important to note at this point, however, is that the ego facilitates the subject's incorporation of scenarios of desire dictated from outside, locating itself and its objects in internal dramas patterned after the plots in which it has been cast by the desiring selves that make up its social world.

Silverman further argues that the drama of desire, in which the ego elaborates its identity, recapitulates the original sacrifice of being to meaning that brought the subject into existence, and that this re-enactment is most acute in the establishment of gender identity. In western culture, Silverman contends, normative gender identity is established by identifying the biologically masculine body with a fictive self-hood that denies and projects the castration that constitutes human subjectivity, claiming for itself instead a delusory wholeness, power, and mastery. The projected castration, lack, and weakness constitute a female subjectivity normatively identified with biological femininity. Thus the common violence we all suffer in the process of becoming human is re-presented as the violent subordination of female to male (Silverman 1988: 1–41).

According to Silverman, this re-presentation is achieved through the exploitation of important ambiguities in the relationship between the anatomical penis and the signifying phallus. The phallus, in Lacanian theory, is a *signifier* and not a bodily organ. As signifier, the phallus stands

> for those things which have been partitioned off from the subject during the various phases of its constitution, and which will never be restored to it, all of which could be summarized as "fullness of being". . . . The phallus is thus a signifier for the organic reality or needs which the subject relinquishes in order to achieve meaning, in order to gain access to the symbolic register.
>
> (Silverman 1983: 183)

Silverman points out, however, that the Lacanian phallus tends to slide from signifying the being which any human subject sacrifices to meaning to signifying specifically "the cultural privileges and positive values which define male subjectivity within patriarchal society, but from which the female subject remains isolated" (1983: 183). In other words, the phallus begins to look a lot like the penis that Lacanians insist it is not. As Silverman's work has developed, she has come to situate this slide within Lacanian discourse as a local manifestation of a misidentification of phallus with penis that constitutes the great enabling fiction of western patriarchal culture (1992a: 15–51). The equation of phallus with penis is what allows the violent subordination of human beings to language to be re-presented as the violent subordination of female to male.[3]

This re-presentation, in Silverman's view, is the basis not only of individual gender identity and of the relations between men and women but also of our culture's entire sense of reality. If the structure of society and the content of culture are fundamentally strategies for dealing with the violence by which human subjectivity is created and with the infinite, objectless desire which is its consequence, then the grand narrative in which the male embodies the all-sufficient while the female embodies irremediable lack is the lynch-pin of western reality. Silverman defines such lynch-pin scenarios as "dominant fictions" (1992a: 15–51).

Now, although dominant fictions do, indeed, dominate, they are not, according to Silverman, invulnerable. The western dominant fiction is shaken at the level of individual subjectivity when, for example, a non-normative mutation in familial or communal structures produces a biologically masculine individual with a subjectivity constructed around representations of lack or a biologically feminine individual whose self-hood is shaped by images of all-sufficiency (1992a: 339–88; 1988: 129–86). At the cultural level, Silverman posits the existence of what she calls "historical traumas": natural or human produced catastrophes that force whole societies to confront the vulnerability and insufficiency of men on the one hand and the power and competence of women on the other (1992a: 52–121).

Silverman turns to Fassbinder's cinematic art to illustrate the theory that I have just sketched. In Fassbinder's work the dialectical relations of ego and object, self and society, gender and the real, eros and political power, take on visceral forms. These forms are determined by an equally visceral conviction that our humanity is conferred on us at the cost of our violent expropriation from our bodies and our environment (1992a: 125–56; 214–96).

One example will have to serve here as a taste of Fassbinder's remarkable output. *In a Year of Thirteen Moons* is exemplary in many ways of Fassbinder's work. Erwin, the central character in this film, has had his genitals surgically removed because the man with whom he has fallen in love will, as a general rule anyway, only make love with women. Erwin does not become a transsexual, however. Neither man nor woman, in different contexts he plays the roles of homosexual, transvestite, heterosexual, and even father in the nuclear family he helped create before his transformation. Erwin has sacrificed his penis and rejected any claim to possessing the phallus, thus fully assuming the burden of symbolic castration. This new creature is a visitor from a utopia beyond the western dominant fiction. Erwin brings havoc and tragedy, but also ecstasy in its most literal sense wherever he goes: in the world of street hustlers and outcasts, in the domestic worlds of his family and friends, in the world of high finance where the man who is the object of his obsession is a major player. Before his suicide which ends the film, Erwin gives both those on screen and those in the theater a vertiginous taste of the fragility of western "reality."

If *In a Year of Thirteen Moons* is quintessential Fassbinder, it is not hard to see why Silverman calls Fassbinder's cinema "an instrument for the ruination of masculinity . . . and for what can only be called, in the strictest sense of the word, masochistic ecstasy" – a way of "returning to the male body all of the violence which it has historically directed elsewhere" (1992a: 9). This return causes the "male psyche" to be "in effect lifted out of the male body and made to feel the pain of other bodies" (1992a:10). In Fassbinder's "ruination of masculinity," Silverman sees a utopian prefiguring of forms of human subjectivity that allows the violence that creates the human subject to be suffered in solidarity by all human beings. When the masculine subjectivity constructed by the denial and projection of symbolic castration is shattered, the forms of domination and abuse endemic to western patriarchal culture come to an end.

And that brings me back to Ezekiel. I want to argue that in the text of Ezekiel we late twentieth-century western readers may see a male subjectivity suffering the effects of a historical trauma and oscillating wildly between the experience of masochistic, ecstatic, utopian ruination on the one hand, and the attempt to defend itself from that experience by sadistically inflicting suffering on women and foreigners on the other. Ezekiel, then, may be viewed as pornographic in the sense that, like Fassbinder's films, it vividly exposes the link between our erotic practices and the violence that constitutes both the human subject and that subject's erotic desires. The exposure of that link between eros and violence breaks the taboos that shore up the western dominant fiction; and thus the book of Ezekiel, like Fassbinder's cinema, reaches and crosses the social boundaries: attaining utopia by the path of pornography.

The text of Ezekiel crosses the social boundaries by shattering male subjectivity and leaving in its wake fragmented prefigurations of a hope not readily distinguishable from nightmare. This shattering and these fragments occur, in Silverman's terms, at the level of both the male fantasmatic and the male ego. The following will indicate some of the aspects of the text of Ezekiel on which a reading might focus in order to recount the shattering and lift up the fragments.

The prophet Ezekiel is also a priest. That is, Ezekiel is not only a male but a male capable of atoning for his people, making good his people's lack. In this sense he is a male who embodies male all-sufficiency to a superlative degree, a degree that makes him capable of conferring the benefits of male subjectivity on his people as a whole. But Ezekiel is a priest in exile. A historical trauma has divided his community and uprooted him from his temple and his holy city. The social setting in which the scenario of atonement can be carried out has been destroyed; the priestly fantasmatic has been shattered.

Ezekiel the exiled priest is also a prophet, subject to divine will. And Yahweh loses no opportunity to degrade, humiliate, and injure the prophet's priestly body: the base of a male subjectivity carefully constructed and defined by its purity, dignity, and wholeness. The priestly ego is shattered (even, indeed, feminized) by being forced to embrace its own vulnerability, insufficiency, and lack – by being forced to incorporate castration. Yet something remains to be purified and transformed by immersion in the paradisal waters flowing from the heavenly temple at the heart of the divinized city (47:1–6). Like the whole house of Israel in the valley of dry bones (chapter 37), the prophet can be reduced to fragments and rebuilt, purified, with a new heart and a new spirit (36:22–28).

Silverman insists that one of the principal functions of fantasmatic scenarios of desire for objects is to establish a place within which subjectivity can articulate itself. "Although the [human subject] is in a sense not only *nothing* but *nowhere*, every subject lives its desire from *some place*, and the fantasmatic is the mechanism through which that subject position is articulated" (1992a: 5). It is precisely this secure positionality that is destroyed for Ezekiel as both priest and prophet.

As priest, Ezekiel is deprived of his position in social reality by his exile. Exile separates Ezekiel from land, nation, city, temple, and sacrifice, which are the objects that construct the scenario of priestly desire. Without this scenario, the priest has no place.

Ezekiel's displacement as prophet, however, is even more radical than his displacement as priest. In visionary ecstasy inspired by the Spirit of Yahweh, Ezekiel is cut loose from all temporal and geographical mooring. The hand of Yahweh drags the prophet, at times quite literally by the hair, back and forth between Jerusalem and Babylon, from the depths of Sheol where Yahweh's enemies perish, to the high heavens where the divine chariot rides. Even when clearly physically located in Babylon, Ezekiel is often forced by Yahweh to act as though he is in Jerusalem, undergoing its indignities and deprivations as it experiences siege, destruction, and dispersion. Likewise, Ezekiel is carried from one point to another in time at the will of the deity, positioned as witness to the past sins of Israel and Judah, the destruction of the northern kingdom, the present undoing of the south, and the future restoration of a paradisal united Israel and a regenerated cosmos.

Deprived of the fictive security of a place within a fantasmatic scene, Ezekiel begins to assume the instability of the primal human subject. The prophet can be whisked anywhere because he *is* nowhere. This shattering of the fantasmatic goes hand in hand with an unraveling of the ego. Positioned *nowhere*, Ezekiel moves toward the condition of speaking with the voice of *no one* out of the ruins of a shattered male body.

Yahweh forces Ezekiel to undergo the fall of the southern kingdom in his own body. The all-sufficient priestly body is subjected to famine, shorn of its hair, and reduced to muteness and paralysis. This degradation of the self, like its displacement, is part and parcel of the prophet's ecstatic submission to Yahweh, a submission and an ecstasy that, given the unmistakably male characterization of Yahweh in the book of Ezekiel, can only be described as homoerotic masochism. Masochism, as readers of Freud will know, is, within the western dominant fiction, the female perversion *par excellence* (Freud 1962: 23–26; 1963b). Just for good measure, it should also be noted that, within the same dominant fiction, paralysis and muteness are important symptoms of hysteria, the exemplary female neurosis (Breuer and Freud n.d.; Freud 1963b).

His male subjectivity in ruins, but still in the throes of a transcendental male homoerotic relationship, feminized but not female, Ezekiel, like Fassbinder's Erwin, is a visitor from the utopia beyond male and female. The return onto male subjectivity of the violence that males usually inflict on females (or on "inferior" males), the return onto male subjectivity of the lack, weakness, and fragmentation males usually project onto females has, for Ezekiel, created a new form of subjectivity: a person with a penis who has renounced any claim to possessing the phallus. This subjectivity bears and lives the violence that gives rise to the primal human subject in solidarity with other selves rather than inflicting or projecting it upon them. This new subjectivity that voluntarily incorporates symbolic castration in a masculine body is not recognizable to western eyes as either male or female.

If this new subjectivity is frightening in its unfamiliarity, the text also offers Ezekiel – and the reader – an alternative subject position that is frightening precisely because it is all too familiar. In chapters 16 and 23, and in the oracles against the nations, Ezekiel identifies with Yahweh to become a super-male: pumping himself up in his all-sufficiency by gleefully inflicting extravagant violence on women, on foreign "others," and on the very community to which the prophet/priest and his God are bound by covenant (since the women of chapters 16 and 23 are figures meant to represent Yahweh's people). Both the masochistic shattering of the male subject in the interest of human solidarity and the sadistic inflation of that subject in the interest of a pernicious dominant fiction are authorized by the word of Yahweh in Ezekiel. And that violent, unresolved contradiction is perhaps the most disturbing thing about this deeply disturbing biblical text.

In conclusion, I want to raise three questions about my reading of Ezekiel, the answers to which cannot be pursued within the confines of a short chapter. First, what are those of us who read the Hebrew Bible out of theological commitment to do with a prophetic book that gives equal divine sanction to the quest for human solidarity and to the human drive for domination? Second, what are the implications of my reading of Ezekiel for women readers of that text? Can a vision of forms of human subjectivity that embrace the violence that constitutes the primal human subject possibly have any liberatory significance for individuals that already bear a double load of violence – the load that all humans must bear as subjects who have sacrificed being to meaning, and the load that males project onto females in order to avoid bearing our share of the burden? Finally, what can be said about what might motivate any given reader to privilege either solidarity or domination in their particular reading of Ezekiel?

This last question, I think, stakes out the frontier of theory. I use the word frontier here in a double sense. First, it indicates the direction in which I believe theory is most urgently called to move in our present political circumstances. Second, it indicates the point where theory pushes against its limits. For the answer to this question lies in the relation between the primal human subject situated in the agonizing gap between being and meaning and our specific, limited human subjectivities. This relation is perhaps more easily explored through sighs too deep for words than in the more brittle medium of academic language.

NOTES

1 To the best of my knowledge, the full text of this interview is available only on film or video in Dieter Schidor's documentary about Fassbinder, *The Wizard of Babylon*.

2 This refusal of an absolute distinction between the Symbolic (the realm of language and culture) and the Imaginary (the realm of visual fantasy, peculiar to the individual, in which the ego and its objects are formed) is one of Silverman's most radical revisions of "orthodox" Lacanian theory. The full implications of this revision are beyond the scope of this chapter. It is sufficient for my purposes here to note that this move is fundamental to Silverman's reduction of the phallus from a universal signifier to an element in the western patriarchal dominant fiction. See also note 3 below.

3 A non-Lacanian reader might reasonably ask why the signifier that stands in for the being that all humans sacrifice to meaning should be called the phallus in the first place. An "orthodox" Lacanian might answer that the penis with its combination of erection and flaccidity offers the best generally available raw material for constructing a signifier for a "fullness" that is both universally desired and universally unattainable. A full consideration of the debate to which this answer gives rise is beyond the scope of this chapter. Here I will content myself with saying that Silverman's demonstration that this answer locates Lacanian theory itself within the dominant fiction of the patriarchal West opens up the possibility of Lacanian psychoanalysis being revised and appropriated for projects such as the present chapter.

11

"AN IMAGINARY AND DESIRABLE CONVERSE"

Moses and Monotheism as Family Romance[1]

Daniel Boyarin

Freud's description of biblical religion in *Moses and Monotheism* has become hegemonic in contemporary criticism. Howard Eilberg-Schwartz has recently well epitomized a major complex of thoughts in the text:

> Freud sees a connection between the fatherhood of God, the prohibi-
> tion on images, sexual renunciation, and the triumph of spirit over the
> senses. He understands the prohibition on images in terms of the
> gender of God, specifically God's fatherhood, and he sees that prohibi-
> tion as linked to masculine renunciation.
>
> (Eilberg-Schwartz 1994: 33)

While the more extreme of Freud's actual historical theses and reconstruc-
tions have been, of course, largely discarded, the broad outlines of his notion
that the Bible represents an advance of the father over the mother, of
abstraction and the spirit over the concrete and embodied, seem to have
taken on a kind of orthodoxy of their own. This historical contextualization
of Freud's reading in the matrix of his own political situation as a male Jew
in early twentieth-century Europe is intended as a move in a strategy to dis-
lodge the regnant view of biblical religion from its place.[2]

In a passage from the "Wolf Man," Freud drew a strong and revealing analogy between the sexual and the political, between the situation of the individual, sexually passive, "inverted," humiliated Jew and the Jewish People as a
whole – and between himself and the collective status of Jews. Freud
describes an incident in which the Wolf Man's sister had played with his
penis when he was "still very small." Freud concludes that the patient had
developed fantasies of active sexual aggression toward his sister that

> were meant to efface the memory of an event which later on seemed
> offensive to the patient's masculine self-esteem, and they reached this
> end by putting an imaginary and desirable converse in the place of the
> historical truth. . . . *These phantasies, therefore, corresponded exactly to*

184

the legends by means of which a nation that has become great and proud tries to conceal the insignificance and failure of its beginnings.
(Freud 1918: 20, my emphasis)

As Madelon Sprengnether has remarked, "Freud's comment on this episode reveals the extent to which he associates it with the kind of sexual humiliation he had experienced at the hands of his own nannie" (Sprengnether 1990: 72). It is the sexual passivity of the male child that feminizes (and paradoxically homosexualizes), not the gender of the "seducer."[3] This transfer takes place within Freud's reading of the Wolf Man. The reality (or fantasy) of female sexual aggression directed at the boy is translated into a "feminine" desire directed at his father. Freud writes: "The boy had travelled, without considering the difference of sex, from his Nanya to his father" (*Standard Edition* XVII: 46). This is the same journey that Freud took in his own psyche, from the nanny to the father, thus representing for us via the Wolf Man his own feminized and thus homosexual desire (Boyarin 1994a).

It does not take a prophet to infer of what nation Freud is speaking, and thus this passage provides the hermeneutic key for a deeper understanding of the politico-cultural situation of the Jews within which psychoanalysis was produced. The memory of a situation that seemed offensive to Freud's masculine self-esteem was effaced by putting an imaginary and desirable converse in place of the historical truth. "Feminine" Jewish passivity, coded as homosexual and experienced as shameful for "real men," was to be rewritten as an originary, "manly" aggressiveness, an imaginary and desirable converse indeed. And Freud's gratuitous political remark is a perfect precis for *Moses and Monotheism*. This is Freud's Family Romance, writ large as the Family Romance of the Jewish People.

Male was written within this culture as spiritual, "abstractly sublime," incorporeal, powerful, and universal, and this is precisely how Freud (and others of his time and place) described the "true" Judaism, directly counter to those representations of it as a feminine religion, primitive, physical, carnal, and weak. One typical account of the time has it that:

> Semites are like women in that they lack the Indo-German capacity for philosophy, art, science, warfare, and politics. They nevertheless have a monopoly on one sublime quality: religion, or love of God. This Semitic monism goes hand in hand with a deep commitment to female monogamy. The masculine behavior of the Indo-German, who masters the arts and sciences in order to dominate the natural world, is met with the Semite's feminine response of passivity and receptivity. As the wife is subject to her husband, so the Semites are absolutely permeable to the God who chose them.
> (Olender 1992: 110, paraphrasing Rudolph Friedrich Grau [1835–1893])

The religiosity and spirituality of the "Semite" are encoded here as a female sexuality. Monotheism equals "natural" female monogamy. The early Nazi theologian Reinhold Seeberg held similar views, writing of "the essential Semite character in its leaning toward religion, whereas the Indo-Europeans lean more to critical scholarly thought. The latter would, so to speak, represent the masculine element, the Semites the feminine" (Seeberg 1923: 111; in Briggs 1985: 250).[4]

Freud's *Moses and Monotheism* is best read as part of a massive sociocultural attempt by German-speaking Jews in the nineteenth century to rewrite themselves, and particularly their masculine selves, as Aryans, especially as Teutons.[5] In order to do so, they engaged in a rereading of the biblical and postbiblical past, emphasizing in that past exactly what traditional rabbinic Judaism had de-emphasized, namely, its martial aspects. The "Jewish" heroes, whether of the Bible or of modernity, are all transformed into mimics of gentile heroes. This point could use some further expansion, because as it stands it sounds both essentialist – "War heroes could not possibly be *really* Jewish" – and counterfactual. What, after all, about Samson and the other biblical warriors? My point is not to deny that there was ever a Jewish martial tradition, nor to assert that being violent is un-Jewish, which would be at best a non-strategic essentialism. As it developed historically, however, Diaspora Jewish culture had little interest in Samson, and its Moses was a scholar. Even the Maccabees were deprived of their status as military heroes in the Talmud. What is significant, therefore, is that as emancipated Jews became desperate to remake the Jewish male in the image of the Anglo-Saxon (in particular) as the ultimate white male of their world, they sought to discover such male models within something they could call Jewish – Hannibal the Semite; a transformed Moses; Massena, an allegedly Jewish general, and ultimately the whole biblical tradition of sovereignty and war-making understood as the antithesis of the Diaspora Jewish wont for passivity. Jewish gymnastic groups in Germany and Austria at just this time took the names of Jewish warriors like Bar Kochba and Maccabee (both quite marginalized and often disparaged in rabbinic Jewish tradition) as their icons (Berkowitz 1993: 108).

These Jews were caught in a terrible double bind, most eloquently described by Gilman: "Become like us – abandon your difference – and you may be one with us," but "The more you are like me, the more I know the true value of my power, which you wish to share, and the more I am aware that you are but a shoddy counterfeit" (Gilman 1986: 2). Since they were vilified as female and opportunistic because of their Jewishness, conversion to Christianity was no escape for these Jews, because it only confirmed the stereotype of opportunism and lack of manliness. The solution that they hit on was to reconstruct themselves, via a reconstruction of the Jewish past, as virtual Aryans, thus providing the impetus for the mimicry that I have been discussing. An entire Jewish collective – including its Orthodox members –

engaged in a project of the assimilation of Jewish culture to *Kultur*, and this included an assimilation of Judaism itself to Protestantism, the sublime faith.[6] Rather than the conversion of the Jews, the total conversion of Judaism was the solution. Without in any way denying that Jewish culture, like any other, was subject to critique and "modernization," I would categorically assert that the efforts of German-speaking Jews at a "purposeful, even programmatic *dissociation* from traditional Jewish cultural and national moorings" was a form of colonial mimicry, such as best anatomatized in Frantz Fanon's *Black Skins, White Masks*, and one that was predicated on an "Orientalist" reification of traditional Jewish culture as a mere "social pathology" (Aschheim 1982: 5–6).[7]

As the terms of antisemitism would predict, the conversion of Judaism involved primarily a gendered discourse, a massive attempt to rewrite the Jewish male of the past as indeed a man. Among the traits that Goethe considered that the Jew would have to give up in order to be acceptable to German society were "wild [read hysterical] gesticulations" and "effeminate movements" (Aschheim 1982: 7). Freud's original title for the work, *The Man Moses and Monotheist Religion*, was much closer to its cultural import (Van Herik 1982: 175), for Freud's whole point was to argue that Hebrew monotheism was a religion of manliness, self-defense, and self-control, to efface the "effeminate" Jewish difference of Judaism and to rewrite it as "manly" Protestantism *avant le lettre*.[8] The analogy between the autobiographical and the political is compelling. Shades of the Wolf Man.[9]

Let us begin as Freud does with Moses himself and his name. Echoing the plausible philological reading of the name as a reflex of the Egyptian *Mose* that forms theophoric names such as Thutmose, Freud then makes a very strange move. He writes:

> Now we should have expected that one of the many people who have recognized that "Moses" is an Egyptian name would also have drawn the conclusion or would at least have considered the possibility that the person who bore this Egyptian name may himself have been an Egyptian. In relation to modern times we have no hesitation in drawing such conclusions, . . . and though a change of name or the adoption of a similar one in fresh circumstances is not beyond possibility.
>
> (Freud 1939: 9)

Freud himself bore an "Aryan" name. His name had been changed, to be sure, but the "original," Sigismund, the name of an early modern Polish king known for his friendliness toward Jews (Klein 1985: 46), was *historically* just as gentile as Sigmund – although in Freud's time it was a stereotypically Jewish name (Gilman 1993b: 70; see also Pellegrini forthcoming). "In relation to modern times we have no hesitation in drawing such conclusions," ergo Sigmund must have been an Aryan. Freud's sublimation of the Jewish child Moses into the Egyptian prince Mose, via the forgetting of his own name, strongly supports the readings of this text as Freud's own family novel (he actually called it *ein Roman*), his own fantasy that he is not the child of the abject Jakob but Oedipus the son of Laius or Hannibal the son of Hamilcar. The implication of Freud's own argument, then, is that he himself "may have been" an Aryan. This family romance for Freud and for the entire Jewish people is borne out throughout the work.

Freud's descriptions of biblical religion are tendentious, to say the least. Thus, near the beginning of the second essay, he writes:

> Some of these differences [between the Jewish religion attributed to Moses and the religion of Egypt] may easily be derived from the fundamental contrast between a strict monotheism and an unrestricted polytheism. Others are evidently the result of a difference in spiritual and intellectual [both = *geistig*] level, since one of these religions is very close to primitive phases [of development], while the other has risen to the heights of *sublime abstraction*.
>
> (Freud 1939: 19)

It is not often noted how wildly inappropriate either of these adjectives is when attributed to biblical (or even later talmudic) religion, which was neither a "strict" monotheism, nor had it risen to the "heights of sublime abstraction."[10] Take, for instance the common misapprehensions that the Bible forbids pictorial representation of any kind and that God is necessarily invisible because wholly spiritual. Neither of these two popular dogmas corresponds to what we actually find in the biblical text, as a result of which the obvious meaning of that text is typically revised by its readers (Boyarin 1990a). The rewriting of the history of Judaism – Kantian, Hegelian, and Platonic-Pauline in its impulses – has been going on for so long and been so successful that we think we recognize Judaism in such descriptions. Thus, typically, Judaism is thought of as the religion of abstract thought and as indifferent or hostile to aesthetics. Renan, however, only a little more than a century ago, thought differently. For him the "Aryan" was characterized by "abstract metaphysics," while the "Semite" represented poetry; the Aryan scientific reason, the Semite religious feeling; the Aryan philosophy, the Semite music (Olender 1992: 78). It is clear how this maps onto Rousseau's and Kant's distinction between the female beautiful and the male sublime (Lloyd 1993: 75). Moreover, as Lloyd further remarks (without noticing the theological subtext), for Hegel, "Divine Law" (i.e., the Jew), insofar as it is concerned with "duties and affections towards blood relatives," is the "nether world" and "is also the domain of women" (81). Freud's narrative both accepts and contests this picture. To be sure, the Jews of Freud's day are "atavistic," "fossilized," caught in a world of superstitious ritual, feminized; but it was not always so. Once they were as sublime as Aryans, and it is that sublime, Aryan-like, true Mosaic tradition that Freud seeks to recover and revive.

As Eric Santner notes, Weininger had written that "It is, however, this Kantian rationality, this Spirit, which above all appears to be lacking in the Jew and the woman" (Weininger 1975: 411). Weininger, of course, was right. Traditional Judaism has very little to do with Kantianism. The desperation to make this not be so becomes nearly an obsession in the writings of Freud's Jewish contemporaries, as in Derrida's paraphrase of Hermann Cohen:

> Let us go directly, by way of a beginning, to the clearest proposition, the firmest and, for us, the most interesting one: the close, deep internal kinship (*die innerste Verwandschaft*) between Judaism and Kantianism. That is to say also between Judaism and the historical culmination (*geschichtliche Hohepunkt*) of idealism as the essence of German philosophy, namely, the Kantian moment, the inner sanctum (*innerste Heiligtum*) which Kantianism is, with its fundamental concepts (the autonomy of universal law, liberty, and duty).
>
> (Derrida 1991: 48–49; 58)

Whatever its other parameters, Kant's sublime comprises also the move toward abstraction that Freud would refer to as sublimation and Lacan as *Aufhebung* (Lacan 1982: 82). Kant himself had written that the commandment against making graven images or idols (Exodus 20: 4) is "the most sublime passage in the Jews' book of laws" (quoted in Olender 1992: 160).[11] In Kant's definition, the "sublime is directly concerned with the *unrepresentable*. It calls for detachment from sensibility (from perceptible forms) in order to accede to the experience of a supersensible faculty within us" (Goux 1990: 141). But as I – and others – have shown in earlier work, the prohibition on graven images of God in biblical religion has little or nothing to do with a putative unrepresentability of God. If, as Goux writes, "nothing that can be the object of the senses can, strictly speaking, be considered sublime," then the biblical God, the seeing of Whom is the *summum bonum* of religious life, can hardly be described as sublime (Boyarin 1990a).

Kant may have been in some ways the "Jewish philosopher", as is sometimes claimed, but his "Jewishness" is only so by virtue of the Kantianism of German Judaism.[12] This sublimation of Judaism is, however, a sort of fetish, recognizing and disavowing at the same time the connections between Judaism and the religions of "primitives," especially insofar as rites like circumcision are shared among these.[13] Eilberg-Schwartz, in *The Savage in Judaism* (1990), has both exposed how inadequate such descriptions of Judaism are and described the cultural processes by which Judaism came to be so rewritten in modernity. Among their tendentious characteristics, such descriptions of the history of Judaism require an assumption – explicit in the work of Wellhausen – that the "priestly" aspects of the Bible, such as food taboos and purity rituals, were the products of a late degeneration of Israelite religion and not its pure fountainhead.[14] It follows, of course, that Orthodox Jewish adherence to such ritual behavior marks Judaism as both "degenerate" and primitive with respect to Christianity, but this is only the late corrupt form of Judaism.[15] Freud at once accepts and defends against this Protestant interpretation of Judaism. For him, as for the German Protestant Bible scholars, the "true Jew" was nothing like the priest-ridden ritualist projected in the Torah. Freud's defense of Judaism ends up almost identical to the antisemitic denunciation of it.

Masculine renunciation and its links to the putative triumph of spirituality over the senses is the essence of Freud's argument in *Moses and Monotheism*. It is the sublimation of the sensible penis in the unrepresentable – thus sublime – (veiled; cf. 2 Corinthians 3:13) phallus that is at issue here, and this implies the sublimation of the Jewish people.[16] Where the Jews have been accused of carnality and, therefore, of being like women, Freud (like Philo before him) would demonstrate that they are more spiritual, and more rational, than the Others, and therefore more masculine than the accusers themselves (Lloyd 1993). In other words, Freud did not set out to explain the prohibition on images of God in a psychoanalytical framework; Freud set out to counter antisemitic charges that Jews are not spiritual but carnal, not male but female. Moreover, as I have argued at length in another place, after the turn of the century, Freud was very busily, almost frantically, engaged in disavowing his own homosexual desires (Boyarin 1994a). This "repression" was produced in the context of the virulent antisemitism and homophobia which were one and the same movement – Adolph Stoecker's "Christian Values" movement in Germany in his time (Fout 1992: 405). The last thing Freud would have wanted to do, at the onset of the Nazi genocide of Jews and homosexuals (Moeller 1994), was to confront the feminization\ homoeroticization of the male Jew in relation to God. Eilberg-Schwartz has provided dramatic confirmation for this reading of Freud's work (1994: 39). He shows that Freud drew back from a conclusion that seems ineluctable from his argument, namely that monotheism predicts representations of the male worshipper as feminized *vis-à-vis* the male God and as a fantasized erotic object for the male God, thus producing the tension that leads eventually to the de-anthropomorphizing – the unmanning, if you will – of the deity. Eilberg-Schwartz explains Freud's reluctance to come to this conclusion as a product of his fear that it would amount to representing Jewish men as feminized, thus playing into the hands of that representation of himself as Jewish male that he was trying so hard to avoid.

I wish here to pursue this reading further. It is not only the case, as Eilberg-Schwartz has it, that Freud seems to hold back from a conclusion to which his own theory leads him, namely, the avoidance of homoeroticism giving rise to the abstraction of God, but more: there is an active contradiction within his discourse. Renunciation of the fulfillment of desire, which is encoded in Freud's text as masculine, is occasioned by a submissiveness *vis-à-vis* a male other, whether it be the "great man" Moses or the deity. But that very submissiveness, the mark of the religious person, was itself feminizing in the terms of nineteenth-century culture. The "higher," that is, the more "masculine," that Judaism gets, the "lower," that is, the more "feminine," its adherents become. Freud's constant skirting and finessing of this issue are the mark of the true tension that generates the text.

In the chapter entitled "Schreber's Jewish Question" in his recent study of the Schreber case, Eric Santner has focussed on another aporia within *Moses and Monotheism*. He writes that

> for Freud, the ethically oriented monotheism of the Jews and the historical condition of diaspora are linked by a series of traumatic cuts: of the deity from plastic representation; of spirituality from magic, animism, and sexual excess; of the passions from their violent enactments; of the people from a territory conceived as proper to them. These various modalities of loss, separation, and departure, which Freud views as so many forms of the instinctual renunciation [*Triebverzicht*] that undergirds the rule of law in the most general sense, procure for the Jews what he calls "their secret treasure," namely a sense of self-confidence and superiority with regard to pagan cultures whose spirituality has remained, as he puts it, "under the spell of sensuality" (Freud 1939: 115).
>
> (Santner 1996)

Santner points out that Freud has a great deal of difficulty, however, in accounting for this "secret treasure," not being able to articulate clearly just why a "set-back to sensuality" should have such a powerful effect in raising the self-regard of individuals or peoples. Freud writes that "We are faced by the phenomenon that in the course of the development of humanity sensuality is gradually overpowered by intellectuality and that men feel proud and exalted by every such advance. *But we are unable to say why this should be so*" (Freud 1939: 118). Freud's final response to this aporia is to discover an "uncanny secretion of *jouissance* within the precincts of the moral law" (Santner 1996), a sensual ascetic rapture [*In einem neuen Rausch moralischer Askese*] in the very renunciations of sensuality. Santner keenly comments then that

> What Freud discovers as a paradoxical kernel of *jouissance* within the domain of an otherwise austere, Kantian moral universe is, as Boyarin has rightly noted, occasioned, *in Freud's narrative*, by submissiveness to a "great man." But that narrative construction was itself generated by an impasse in his argument apropos of the Jewish valuation of *Geistigkeit*. Freud was unable to imagine a resolution of that impasse – the impossibility of accounting for the value of this value – outside the

191

terms of the "father complex." Freud's "great man" fills a gap, a missing link in his argumentation about the emergence of a new cultural value. But to follow Freud here, as I think Boyarin does, is to miss, once more, the encounter with this missing link. To interpret Freud's failure as the avoidance of a homoeroticism implied by his own narrative is to domesticate the impasse on which Freud's interpretation founders, the impasse that called his narrative into being in the first place.

(Santner 1996)

Santner's comment is profoundly satisfying, revealing a dimension in the European imaginary of the gay man, the woman, and the Jew as an "abjection, the experience of something rotten within that signifies a cursed knowledge of *jouissance* which only by way of a kind of secondary revision becomes legible as 'homosexuality,' 'femininity,' or 'Jewishness'" (Santner 1996). This "secondary revision," however, is only for Schreber the Aryan, for the one to whom femininity and Jewishness can be put on. The Jew Freud is mostly too busy trying to get the Aryan phallus, to get "invested" with it, in order to experience such cursed knowledges – except, of course, for the one very significant moment that Santner spotlights, that brief opening when *Jewissance* is glimpsed by Freud.

Freud's impasse is occasioned by his very assumptions that Judaism is to be characterized as a compelling renunciation of the senses (the mother) for the spirit (the father, phallus, logos), and that this renunciation has generated in the Jew, *from the time of Moses*, a sense of superiority with respect to pagans, that is, a sense of profound well-being in a world which is hostile and threatening to Jews; but there is hardly any reason to think that this was the way ancient Israelites imagined themselves – neither as superior by reason of renunciation nor as particularly threatened. I think, rather, that it is, if anything, a childlike or erotic intimacy with God that would have described their sense of superiority – Gott der Tatte, not Gott der Vater. In other words, the first point that should be absolutely clear and obvious is that Freud is concerned not at all with Moses or the Bible but with the situation of Jews in his own time, and the situation of German-speaking Jews at that. Freud first has to posit Judaism as "a posture of severe self-control grounded in an endless series of instinctual renunciations," *because he must ward off Weininger* and the latter's argument that "the (masculine/Christian) point of view of Kantian critical philosophy was as foreign to the (feminized) Jewish psychic and moral constitution as was Wagner's *Parsifal* to the Jewish aesthetic sensibility" (Santner 1996). Freud's very description of Moses's "advances" and the aporia that it produces for him is, in the first instance, a desperate grab for this Spirit (phallus) that Weininger had denied the Jew, a signifier of his profound need to defend against not so much homoeroticism, as in Eilberg Schwartz's account, but femininity. Freud is

192

then genuinely troubled by the question of why, having misread Judaism as such an austere, dessicated, incorporeal renunciation of the senses, Jews should feel good about it at all, why they should not be denied all *jouissance*, but he knows, of course, that they do, that at least for the *Ostjude* being Jewish is a source of secret joy. And then through this misprision, Freud reveals/conceals the secret of abject *jouissance* that Santner saves in Schreber's discourse from Freud's attempt to hide it again. But at the first level, the question remains what it is that occasioned the originary misreading, and I suggest that it is Freud's dire need to be manly, to discover a manliness at the origins of Jewishness, Moses, and the Bible.

This desperation becomes manifest, I suggest, at a particularly bizarre and telling moment in *Moses and Monotheism*. Immediately after his discourse on the great man as Aryan father, Freud produces the following utterance:

> Why the people of Israel, however, clung more and more submissively to their God the worse they were treated by him – that is a problem which for the moment we must leave on one side. It may encourage us to enquire whether the religion of Moses brought the people nothing else besides an enhancement of their self-esteem owing to their consciousness of having been chosen. And indeed another factor can easily be found. That religion also brought the Jews a far grander conception of God, or, as we might put it more modestly, the conception of a grander God. Anyone who believed in this God had some kind of share in his greatness, might feel exalted himself. For an unbeliever this is not entirely self evident; but we may perhaps make it easier to understand if we point to the sense of superiority felt by a Briton in a foreign country which has been made insecure owing to an insurrection – a feeling that is completely absent in a citizen of any small continental state. For the Briton counts on the fact that his Government will send along a warship if a hair of his head is hurt, and that the rebels understand that very well – whereas the small state possesses no warship at all. Thus, pride in the greatness of the British Empire has a root as well in the consciousness of the greater security – the protection – enjoyed by the individual Briton. This may resemble the conception of a grand God.
>
> (Freud 1939: 112)

This bizarre analogy provides the final moment in Freud's attempted appropriation of the sublime (Kantian) phallus for Jews, and it renders crystal clear what the political background for that attempt is. The Jew is the epitome of the citizen of the small state with no warships, indeed "he" is not a citizen of any state at all. Freud is arguing that the Jews' "grander [more sublime] conception of God" as their sublimation [masculinization] of physicality and desire, the vaunted "advance in *Geistigkeit*," provides them with an alternative asset for the warships and state-power that they do not

193

possess. At this point it is obvious that the Zionism of Freud's contemporary, Theodor Herzl, was another answer – more direct and more responsive to new and emerging paradigms of the masculine, viz., "Muscular Christianity" (Hall 1994) – to this same Jewish question. Where Freud sought for Jews a compensation for the lack of imperial power, Herzl pursued imperial power itself (Boyarin forthcoming). It is immediately in the next paragraph after this encomium to imperial power that Freud invokes the prohibition against making images of God as a sign of the "triumph of *Geistigkeit* over sensuality, or strictly speaking, an instinctual renunciation." These are the characteristics encoded as sublime, male, and Protestant in Freud's cultural world. In the next paragraphs Freud writes of "our children, adults who are neurotic, and primitive peoples," and, together with these, of the succession of the matriarchal social order by the patriarchal one. The connections between these expressions are clear, but it is vital to remember that it was the Jews who were branded as neurotic, primitive, sensual, and female in *fin-de-siècle* central Europe. We now see Freud's claims for the "superiority" of the Jews in a different light. Key to my interpretation is the recoding of "submissive" from feminine to masculine within the space of this passage. By reading the "inclination to intellectual interests" as a product of the dematerialization or sublimation of God, Freud accomplished another brilliant defensive move. What has been stigmatized as the femaleness of the Jewish male, both his circumcision and his devotion to the interior, "female" pursuits of study, actually marks him as more masculine than the (male) Greek, who in his very muscularity is less restrained, less able to "renounce instincts" (Freud 1939: 115 and esp. 116), and thus paradoxically less "manly" – than the (male) Jew.[17] Jewish carnality, adherence to a law characterized by its passionate attachment to blood and flesh and thus described by antisemites (Hegel) as feminine, is transvalued by Freud precisely into a very masculinist *Geistigkeit* or denial of the body itself.

This masculinity is extruded by the infamous analogy that Freud draws between "declaring that our God is the greatest and mightiest, although he is invisible like a gale of wind or like the soul" and the "deciding that paternity is more important than maternity, although it cannot, like the latter, be established by the evidence of the senses" (118). Freud thus sought to reinvest (male) Jews with the phallus in an almost pathetic quest for the "self-regard" (116) notably lacking in the nineteenth-century "emancipated" Jew of Austro-Germany. Freud's desire – characteristic of Jews of his time and place – projected onto Moses and the entire Jewish People is recorded here, for Freud is registering the absence of an asset, one prohibited to Jews, and not its presence.

Freud, however, remains quite ambivalent about all this, as one can easily see by his dual comments within the space of a page about "more and more instinctual renunciations" as leading "in doctrine and precept at least – [to] ethical heights which had remained inaccessible to the other peoples of antiquity," but these very same renunciations "possess the characteristic of obsessional reaction-formations" (134–35).[18] Moreover, we can locate this fault line in his psychodynamic theory itself at the site of the ambiguity surrounding the term sublimation *vis-à-vis* reaction formation, aim-inhibition, and repression. Laplanche and Pontalis note somewhat dryly that in Freud's writings, "there are only the vaguest hints of dividing lines between sublimation" and repression, obsession, and aim-inhibition, but "the capacity to sublimate is an essential factor in successful treatment" (Laplanche and Pontalis 1973: 433). Since obsession and repression are part of what there is to be treated in a successful treatment, the cure and the disease become hard to distinguish. This famous moment of incoherence in the dynamic theory is the product, I suggest, of the pervasive ambivalences I have been exploring as products of Freud's *fin-de-siècle* sexual-political situation; it is indeed, almost emblematic of a liminality that Freud manifests.

This equivocation or tension lines up with other points of constant pressure in Freud's writing. Freud remained ambivalent about the civilizing mission of colonialism almost to the very end, and his ambivalence is marked by a series of equivocations in his writing. In 1908 he described female neurosis as being the product of libidinal renunciation: "Anyone who is able to penetrate the determinants of nervous illness will soon become convinced that its increase in our society arises from the intensification of sexual restrictions" (Freud 1908: 194). And even: "The cure for nervous illness arising from marriage would be marital unfaithfulness" (195). In this text, then, the primitive is written as the healthy libido unrepressed by civilization – Gauguin's Tahiti. At the same time, however, a parallel and opposite tectonic movement takes place in Freud's writing. As Marianna Torgovnick has remarked, in a text published in 1915, "Thoughts for the times on life and death," Freud fathomed the deleterious aspects of civilization but still claimed that "the great ruling powers among the white nations" should, in fact, rule over the others in order to civilize them (Torgovnick 1990: 197). The year 1913 saw the publication of *Totem and Taboo*, which concerns itself with "some points of agreement between the mental lives of savages and neurotics" (Freud 1913).[19] In the late 1920s, when *Civilization and its Discontents* was being written, civilization, with its demanded instinctual renunciations, was seen as the source of neuroses (Freud 1930: 87, 97, esp. 139) and Freud could write that "civilization behaves towards sexuality as a people or a stratum of its population does which has subjected another one to its exploitation" (57).

There is, accordingly, an enormous tension in Freud's writing on the relation of the civilized to the primitive, a tension that reaches its highest pitch in the discrepancies on this score between *Civilization and its Discontents* (1930) and the only slightly later *Moses and Monotheism* (1939). In this contradiction, I theorize, we can discover the force that generates the tension. As Bram Dijkstra has perceptively written,

The truly psychotic, rather than merely neurotic, idealization of a supremely evolved white male and the concomitant assumption that somehow all others were "degenerate" had, as Freud was writing [*Civilization and its Discontents*], begun to reap its most evil harvest. Even the most casual reader of the theoretical disquisitions of the later nineteenth-century exponents of the science of man must at once perceive the intimate correlation between their evolutionist conclusions and the scientific justification of patterns of "inherent" superiority and inferiority in the relations between the sexes, various races, and the different classes in society.

(Dijkstra 1986: 160)

The ambivalence in Freud's disposition *vis-à-vis* civilization and the primitive is generated precisely by the ambiguity of his position as "white male." Freud as the Jew, the "black," the unacknowledged (by him) object of the racist discourse of evolution, sees well the horror of colonial domination, but when Freud identifies himself with the "white man," then he perceives the great virtues of the civilizing mission. This tension was always present, but resolves itself most definitely in the gap between *Civilization and its Discontents* and *Moses and Monotheism*. While still in the killing field of the "evil harvest," Freud perceives the violence of civilization. Safe, however, among the "great[est] ruling power among the white nations," in *Moses and Monotheism* Freud ruminates that it is the "primitive" who has not (yet) undertaken renunciation of libidinal strivings who is most similar to the neurotic and the female, and renunciation thus has become a sign of greater psychic health. Now the "Jew" has to be demonstrably on the side of civilization.

Rather than reading these tensions symptomatically, Judith Van Herik attempts to resolve the contradictions by assuming that Freud's negative estimations of civilization, especially *The Future of an Illusion*, are about Christianity, while *Moses and Monotheism* is about Judaism. This founding postulate of her thesis is based on the fact that in the former work Freud explicitly writes that he is describing "the final form taken by our present-day white Christian civilization" (Van Herik 1982: 143). She understands "Christian" in that sentence to be in contrast to "Jewish." This interpretation, however, seemingly so inescapable, just does not finally hold. The characteristics of that civilization that Freud delineates in the context are not at all distinctive to Christianity as opposed to Judaism but are common to them: moral laws, reward for good and evil, life after death, *Chosen People*. Freud is rather using "our present-day Christian civilization" in the way that a postwar American might refer to "Judaeo-Christian" civilization, and Freud's point is that when he speaks of "religion" he refers only to Western religion, as opposed, for example, to the religions of India, China, or Africa. He is dubbing it "*our* present-day white Christian civilization," because of the cultural and political hegemony of Christianity within it and not to distinguish it from Judaism.

Van Herik depends, on her own account, on the agreement of anonymous "commentators" that "Freud singled out and treated contemporary central European Catholicism" in *Future of an Illusion*, but at the same time she wonders why "he emphasized the wish fulfillments offered by Catholicism when any historical survey would show that it had also imposed renunciations. Similarly, he emphasized the renunciations which Mosaic monotheism imposed when even in his own view Judaism had also fulfilled wishes" (150). This seeming arbitrariness can be removed, in fact, by abandoning the thesis that the two texts are about the two religions. We cut the gordian knot by remarking that there is no internal evidence in *Future* to indicate that Freud intends in that work to distinguish between Catholicism and Judaism at all. It is (western) religion in general which is the subject of his discourse, and so the supposed paradox vanishes. The consensus of commentators is, I suggest, specious. In his own autobiographical reflections, Freud indicated that he saw *Moses and Monotheism* as replacing the earlier work as a statement about religion:

> In *The Future of an Illusion* I expressed an essentially negative valuation of religion. Later, I found a formula which did better justice to it: while granting that its power lies in the truth which it contains, I showed that truth was not a material but a historical truth.
>
> (Freud 1925b: 72)

Van Herik writes that, for Freud, "Whereas Christian beliefs restricted intellectuality and morality, Mosaic beliefs advanced them" (1982: 178). Freud never drew such a contrast, and only the assumption that the distinction between *Future* and *Moses* is between Christianity and Judaism would support it. But it is clear from this statement of Freud's that he himself considered the two texts to be about the same object, and that the earlier text had ignored an aspect of value that the later one revealed. Unless we suspect Freud of deliberate obfuscation, then, how could it be that the two works intend a contrast between two different religions? Torgovnick comes much closer when she writes "In Freud's work, the feminine often functions as the primitive does *and as religious Judaism does* – as something the 'Roman citizen' rejects and controls in his march toward civilization" (Torgovnick 1990: 204). She even more acutely notes that the link between 'the oceanic' and the female" is treated by Freud "in a way that reveals how ['the oceanic'] was for him, like religious Jewishness and the primitive, a category he wished to suppress and leave behind" (205). I do, of course, grant that in *Moses* Freud writes explicitly that in certain respects Christianity was a "regression" towards polytheism from the heights of monotheism (Freud 1939: 88). We must not forget, however, that he ascribes a similar regression to the Jews and their priests who invented the rituals of Orthodox Judaism

197

(47), and, on the very same page in which he argues that Christianity was a "regression" towards polytheism, writes as well that it had "restored a feature of the old Aten religion."

Freud's comments about Paul also hardly support a reading of the text as simple Jewish triumphalism:

> Paul, who carried Judaism on, also destroyed it. No doubt he owed his success in the first instance to the fact that, through the idea of the redeemer, he exorcised humanity's sense of guilt; but he owed it as well to the circumstance that he abandoned the 'chosen' character of his people and its visible mark – circumcision – so that the new religion could be a universal one embracing all men. Though a part may have been played in Paul's taking this step by his personal desire for revenge for the rejection of his innovation in Jewish circles, yet it also restored a feature of the old Aten religion – it removed a restriction which that religion had acquired when it was handed over to a new vehicle, the Jewish people.
>
> (Freud 1939: 87–88)

Of course, the next paragraph within which Freud treats Christianity as a "cultural regression" and a "fresh victory for the priests of Amun over Akhenaten's god" is much more notorious, but it will be seen that there is, at least, great ambivalence in Freud's account of the relation of the two faiths to each other. Once again, in the next paragraph, the same ambivalence (or is it a contradiction?) reappears when, in accounting for the Jews' tenacious adherence to the monotheist idea, Freud argues that it was the result of "acting out," and thus neurotic, as opposed to the therapeutic progress of Paul. The Jews "remained halted at the recognition of the great father and thus blocked their access to the point from which Paul was later to start his continuation of the primal history" (89). Narratives of evolution and devolution jangle each other here with almost no attempt at harmonization. I would suggest that it is the discontinuities of Freud's own ambivalent desire for Christianness and his own tenacious refusal to abandon Jewishness that are clashing here. In my reading of the "My Son the Myops" dream I have found the same dissonance (Boyarin forthcoming). Further evidence for Freud's investment in this discourse might be found in his reference to "the murder of Moses" but "the supposed judicial murder of Christ" (100). The former is marked as more certain than the latter, an inconsequence that I take to be simple Jewish defensiveness against the charge of Christ-killing (although others might read it in a more sinister light). It would be a strange triumphalism indeed that would credit, as Freud does, the Christians' charge against the Jews that they have murdered God (136), even in the somewhat disguised form in which he does so. I, accordingly, quite reject the consensus upon which Van Herik depends and agree entirely with Lyotard, who writes, "Freud is attacking not only Christianity, reclassified (as in *Totem and Taboo*) as a totemism, but also primitive Judaism" (Lyotard 1984: 67). It is important to emphasize only, as Lyotard does not, that "primitive Judaism" means, in fact, Judaism as traditional Jews – and I myself – live it until today. Le Rider seems to me absolutely on the mark in his characterization of *Moses and Monotheism* as a psychopathology of Judaism – that is, of actual Judaism, and not the fantasy of Judaism as Kantian *Aufklärung*, that desirable and imaginary converse. As he remarks, in *Moses* Judaism is presented as a genuine psychosis and not merely as a neurosis, as is religion in general (Le Rider 1993: 236–38). Strange triumphalism indeed!

Seen in this light, Freud's apparent (if ambivalent) rapport with the civilizing mission, as well as his acceptance of the bromide that ontogeny recapitulates phylogeny, is a much more complex political move than it might first appear, for the "primitives" to which he addresses himself are as much Jewish primitives – indeed, first and foremost Jewish primitives, primitives within – and only secondarily the contemporary objects of the civilizing mission of colonialism. Freud's apparently guileless use of the phrase "A State Within a State" as a metaphor for "pathological phenomena" (Freud 1939: 76) is telling here, since, of course, that phrase was coined for women and Jews, the twin primitive others within the German state (Geller 1993: 56). Freud had apparently, almost against his will, internalized the antisemitic ideology that Jews were a people both out of time and out of place. Other Jews in his milieu had also incorporated such views, most notably the western European Zionists of Herzl's movement (Boyarin forthcoming). Although Freud was not, certainly by 1939, a Zionist in the sense of being a supporter of Jewish settlement in Palestine and the founding of a Jewish state there, his interpretation of Jewish history was exactly the same as the Zionist interpretation – ancient glory followed by thousands of years of degradation producing moral, spiritual, and aesthetic distortions in the oppressed people. The "high" religion of the Egyptian Moses, the purely spiritual monotheism, was the production of a "fortunate period of established possession"; that is, "In Egypt, so far as we can understand, monotheism grew up as a by-product of imperialism" (Freud 1939: 65), but as the Jewish people underwent the trials and sufferings of the Diaspora, "their god became harsh and severe, and, as it were, wrapped in gloom . . . they increased their own sense of guilt in order to stifle their doubts of God" (Freud 1939: 64). Freud explicitly echoes the best of German Protestant Bible scholarship: "Institutions such as the ritual ordinances, which date unmistakably from later times, are given out as Mosaic commandments with the plain intention of lending them authority" (Freud 1939: 65). The great ideals of the true Mosaic religion remained dormant within the people, but the priests with their "ceremonials" became increasingly the dominant force.[20]

Freud went beyond most of his contemporaries, however, by actually splitting Moses and thus Judaism into two different antithetical and antagonistic groups with two different Moseses and two different religious traditions. The "true" Moses, the Egyptian one, is remarkably like the ideal Protestant. Freud's Moses fantasies and dreams provide important backing for this thesis. When he dreams he is on a mountain looking yearningly at "the Promised Land," it is not the Land of Israel, but Rome, like Hannibal at Lake Trasimeno (Freud 1900–01: 194; cf. Masson 1985: 285), and this is emblematic of the metamorphosis of the man Moses at his hands. In the early essay on the *Moses* of Michelangelo, Freud discovers that Moses is not about to throw down the tablets of the Law, but is, in fact, checking that impulse and that, therefore, Michelangelo has

> added something new and more than human to the figure of Moses; so that the giant frame with its tremendous physical power becomes only a concrete expression of the highest mental achievement that is possible in a man, that of struggling successfully against an inward passion for the sake of a cause to which he has devoted himself.
>
> (Freud 1914a: 233)

Moses is now the very model of a masculine spirituality and renunciation – as well as a "manly" aggressiveness: "in contrast to the meditative king, he was energetic and passionate" (Freud 1939: 60). Bluma Goldstein has shown how identified Freud was himself with this gentilified Moses:

> In 1900 Freud characterized his own adventurous nature in terms of conquest: "I am actually not at all a man of science, not an observer, not an experimenter, not a thinker. I am by temperament nothing but a *conquistador*, an adventurer, if you wish to translate this term – with all the inquisitiveness, daring, and tenacity characteristic of such a man." Whether in the guise of *conquistador* or Semitic warrior, Freud apparently conceived of himself at that time as conquering Rome in the name of Jewry, which the Roman Church, in his view, had persecuted and continued to threaten. But what did happen when he finally reached Rome?
>
> (Goldstein 1992: 76)

According to Goldstein's brilliant reading of Freud's essay on Michelangelo's *Moses*, what happened was that Freud discovered a Moses who embodied all of the values and traits of European Christians, indeed who was a central monument of European Christianity in the heart of Rome itself, another, like Hannibal, un-Jewish Jew (not the same thing, of course, as a non-Jewish Jew).

The other Moses, the second Moses, was, on the other hand, all-too-Jewish, and the religion that he founded was obsessed with "neurotic" ritual observances and not with "sublime abstractions." "Everything in the [Egyptian] Mosaic god that deserved admiration was quite beyond the comprehension of the primitive masses" (Freud 1939: 63). On Freud's own theory that such ancient fault lines reappear in later splits within a people (38), could we not read this as a covert (perhaps unconscious) representation of the distinction between German Jews and their embarrassingly primitive relatives, the *Ostjuden*, the "black" Jews, the Jews who spoke a language one converted German Jew referred to as "Hottentot" (Gilman 1986: 99)? Such a "family romance" was not unprecedented among Viennese Jews of Freud's generation. Theodor Herzl went so far as to write explicitly that the *Ostjude* was of a different "race" from the "evolved" German Jew (Boyarin forthcoming). Freud's account of how the ideas of the original Moses, "the idea of a single god, as well as the rejection of magically effective ceremonial and the stress upon ethical demands made in his name" (Freud 1939: 66), were suppressed but hundreds of years later would reappear as an allegory of the reappearance of such "high" ideas of religion among the German Jews after centuries of their abeyance among the *Ostjuden*. As one of Freud's Bnai Brith lodge brothers couched it: "We Jews ... are not constrained by dogma. In his inner being the Jew, the true Jew, feels only one eternal guide, one lawgiver, one law, and that is morality" (Ludwig Braun 1926, quoted in Gilman 1993a: 75). Gilman appropriately glosses this: "This image of the Jews as following only 'natural law', rather than the complicated rules and rituals of traditional Judaism, imagines them as the ultimate rationalists, at one with God and nature." Hiding behind the second, "too Jewish," ritualist Moses is none other than Mauschel, "little Moses" (Ikey), the malicious name that German antisemites, both Jewish and gentile, applied to east European Jews (Gilman 1986). Mauschel is obsessed with his primitive, atavistic, and irrational rituals. If the first Moses is Mendelssohn, the second is Mauschel. Indeed, one might almost wish to rename the work *Mauschel and Monotheism*.

The crisis of the early 1930s so heightened this strain that it gave way finally in a "personality split" within Moses and the Jewish People: *Moses and Monotheism*.[21] Each of the "religious" categories which Freud projects is, like Rome, split and doubled. Judaism is not identical with itself, and neither is Christianity. The split between the "queer effeminate" Ostjude and the "straight male modern" Jew (Brenkman 1993), between Mauschel and Mendelssohn, seems to be repeated in a split between the Austrian Catholic and the German Protestant as well, suggesting further Freud's complicated identifications of self and other – all within. Another way of saying this would be that the evolutionary narrative is from Catholic to Protestant Christian – and from Catholic to Protestant Jew (with some temporary devolutions along the way). "Maimonides is, within Medieval Judaism, the revealing mark of Protestantism," wrote Hermann Cohen (quoted in Derrida 1991: 53; 65), and Freud's description of the religion of sublime abstraction is surely much more like that of Moses Maimonides – and Hermann Cohen – than like that of the biblical Moses.

NOTES

1 A longer version of this chapter, including a close reading of Freud's "My Son the Myops" dream and attending to the situation of Freud in the context of a virulent homophobic movement, is due to appear in Benigno Sanchez-Eppler and Cindy Patton's edited volume, *Queer Diasporas*, forthcoming from Duke University Press. I wish to thank the following who read earlier versions of this argument and helped me along considerably: Robert Alter, Homi Bhabha, Jonathan Boyarin, Howard Eilberg-Schwartz, Jay Geller, Stephen Greenblatt, Martin Jay, Thomas J. Luxon, Juliet Mitchell, Ann Pellegrini, Michael Rogin, Eric Santner, and Kalpana Seshadri-Crooks, all of whom are responsible for something here and none for all of it.

2 Eilberg-Schwartz (1994) and Boyarin (1990a) represent previous moves in this same direction.

3 It should be carefully noted here that the terms "active" and "passive," and their correlations with masculine and feminine and notions of inversion invoked throughout this text, are Freud's – not mine. In fact, of course, they are not Freud's but a general aspect of his sociolect.

4 For Seeberg's Nazi-sympathies, see Briggs (1985: 251).

5 Note Freud's comment that the Jews were in Cologne, where he fantasized his own ancestors came from, before the Germans (1939: 90)!

6 To be sure, Freud lived in Catholic Vienna, but I think it is not inaccurate to suggest that the kind of religiosity that he admires and constructs as originally "Jewish" in *Moses and Monotheism* is more like German Protestantism than Austrian Catholicism. See below.

7 In other words, I agree completely with Seshadri-Crooks (1994: 192) when she writes that "[Freud's] easy condensation of totemic rites as being 'the same thing' as present day neuroses also elides the glib pathologization of non-Western cultures." My intervention is to claim that for Freud the traditional Judaism of the *Ostjude* is in the same category of the non-western and primitive as totemic rites, and is equally pathologized.

8 I do believe that it was the Protestantism of high German *Kultur*, understood as *Aufhebung* of all previous cultures, that was Freud's model, in spite of his dwelling in Catholic Austria, or perhaps because of it. But again, let me emphasize, Freud's was an assimilationism like Herzl's Zionism (for which, see Boyarin forthcoming), one that sought not to erase the name Jew but rather to reconfigure Jews as identical to Gentiles and as such in origin. The "Egyptian" Moses is a perfect figure for this move. Therefore, arguments that Freud was not "ashamed" of his Jewishness or was pugnacious against antisemites are precisely beside the point.

9 Freud returned to this view in his analysis of the Schreber case in which he argued that Schreber's fantasies of being the Redeemer followed his feminization, *Entmannung*.

> For we learn that the idea of being transformed into a woman (that is, of being emasculated) was the primary delusion, that he began by regarding that act as constituting a serious injury and persecution, and that it only became related to his playing the part of Redeemer in a secondary way. There can be no doubt, moreover, that originally he believed that the transformation was to be effected for the purpose of sexual abuse and not so as to serve higher designs. The position may be formulated by saying that a sexual delusion of persecution was later on converted in the patient's mind into a religious delusion of grandeur.
>
> (Freud 1911: 18)

The two passages provide striking commentary on each other and together a hermeneutic key for the reading of *Moses and Monotheism*.

10 Freud himself realized how malapropos these descriptions are of actual biblical religion, but ascribed all of the "primitive" characteristics to the religion of the "Midianite Moses," as opposed to the spiritual religion of the "Egyptian Moses [who] had given to one portion of the people a more highly spiritualized notion of god, the idea of a single deity embracing the whole world, who was not less all-loving than all-powerful, who was averse to all ceremonial and magic and set before men as their highest aim a life in truth and justice" (Freud 1939: 50). See also Robert Alter, "Freud's Jewish Problem," *Commentary*, January 1992.

11 Hegel's description of Judaism as "the religion of the sublime," of which Jay Geller has reminded me, seemingly follows from this point.

12 This provides quite a different spin on Kant's alleged "innermost affinity with Judaism," as recently discussed by Harpham (1994: 530). Precisely the point of the *construction* of such an affinity by figures like Hermann Cohen would be to *produce* identity between "Judaism" and the German Spirit. Harpham also quite curiously seems to dramatically underplay Kant's own quite spectacular expressions of antisemitism. On the other hand, he fathoms acutely that "from serene thoughts of reason it is but a short step to critical terrorism in the service of revolutionary fantasies of the essential unity of mankind" (531–32). Harpham brilliantly explores the contiguities between Inquisition and Enlightenment; I would locate the sources of the Kantian Universal – with both its light and dark aspects – further back, in Paul (Boyarin 1994b). My point is that Enlightenment and Difference are structurally, systemically antithetical, which does not yet mean that we can do without either Enlightenment or some kind of Universal. For further articulation of the paradox see Boyarin and Boyarin (1993).

13 Gilman (1993b: 188) should be compared here both for the ways in which my reading of *Moses and Monotheism* is similar to his and for the equally considerable ways in which we differ.

14 This view, which was the scholarly consensus about the history of Judaism among German Protestant scholars, is directly evinced in Freud (1939: 51). This historiography of Judaism was enshrined in German Reform Judaism as well.

15 It is for this reason that Solomon Shechter referred to the Higher Criticism of the Bible as the Higher Antisemitism.

16 Gilroy, on the other hand, remarks on the "dangers for both blacks and Jews in accepting their historic and unsought association with sublimity" (1993: 215–16). See also Boyarin and Boyarin (1993).

17 It is symptomatic that when Freud writes of the legendary founding of rabbinic Judaism in R. Yohanan ben Zakkai's escape from besieged Jerusalem, he mentions only the "masculine" pursuit of intellectuality that it presaged and not the notoriously "feminine" mode of escape through trickery, in a coffin (Freud 1939: 124).

18 Cp. the somewhat similar reading of another aporia in Freud's text by Geller (1993: 62).

19 Freud is certainly aware that "savages" hedge sexual life with prohibitions and taboos, as he explicitly writes in the first chapter of *Totem and Taboo*. I think, nevertheless, that he not infrequently imagines the "primitive" as a space of unrepressed libido, as in Gaugin and Douanier Rousseau.

20 Cp. the description by Manuel of German Reform Judaism: "Reform Judaism, which had distanced itself from traditional rabbinism, owed something to the Christian idealization of ancient Judaism, the object having molded itself to fit the image in the mind of the beholder" (Manuel 1992: 263). Manuel points out that Herder had described biblical religion as "sublime" (264). Manuel also refers to the

Christian tradition dating back to the thirteenth century which admired "the Mosaic law but despised the legalistic accretions of the Talmudists" (266–67). Freud is not far here from such views, and that is, I suggest precisely the point.

21 Torgovnick shrewdly sees the same split in the 1930 preface to the new edition of *Totem and Taboo*, not associating it, however, with *Moses and Monotheism*. The difference between my reading and Torgovnick's is that whereas she sees a rather simple contrast between the way in which Jew is portrayed by the antisemite and Freud's attempt to counter it, I see much more equivocation within Freud himself. Torgovnick does not cite the very early valorization of the "primitive" in "Civilized" and thus misses, I think, an opportunity to see a layer of identification with the "primitive" Eastern Jew long before "the pressure of Naziism" (Torgovnick 1990: 201). Otto Rank was more consistent than Freud. For him the "essence of Judaism" was in its avoidance of repression and its "stress on primitive sexuality," which was a positively marked term (Rank 1985, and see Gilman 1993: 176).

PART III

GLEANINGS

It might seem, methodologically, not to matter from which testament one takes one's examples; but in fact it does matter. For the problem of psychoanalytic method proves to concern most particularly the question of two testaments, two religions; and we shall not be able to avoid [the topic of] Christian, and New Testament, anti-semitism.

David Jobling

The blank page – as vast and unbearable as it is, like the desert wherein Israel began to write the voice of God – is the place where writing can begin again.

Tod Linafelt

We cannot and never have interpreted without re-creation. . . . What biblical scholars must come to recognize and accept is that this has always been the case, even with the sacred texts that they put a wall around.

Kyle Keefer

As much as it seeks uniformity, univocality, closure, and stability, text criticism produces multiformity, multivocality, open-endedness, and instability. If text criticism can prioritize difference and so shore up the singularity of both Bible and Faith, it can surely multiply Bibles and in doing so fracture the Faith.

David M. Gunn

TEXTUAL BODIES

What text are we reading, and what difference does that question make to how we read? What text are we writing, for that matter? Here questions of textuality, authorship, and "The Book," which have been emerging throughout this volume, come more sharply into focus. What is the Bible? Is it a book? Has it a text? Where are its textual limits? What assumptions operate in contemporary thinking about this particular "book" as text and its relation to the political? When such questions are addressed to Scripture, to a body of "canonical text" with a literary history — in terms of both composition and reception — of arguably unparalleled length and complication, the problematics of textuality which infuse postmodern critical theory are compellingly compounded.

12

TRANSFERENCE AND TACT
IN BIBLICAL STUDIES

David Jobling

To declare my interest, I want to encourage a practice of psychoanalytic reading of the Bible integrated into a genuinely *critical* approach, as opposed to a pseudo-criticism that doesn't criticize anything (Bal 1991: chap. 3). This implies, first of all, that psychoanalytic method be kept in a tense relation of *mutual* critique with the other methods, not automatically submitted to another law than its own, as when some dominant method admits it, but only as subsidiary or secondary, forgetting that psychoanalysis has its own thing to say about submission to the law.[1] (Psychoanalytic method is here exemplary of a range of "new" methods, literary, etc., about which I would say the same thing. I stress that I am *not* advocating rejection of historical-critical methods, but rather a critical view of how methods interact with each other.) Second, this implies a psychocritique which, in line with current theory, does not exclude the critic from the criticism, living up to Jürgen Habermas's characterization of psychoanalysis as "the only tangible example of a science systematically incorporating self-reflection" (Habermas 1971: 214, and cf. the whole chapter; see also Bal 1991: 35–36). This means coming to terms, in interpretive work, with the reality of transferential and counter-transferential relationships at all levels.[2] The results of interpretation are at no point separate from the unconscious reasons why I am doing it – though the interpretation always pretends to such separation, to objectivity (as biblical studies amply confirm). I find a superb model in Jane Gallop's *Reading Lacan* (Gallop 1985), which never loses touch with what is going on between Lacan and Freud (whom to interpret was Lacan's life's work), *or* with what is going on between herself and Lacan.

In line with Gallop's decision to read precisely Lacan, I decided to read as authoritative a work as I could find on the use in biblical studies of psychological approaches: Gerd Theissen's *Psychological Aspects of Pauline Theology* (1987). Thus in this chapter[3] I am a refugee from my home turf of Jewish Bible studies, on the terrain of scholars of the "other" Testament. It might seem, methodologically, not to matter from which testament one takes one's examples; but in fact it does matter. For the problem of psychoanalytic method proves to concern most particularly the question of two testaments, two religions; and we shall not be able to avoid a topic which Canadian scholars[4] have a commendable record of taking up – Christian, and New Testament, anti-semitism (Richardson and Granskou 1986; Wilson 1986).

There will, though, be other texts. The choice of Theissen immediately implicates the Apostle to the Gentiles, from whom I have chosen 2 Corinthians 3:4–4:6, one of the sections Theissen reads, and one with which I know myself to have a largely unexplored transferential relationship. For I find myself saying, in a sermon of 1977, "In my personal wanderings around scripture, which take me more often to the Old than to the New Testament, [this] section of 2 Corinthians . . . has, I don't know why, for many years been 'home,' the center of the Bible." I must say that this predilection seems to have disappeared from my conscious since 1977! I shall also, after reading Theissen, draw by way of commentary on a few other texts, notably Walter Wink's *Transforming Bible Study* (1989b) as well as his review of Theissen (Wink 1989a), Richard Rubenstein's *My Brother Paul* (1972), and, going farther afield, Peter Gay's *A Godless Jew* (1987).

HISTORICAL-CRITICAL FATHERS

The upshot of Theissen's reading of the 2 Corinthians text is that Paul, while at the conscious level rejoicing unboundedly in his conversion from Judaism to Christianity, has unconsciously a hard time *achieving* it, as shown in his ambiguity about the law of Moses. At the level of interpretation, I find this well done. At the level of transference, I find nothing – Theissen absents himself from his own text, giving no indication of where *he* stands *vis-à-vis* Paul's conversion.

The line I shall take is based on my own experience of methodological conversion. For me, as for many others, the move from the historical criticism in which we were trained into current critical theory has been a rebirth. Transference with Paul and his Damascus experience! My main gut reaction to reading Theissen is that this creative critic, recognized as a leader in the broadening of methodology in biblical studies (see also Theissen 1978; 1985), does *not* express himself in the language of such a methodological conversion, does not accept the transferential invitation.

Let me read an exemplary page, 146. Theissen has been referring to Paul's language of human transformation (1987: 143) and is now discussing what, in Paul's view, prevents this transformation: "What remained hidden from the Israelites is . . . the killing power of the law – in psychoanalytic terms, the aggressivity of the internalized norm." The writing here is confident and creative. But he quickly pauses (as he often does) to ask himself, "Can an interpretation of this sort be made historically plausible?" How, I ask myself, can he fail to see that he is himself, at such a point, subject to the aggressivity of an internalized norm, the norm of historical criticism! The transferential invitation seems (from my perspective, the veil having been removed [2 Corinthians 3:16]) to be so obvious! Why does he never tell me what transformation his pioneering of psychological approaches has wrought in him? Why does he not, like Paul, contrast his being as a biblical interpreter pre- and post- the great event of his discovery of these approaches? Does it not seem to him *at all* that there is "a veil over the minds" (2 Corinthians 3:14–15) of the historical critics when they read Moses, or Paul?

Apparently not. But why can I not simply accept that Theissen has had an experience different from mine, and chooses to take up a different position *vis-à-vis* the new methods, and leave it at that? Aside from theoretical problems with this ideology of choice, I hear Paul saying: "*Necessity* is laid upon me. Woe is me if I preach not the gospel" (1 Corinthians 9:16). I suspect that Theissen *does* have this sense of evangelical necessity to broaden biblical methodology – why, otherwise, all his books? – but that he is prevented from so expressing himself precisely by "internalized norms."

I want, in fact, to posit not one but several related levels on which Theissen evokes processes which one might think of in terms of conversion, though *he* does not think of them so. The first level is from historical to psychological method in biblical studies. Theissen is clear that any use of the psychological must be preceded by, and grounded in, the historical. Each of his textual analyses proceeds in this order, and he repeatedly asks about the historical plausibility of a psychological datum. This, in effect, denies to psychological methods the slightest autonomy. For example, he makes a valuable comparison between certain psychological aspects of Paul and Philo, but at once, by a knee-jerk reaction, turns the discussion to the possibility of their historical relatedness (Theissen 1987: 133–37), conveying no sense that psychological method might entail a different, synchronic view of how such comparisons ought to be made.

The second level is within the category of the psychological, from psychodynamic (what I call psychoanalytic) to cognitive approaches. Theissen refers to a recent "trend to cognitive theories" (1987: 4) which, in a passage I find important, he puts in a historical framework; he sees the psychodynamic approach as resonating with "the European catastrophes of this century," while the cognitive "corresponds to a general renaissance of Enlightenment traditions in the period of economic and social stabilization of western democracies between 1950 and 1980" (1987: 43). Theissen prefers the cognitive.

The third level is within the category of the psychodynamic, from Freud to Jung. Theissen prefers Jung.

These choices, all of which seem to me to be implicated in a rejection of the radicality of psychoanalysis, rule out the possibility of Theissen's getting seriously into current methodological debate. To give him his due, he does, whether from influences not acknowledged or out of his own intelligence, come close to several *topoi* of current theory. The discussion just mentioned, of the cultural climates conducive to the different psychological methods, is attuned to current culture-critique, and the treatment of "textuality" (Theissen 1987: 45–49) has a postmodern ring. But there are places he won't go – no Lacan or French theory, no overt reference even to Habermas. And he lacks the postmodern instinct: he *worries* about anachronisms and mistakes, where a Mieke Bal thinks first of their meaning-producing potential.[5] In relation to the methodological conversion some of us have experienced, and to the new interpretive communities being formed, Theissen's role is analogous to that of the Judaizers!

Yet I perceive at each level the symptoms of what he is repressing. As regards the first level, and the whole aim of his book, let us look (in line with postmodernism's concern with the "frame") at his preface (for what follows, see Theissen 1987: xii). Theissen is referring to his wife. She is a psychologist. (*My* wife, by the way, is a psychiatrist.) He makes the usual academic gesture, but oddly. He acknowledges her help, and adds, "Yet I cannot hold her responsible for my mistakes." He goes on, "I am myself responsible," and we expect, "for any mistakes"; but what we actually read is "for the application of psychological theories to religious texts and phenomena."

I shall read, here and elsewhere, *à la lettre*, as Lacan puts it, "to the letter" (the translation "literally" misses the point wonderfully).[6] Recall, for example, the insistence on the *letter* of the dream in Freud's classic analyses (Freud 1976). More than once, when referring to Lacan's procedure here, Gallop alludes to the *locus classicus* in the Pauline text before us: "the letter kills, but the spirit gives life" (2 Corinthians 3:6). But psychoanalysis reverses this: "Freud discovered that truth manifests itself in the letter rather than the spirit" (Gallop 1985: 22, cf. 115). So my reading is at odds with Paul – or, shall we say, on the Jewish as opposed to the Christian side.

À la lettre, Theissen's preface can only imply that "applying psychological theories to religious texts . . . ," the aim of his book, is itself a mistake. What, we wonder, is the significance of this slip? To this symptom, I would join another. I am amazed how, in the psychological sections of his textual readings, the dialogue in the footnotes continues to be almost exclusively with historical critics, rather than with his predecessors in psychological interpretation. My thought is that Theissen is working out his relationship with his academic fathers. They are historical-critical, not psychological fathers. His worry is that his conversion has been too great and threatening a one, that the application of psychological methods to the Bible is, indeed, a big mistake.

In his other major choices, psychodynamic versus cognitive, Freud versus Jung, Theissen seems to me to want to soften the impact of psychological methods on traditional biblical studies; but more symptoms are present. In the part of the preface already referred to, he displaces his preference for the cognitive onto his wife: "Her professional knowledge has opened up to me . . . cognitive conceptions of psychology; I have to thank her for a critical distance on the psychodynamic currents . . ." (Theissen 1987: xii). Is the preference for the cognitive really *his own*?

Theissen's preference here often seems more like a hang-up, for he cannot get away from the unconscious, and, as he says, its special relevance for religious phenomena. He tells us that he has deliberately chosen Pauline texts "in which confrontation with the unconscious is visible" (1987: 53), and ascribes to unconscious motivation key phenomena in the texts, such as Paul's misquoting scripture (1987: 130). Indeed, "Interpreters always put something of themselves into the text to be interpreted. This occurs unconsciously . . ." (Theissen 1987: 46; he fails to apply this insight to himself). There is perceptible tension, then, between the choice for the cognitive and a sense of the necessity of, or a fascination with, the psychodynamic. Most revealing is the final, "cognitive," section of the analysis of 2 Corinthians 3–4. What Theissen characterizes as *cognitive* is Paul's rationalizing and self-deception, in finding a way to continue to respect the law from which he has been converted (Theissen 1987: 153–58). Psychoanalytically, this is simply a way of saying "regression" – Paul draws back from the extremity of the change he is experiencing. Is the cognitive, for Theissen, a regression from the change threatened by psychoanalysis? More generally, in view of his discussion, mentioned earlier, of the modern cultural contexts of different psychological approaches, does the "trend to the cognitive" in recent decades constitute a recovery from the psychoanalytic, or a regression from it?

As for Freud versus Jung, suffice it to say for now that Theissen expresses the contrast in terms both immoderate and going beyond the historically justifiable: the unconscious is, for Freud, "a swamp that must be drained," for Jung, "a vivifying spring" (1987: 12).

In sum, Theissen's text suggests how radical a conversion it is to go from historical-critical to psychological methods. The existence of his book establishes how necessary he believes the move to be, but all his conscious choices tend to diminish the radicality. A variety of symptoms, however, indicate that much more is going on than conscious choices, and that Theissen's repression of the fundamental conflict is incomplete.

For further light on the conflict, I turn briefly to Walter Wink's *Transforming Bible Study*. This book describes the use of the Bible in group therapy to which Wink devotes much of his life. So one might expect that he would grant to psychological approaches to the Bible their own autonomous place, especially in view of his title, which suggests a conversion paradigm for what is happening in biblical method. This expectation is utterly disappointed. Wink repeats all Theissen's gestures, even exaggerates them. "The value of the critical method is that it defends the text from our projecting on it our own biases, theologies, and presuppositions" (Wink 1989b: 39) – as if no "biases," etc., were enshrined in the "critical method" itself. This is a criticism that not only doesn't criticize anything, but exists specifically to defend the Bible from our critique. The extreme expression of Wink's view comes in his appendix, "On Psychologizing." It is for applying psychological theory without "psychologizing" that Wink, in his review, commends Theissen so highly (Wink 1989a: 41; cf. 40, "the spectre of psychologism"), and in his own book this verb indicates for Wink a danger so great that we seem to be in the realm of taboo. "The hazards of psychologizing are not to be minimized. . . . *Not the text, but we ourselves are the object of analysis*" (Wink 1989b: 164, his emphasis). The taboo extends to some interpretations which seem not unuseful, at least as trial balloons, including one which I cannot resist quoting:

> It would be psychologizing to argue, on the basis of Jesus' use of 'Abba' ('Daddy') as a metaphor for God, that he had an Oedipal complex, or was perhaps a bastard who was compensating for not knowing his earthly father. Such questions are *illegitimate*.
>
> (Wink 1989b: 163, my emphasis)

There is nothing so anal-retentive as this in all of Theissen! Wink repeats Theissen's contrast of Jung and Freud, surpasses him in his sense of the danger of anachronism, and so on. In a word, he utterly submits psychological method in biblical studies to an alien law.

Where Theissen and Wink, for opposite reasons, exclude the drama of transference and counter-transference in interpretation – Wink because he excludes the text, Theissen because he excludes himself, from analysis – someone who gets it right is Richard Rubenstein, in *My Brother Paul*. The very first topic of his book is the impossibility of objective interpretation, in which context he points precisely to Freud's discovery of the counter-transference (Rubenstein 1972: 1–22, esp. 22). Relating Paul to Freud is not, for him, the anxious business it is for Theissen. Depth psychology possesses, in Rubenstein's view, the tools appropriate for understanding Paul, who is even Freud's precursor (Rubenstein 1972: 22)! And, much to my purpose, Rubenstein notes how rebirth, conversion, can come as well through psychoanalysis as through religion (Rubenstein 1972: 7).

JEWISH FATHERS

But Rubenstein is a Jew, and at this point I want to raise the stakes by suggesting that Theissen is also co-implicated with Paul in that special type of father-conflict which is Christian anti-semitism – though not, I hasten to add, at any conscious or overt level. In his preference for Jung over Freud, Theissen makes nothing of the one being a Christian, the other a Jew. But this contrast assumes importance when he contrasts Jung's view of early Christianity favourably with Freud's. Jung suggested that Jesus and early Christianity achieved the reawakening of buried "archetypal tendencies" in the human psyche (Theissen 1987: 15–17, with reference to Jung 1958: esp. 152–57), whereas Freud viewed the same phenomena as achieving a resolution of the primal scene, father and sons, by vicarious sacrifice (Theissen 1987: 19–21; cf. Freud 1950). But if Christianity achieves the reawakening of the repressed, this inevitably implicates Judaism as the cause of the repression. To this I would add that Theissen's view of twentieth-century history is open to the suspicion of "forgetting the holocaust," if, as I have suggested, his cognitive "recovery" from twentieth-century catastrophes implies repression of what the catastrophes were about.

This admittedly slight basis in Theissen's text can be consolidated from other directions. I begin with the thesis explored, though partly rejected, by Peter Gay in *A Godless Jew*. Gay's title is from a letter of Freud to his friend Oskar Pfister. "Quite by the way," Freud asks, "why did none of the devout create psychoanalysis? Why did one have to wait for a godless Jew?" (Gay 1987: vii). Again *à la lettre*, what is here being opposed to "devout"? Not "godless," but "godless Jew." Is devoutness contrary, for Freud, not (only) to godliness, but (also) to Jewishness? The question gains some point from the fact that Pfister was a Christian pastor (see Gay 1987: 73–87, for an account of this extraordinary friendship). The thesis, at any rate, is that psychoanalysis had to be invented not only by an atheist, but by a Jewish one – the reason being (and here I depart from Gay) that Judaism is what Christianity must repress in order to constitute itself, and repression cannot be perceived by those doing the repressing.

Such speculation receives further encouragement from Wink, in his review of Theissen. In that highly positive review, his only critical point is that Theissen fails to "critique" (as opposed to "recover") Pauline psychology. "In Pauline theology," Wink asks, "does one ever become fully conscious of the depth of human hatred toward God?" (1989a: 41). Paul, and the Christian tradition after him, are implicated in whitewashing the wrathful biblical God. "Paul did not dare raise this conflict to consciousness. As a consequence, Christianity has been unable to rid itself of a monstrous hidden aggression, displaced from God to scapegoats like *Jews* . . ." (Wink 1989a: 42, my emphasis). *À la lettre*, an implication of Theissen's text in anti-semitism.

Encouragement of a different kind comes from Rubenstein, throughout whose book appears a sense of understanding, even ownership, of psychoanalysis. To what I have already said, I may simply add that Rubenstein, of course, has written much on the Holocaust, and sees recovery from it to lie in the direction of going deeper into psychoanalysis, rather than in regressing from it (Rubenstein 1966, esp. chap. 1).

A case can therefore be made, with more than a show of plausibility, that Theissen's struggle with the psychoanalytic is very much linked with Paul's struggle with Judaism, and that Theissen has not come to terms with his relationship to Paul's invention, in that struggle, of Christian anti-semitism.

TACT

Finally, my title promises "tact" as well as "transference." By this I intend to ask, very briefly, what a transferential style of biblical interpretation might look like, and what limits are to be set to it. Is biblical scholarship to become one big therapy session? I pose my question in terms of tact because of one final reference in Theissen,[7] in which he threatens to come out of his shell, but again oddly (when read *à la lettre*): "*We* not only understand *ourselves and one another*, but also explain. . . . Human tact presupposes the ability to make intelligible the bizarre behavior, sore points, and personal limitations *of others* . . ." (1987: 42, my emphasis). Interpretation has to do, then, with real human problems, even real human *illness*. This, at last, looks like a limit to the tact of Theissen's objective scholarship. But even here, he tactfully diverts the point from "we" to "others." Wink, outside of biblical scholarship as normally defined, advocates a therapeutic breaking of tact in controlled conditions; but I have discerned in his position some methodological falseness. Rubenstein simply starts to talk about himself, his Jewish upbringing, in the most natural way, as he starts to talk about Paul – how else should it be, with a brother? We won't find it hard to invent styles, or technique, for talking in tactful ways about our transferential relationship to what we do, once we are converted.

POSTSCRIPT

With a few cosmetic changes, the foregoing is the text of a paper which I read to the Canadian Society of Biblical Studies in 1990, and which I thought to rewrite for an issue of *Studies in Religion* devoted to postmodernism. When I set about this, though, I found that the paper resisted being rewritten and insisted, rather, on being reread. It had become a text, like the ones which it itself read. What mainly prompted a serious rereading was the extent to which I found the 1990 paper to be enmeshed in the problematic which it was supposed to address. I discovered that I had unconsciously repeated the gestures which I had exposed in Theissen.

There is perhaps nothing so characteristic of postmodernism, or so detested by its detractors, as its inability to talk about anything without immediately talking about talking about it. Self-reflection, metadiscourse, iteration – the terms are many – is part of the postmodern habit of mind. Postmodernism often proceeds by (re)reading texts, especially authoritative, "classic," texts – most of Derrida and Lacan consists of such readings. It does not claim to be new, to advance or expand knowledge, but to be a way of inhabiting what is already there, of retreading roads already trodden, of indicating roads not taken. It is "metacritical," refusing the distinction between text and commentary, reading everything as text. It is self-critical, accepting and tracing its own involvement in the problematics it exposes.

So this postscript is a reading (or rather, a brief sample of one) of what was already a reading of Gerd Theissen's reading of a passage from Paul. At least for the converted, this critique of my 1990 paper will represent not a weakening, but a transferential strengthening of what I was trying to say then. But the new version will itself be just a text, inviting reading.

Already in 1990 I *was* vaguely aware of the major problem – that I had not improved much on Theissen in self-reflection. I too was largely absenting myself from my own text. This sounds odd, given the frequency with which "I" appears there; but it is an I which critiques others rather than reflects on its own status – the I of the beholder. Let me now say a little more about that "I." I was aware of the importance of psychoanalysis in postmodern discourse, especially in developments around Lacan, and the use of him by literary critics. I was intrigued by the link with feminism – how both in France and in North America the most creative responses to Lacan had been by women.[8] But I lacked models for doing biblical study along these lines. I had read Mieke Bal on Samson and Delilah (1987: chap. 2), but could not generalize from it. I was also conscious of the dead weight of an old-style "Freud and the Bible" approach, based on mutual suspicion if not contempt, in which a few psychoanalytic enthusiasts used their models to explain biblical data, but were firmly rebuffed by biblical scholars. The dynamics of this encounter were tedious in the extreme. Psychoanalysis, assuming the validity of its models, came to the Bible with a desire not for mutual critique but for domination, while historical-critical scholarship resisted out of an ignorance and fear which only masked its own parallel desire. Psychoanalysis dealt with this resistance in its own terms, and the whole issue went round in circles.[9]

It was reading Gallop's *Reading Lacan* which gave focus to my interest in the possibility of psychoanalytic approaches to the Bible. Attention to transference makes for an endlessly fluid application of psychoanalytic theory to acts of interpretation, as opposed to reading texts as exemplifying fixed psychological structures. For example, we can shift our interest from the correctness of Freud's theory that Judaism (and Christianity) is a working out of the relationship to the father, to the role played *by* the working out of the relationship to the father in the building of the theory (see The Bible and Culture Collective 1995: 187–224). To pose the question in the most general terms, how are the dynamics of biblical texts replayed in the drama of their interpretation?

I conclude with two examples of how my 1990 paper evidences the same anxieties I discerned in Theissen. First, I find that I told there a quite fictitious story of how the paper came to be written, a story in which I *started* with a fully conceived aim, to demonstrate transference in biblical interpretation, and chose Theissen, "as authoritative a work as I could find on the use in biblical studies of psychological approaches," as an apt site for the demonstration. In fact, I don't recall why I read Theissen, but it certainly was not to demonstrate transference! I did not at all anticipate what I found, but doubtless I found it because I was reading with eyes that Gallop had prepared. This fits my experience of postmodernism, that it is a theoretically productive style or even habit of reading, an openness to serendipity or, if you prefer, to intertextuality. Why, then, did I unconsciously displace this story of serendipity into a story of intentionality, of properly organized research? Out of the same sort of anxiety, no doubt, that I impute to Theissen, anxiety about the impression I create among my colleagues. I ought to add that I felt from the start some animus against Theissen. The worst crime I attribute to *my* academic fathers is that they directed me, for my overseas study in the 1960s, to Germany, whose dominance in biblical studies was ending, rather than to France, where the intellectual action was. That we should still, in the 1980s, be turning to a rather moribund German biblical scholarship for guidance in a cutting-edge area like psychological approaches annoyed me. So my "choice" of Theissen was no more part of an objective research design than was my choice of 2 Corinthians among the passages he deals with.

Second, I note that near the beginning of the 1990 paper I use the word "home" in contrary senses. In the opening courtesies, I refer to myself, a Jewish Bible scholar addressing a group of New Testament scholars, as "a refugee from my home turf." But shortly thereafter I quote my 1977 self as finding its "home" in the New Testament, with the implication that the career I was making in the study of the Jewish Bible was a "wandering." I find it now scarcely credible that I should have been unconscious, in 1990, of the collision between these two passages. Were I to analyze the anxiety of which this repression is a symptom, I would surely find myself retracing the same ground – that of the impossibility of finding appropriate ways to relate, as a Christian, to Judaism – that I found it necessary to explore in relation to Theissen.

NOTES

1 I have in mind, of course, Jacques Lacan's "Law-of-the-Father" (1977: chap. 6).
2 For psychoanalytic definitions, see Laplanche and Pontalis (1974). For Jane Gallop's use of "transference," and mine, see Felman (1985: 159–83).
3 This part of the present chapter was originally a paper read to the Canadian Society of Biblical Studies. See my "Postscript" below.
4 See the preceding note.
5 Bal advocates a methodological use of anachronism – exploring the heuristic value of looking at the texts from perspectives alien to them. See Bal (1991: 227–28, 240–41; and 1987 131–32), and cf. Jobling (1991b: 6–7).
6 See Lacan (1977: 147) and the translator's note (176). Gallop's discussion (1985: 115) is charming.
7 One could similarly develop the reference to "an offense against . . . good manners" (Theissen 1987: 1).

8 In addition to Gallop (1985), see, among others, Felman (1987), Grosz (1990), Ragland-Sullivan (1987). Let me add that I made from the outset a conscious decision not to pursue feminist issues in my paper. The invitation to do so is hard to resist; it lies in the "Excursus" to Theissen's psychological analysis of 2 Corinthians 3–4 (Theissen 1987: 158–75), which he devotes not to this text at all, but (by a displacement based on "veil" in 3:13–16) to the need for *women* to be veiled in 1 Corinthians 11. What I find alarming is not the displacement itself, but the extraordinary length of the excursus – longer, allowing for the small print, than the chapter to which it is appended, so that the discourse on the primary text seems to get overtaken or consumed by the discourse on the secondary text. But I decided that if I pursued this line, I would not be able to keep my paper within reasonable limits.

9 Cf., e.g., the way Howie (1950: 69–79) simply dismisses the psychoanalytic approach of Broome (1946). On this history, see now Halperin (1993: 7–38).

13

MARGINS OF LAMENTATION,
Or, The Unbearable Whiteness of Reading
Tod Linafelt

*There is the white space before the event and the white space after.
But who could tell them apart?*

*So the event is perhaps only the unexpected shattering of the white
space within the indefinite space of the book.*

(Jabès 1993: 91)

I begin with an epigraph from Edmond Jabès. But of course that is not true.
I begin rather with a blank space, into which Jabès's words intrude. There is
white space before and white space after. Writing gives us only a brief
reprieve from this unbearable whiteness, this ever-present absence. Yet even
in filling the white space with writing, absence persists.

*. . . do we not need the blank space, the fraction of silence between
words to read or hear them? – words have no tie to one another except
this absence.*

(Jabès 1993: 174)

Without the white spaces between letters and words our writing would be
illegible. The claustrophobia of language requires *Lebensraum* in order to
thrive. (Even the black fire of the Torah letters depends on the white fire as a
background.) Absence is the one thing we can count on always to be present.

– the space, you know, the space we dread by day and night.

(Jabès 1993: 68)

Is this absence anywhere more apparent than in the book of Lamentations? "There is none to comfort her . . ." (1:2), "with none to help her . . ."
(1:7), "with none to comfort her . . ." (1:9), "she has no one to comfort her
. . ." (1:17). Absence pervades this brutal book. The reader is told again and
again that Zion has no one to comfort her. Jerusalem has been destroyed;
God has abandoned the city of David and God's own chosen people.

*"Vertiginous space between the lines! We need only to look at a page of
writing,"* he said, *"to realize that our roads are bridges thrown from*

one point of absence to another, from an absence rich in promises, to an
absence that is desolate."

(Jabès 1993: 55)

From promise to desolation: this is the story told by Lamentations. *Heils-*
geschichte become *Fehlgeschichte*. There is no space here for Gerhard von
Rad's schema of promise – fulfillment. But perhaps for Jabès? Can this distinctly Jewish, distinctly postmodern (*I talked to you about the difficulty of*
being Jewish, which is the same as the difficulty of writing. For Judaism and
writing are but the same waiting, the same hope, the same depletion [cited in
Gould 1985: 3]) thinker/poet/philosopher/writer help us to understand the
book of Lamentations? To understand it without betraying the suffering it
portrays?

Harsh words of lament and accusation in the Hebrew Bible are not unique
to the book of Lamentations of course. The Psalms too contain numerous
laments, on which biblical scholars have expended a great deal of interpretive
energy. They have typically focused on the structural movement of the
Psalms from complaint to petition to divine response to praise.[1] To be sure,
this structure is apparent in the majority of the laments in the Psalter (Psalm
88 being one notable exception), but the overriding emphasis on the movement to praise threatens to betray the memory of suffering preserved in the
candid language of lament.

So white was the cry we had reason to think that pain simply meant
feeling the stages of whiteness.

(Jabès 1993: 95)

Claus Westermann's analysis of Israelite worship, for example, is no doubt
susceptible to Walter Lowe's diagnosis (1993: 2–6) of "ready-made enlightenment." According to Westermann, the primary mode of worship for ancient
Israel was that of praise. This was interrupted only in times of danger, at
which point the community would switch into the "lament" mode until the
trouble was resolved. Then the community would return to its normal mode
of praise.[2] In the liturgy, so the hypothesis goes, the assurance that the
trouble would be resolved was provided by a "salvation oracle." That is, a
word from the LORD ("fear not") was spoken by the priest or other official at
the appropriate point in the lament.

What is troubling about this move from lament to praise can be summed
up in Adorno's dictum, "the need to let suffering speak is the condition of
all truth" (in Cornell 1992: 13). Or, as Walter Brueggemann (1984: 52) has
written about contemporary liturgical usage of the Psalms, "It is clear that a

church that goes on singing 'happy songs' in the face of raw reality is doing something other than the Bible itself does." Bounded on both sides by praise, or what Brueggemann calls "orientation" (1984: 19–23), the disorientation of the lament appears to be tamed, controlled – not unlike the experience of watching the television news, where unspeakable violence appears safely contained within the frame around the screen. Try as we might, we can never really convince ourselves that it is contained. Eventually the television is turned off and the blank screen leads us to look outside its electronic borders.

> *Leaving the book, we do not leave it: we inhabit its absence. . . . The absence of the book is located both before and beyond the word. But it is also written in the margin of writing, as its erasure.*
>
> (Jabès 1993: 41)

Are these poles of orientation really the *archē* and *telos* they seem? Or are they also bounded by absence "before and beyond"? Indeed, the schema suspiciously resembles Lowe's idealist diamond: "a full blown narrative which proceeds in three parts: the *archē* of a primal unity, an original innocence; the division or fall into disunity and alienation; and the *telos* of hope and reunification" (Lowe 1993: 25). The diamond, however, must be cut.

> *No borders for oblivion.*
>
> (Jabès 1993: 64)

Lowe (1993: 27) notes: "the diamond attempts to capture history, but history withdraws from it like the tide." Are we justified in suspecting that the pain of lament likewise withdraws from the *archē* and *telos* of orientation and orientation?

Turning to the book of Lamentations, these suspicions prove grounded.[3] Before the move from lament back into praise could be made, according to Westermann (1980: 42), "first the most important thing had to occur: God's answer." But in Lamentations, God's answer is not so readily available. Indeed, God's voice is most conspicuously absent.

> *Leave it to God to die of God where He is silent.*
>
> (Jabès 1993: 134)

The voice of God never intrudes into the poetry of Lamentations. The move to praise is indefinitely postponed, though not for lack of passion or artistry on the part of the poetry. From beginning to end the book of Lamentations affronts God with suffering in hopes of eliciting a response. Particularly poignant is the figure of the mourning Mother Zion in chapters 1 and 2. Let us attend to her in our quest to remain true to the memory of suffering. In so doing we follow in the trace of Jabès's godchild Jacques Derrida: "I am (following) the mother. The text" (Derrida 1986: 116). As Drucilla Cornell notes in her reflections on Derrida's *Glas*, "It is the Woman who mourns" (1992: 75).

LAMENTATIONS 1

The book of Lamentations opens with the voice of the poet employing the exclamatory *'ekah* ("Alas!"/"How?"), then offering parallel, ironic reversals to describe the city of Jerusalem.

> Alas!
> She sits alone, the city once great with people.
> She is like a widow, her once great among the nations.
> A leader among provinces, has come to forced labor.[4]

In the verses that follow the poet elaborates on the state of fallen Jerusalem, citing the LORD as the source of the destruction (verse 5) and justifying it as a punishment (verses 5 and 8).

Verse 9 begins as if to carry on the general sentiment expressed to this point by the poet. But there occurs a radical shift at the end of verse 9 when what is unmistakably the voice of Zion interrupts the poet:

See, LORD, my affliction; how the enemy magnifies himself.

This interruption is short, only two cola, but nonetheless compelling. Cornell (1992: 84) writes: "'There is' disruption of totality. The Other [Mother?] cannot completely be eliminated in any given representational system. The Other survives." The poet's monopoly on the reader is momentarily broken; the one spoken about now becomes the one who speaks. Likewise, while the poet has spoken *about* the LORD, it is Zion who first speaks *to* the LORD. Theology is put on hold, as Zion challenges the LORD (and the reader) to look upon her affliction, rather than to explain it.

No sooner has the reader realized that Zion is speaking than she is silent once more.

A sound – uttered by whom – and then nothing.

(Jabès 1993: xi)

No answer from God. The speaking voice reverts to the poet. Yet there is an indication that the poet has been affected by the interruption – albeit brief – of the voice of Zion. For in verse 10 the poet uncharacteristically addresses God directly, as did Zion, using the second person:

She has seen nations come into her holy place;
about whom you commanded, they shall not come into your assembly.

Verse 11 is the final verse of the first half of the poem, and represents a climax and a transition:

> They have given their precious things [*mahmad*] for food,
> in order to restore their lives.

The sense of *mahmad* ("precious things") here is debatable, but the bitter irony of the line is better exploited by emphasizing the connotation of children as the "precious ones."[5] Furthermore, it anticipates 2:20 and 4:10, where children themselves are eaten by their mothers.

This, it seems, is too much for Zion. The poet is once again interrupted by the voice of Zion, with the same imperative as verse 9c: "see, LORD!" (*re'eh yhwh*). The transition is a major one, with the voice of Zion dominating for the remainder of the chapter (with a brief interruption by the poet in 1:17). Alan Mintz (1984: 25) writes: "[Zion's speech] has the effect of a mute and distantly observed object suddenly springing to life and coming forward to speak. What has been a personification becomes more like a person."

> *A face of which only wrinkles are left. A face with its daily life shattered, its eternity blurred.*
>
> (Jabès 1989: 75)

Faced with the testimony of a woman raped and tortured, questions of just punishment are ludicrous.

> *What is destroyed inspires relief or regret, but never causes fright. A stubborn perseverance, on the other hand, is daunting in its insolence.*
> (Jabès 1989: 76)

So, for the moment at least, the reader (and the poet) are forced to consider only the lived pain of the widow Zion.

In verse 16 we find the climax to Zion's first speech. In response to the terrifying situation she has just described, Zion cries out:

> For these things I weep . . . My eyes, my eyes!
>   They pour out tears.
> How far from me is one to comfort,
>   one to restore my life.
> My children are ravaged;
>   O, how the enemy has triumphed.

Thus the section culminates with a mother wailing over the loss of her children. She is alone, with no one to offer comfort, no one to share the pain. "Most direct of all responses: the scream which emerges from the gap in every word" (Gould 1985: xvii). With Zion momentarily overcome by grief, the poet interjects in verse 17, repeating the by-now familiar refrain, "there is no one to comfort her." Zion regains her voice in verse 18, taking a different tack this time to elicit a response from YHWH. She begins by acknowledging Y<small>HWH</small>'s justice and her own rebelliousness (referred to again in verse 20). We may note that the character of Zion, for all her challenging of Y<small>HWH</small>, never claims complete innocence. But she does shift the rhetoric to the experience and extent of pain, and in this final section of chapter 1 she does not let up, despite her initial admission of rebelliousness.

LAMENTATIONS 2

The voice of the poet begins chapter 2 with the same word as chapter 1, *'ekah* ("Alas!/How?"). But this time it is freighted with all that has come in chapter 1, and with this opening the poet weighs in firmly on behalf of Zion. Picking up the cue from Zion, the poet portrays God, in line after line, as an enemy warrior.

> *God, an obliterating tyrant? World and man perish where the Word rages.*
>
> (Jabès 1983: 214)

The reader of 2:1–4 is confronted by a poetic whirlwind of wrath and fire. Verse 1: the L<small>ORD</small> in "his wrath" (*'aph*) has shamed Zion, and has forgotten his footstool on "the day of his wrath" (*yom 'aph*). Verse 2: "In his fury" (*'ebrah*) the L<small>ORD</small> has razed Judah's defenses. Verse 3: the L<small>ORD</small> has cut down "in blazing wrath" (*bohari-'aph*) the horn of Israel, and has "burned [*ba'ar*] against Israel like a blazing fire [*'esh lehabah*], consuming [*'akal*] on all sides." Verse 4: the L<small>ORD</small> pours out against Zion "his wrath [*'aph*] like raging fire [*'esh hamah*]." The English language is exhausted in an attempt to describe the destructive inferno unleashed by God's anger.

After recounting the state of the vanquished city in verses 5–10, in verse 11 the poet brings us to the halfway point of the second poem. Like the first poem, it marks a climax and transition. In light of the suffering figure of Zion, the poet finally breaks down:

> My eyes are spent with tears, my stomach churns;
> my bile is poured out on the ground,
>   at the destruction of the daughter of my people;
> as the children and the infants collapsed
>   in the squares of the city.
> They kept saying to their mothers,
>   "Where is bread and wine?"
> as they collapsed as if wounded
>   in the squares of the city,
>   as their lives ran out in the bosoms of their mothers.

The poet again echoes the words of Zion. Even as Zion's eyes flowed with tears, so the poet's eyes are spent with tears. And the poet employs the same phrase Zion used in 1:20, "my stomach churns," to describe his physical and/or emotional state. But most significantly, it is the children perishing in the street that finally prove too much for the poet, even as they did for Mother Zion (1:16). Adorno wrote that after Auschwitz poetry is barbaric (Adorno 1981: 30). He was, perhaps, anticipated by the writer of Lamentations.

Irving Greenberg (1977: 23) offers the following as a working principle for discourse after the Holocaust: "No statement, theological or otherwise, should be made that would not be credible in the presence of the burning children." Given this criteria, there is no speech adequate. Perhaps Greenberg, too, was anticipated by Lamentations.

> What can I say for you, to what can I compare you,
>   daughter Jerusalem?
> To what can I liken you, that I may comfort you,
>   daughter Zion?
> For your breach is as vast as the sea;
>   who could heal you?

(2:13)

The questions are rhetorical. Nothing can be said; there is no comparison; no one can heal a breach as vast as the sea.

> *Who could ever measure the extent of a suffering which has forgotten even its origin . . . ?*

(Jabès 1985: 28)

The poet is caught in the survivor's dilemma: to speak is to betray the memory of the dead, for there is no adequate language; but to remain silent is a worse betrayal. So the poet continues, as even Adorno conceded must be done.[6]

With verses 18 and 19 we come to the end of the poet's speech, and a final intensification of rhetoric. Having taken up the cause of Zion, but able neither to find a comforter nor to comfort Zion adequately himself, the poet urges Zion to cry out once again to the LORD.

> Cry out to the LORD from the heart,
>   wall of daughter Zion.
> Shed tears like a torrent,
>   day and night!
> Give yourself no rest,
>   and do not let your eyes be still.
> Arise! Wail in the night, at the beginning of the watches.
>   Pour out your heart like water in front of the LORD.
> Lift your hands to him, for lives of your children,
>   who collapse from hunger at the corner of every street!

The rhetorical move imagined by the poet is for Zion to affront Yhwh with the intolerable suffering of children.

> *Every human word is an affront to the Word of God, not because of rising up against it, but because it forces the latter to repudiate it.*
>
> (Jabès 1989: 24)

It is exactly this, we may recall, that led to Zion's breaking down into tears in 1:16. It is also the perishing children that lead to the poet's own breakdown in 2:11. Perhaps, then, the "lives of the children" will be enough to move even God.[7]

Zion responds to the urging of the poet, beginning with the most accusatory passage in the book:

> See, LORD, and consider who it is
>   you have so ruthlessly afflicted!
> Alas! Women are eating their offspring,
>   the children they have borne!
>
> (2:20)

Zion employs the same imperative as she did at the end of 1:11 in an attempt to command the attention of God. The verb *'alal* ("afflicted") is sardonically placed here in a parallel position with *'olal* ("children"), contrasting the ruthlessness of God with the suffering of children, and making clear that these are whom God is afflicting.

Mother Zion continues in this final section to elaborate on the suffering of the population, and employs ironically the language of sacrificial worship. But it is a gruesome perversion of the temple cultus that affronts the reader in the last line of verse 22: "those whom I bore and reared, the enemy has consumed!" Zion's final speech of 2:20–22, bounded at beginning and end by the cannibalizing of children, is the last we here from her in the book of Lamentations.

> *Death is near.*
> *How do you know?*
> *It has fallen silent.*
>
> (Jabès 1985: 32)

Her penultimate line in verse 22 rings fitting as a summary: "none survived or escaped."

Zion gets no response from God. The book struggles on, of course, attempting to stave off the silence, the white space, employing a number of rhetorical strategies to express the grief and anger of the community and to elicit divine response.

. . . a silence charged with intense emotion has suddenly come to stop all words, interrupt all talk . . .

(Jabès 1993: 140)

In the final chapter, the community speaks in a first person plural voice, addressing God directly. The book ends with their plaintive appeal:

> Why dost thou forget us forever,
> why dost thou so long forsake us?
> Restore us to thyself, O LORD,
> that we may be restored!
> Renew our days as of old!
> Or hast thou utterly rejected us?
> Art thou exceedingly angry with us?

(5:20–22; RSV)

This appeal, like those of Zion and the poet, remains unanswered. The voice of God never sounds in the book.

All that finally remains of the completed book is a gaping hole.

(Jabès 1993: 65)

With the book of Lamentations, then, it seems that we must question the *arche* and *telos* of orientation. The idealist diamond has been cut; without the salvation oracle of God's response, there is no movement back to praise. Instead, there is only white space.

a space so vast to the eye, so crushing to thought

(Jabès 1993: 132)

Is there anything so unbearable as this blank space?

From the opening portrayal of the city as an abandoned widow, to the broken man of chapter 3, to the final unanswered communal lament of chapter 5, the reader is not so much engaged by the book of Lamentations as assaulted by it. We are compelled nonetheless to continue reading – to follow Mother Zion – for

a blank means passage into death

(Jabès 1993: 166)

If there were anything worse than the brutal rhetoric of destruction it would be the blankness of God's non-response. We continue to read because the absence of God in the face of Zion's lament over dying children is intolerable. We continue to read because we know that when the words run out God's response will no longer be possible.

The murder of God is an illegible murder.

(Jabès 1993: 51)

Of course our desire is frustrated. Our reading always stops short of presence. We are somehow able to negotiate the white between the letters, the blanks between the words, the absence at the core of writing, but the void that confronts us after the book's final questions appears insurmountable . . .

> *The white there.*
> *The page*
> *after all this white.*

(Jabès 1993: 84)

"Why have you forsaken us for all time? Have you rejected us? Are you bitterly angry with us?" So the book of Lamentations ends – or, rather, does not end. For these unanswered, "final" questions echo in the absence of God's response.

> *And I say to myself, this must be the way books die, given that they begin with words taking wing toward the sky.*

(Jabès 1993: 106)

Words directed toward the sky – the passion of Mother Zion, the pathos of the poet – fall back to the ground and disappear into the whiteness. No, the idealist diamond offers no solace to the reader of Lamentations and certainly not to the mother mourning the murder of her children. The biblical scholar's penchant for closure in praise cannot be accommodated in the vast margins of Lamentations.

Edmond Jabès has lurked among the white spaces of this chapter, interrupting sporadically to unsettle the course of my exegesis, subverting any theodicy of disengagement fostered by academic discourse. Attempting to maintain the otherness of his presence (?), I have relegated him to marginal status. Perhaps now it is time to introduce Jabès properly, and to request his help more formally in relating the sense of reading Lamentations without sublating the unrelieved suffering therein.

A Jew born in Egypt, Jabès has come to epitomize the exilic nature of language for poststructuralist thinkers. Wandering words, cut off from a homeland preserved only in a distant memory, are the legacy of Jabès. Derrida's two essays in *Writing and Difference* dedicated reverently to the work of Jabès (where he refers to Jabès's *The Book of Questions* as "the poetic revolution of our century") no doubt began the canonization of this unlikely icon of postmodernism. Unlikely, because his work is non-polemical, poetic in style, and, above all, concerned with the question(ing) of God.

But with the ubiquity of the Holocaust in Jabès's writing, God is often as not a problematic absence. In his introduction to Jabès's posthumous *The Book of Margins* (1993: xiv), Mark C. Taylor writes: "God never speaks directly but only approaches indirectly in the faults of language and silence of words." Jabès himself writes:

Wide, the margin between carte blanche and white page. Nevertheless it is not in this margin that you can find me, but in the yet whiter one that separates the word-strewn sheet from the transparent, the written page from the one to be written.

(Jabès 1993: 124)

These concerns – for absence, silence, incompleteness, the blank – make Jabès's writing resonate with the book of Lamentations. What then can Jabès teach us that the credentialed biblical scholars cannot?

There are two kinds of discoveries in literary matters: the work that is complete in its very incompletion – an incompletion ineluctably carried to term – and the work that has come only halfway toward its always deferred completion.

(Jabès 1993: 115)

Jabès does not labor under the illusion of a *telos*. He knows all too well of the exile of the wor(l)d without end. The two possibilities are: an incompletion that somehow allows one to move on, or an incompletion whose deferral is ever-present (compelling as no *telos* can be). The non-ending of Lamentations is certainly of the latter sort.

We also learn from Jabès to dwell in the emptiness . . .

Under this blank we repose.
Under this immaterial blank face.

(Jabès 1993: 166)

. . . for, as he writes to Emmanuel Levinas,

There is no trace but in the desert, no voice but in the desert.

(Jabès 1993: 160)

The blank page – as vast and unbearable as it is, like the desert wherein Israel began to write the voice of God – is the place where writing can begin again.

*Though the pen grow weaker and weaker, the book nevertheless writes,
in white letters, on to its end. Making a book could mean exchanging the
void of writing for the writing of the void.*

(Jabès 1993: 106)

This tracing of the void has already begun in the margins of Lamentations.
The written text of Lamentations, to borrow a phrase from Derrida (1982:
xxiii), "overflows and cracks its meaning." In the margins of Lamentations,
where there should be only white space, there is (already) writing. Jewish
liturgical tradition, for example, has longed for a supplement, and has tried
to answer that longing by repeating the more positive verse 21 after the non-
ending of verse 22. So into the blank space opened up by the scroll intrudes
the supplement of writing. There is here no pretense to replace the absent
voice of God; rather, "the Jew . . . weeps for the lost voice with tears as
black as the trace of ink" (Derrida 1978: 7), and with these inky tears begins
to write in order to survive.

*Faced with the impossibility of writing that paralyzes every writer and
the impossibility of being Jewish, which for two thousand years racked
the people of this name, the writer chooses to write, and the Jew to
survive.*

(Jabès 1993: 176)

This writing of survival does not end in the margins of Lamentations. The
tentative

writing of the vertigo where book opens to book

(Jabès 1993: 20)

which we find in the liturgical tradition is expanded elsewhere. In the
Targum to Lamentations (its translation into Aramaic) there are numerous
textual expansions focused on the dying children. Likewise, we find in Isaiah
a number of passages which attempt to "answer" Lamentations.[8]

*To set out to discover the trace means perhaps to continue writing, to
circle around the unfindable trace.*

(Jabès 1993: 166)

The writing of survival becomes the survival of writing. None of this writing
represents a closure, or *telos*, to the book of Lamentations, however. It witnesses instead to the truth of Derrida's statement (1978: 73) that, "within original aphasia, when the voice of the god or the poet is missing, one must be
satisfied with the vicars of speech that are the cry and writing."

Remains from the book of Lamentations: the cry and writing. The cry of Mother Zion for her lost children . . . the writing by which that cry may be kept audible.

Derrida: "Remain(s) – the mother".

(1986: 115)

Jabès: "The blank remains. Read the blank".

(1993: 166, xi)

NOTES

1 See Westermann (1980: 35–43) for a summary of lament psalm structure.
2 See his summary in Westermann (1980: 10–11), as well as his earlier, more complete treatment (1977).
3 Much of the exegetical material in what follows was first published in Linafelt (1995).
4 Unless otherwise indicated, all translations from the Hebrew are my own.
5 Gottwald (1954: 8) and Meek (1956: 11) take it to mean "possessions," Hillers (1992: 87) argues that it refers to children, and Provan (1991: 47) allows either.
6 Adorno's famous remark, "To write poetry after Auschwitz is barbaric," was written in 1949 (see Adorno 1981: 30). In *Negative Dialectics* (1973: 335) he wrote, "Ceaseless suffering has as much right to express itself as does the victim of torture to screaming. Therefore it may have been false to say that after Auschwitz one cannot write poetry. But it is not false to ask . . . whether after Auschwitz it is possible to live at all."
7 The rhetoric is forceful, but it is not without its more subtle artistry. The occurence of *shaphak*, "pour out," at this critical point in the poem represents a nexus of inter-relations between the characters. Indeed, we may say that each character is defined by what s/he is said to "pour out." Mother Zion is told here to "pour out your heart like water . . . for the lives (*n-ph-sh*) of your children." In 2:12 it is precisely the "lives [*n-ph-sh*] of the children" that are being "poured out [*sh-ph-k*] in the bosoms of their mothers." Moreover, in that same passage it is the pouring out of the children's lives that move the poet to "pour out" (*sh-ph-k*) his grief (literally, *kibed*, "liver"). In sharp contrast, when the word *shaphak* is used to describe YHWH in 2:4, it describes the "pouring out" of YHWH's "raging fire."
8 See Linafelt (1995) for a more in-depth treatment of the "survivals" of Lamentations in the Targum and in Isaiah 40–55.

14

A POSTSCRIPT TO THE BOOK

Authenticating the Pseudepigrapha

Kyle Keefer

Among the humanities, biblical scholarship is one of the more well-defined fields. Unlike English departments, biblical studies does not continually face a redefinition of canon. While philosophers write philosophy and historians write history, biblical scholars do not write the Bible. The main purpose that drives most biblical scholars is almost a uniform one – to explicate and clarify, through commentaries and articles, what the biblical texts are saying. Despite the vast proliferation of biblical scholarship in the last few decades, and despite a great deal of research in closely related fields (archaeology, sociology, etc.) which have been employed by biblical scholars, most biblical scholarship continues to display a tacit assumption that it is dedicated to a corpus of either 39 (Hebrew Bible) or 66 (Hebrew Bible/Old Testament plus New Testament) writings, and that the scholarly output is parasitic and secondary to those writings.

Much of contemporary literary theory questions these primary tenets of biblical scholarship. Julia Kristeva and Jacques Derrida, for example, have raised serious doubts about the sharp boundary between text and commentary (see, e.g., Kristeva 1980: 65–66; Derrida 1976). They have concurrently redefined interpretation as a matter of re-creation. Their forceful and convincing arguments can contribute to a new way of describing the activity of biblical scholarship. As a way of getting at this point, I want to bring some of the documents from Second Temple Judaism, written sometime between 200 B.C.E. and 200 C.E., into conversation with contemporary literary theory. These non-canonical, pre-rabbinic documents are usually grouped under the title Pseudepigrapha, or "false-writings," the epithet deriving from the large number of pseudonymous works in this collection. This collection of literature[1] includes a wide variety of styles and genres, including apocalyptic writings, poetry, testaments, wisdom literature, and legendary material. What interests me here are those works that are closely connected to the Torah (or Pentateuch – Genesis through Deuteronomy) and are defined loosely as "expansions of the Old Testament" (Charlesworth 1983: 5). Two of these writings, Pseudo-Philo (Biblical Antiquities) and Jubilees, are particularly pertinent for the present discussion because of the questions they raise about textuality, canon, and interpretation.

By the time Pseudo-Philo and Jubilees were written, the books of the Torah were almost certainly considered canon (Collins 1983: 12). The translation of the Hebrew Bible into Greek had already occurred, and the first five books of Moses had come to be a defining symbol for Jews throughout the Mediterranean world. In the period after 200 C.E., after the Mishnah (the text of the oral Torah) reached its final form, it is obvious that the books of the Hebrew Bible formed the backbone of rabbinic interpretation (Neusner 1987b: 8). The rabbis and sages in the period after 200 C.E. quoted from Scriptures and then expounded on them in order to make their meaning and application clear for their present circumstances. In the time of the Mishnah and Talmuds, a distinction between the canonical written Torah and the oral Torah (oral tradition believed to go back to God's revelation at Sinai and finally written out in the Mishnah) was firmly in place (Neusner 1987a: 15). Before 200, though, in the period in which most of the Pseudepigrapha were written, written Torah did not apparently have the same distinctive status.

James Charlesworth has attempted to clarify the relation of the Pseudepigrapha to the Hebrew Bible in an essay entitled "In the Crucible: The Pseudepigrapha as Biblical Interpretation." There he points out ways in which the Pseudepigrapha have been miscategorized and proposes new paradigms for investigating the myriad documents. Against those who would dismiss the Pseudepigrapha as inconsequential forms of exegesis, Charlesworth makes the point that just because these writings do not always employ direct quotations (as the later targumim and midrashim do), this does not minimize their importance as interpretive documents (Charlesworth 1993: 27). Thus on the one hand he valorizes these writings as inherently worthy. Yet, on the other hand, he still very clearly holds the position that the Pseuedepigrapha are secondary to the Torah. He makes this observation, however, more as a *de facto* statement than as an argument. After asserting the canonicity implicit in Hebrew script at Qumran, he states, "The new was an exegesis of the old; the latter elevated the former. I am convinced the same phenomenon characterizes the Pseudepigrapha" (1993: 25). Although he claims that in this essay he will argue against the position that the Pseudepigrapha were intended to replace what became canonical Hebrew Scripture (the Tanak – Torah, Nevi'im, Ketuvim), he never does so. In the face of evidence which he clearly recognizes, he continues to assert a clear line of division between biblical canon and pseudepigraphal interpretation, as well as the primacy of the former over the latter:

> The Pseudepigrapha tend to treat the Tanach in ways that are shockingly cavalier to modern biblical critics. It seems obvious that the text was considered divine, but the spirit for interpretation allowed the

Jewish exegete to alter, ignore, expand, and even rewrite the sacred scripture.

(Charlesworth 1993: 39)

Charlesworth's essay provides a starting point for my observations because he clearly defines the rock and the hard place that the Pseudepigrapha are caught between. It would, as he asserts, be difficult to deny the importance of Torah for these writers. At the same time, the "shockingly cavalier" methods of interpretation that the pseudepigraphical writers demonstrate do not allow for the confidence that Charlesworth has in the "divine" autonomy of the text. Categories more nuanced than simply "text" and "interpretation" (or "old" and "new") are needed to define the phenomenon that we see at work in Jubilees and Pseudo-Philo.

The book of Jubilees receives its title from its prologue:

> This is the account of the division of days of the law and the testimony for annual observance according to their weeks (of years) and their Jubilees throughout all the years of the world just as the LORD told it to Moses on Mount Sinai when he went up to receive the tablets of the Law and the commandment by the word of the LORD, as he said to him, "Come up to the top of the mountain."[2]

Following this prologue, the document relates the biblical stories of Genesis and the early chapters of Exodus, with special emphasis – as the prologue implies – upon feasts, observances, and other tendencies of the source generally known as the Priestly (P) source. The opening to Jubilees, therefore, recasts the biblical story within the framework of the Mosaic law. The text deftly weaves the material of Genesis (which precedes the law) into the law so that the figure of Moses and the place of Sinai tower over the events from creation to the Passover. That which does not impinge upon the Mosaic law is left out, and that which is only tangentially related to the law becomes inextricably tied to it.

At the beginning of the book, before the creation story is recounted, the focus falls entirely upon Moses and God's command to him to write down "both what (was) in the beginning and what will occur (in the future)" (1:4). The first chapter, then, serves as both introduction and prologue – giving away the conclusions through a prediction of Israel's rejection of the law. Not content to allow readers free reign with the Genesis account, the text's introduction supplies the key for its own reading. This is not a dispensable preface separate from the main body of the document but rather a guideline for reading and interpretation.

The introduction, however, does not provide the only means by which this author recasts Torah into a cultic document. From creation to the ten plagues, Jubilees highlights the special concerns of the priestly class by creating a narrative that fuses the Genesis/Exodus account with commentary and

234

expansion, though without any hint that the canonical text has priority. This is a procedure that occurs throughout the document. The story of Abraham provides a good example of this kind of redaction of the Genesis material. Abraham serves as the central focus from Jubilees 11:1–23:8, and this story basically follows the chronology of Genesis 12:1–25:18. Between major scenes pulled verbatim from Genesis, though, one finds carefully placed commentary on these events. Jubilees 15:23–24 parallels Genesis 17:23–27, recounting how Abraham circumcised himself, his son Ishmael and all his servants according to God's commandment. In Genesis the narrative moves immediately to the story of Sarah's laughter at the prediction of her bearing a son. In Jubilees, however, sandwiched between these two scenes is an excursus upon the laws of circumcision. So that the importance of Abraham's action is not lost on the reader, the author of Jubilees writes:

> This law is for all the eternal generations and there is no circumcising of days and there is no passing a single day beyond eight days because it is an eternal ordinance ordained and written in the heavenly tablets. And anyone who is born whose own flesh is not circumcised on the eighth day is not from the sons of the covenant which the LORD made for Abraham since (he is) from the children of destruction.
>
> (15:25–26)

This explanation of circumcision displays the historicizing tendencies of this document. Not only does it conflate the Levitical laws with their etiological explanation in Genesis (cf., e.g., 6:1ff.; 21:1–20), it also uses the Abraham story to highlight one of the major boundary markers for Jewish identity. The book of Jubilees uses the Genesis and Exodus accounts as ammunition in a battle directed toward those who do not follow closely the Levitical laws and holidays. By incorporating a polemical stance toward uncircumcision into Genesis (a less than polemical narrative), the author contemporizes the text and gives it a strong didactic force (Endres 1987: 235).

Along slightly different lines, but displaying a similar writing technique, is the text known as Pseudo-Philo or Biblical Antiquities. Daniel Harrington (1983: 297) aptly describes it as "an imaginative retelling of parts of the Old Testament story. It interweaves biblical incidents and legendary expansions of these accounts." Unlike Jubilees, Pseudo-Philo does not reflect a strong ideology of the author. It is neither sectarian nor polemic. This leads Harrington to postulate that Pseudo-Philo "seems to reflect the milieu of the Palestinian synagogues at the turn of the common era" (1983: 300). It both synopsizes and expands the Old Testament narrative from Adam to the death of Saul without any discernible pattern to its omissions or additions. To return to the figure of Abraham, Pseudo-Philo portrays him as the hero of a greatly expanded Babel story (6:1–7:5), in which he survives an ordeal in a fiery furnace. Immediately following this, the text compresses the rest of

Abraham's life into a few sentences, comprised of a mishmash of verses from Genesis:

> And God appeared to Abram, saying, "To your seed I will give this land, and your name will be called Abraham, and Sarai, your wife, will be called Sarah. And I will give to you from her an everlasting seed, and I will establish my covenant with you." And Abraham knew Sarah, his wife, and she conceived and bore Isaac.
>
> (Pseudo-Philo 8:3; cf. Genesis 13:15, 17:1, 5, 7, 8, 15)

Pseudo-Philo exhibits neither a consistent cultic legalism, as does Jubilees, nor explicit exhortation, as do the Testaments of the Twelve Patriarchs. The result is a long, rambling document without much coherence or texture. The legends that are added, the most prominent being Abram at the Tower of Babel and the deeds of Joshua's successor Kenaz, seem happenstance. Furthermore, the description of God in the document is as variegated as it is in the Pentateuch and Deuteronomistic History; this author did not try to mold sources into a strict pattern. What results is both a theological and a narratological amalgamation which serves to capture the broad history of Israel and the numerous pictures of the relationship between God and humanity.

Of course, with regard to narrative content, one might also describe Pseudo-Philo as uninteresting. Though the legends of Kenaz and the expanded story of the Tower of Babel may be of curious interest, the overall content of this book is rather bland. Yet what makes it interesting, and worth further reflection, is the manner in which it deals with the canonical text, for it appears in Pseudo-Philo that simply the phenomenon of the text is of more importance that its content or presentation. Pseudo-Philo reads like the *Reader's Digest* condensed version of Genesis to 1 Samuel with a few points of expansion. If, as Harrington has suggested, Pseudo-Philo finds its roots in the early synagogue, this writing broadens our portrait of biblical interpretation in the Second Temple period. It does not take a great imaginative leap to consider a book such as this as popular Torah. If this were true, it would undercut any attempt to map contemporary ideas of canon and authority back onto this segment of Second Temple Judaism.[3]

Although dealing only briefly with the Pseudepigrapha, Michael Fishbane's *Biblical Interpretation in Ancient Israel* frames the issue of biblical interpretation by speaking of the *traditum*, the content of tradition, and the *traditio*, the process by which that tradition is transformed (1985: 6). Fishbane finds that within the Hebrew Bible, various authors reinterpret passages from the now-canonical texts, resulting in what he calls innerbiblical exegesis. This phenomenon in the Hebrew Bible, therefore, provides a precedent for various pseudepigraphical authors to follow. Both innerbiblical exegesis and interpretations such as those found in Pseudo-Philo and Jubilees are "complex blends of *traditum* and *traditio* in dynamic interaction, dynamic interpretation, and dynamic interdependence. They are, in sum, the exegetical voices of many teachers and tradents, from differ-ent circles and times, responding to real and theoretical considerations as perceived and as anticipated" (1985: 543). Though I do not think "exegesis" adequately describes the phenomenon Fishbane speaks of, his characteriz-ation of the relationship between received text and commentary incisively points out the difficulty of separating the *traditio* from the *traditum* in sharp, clear lines. In the passages I have discussed from Jubilees and Pseudo-Philo, one cannot tell from internal evidence what belongs to the *traditio* and what belongs to the *traditum*. To put it another way, epigraphon differs little from the pseudepigraphon. Only because the *traditum* has survived in a canonical form can these distinctions be made. If Fishbane is right in point-ing out that this blending of commentary and text into a *tertium quid* pervades in the Hebrew Bible itself, Jubilees and Pseudo-Philo handle their texts according to the pattern already laid out in those texts.

Lest the pseudepigraphical books that I have highlighted seem anomalous in their approach to (inter)textuality, later Jewish interpretations support the evidence that the hypostasized text of contemporary exegesis was not the pattern which governed their methods. In his book *Intertextuality and the Reading of Midrash* (1990b), Daniel Boyarin describes the rabbinic mid-rashim in a manner that is very close to how I want to describe the Pseudepi-grapha. He begins by seeking an understanding of the hermeneutics of midrash through a close reading of the text: "My question is not posed as: given that we know what reading is, why does midrash deviate from it, but rather, seeing how midrash reads, what theoretical concepts are useful for understanding it?" (1990b: x). By framing the question this way, Boyarin can read midrash through an exploration of how the poststructural terminology of intertextuality both illumines and is illumined by the midrash Mekilta of the third century. According to Boyarin, the rabbis saw gaps in the biblical text which almost cried out to be filled (1990b: 41). They filled them by read-ing the Bible as a self-glossing book, by relating texts to other texts within the canon. This way of reading was, therefore, "not allegorical – relating signifer to signified – but intertextual – relating signifier to signifier" (1990b: 115). In this schema, interpretation works horizontally rather than vertically; that is, one finds the meaning of the text by looking not for a deep structure but for a significance within the interstices of the Torah.

The importance of Boyarin's work for my chapter is twofold. First, I want to suggest that, like the rabbis, the authors of Pseudo-Philo and Jubilees fill in gaps they perceive in the biblical text with allusions to other texts. This is especially noticeable in Jubilees's conjoining of legal and narrative Penta-teuchal material. Second, again like the rabbis, the pseudepigraphical writers make the text contemporary to their own concerns. Ancient forms of inter-pretation usually are described over against modern forms of interpretation because of their relative fancifulness regarding the text. The upshot of both Boyarin's and my analysis is that this charge can only be made by assuming that an objective exegesis of text exemplifies the correct mode of interpretation.

Informing Boyarin's conception of intertextuality are the writings of Kristeva and Derrida, which he occasionally quotes. The following passage from one of Derrida's essays devoted to Edmond Jabès (a writer familiar with the difficult questions of writing, interpretation, and the book in Judaism) is especially appropriate to the present discussion:

> The necessity of commentary, like poetic necessity, is the very form of exiled speech. In the beginning is hermeneutics. But the *shared* necessity of exegesis, the interpretive imperative, is interpreted differently by the rabbi and the poet. The difference between the horizon of the original text and exegetic writing makes the difference between the rabbi and the poet irreducible. Forever unable to reunite with each other, yet so close to each other, how could they ever regain the *realm*? The original opening of interpretation essentially signifies that there will always be rabbis and poets. And two interpretations of interpretation.
>
> (Derrida 1978: 66)

In another essay, also from *Writing and Difference*, Derrida elaborates further on the two ways of the rabbi and the poet mentioned here: the rabbinic seeks closure, cutting off the freeplay of the text to achieve some sort of stability, while the poetic affirms the freeplay and revels in the possibilities of becoming that are nascent in textuality (1978: 292). He goes on to write, however, that "although these two interpretations must acknowledge and accentuate their difference and define their irreducibility, I do not believe that today that is any question of *choosing*" (292). Interpreters, who perform their acts without the ability to reside decisively in either of these arenas, work in a tenuous interplay between the two.

Derrida's two types of interpretation are integral to the interpretation we find in the Pseudepigrapha. The interpretive practices of Second Temple Judaism live in this tension-filled space (the space of exile?) between the rabbinic and poetic. The authors of both Jubilees and Pseudo-Philo recognize the lack in the biblical texts which their interpretation supplements and thus participate in the "interpretive imperative." Bringing Derrida to bear upon the pseudepigrapha, however, raises problems. His labelling of interpretation that seeks closure as "rabbinic" and of affirmation of freeplay as "poetic," may be misnomers for these documents. As Boyarin has shown, rabbinic interpretation displays precisely those aspects which Derrida calls poetic. The pseudepigraphical writings affirm freeplay with their refusal to be chained to the literal form of the text they interpret. While these examples do not negate the "irreducible difference" of the two ways of interpretation that Derrida highlights, they do call into question the labels "poetic" and "rabbinic." Implicit in Derrida's categorization is a denigration of the rabbinic and an elevation of the poetic. In traditional biblical scholarship, these poles are reversed; closing off freeplay is much more desirable than imaginatively engaging texts (the "cavalier" attitude Charlesworth sees in Jubilees and Pseudo-Philo). Derrida's observation – which he partially undermines through his terminology – that the rabbinic and poetic cannot exist in isolation serves as a guard against overemphasizing either aspect.

My brief analysis of these pseudepigraphical books with respect to their intertextual relationships with Hebrew Scripture does not, on one level, present any astounding conclusions. If Kristeva and Derrida are right about the all-pervasiveness of intertextuality, claiming that many of the Pseudepigrapha display an intertextual reading of the Torah becomes a tautology. Furthermore, the two documents I have chosen do not stand out as aberrant in their treatment of the canonical text, and scholars have long noticed the ways they reshape and re-create biblical texts. Jubilees, Pseudo-Philo, and other documents such as the Testaments of the Twelve Patriarchs, to a great extent prefigure midrashic interpretation, and their reconfiguring of the text has many similarities to documents found at Qumran, especially Genesis Apocryphon and the Pesher on Habakkuk.[4]

What makes a difference is that the implications of these observations, however obvious, have been overlooked. In Charlesworth's article, he observes the same aspects of the Pseudepigrapha that I do – a looseness in dealing with the text and a respect for it as an important document – but he still can somehow claim that they had a "high" view of Scripture analogous to that of contemporary Judaism or Christianity. A reluctance to admit to a "lower" view of canon is evident not only among biblical scholars but also among some of the theorists that I have referred to. Derrida's description of rabbinic interpretation as "that which attempts to close off freeplay," along with common assumptions of the Bible as a univocal document of monotheism (e.g., Kristeva 1982: 90–94), appear quite problematic in light of the evidence I have presented. My argument is largely a historical one: that these authors, in their reading of Scripture, proleptically affirmed Derridean freeplay and Kristevan intertextuality as it resided both in the Bible and in their interpretations. In this sense, these documents from the pre-critical period display a surprisingly postmodern stance. The period from 200 B.C.E. to 200 C.E. was possibly the most fecund time for Jewish biblical interpretation in all of history. The texts now considered canonical certainly had some sort of consensually conferred authority, but not an authority which they would later have under Tannaitic Judaism or orthodox Christianity. From Jubilees to Pseudo-Philo to the Qumran community to the rabbis to Paul and the nascent Christian movement, Torah was both fixed and fluid, and various interpreters almost revel in that fluidity.

In addition to making this historical argument, however, I have been attempting to put the Pseudepigrapha into a discussion of contemporary biblical criticism. Like the pseudepigraphical writers, biblical critics find themselves with an imperative to interpret texts. No biblical critic can fulfill this imperative without engaging in both "rabbinic" and "poetic" modes. In other words, all commentary, however much it may try to be strictly exegetical, always slips into rewriting. In the language of pragmatism, "interpreting something, knowing it, penetrating to its essence, and so on are all just various ways of describing some process of putting it to work" (Rorty 1992: 83).[5] This description of the interpretive act exposes a blindspot that characterizes much of contemporary biblical criticism, the assumption that biblical critics are *just* in the business of finding textual meaning. It is commonplace for biblical scholars to criticize certain interpretations for being eisegesis and not exegesis. All interpretion, though, performs both functions and need not be apologetic about doing so. Embarrassment over this situation stems from an unattainable desire for a pristine center, and this fixation has very likely contributed to the moribund nature of much of current scholarship.

On this point, Derrida, Boyarin, Jubilees, and Pseudo-Philo converge. We cannot and never have interpreted without re-creation. Whenever the phrases "*the* biblical" or "*the* Bible" appear, therefore, they connote a fallacious univocality that does not exist and never has. Neither should biblical interpretation try to find it. What biblical scholars must come to recognize and accept (as have Fishbane and Boyarin) is that this has always been the case, even with the sacred texts that they put a wall around. Biblical scholarship would do well to see — as did the pseudepigraphical writers — that the canon cannot be closed as long as interpreters exist.

NOTES

1 Collected in the two-volume *Old Testament Pseudepigrapha* (1983; 1985), edited by Charlesworth.
2 All quotations are from Charlesworth (1983).
3 I am grateful to Carl Holladay of Emory University for his suggestions on this point.
4 For an excellent discussion of the mode of interpretation at Qumran, cf. Talmon (1991). He argues, similarly to me, that interpretation for the Qumranites was primarily a means of making the text contemporary by pointing out how it spoke directly to them.
5 For the most part, deconstruction has not interacted fruitfully with pragmatic insights. Some exceptions would be Christopher Norris's sustained debate with Richard Rorty or Jonathan Culler's occasional discussion of deconstruction alongside a pragmatic hermeneutic (see, e.g., Culler 1982: 152–54). Even in these exchanges, however, the debate takes place largely at a polemical level. Derrida himself has provided the best exchange between these philosophical points of view in *Limited, Inc.* (1988). See especially this tantalizing footnote to the Afterword:

Grammatology has always been a sort of pragmatics, but the discipline which bears this name today involve [sic] too many presuppositions requiring deconstruction, very much like speech act theory, to be simply homogeneous with that which is announced in *De la grammatologie*. A pragrammatology (to come) would articulate in a more fruitful and more rigourous manner these two discourses.

(Derrida 1988: 159)

As far as I know, this "pragrammatology" is still "to come."

15

WHAT DOES THE BIBLE SAY?

A Question of Text and Canon

David M. Gunn

What I want to know is simply this: What does the Bible say about how young David killed Goliath – the giant, the shaft of whose spear was like a weaver's beam? Everyone knows from childhood that he did it with a sling and stone. And we only have to look at Michelangelo's marble David, sling hanging over his left shoulder, or Bernini's David, about to let the stone fly, to be assured that this is indeed the case. On the other hand, if we're talking about Florentine art, we can hardly avoid noticing that Donatello's master-piece in bronze stands sword in hand, one foot resting upon Goliath's severed head (though, to be sure, on close inspection we discover a stone tucked in the boy's left hand). Actually Western art until modern times has had something of a predilection for images of David with the giant's head – cutting it off with a sword, holding it aloft, or otherwise displaying the grue-some trophy. Killed with a stone or a sword? Or did David bring the giant down with the sling and then finish him off with the sword? A question about one of the great religious and cultural icons of the West: exactly how *did* David kill Goliath?

Well, what does the Bible say?

(38) Then Saul clothed David with his armor; he put a helmet of bronze on his head and clothed him with a coat of mail. (39) And David girded his sword over his armor and he tried in vain to go, for he was not used to them. Then David said to Saul, "I cannot go with these; for I am not used to them." And David put them off. (40) Then he took his staff in his hand, and chose five smooth stones from the brook, and put them in his shepherd's bag or wallet; his sling was in his hand, and he drew near to the Philistine.

(41) And the Philistine came on and drew near to David, with his shield-bearer in front of him. (42) And when the Philistine looked, and saw David, he disdained him; for he was but a youth, ruddy and comely in appearance. (43) And the Philistine said to David, "Am I a dog, that you come to me with sticks?". . . . (45) Then David said to the Philistine, "You come to me with a sword and with a spear and with a

javelin; but I come to you in the name of the LORD of hosts, the God of the armies of Israel, whom you have defied. (46) This day the LORD will deliver you into my hand, and I will strike you down, and cut off your head . . . (47) that all this assembly may know that the Lord saves not with sword and spear; for the battle is the LORD's and he will give you into our hand."

(48) When the Philistine arose and came and drew near to meet David, David ran quickly toward the battle line to meet the Philistine. (49) And David put his hand in his bag and took out a stone, and slung it, and struck the Philistine on his forehead; the stone sank into his forehead, and he fell on his face to the ground.

(50) So David prevailed over the Philistine with a sling and with a stone, and struck the Philistine, and killed him; there was no sword in the hand of David. (51) Then David ran and stood over the Philistine, and took his sword and drew it out of its sheath, and killed him, and cut off his head with it. . . . (54) And David took the head of the Philistine and brought it to Jerusalem.

(1 Samuel 17:38–54; RSV)

At the risk of sounding pedantic, there is a problem here. The Bible seems to say two things: first, that he struck and killed the Philistine with the stone from his sling and specifically *without* having a sword in his hand (verse 50) and, second, that then he ran and drew his (own or the Philistine's?) sword and *with* this sword killed him and cut off his head (verse 51). It sounds like a flat contradiction: he killed him first with the stone and then with the sword. Nor is it entirely clear whether he killed him with the sword *and then* cut off his head or whether he killed him with the sword *by* cutting off his head. There is even ambiguity over whether the sword belonged to Goliath or to David.

Perhaps my translation fails me. Like many liberal Protestants of my age I turn instinctively to the Revised Standard Version (RSV), the Bible of my Presbyterian upbringing. Would I be better served by a more recent Bible, the New RSV perhaps? But while its English replaces the repetitive "ands" of Hebrew paratactic style with typical English syntax, the only clarification of substance I find concerns the potential ambiguity of the end of verse 51: this Bible is absolutely clear: "he grasped his sword, drew it out of its sheath, and killed him; then he cut off his head with it" (NRSV).

The television preachers (and many Protestants in the USA) would undoubtedly urge upon me to turn to the Řeal Bible, the so-called King James Version (properly the Authorised Version). It turns out, however, only to raise another ambiguity:

So David prevailed over the Philistine with a sling and with a stone, and smote the Philistine, and slew him; but *there was* no sword in the hand of David. Therefore David ran, and stood upon the Philistine, and took his sword, and drew it out of the sheath thereof, and slew him, and cut off his head therewith.

(KJV)

Now I am stuck with the meaning of "therefore" in the clause, "Therefore David ran...." He ran to kill him with a sword *because* (for the reason that) he had just killed him with a stone or because he did not have a sword and needed Goliath's sword to kill him? Or in 1611 did the term "therefore" signify sequence rather than consequence? To proceed further I need my Oxford English Dictionary.

Instead let me turn to another Bible that purports to be in a language closer to my own, the (liberal Protestant) New English Bible. The part about the initial encounter with the sling reads much like the RSV, NRSV, or KJV. But then:

So David proved the victor with his sling and stone; he struck Goliath down and gave him a mortal wound, though he had no sword. Then he ran to the Philistine and stood over him, and grasping his sword, he drew it out of the scabbard, dispatched him and cut off his head.

(NEB)

Now indeed we have progress, for the contradiction has turned out to be more apparent than real. The stone did not kill the giant; it gave him a "mortal wound." KJV's "therefore" becomes "then," unquestionably indicating sequence. And "dispatched" conveys better than "killed" the sense of "finishing him off." But is this the *true* biblical text? Does it finally tell me what the Bible says? Certainly the more recent revision of the NEB, the Revised English Bible (REB), sticks with this translation on the crucial points. For further verification, I look to another contemporary language Bible, the Good News Bible (Today's English Version), a "dynamic equivalent" translation. The combatants meet each other. Then David

reached into his bag and took out a stone, which he slung at Goliath. It hit him on the forehead and broke his skull, and Goliath fell face downward on the ground.

"Broke his skull?" This looks like preparation for a "mortal wound" account in the following, troublesome verse and hence confirmation of the NEB. But no, the translation continues unblinkingly:

And so, without a sword, David defeated and killed Goliath with a sling and a stone! He ran to him, stood over him, took Goliath's sword out of its sheath, and cut off his head and killed him.

The contradiction is back again, though the secondary question, whether decapitation caused or was consequent to death, is answered this time by reversing the verbs: David "cut off his head and killed him."

The (conservative Protestant) New International Version, however, uses the same transposition of those last verbs to create an ambiguity which could stretch to cover the contradiction: yes, David killed the Philistine without a sword in his hand, and "*after* he killed him" he cut off his head with the sword:

> So David triumphed over the Philistine with a sling and a stone; without a sword in his hand he struck down the Philistine and killed him. David ran and stood over him. He took hold of the Philistine's sword and drew it from the scabbard. After he killed him, he cut off his head with the sword.
>
> (NIV)

The new Jewish Publication Society's translation ("The Holy Scriptures, According to the Traditional Hebrew Text"), TANAKH, seems to be clear that David killed the Philistine with sling and stone:

> Thus David bested the Philistine with sling and stone; he struck him down and killed him.

But then it nuances the clause about David having no sword in his hand differently from, for example, the NIV or RSV, and rather more like one of the possibilities for reading the KJV. It connects the clause to the following sentence rather than the preceding one:

> David had no sword; so David ran up and stood over the Philistine, grasped his sword and pulled it from its sheath; and with it he dispatched him and cut off his head.

And finally it uses the same term, "dispatched," as the NEB and REB used to speak of David's action with the sword. Now am I being led towards a "mortally wounded" view, but with a difference? Is "struck him down and killed him" a summary statement referring back to the stone ("struck him down") and forward to the sword ("and killed him")?

So where am I with regard to my initial question? I can hardly say that I have heard one unambiguous "biblical" voice in reply. Any number of more or less precise answers seems possible. Perhaps it is time to do the scholarly thing, abandon these English Bibles for the moment, and look at a Hebrew one, the text as printed in the standard scholarly edition, Biblia Hebraica Stuttgartensia (BHS), based on one of the earliest extant manuscripts of a "complete" Bible in Hebrew, namely the early eleventh-century C.E. Leningrad Codex. There are some obvious points to be made: this Hebrew text, as in normal Hebrew narrative prose, does not have specific words for "thus" or "so" or "therefore" or "then," but merely a sequence of finite verbs linked with "and." The verbs of killing are slightly different forms of the same root, a common verb of killing, but it is likely that the second form does have the sense of "dispatching" or "finishing off." The order of the final

DAVID M. GUNN

verbs is, literally, "and he killed [dispatched] him and he cut off his head."
The posessive pronoun "his" in "he took his sword" has as its closest antecedent, in Hebrew as in English, the third person subject of the verb "he took"
(in the sequence "he ran," "he stood over" and "he took"), which would
suggest David as the possessor, though the "the Philistine" is the closest
explicitly named antecedent, which, as in English, could allow "his" to mean
"the Philistine's" if the reader, for larger contextual reasons, so determined.

What would it avail me to offer my own translation of the passage?
I would be confronted with the same contradictions, ambiguities, and inter-
pretive choices that have become manifest in my review of English Bibles.
Inevitably I would be generating yet another Bible.

Might some other ancient texts help me? What of the Latin Vulgate, the
standard text of the Roman Catholic Church for centuries? After David lets
fly the stone we read that

> striking the Philistine he killed him [*percussumque Philisthaeum
> interfecit*].

Like KJV and TANAKH the Vulgate attaches the next clause to the following, instead of preceding, sentence; yet its meaning is different, a matter of
description rather than motivation:

> And without having a sword in his hand, David ran and stood over the
> Philistine [*Cumque gladium non haberet in manu David, cucurrit, et
> stetit super Philisthaeum*].

For the rest, the primary contradiction remains:

> and he killed him and cut off his head [*et interfecit eum, praeciditque
> caput ejus*].

Indeed the contradiction is the more apparent, since, like many of the
English Bibles, this Bible uses the same verb of killing (*interfecit*) in each of
the relevant clauses.

The Aramaic Targum, a paraphrase of the Bible deriving from as early as
the first century C.E., turns out to offer nothing new on the crucial point.
On the other hand, Josephus, the first-century C.E. Jewish historian, writing
in Greek, does make a contribution to the issue:

> But the youth went out to meet [him], together with an ally invisible
> to the foe – this was God. And drawing out of his wallet one of the
> stones from the stream which he had placed in it, and fitting it to his
> sling, he shot at Goliath, into his forehead; and the missile penetrated
> his brain so that Goliath, instantly stunned, fell on his face. Running,
> he stood on his prostrate foe and, with the latter's broadsword, since
> he did not himself have a sword, he cut off his head.
>
> (Josephus, *Biblical Antiquities*, VI, 189–190)

246

So here we have, together with a nice theological touch about the Divine presence, confirmation of the "mortally wounded" account – an account of what the Bible says with an apparently long pedigree.

Indeed, if I read a little further in first-century C.E. literature I find something similar, if a little more expansive, in the *Biblical Antiquities* of Pseudo-Philo where the Divine presence takes on angelic form:

> And David put a stone in the sling and struck the Philistine on his fore-head. And he ran up to him and drew his sword. And Goliath, while he still had life in him, said to him, "Hurry and kill me, and then rejoice." And David said to him, "Before you die, open your eyes and see your slayer, the one who has killed you." And the Philistine looked and saw an angel and said, "Not you alone have killed me, but also the one who is present with you, he whose appearance is not like the appearance of a man." And then David cut off his head.
>
> (Pseudo-Philo, *Biblical Antiquities*, 61)

Well, now we have God well and truly the instrument of destruction (which is what David in his pre-contest speech to Goliath in our other Bibles – missing from Pseudo-Philo – seems to have been at pains to suggest); and we have the ambiguity resolved: the stone stuns, the sword dispatches.

But are these versions truly The Bible? On the one hand, in the way they deal with the contradiction, they have a close affinity with the likes of the New English Bible. And I cannot say how many times I have read or been told that what the biblical text says is that David won the victory because God accompanied him. On the other hand, materially speaking, these sentences about the Divine presence seem to differentiate these texts from the others. The others may imply some such sentences; they do not actually contain them. And no scholars or religious traditions claim that the *Antiquities* of Josephus and Pseudo-Philo *are* the Bible. So though we have obviously reached a rather fine line in distinguishing between the "biblical" and the "non-biblical", let me return to a text that I believe my colleagues would assure me *is* the Bible.

Representing modern critical scholarship in the Catholic Church in North America, The New American Bible (NAB), like the NEB and the REB, uses the "mortal wound" strategy to smooth the disjunction. At the same time, however, my edition of this version makes a move in the opposite direction: it brackets the problematic verse 50 to indicate that, along with substantial other material, the verse is lacking in the "oldest [ancient] Greek translation."

> David put his hand into the bag and took out a stone, hurled it with the sling, and struck the Philistine on the forehead. The stone embedded itself in his brow, and he fell prostrate on the ground. [Thus

David overcame the Philistine with sling and stone; he struck the Philistine mortally, and he did it without a sword.] Then David ran and stood over him; with the Philistine's own sword [which he drew from its sheath] he dispatched him and cut off his head.

Now here is a can of worms. Do the brackets mean that I should bracket *out* this material that is lacking in the ancient Greek translation (the fourth-century C.E. Codex Vaticanus = LXX[B]) but present in the traditional Hebrew (Masoretic Text = MT; represented most notably by the tenth-century C.E. Aleppo Codex and the early eleventh-century C.E. Leningrad Codex)? If I do bracket out this material I find that while my question has gone a long way to being answered, more than one third of the David and Goliath story as told in these English Bibles is missing. One third! On the other hand, having moved me to consider that the contradiction concerning killing by stone or sword might be the result of a poor editing job on the part of some ancient redactor, the NAB hastens to assure me that the English language Bible that I am reading right now, bracketed material and all, is nonetheless the True Bible: "Though square brackets are used in the edition to indicate the passages lacking in the oldest translation [i.e., the LXX], this is meant only to let the reader follow one account at a time. Both are equally part of the inspired text. . . ."

I have another problem. If the LXX[B] is to be our guide, why does the NAB bracket what the Greek text lacks but does not translate all that it contains? A small point, to be sure, but I am interested in how David killed Goliath. The NAB translates, "The stone embedded itself in his brow"; the LXX[B] says "And the stone penetrated through the helmet into his brow." So what happened to the helmet?

Kyle McCarter in the Anchor Bible, a recent translation and commentary, takes the fact of this major textual difference here between LXX[B] and MT one step further: he lays out his translation as two separate stories. The first is based on the ancient Greek Codex Vaticanus (LXX[B]), and includes 17:1–11, 32–40, 42–48a, and 51–54 (together with the sequel 18:6–8a, 9, 12a, 13–16). The second is formed from what he terms the "additional" material found in the received Hebrew text, the Masoretic Text (MT), and includes "redactional" (i.e., editorial) material designed to harmonize the two stories when they were combined. It comprises 17:12–31, 41, 48b, 50, 55–58 (together with 18:1–5, 10–11, 17–19, 29b–30). Thus in the case of verses 51 and 52 the apparent conflict between them is put at one remove by separating them into two "originally independent" accounts (see McCarter 1980: 285, 300).

From First Account: Then the Philistine rose up and came toward David. David reached into the bag, took out a stone and slung it, striking the Philistine in his forehead. When the stone sank into his forehead, he fell on his face to the ground. David ran up and stood beside him. He took his sword and dispatched him, cutting off his head.

$$(<LXX^B)$$

From Second Account: Then as the Philistine, with the man who carried his shield in front of him, drew closer and closer to David (v. 41), David ran quickly to the battle line to meet [him]! Taking hold of sling and stone he struck down the Philistine and killed him – though there was no sword in David's hand!

$$(<MT \text{ "additions"})$$

What we see here is a convergence of two critical methods for dealing with disjunction – textual criticism and source (or what used to be called "literary") criticism – that have been staples of biblical scholarship for at least two centuries. Both are concerned to discover an "original" text. Text criticism seeks to establish the "original" text of the Bible by reconstructing a history of textual transmission, that is, by writing a new story of the text which moves from "now" (multiple extant texts) to "then" (single "original" text). Source criticism attempts to discover the "original" text(s) *behind* the (reconstructed) "original" text by reconstructing a history of composition, that is, by writing a new story of the text which moves from "then" to "before then"; it is a story of original components (authentic parts), add-ons, and modifications. That is to say, a fundamental impulse of both types of critical endeavor is the modernist impulse to lay bare the Truth, in this case understood as the Original.

McCarter makes this program clear in his own source analysis. He summarizes "the growth of the story of David and Goliath" as one of several stages:

1 a "foundation story" of David's role in an Israelite victory over the Philistines was incorporated into a larger story of David's rise (itself a [re]construction of modern scholarship);
2 a popular legend of young David's victory over a Philistine champion (the First Account) largely displaced the first story;
3 certain details – the name of the Philistine and the description of his spear – were "attracted" to the story from a similar legend about one of David's heroes; and
4 a "complete, alternative" account (the Second Account) was interpolated "somewhat heavy-handedly" into some manuscripts of the completed story (see McCarter 1980: 298).

For the most part, scholars have not needed manuscript differences to spur them to reconstruct the text's compositional (source and editorial) history; more often the kind of apparent discrepancy with which we started (sword or stone?) has been sufficient warrant. Here, however, an important ancient version provides what appears to be tangible evidence for both compositional and transmissional development. McCarter's story of the text here in 1 Samuel involves a Hebrew original represented by (or "behind") the Greek LXX^B, to which further material has been added so as to produce the received Hebrew text (MT). It is this reconstructed text rather than the MT which is the authentic Hebrew text. McCarter's story of sources and composition includes this story of (inauthentic?) "add-on" along with other additions and modifications to the core "foundation story."

McCarter's story of composition and transmission appears to be a story of "from history to legend." To determine the original "foundation story" behind the elaborated legend, McCarter employs here as elsewhere in his book the method of source criticism, one of the primary methods of what biblical critics call "historical criticism." This is the dominant method of biblical scholarship in the modern period employed to trace both the history of biblical literature and the history of ancient Israel. Given this method, then, together with McCarter's interest elsewhere in the commentary in reconstructing the historical roots of the biblical material, the distinction between "foundation story" and supplanting "legend," and the sparse terms in which he describes this original story (which does not read as a story as such – it has, for example, no plot – but as the simple report of an event), I am inclined to take McCarter to mean that behind this story lies (authentic?) "history." What does the Bible say about David killing Goliath? Read critically on what appear to me to be its own terms, then, the (Anchor) Bible tells me simply of a "battle" near "Socoh" between the "Israelites" and the "Philistines" in which "David" played some part. By pursuing my question in the context of the historical critic's story of text and composition, my RSV story of David and Goliath has been reduced from some fifty sentences to one.

But now the questions are coming hard and fast. What kind of a "battle"? Where is "Socoh"? And not least of all, who are these "Philistines," "Israelites," and "David"? What meaning have these terms in the text if they are so stripped of their biblical context? Words without a language? Bones without a body? If history as "what originally happened" is my goal and my source of biblical authenticity then I am in for some bereavement. For when I look beyond the Bible for textual information about David in antiquity, I discover that – with the possible exception of one hotly contested reading of the phrase "house of David" in a recently discovered inscription – there is none that is not already dependent upon the Bible. As "history," my quest dies an early death.

Let me back away from "history" as the location where I might find "what the Bible says," and construe McCarter's meaning somewhat less radically. Another way of understanding him would be to locate the authentic literary text of the Goliath story in a Hebrew text lying behind, or represented by, the LXX^B, a text which to date is represented materially in the case of our story by a Qumran fragment of 1 Samuel 17:3–6 from Cave 4 (= 4 Q Sam^a), but which otherwise exists only through scholarly retro-translation.

But how can I be sure that this reconstructed text is the *authentic* text, the one that will tell me what the Bible says? Certainly a reasonable case has been made by McCarter and others for considering the non-LXX^B material found in the MT (and in other texts, such as LXX^A) to be an addition to a LXX^B type text as opposed to the LXX^B or its underlying Hebrew text(s) being an abridgement of a MT type text. On the other hand, David Gooding makes, in my view, an able case for the reverse hypothesis (Barthélemy *et al.* 1986). Gooding's argument for the "integrity" of the MT turns on his rhetorical (literary) analysis of the story as it appears in the MT, illustrating nicely the point that much of the historical critical program of the last two hundred years has turned on (often unexamined and certainly culture-bound) assumptions about esthetics and the poetics of biblical literature. In the matter of the "contradiction" that concerns us here, Gooding adopts the "mortal wounding" reading, and views verse 50 as an essential thematic summary statement, with the phrase "there was no sword in David's hand" doing double function as a bridge into the final action of decapitation. My reader will recognize the ingredients of this reading already in some of the versions we have perused.

I do not wish to decide the issue myself. Rather, for the purposes of the discussion and Gooding's argument notwithstanding, let me go along with McCarter and others and allow that LXX^B represents a "prior" stage of textual development relative to the MT. I find my difficulty in determining what the Bible says about David and Goliath still unresolved. Instead I am faced with two unsettling questions concerning what such a decision about the priority of LXX^B implies concerning the Bible.

First, let us say that the LXX^B text is superior to the point of necessitating printing in the Anchor Bible two separate stories, one translating a text based on a Hebrew text based on LXX^B (the "first account") and one based on the postulated MT "additions" (the "second account"). Why then print the secondary text in such a way typographically that, despite notes to the contrary, it appears materially to rank in importance with the first primary text? Elsewhere "inferior" textual readings are consigned to the notes. So does LXX^B here not represent the Bible after all?

Second, let us accept some such reconstructed history of composition as McCarter lays out, showing multiple stages of development in the text. In that context, a decision to treat the received MT in 1 Samuel 17 as inferior to, and therefore subsequent to, the reconstructed Hebrew behind LXX^B underscores the question: Why stop at one particular stage and not another? Historical criticism is replete with judgments concerning well or poorly executed redactions, early or later stages in the growth, of what it still calls the "biblical" literature. Hence, even if MT can be shown to be inferior to LXX^B in narrative quality and posterior in editorial development, why prioritize LXX^B here as the Bible and not MT? (And if MT is prioritized, the same question can be asked.)

The goal of text criticism is to understand the history of transmission of the text and to reconstruct the text "in its most authentic and original form," as John Hayes puts it (1979: 47). And McCarter appears to share those goals. Yet it is clear that something is awry: the critic's postulated "original" text turns out to be neither unambiguously original nor, for that matter, exclusively authentic, if by "authentic" is meant anything like the one, true, genuine, biblical text. Actually Hayes himself is quick to signal recognition of deepseated problems in the text-critical program by immediately qualifying these goals as "perhaps unattainable" and by citing Shemaryahu Talmon's list of three basic complicating factors. First is the fact that "not one single verse of this ancient literature has come to us in an original manuscript" and even the earliest manuscript evidence is "removed by hundreds of years from the date of origin of the literature recorded in them." Second is the great diversity and complexity of the history of transmission of the biblical text relative to other extant texts, ancient or modern. Third is the observation that

> The further back the textual tradition of the Old Testament is followed, i.e., the older the biblical manuscripts perused, and the more ancient the records which come to the knowledge of scholars, the wider is the over-all range of textual divergence between them. . . . In other words, the later the witnesses which are reviewed, the more pronounced their conformity, and the fewer their divergences, both in number and type.
>
> (Hayes 1979: 47–48; Talmon 1975a: 3–5)

The first of these remarks raises again the problem of what is meant by the term "the original" in a literary corpus marked by composite authorship and/or radical editing over a period of many years and perhaps centuries. Likewise, what would count as "the date of origin" of the literature recorded in the extant manuscripts? Let us take McCarter's analysis of 1 Samuel 17 as a case in point. If the "original" text is deemed to be the hypothetical Hebrew text lying behind LXX^B (but why this one and not some other?) then would the date of its authorship/editing be the "date of origin" of the literature or would that be rather the date(s) of the legend it contains (the first time it was told? – or the second time, . . .? – or when it was written down? – the first time, second time, . . .?) or perhaps the "foundation story" or even the "battle near Socoh" (which depends for a date on the literature which we are trying to date, which the historical critic has shown to be mostly historically unreliable). Hayes comments:

Where textual traditions are so different, is it really possible to speak of the original, authentic text? To do so implies that at one time there existed the text of the book from which the various traditions or recensions developed. However, is it not possible that differences already existed in the tradition before it came to be written down? Or that from the beginning, when the materials were not yet considered as "scripture," there already existed a variety of traditions?

(Hayes 1979: 79)

Talmon's third observation helpfully draws attention away from the pursuit of the "original" and towards a factor that is fundamental to understanding the pursuit of the "biblical." We might have expected that the longer the period during which texts were copied and recopied the more diversity we would come to see. Hence the earlier we go in our search the more uniformity we might expect to find. Talmon observes that the opposite is the case. Why is this so? Why is there a narrowing instead of a broadening of transmission?

The answer has to be the intervention of the concept of a "canon," or definitive and authoritative religious "scripture," coupled with a technological innovation, namely the codex, which made regulating such a body of writing more feasible because it allowed for a large number of texts to be bound together in one "book." We know about as much (or as little) concerning the emergence of canon in connection with biblical literature as we know about the early texts of that literature. In large part the evidence comes from the century or two before and after the beginning of the common era and it suggests that by later in the second century C.E. *some* Jewish communities *might* have had a list of specially authoritative books that looked *something* like this (cf. Beckwith 1985: 181–234):

Genesis, Exodus, Leviticus, Numbers, Deuteronomy
Joshua, Judges, Samuel, Kings, Jeremiah, Ezekiel, Isaiah, The Twelve
Ruth, Psalms, Job, Proverbs, Ecclesiastes, Song of Songs, Lamentations,
    Daniel, Esther, Ezra, Nehemiah, Chronicles.

And *some* Christian communities *might* have had a list that looked *something* like this:

Genesis, Exodus, Leviticus, Numbers, Deuteronomy
Joshua, Judges, Ruth, Samuel, Kings, Chronicles, 1 Esdras, Ezra,
    Nehemiah
Psalms, Proverbs, Ecclesiastes, Song of Songs, Job, Wisdom of Solomon,
    Ecclesiasticus
Esther, Judith, Tobit
The Twelve, Isaiah, Jeremiah (with Baruch, Lamentations, and the Epistle
    of Jeremiah), Ezekiel, Daniel (with Susanna and Bel and the Dragon)

It is clear, too, that the Jewish collection may have become authoritative as much as a century or more before this time, and that Christians, as a sect that grew out of early Judaism, borrowed their list and probably the very notion of such a scriptural collection from Jews and Jewish literature.

Strictly speaking, then, to talk about the "biblical" text is to talk about the "canonical" text, since prior to the canonical Bible there is no "biblical text." It is in this canonical sense that McCarter's claim to the authenticity of LXX^B as "the biblical text" can be assessed. In this sense of "biblical" we can say that it was (probably) used by some Greek-reading Christians in the fourth century C.E. as part of their Bible; and that a possibly comparable version in Hebrew (4 Q Sam^a) may have been considered to be "sacred" by some Hebrew-reading Jews of the first century B.C.E. and/or the first century C.E. On the other hand, McCarter knows that at the time of the Qumran text other versions of the text existed, including versions not unlike the later Masoretic Text; and that the Qumran caves have yielded a fragment of 1 Samuel that seems to belong to the MT type of text rather than the LXX^B type. So was that text, too, considered "sacred" or "biblical"? As Hayes observes, "That religious communities were quite willing to live with diverging traditions is illustrated by the inclusion of Kings and Chronicles within the canon in spite of their divergent presentations of Israelite history" (1979: 79).

Text and canon are inseparable issues in biblical criticism. Summing up a wonderfully stimulating formal interchange concerning the text criticism of 1 Samuel 17 between Dominique Barthélemy, David W. Gooding, Emanuel Tov and himself, Johan Lust concludes:

> When Old Testament textual critics try to establish 'the final text' of the Bible, what do they mean by that? The [seminar] participants agreed that for several biblical books more than one text must have existed. To a certain extent the final character of such a text depended on its functioning and its acceptance by a religious community. This observation led to a discussion concerning the impact of the canon and to the appraisal of the MT and the LXX as two different canonical forms of the text.
>
> (in Barthélemy et al. 1986: 156)

The discussion could have taken a bolder turn. For while the divergences in the books of Samuel, Job, and Jeremiah, say, may be most noticeable, there is no biblical book untouched by the problem of textual divergence or (with the possible exception of Genesis, Exodus, Leviticus, Numbers, and Deuteronomy) canonical arrangement. Not "several" biblical books but all biblical books participate in the multi-textuality and multi-canonicity of the Bible.

I mention canonical "arrangement." It is well known that the contents of the canonical lists were subject to debate and disagreement in the first centuries of the common era, more particularly in Christianity where discussion continued for many years over the status of the books of the Apocrypha and the so-called Apocryphal "Additions" to the MT. It is also well known, but more usually ignored in discussion of "the biblical text," that just as with text types, largescale divergences in the arrangement of the Bible have existed from earliest times. I listed above typical canons of the Jewish Bible (MT) and the Christian Old Testament (LXX). But that table is itself a simplification (see, e.g., the tables in Beckwith 1985: ch. 5). In fact, both Hebrew and Greek manuscripts, from the earliest exemplars, frequently vary this order. In the case of Samuel, if we are reading from a Bible based on Jewish Scripture order(s) we read the book as part of a larger story running from Genesis through Kings, in which Samuel follows immediately upon the picture of chaos at the end of Judges; when we read in a Bible based on Christian Greek and Latin scripture orders (including almost all contemporary Protestant Bibles, which purport to be based on the Hebrew Bible) we find Samuel in the same general place in the larger story, but now it follows specifically the much more up-beat book of Ruth, which now appears between it and Judges. If we are interested in what the Bible means, and meaning is contextual, then it is clear that this difference in order translates into two significantly different Bibles.

To return, then, to Talmon's point about the unexpected "narrowing" of texts: we can say that this is due to the emergence of the very notion of "the Bible" itself, as Judaism and Christianity define themselves over against each other, and as Roman Christianity gains hegemony in Christendom. So in the West we have a narrowing of the allowable range of Hebrew texts and Latin texts, with the Greek texts being increasingly supplanted. Yet even though the codex brings a measure of control to the general contents of The Book, it is very difficult to control the smaller differences spawned by copyists in a manuscript transmission. In the fifteenth century the situation begins to change radically. Printing brings about the possibility of control over text and canon in a way never before imagined: one version of the Bible could be disseminated in large numbers of exactly similar copies, enough quickly to obtain a monopoly. This is the story of the eventual dominance of the King James Version in the English speaking world. On the other hand, printing made it possible to produce with relative ease new and different versions of the Bible and give these wide distribution. Talmon's comment requires modification, at least in connection with Christian texts. Taking simply English versions as an example: these grew in number through the closing decades of the sixteenth century before control was exerted (not least against the popular Calvinist "Geneva Bible") by the Crown and the Church of England in the form of the KJV (published in 1611, it took a generation to displace the Geneva Bible). But today in English there are far more versions than one hundred years ago, a fact directly related, I believe, to the fissuring of ecclesiastical power in the English speaking world over the past two centuries.

I have moved from canon to technology and have now begun to talk of control and power. I believe it is important to recognize these as "basic factors" (Talmon's term) in the construction of the "biblical" text. In Christian western Europe the rise of text criticism, the rejection by many of the Latin Vulgate Bible as The Bible (as it had been in the Church for centuries), the proliferation (through printing) of varying vernacular Bibles, the social and intellectual upheavals called the Renaissance and the Reformation, are concurrent and not coincidental.

As noted earlier, Lust's seminar participants, agreeing that the LXX^B and MT of 1 Samuel 17 point to two quite different early texts, recognize that "to a certain extent the final character of such a text depended on its functioning and its acceptance by a religious community." This observation, continues Lust, led to a discussion concerning the impact of the canon and to the appraisal of the MT and the LXX as two different canonical forms of the text. In other words the participants recognized that what makes a text authentically "biblical" is not necessarily to do with which text is "original," "earlier," or "superior" (the vocabulary of text critics) but rather a matter of use, which is to say, canon. The politics of use are crucially determinant — and not just "to a certain extent" — in establishing what *is* the Bible. Origen put his finger on it memorably, when he was challenged by Julius Africanus to discount the story of Susanna which appeared in the Greek text of Daniel, on the grounds that what is not in the Hebrew text is not genuine (see Beckwith 1985: 393). Origen, Hebrew scholar and sometime champion of the Jewish canon, replied:

> In answer to this, I have to tell you what it behoves us to do in the cases not only of the History of Susanna, which is found in every Church of Christ in that Greek copy [of the Bible] which the Greeks use, but is not in the Hebrew, . . . but of thousands of other passages also which I found in many places when with my little strength I was collating the Hebrew copies with ours: . . . In all these cases consider whether it would not be well to remember the words [Proverbs 22:28]: "Thou shalt not remove the ancient landmarks which thy fathers have set."

> (Origen, *Letter to Africanus*, paras 2 and 5)

A millennium later, in a radical move (which took, however, more than a century to become a matter of strict orthodoxy), the Reformers were able to displace the Apocryphal books from their canon, whether by separation into a discrete section or by complete exclusion. Yet, for the most part, they did not (could not?) change the traditional order of the Latin Bible they so denigrated. In other words, their Bibles were hybrids.

Today the Bible is like no other book in the West; the investment of religion and culture in this book is profound. To "change" this book constitutes for many people an outrage. (The vituperative reaction to Polebridge Press's recent *The Complete Gospels* – including the Gospels of Thomas and Mary, among others – and *The Five Gospels* – including Thomas – is a case in point.) Most text critics themselves, even if they hold posts in secular institutions, have some significant link with the religious traditions that claim The Bible as sacred and singular. Equally important, publishers are understandably wary of venturing too far from the status quo, the *textus receptus*, unless they can be persuaded that their new Bible has a market of new "users." Could this be the answer, then, to the question I asked earlier about the typography of McCarter's text? Is this why the Anchor Bible prints the "inferior" text as equivalent to the "superior" one? Is it a matter of the politics of use? We might well suppose that a proposal to footnote upwards of a third of a chapter of the received/traditional (for Jews and Christians of all denominations) text would meet with no little resistance. (Attractive as it might appear at first, Eugene Ulrich's claim that "for both Judaism and Christianity, it is books, not specific textual forms of the books that are canonical" [1992: 36] does not bear close scrutiny, as both the Origen-Africanus debate and the case of 1 Samuel 17 make clear.) Publishing Bibles is, like all publishing, a political act and a particularly sensitive one. There is only so much one can change at a time when it comes to the "traditional" text of the Bible. Critics of biblical text and canon work with ancient landmarks.

The actual or potential relation of the criticism to the landmark is not always in the forefront of the discussion. Hayes acutely observes many of the reasons why a search for the "original" biblical text is an illusory pursuit. He recognizes that the *textus receptus* Bibles came into being at the earliest with early Christianity, rabbinical Judaism, and Samaritan Judaism, and so obviously recognizes the historical place of the Greek Old Testament as the Bible for many Christians (and possibly, in early times, many diaspora Jews). Yet he still insists that textual criticism must start with the MT: "This tradition is, after all, the canonical form of the Hebrew scriptures" (Hayes 1979: 79–80). How curious. A Jewish or a Christian "original" canon? Why should one take priority over the other, as Hayes would appear to be urging (at least implicitly), unless it be to give expression to the prioritizor's canonical politics? Why should Hayes, a Christian, writing in a book whose title, *Introduction to Old Testament Study*, would seem to indicate a Christian Bible, urge the "canonical form of the Hebrew scriptures" as the basis of textual criticism of the biblical text? (I should make clear that this is the "received" position in modern scholarship.)

Another Christian, Roger Beckwith, in his recent book, *The Old Testament Canon of the New Testament Church* (1985), offers one convincing reason as he explains his own attempt to claim for the Hebrew Bible originary canonical status. It is a matter of church and theological politics: the issue is the Reformation and the Reformers' challenge to the authority of the Roman church.

To break the church's monopoly on the interpretation of scripture through appeal to "tradition," the Reformers countered with a doctrine of *sola scriptura*, decreeing that the Bible and the Bible alone, interpreted through the Holy Spirit, was the rule of faith and practice for the true church. Further undermining the Roman Catholic position, they argued *against* the Latin Vulgate and the *de facto* canon of the Roman tradition which included books contained in the Greek and Latin Bibles and known as the Apocrypha, as well as the books found in the Jewish scriptures. (The Catholic Council of Trent in 1546 officially pronounced all these books "biblical.") The Reformers argued *for* the priority of the "original" Bible, which in the case of the Old Testament they deemed to be the scriptures in Hebrew, in practice a canon of books common to the Greek, Latin, and Hebrew Bibles but following a basically Greek and Latin order, and a text which was the contemporary (sixteenth-century) Jewish *textus receptus* known today as the Masoretic Text. (Lutherans, however, continued to accept as "edifying" and fitting to be read in church traditional "apocryphal" books, while Calvinists insisted on the Jewish canon alone).

Politically the Reformer's position made excellent sense. Logically, however, it was open to serious challenge, as Beckwith reminds us, in the form of Bellarmine's famous objection (formulated at the end of the fifteenth century): "that though Protestants may base everything else which they believe on the authority of Scripture, they base their very canon of Scripture on the authority of tradition, and so overthrow the foundations of their own theology" (Beckwith 1985: 5). And this was the case: despite all their talk about locating the sources of tradition, the Protestants found their very notion of canon as well as their arguments (the words of Jerome and Augustine, for example) *in* the traditions of both Church and Synagogue. Beckwith, unusually, does bring his politics into the foreground. He is frank: he is concerned to rescue Reformed theology from Bellarmine's objection. His strategy is to show that the Reformers "were right in thinking that one can find firmer grounds than tradition on which to base the canon, namely, the teaching of Jesus and the apostles" (1985: 6).

Protestant scholarship and the Masoretic Text have a long political connection. In this light, the often criticized (as illogical) commitment of Brevard Childs to the priority of the MT in the course of his propounding a mode of (Christian) "canonical criticism" which among other things attends seriously to the meaning of canonical arrangement, makes perfect sense. Childs is a theologian in the Reformed (Calvinist) tradition, and he, like Beckwith, is not anxious to move his Reformed Fathers' landmarks.

Beckwith's argument is instructive. Like many a text critic, this canon critic launches us on a search for the Original and True Canon, in this case, The Bible of Jesus. Yet some five hundred pages later (of richly informative discussion) I find myself no closer to the goal. Rather I am so much the more forcibly reminded of the parallels between the quests of canon and text.

The further into antiquity one seeks, the more diversity one finds.

Attempts to locate some definitive time and place, prior to Jesus, when The Canon was established are no more convincing than attempts to determine when the "original" text of 1 Samuel was produced; instead we find elusive witnesses to processes extending over centuries rather like McCarter's postulated growth of the David and Goliath story.

Beckwith's appeal to "the teaching of Jesus and the apostles" no more dispenses with the perceived overlay of "tradition" than McCarter's appeal to an "original" Hebrew text underlying both LXX^B and MT. Like McCarter, Beckwith merely pushes the "original" back one stage in the "tradition." He strains every sinew in arguing that the Jewish canon was essentially fixed prior to the ministry of Jesus, and then tells us that Jesus and his disciples believed that this postulated canon was the true and inspired Scripture. Only he treats the New Testament text as though it were somehow "traditionless," a transparent window into "history," a direct source of true information. And he leaves hanging over his argument the awkward implication that somehow, despite this apparently fixed canon that Jesus unambiguously endorsed as The Bible, the early Christian Church went ahead anyhow and invented a different canon, a *new* Bible – which included the story of how Jesus believed there was already in existence a One True Fixed and Authentic Bible!

The pursuit of the original. The scholar's ability to sunder successfully the subject and object of the search, so as to starkly render its goal, "history" – namely, the very beliefs of Jesus. The idea that the pursuit itself, the interpretive endeavor, can indeed be "traditionless," somehow separate from the language and modes of operation that construct the search in the first place. Beckwith's is a very modern canon criticism. Bellarmine, I believe, has a better chance of engaging in a postmodern conversation.

Both Beckwith and McCarter are in the business of designating "authentic and original" texts. That desire for the "original," like the myth of presence or pure origin (Derrida), is a characteristically modern one. It also taps into the politics of singularity, a powerful politics in the West. As there is One God, there is One Word of God, One Scripture. For text critics of the Jewish Scripture/Hebrew Bible or Christian Old Testament this pursuit often involves postulating "original" texts that are centuries (and who knows how many versions) distant from the time when anything like "the Bible" came into being. And at the same time the same critics are frequently busy collapsing the difference between "original" and "biblical" so that the One biblical text may not become Several. Yet, as both Beckwith and McCarter illustrate for us, text critics who are dedicated to narrowing the divergences between Bibles into earlier or later, superior or inferior, original or spurious, are at the same time in the business of creating Bibles which are different from the received "biblical" texts. Hence McCarter prints the story of David and Goliath as doublets; Beckwith makes a case for an English

Bible that follows a traditional Jewish order, something that (to my best knowledge) no publisher of a Christian Bible in English has yet been willing to do, despite the lavish assurances that accompany virtually every major version since the English Reformation that the Old Testaments are based on, and translated directly from, the Hebrew (and Aramaic). This is the politics of use – one can hear already the howls of anguish from the folks in the pews as they scramble to find the Book of Ruth in a strange place in a strange Bible.

Biblical text criticism is a conflicted enterprise. As we have seen, it drives towards the One. We can see the same drive also in the production of "standard" editions of the Hebrew text, mandatory for use by scholars like myself if we wish to be taken seriously in the guild. The Old Testament/Hebrew Bible/Jewish Scripture scholars' Bible. Whatever the scholarly, "text-critical," reasons for making this the "standard" text, one must admit it is just plain useful for the business of scholarly interchange to have a single standard edition. But, paradoxically, biblical text criticism also drives towards the production of ever more texts. McCarter on 1 Samuel 17 is nicely representative: like many other critics persuaded of the merits here of LXX^B, he nevertheless does not follow this version slavishly (e.g., like NAB, he omits the pierced helmet). Modern text criticism is essentially eclectic, which is to say that it is suspicious of affording any one manuscript or version absolute priority, though it will, as a matter of convenience, allow one text a relative priority (by printing it in the body of the text, and then emending it in the appended textual apparatus). Rather it places a premium on critical choice by the text critic, a priority which hardly surprises given the professional location of most text critics in academia. Already in my scholarly lifetime I have worked with two "standard editions" (Kittel's Biblia Hebraica, 3rd edn, and the Biblia Hebraica Stuttgartensia). The next is only a matter of time and (considerable amounts of) money away. In the meantime new readings abound as scholars seek out and (not insensitive to the job requirements of academia) publish the ever-expanding evidence, with the Qumran texts being the most recent boost to this proliferation. (And remember that the further back, the more divergent the evidence.) In short, as hard as it presses towards the One True Text, it produces instead innumerable Variant Texts, a proliferation to add to that of the extant manuscripts. As much as it seeks uniformity, univocality, closure, and stability, text criticism produces multiformity, multivocality, open-endedness, and instability. If text criticism can prioritize difference and so shore up the singularity of both Bible and Faith, it can surely multiply Bibles and in so doing fracture the Faith. And yet, as McCarter's printed doublets remind us, while it is the task of the text critic to determine the limits of The Bible, the text critic is limited because this decision has already been made, or will be remade, elsewhere; without The Biblical Text as a given, the biblical text critic would have nothing to talk about. The Biblical Text is always a given.

I watched in awe recently as a television preacher held fast to his King James Version and passionately defended The Bible against the depredations of a panel of conservative Christian text critics and translators who vainly ventured observations about differences between the "original" Bible, whether Greek (New Testament) or Hebrew (Old Testament), and the KJV. The preacher already had The Bible in his hand and his line in the sand. Yet, while I understood exactly what the text critics were saying and shared their bemusement, I wondered whether they perhaps shared, more than they acknowledged, in his project. Did they, too, desire the One, the Original, and merely trail some steps behind their fellow panelist who already believed he grasped the object of his passion? Or, on reflection, was it possible that they were sowing seeds of division, conservative (but contextually radical) voices for multivocality, against an encroaching crop of Christian fundamentalism in the USA which calls for one variety, one voice on Bible, politics, and morality?

It occurs to me that I have moved a long way from my question of sword or stone. I have found no solution to my question. Rather I have found different Bibles offering different information, in varying ways either entertaining or eschewing the appearance of contradiction. More than that, my quest has confounded my question. What do I mean when I say, what does the Bible say? Which text, which canon, which Bible am I talking about? And why do I persevere with the question – what politics drive my essay? But now, as the search turns in on the searcher, let me fend off that question and backtrack to the beginning. What if I have been too cavalier, too intent in my gaze on the text of 1 Samuel 17 to see the wood for the trees? For purposes of the argument, let me return to my starting point, my "received text." In my search I moved from talk of text to canon. Why stop at 1 Samuel 17? The Bible is larger than that chapter. So what else does the Bible (which is to say, my Bible) say about Goliath that might help me with my question?

A concordance takes me to two passages:

And there was again war with the Philistines at Gob; and Elhanan the son of Jaare-oregim, the Bethlehemite, slew Goliath the Gittite, the shaft of whose spear was like a weaver's beam.

(2 Samuel 21:19)

And there was again war with the Philistines; and Elhanan the son of Jair slew Lahmi the brother of Goliath the Gittite, the shaft of whose spear was like a weaver's beam.

(1 Chronicles 20:5)

And I thought I had a problem discovering whether it was by sword or stone.

BIBLIOGRAPHY

Ackroyd, Peter R. (1975) "The Verb Love – *'āhēb* in the David–Jonathan Narratives – A Footnote," *Vetus Testamentum* 25,2: 213–14.

Adorno, Theodor W. (1973 [1966]) *Negative Dialectics*, New York: Continuum.

—— (1981) *Prisms*, trans. S. and S. Weber, Cambridge MA: MIT Press.

Aletti, Jean-Noel (1977) "Seduction et Parole en Proverbes 1–9," *Vetus Testamentum* 27: 129–44.

Allen, Leslie C. (1976) *The Books of Joel, Obadiah, Jonah, and Micah*, London: Hodder & Stoughton.

Allen, D., Bartow, C., Loder, J., Mauser, U., McCormack, B and Willis-Watkins, D. (1994) "An Open Letter to Presbyterians: Theological Analysis of Issues Raised by the Re-Imagining Conference," unpublished manuscript.

Alt, Albrecht (1989) "The Formation of the Israelite State in Palestine," in *Essays on Old Testament History and Religion*, trans. R. A. Wilson, Sheffield: JSOT Press.

Alter, Robert (1992) *The World of Biblical Literature*, New York: Basic Books.

Althusser, Louis (1971) *Lenin and Philosophy*, trans. B. Brewster, London: Monthly Review.

Anderson, Gary (1992) "The Garden of Eden and Sexuality in Early Judaism," in H. Eilberg-Schwartz (ed.) *People of the Body: Jews and Judaism from an Embodied Perspective*, New York: SUNY.

Aschheim, S. E. (1982) *Brothers and Strangers: The East European Jew in German and German Jewish Consciousness, 1800–1923*, Madison: University of Wisconsin Press.

Aschkenasy, Nehama (1986) *Eve's Journey: Feminine Images in Hebraic Literary Tradition*, Philadelphia: University of Philadelphia Press.

Bal, Mieke (1987) *Lethal Love: Feminist Literary Readings of Biblical Love Stories*, Bloomington: Indiana University Press.

—— (1988a) *Death and Dyssymmetry: The Politics of Coherence in the Book of Judges*, Chicago: University of Chicago Press.

—— (1988b) *Murder and Difference: Gender, Genre, and Scholarship on Sisera's Death*, trans. M. Gurmpert, Bloomington: Indiana University Press.

—— (1991) *On Story-Telling: Essays in Narratology*, ed. David Jobling, Sonoma: Polebridge.

—— (1993) "Metaphors He Lives By," *Semeia 61*: 185–208.

Barr, James (1959) "Theophany and Anthropomorphism in the Old Testament," *Vetus Testamentum Supplements* 7: 31–38.

—— (1968/69) "The Image of God in the Book of Genesis – A Study of Terminology," *Bulletin of the John Rylands Library* 51: 11–26.

Barthélemy, Dominique, Gooding, David W., Lust, Johan, and Tov, Emanuel (1986) *The Story of David and Goliath: Textual and Literary Criticism*, Orbis Biblicus et

Orientalis 73, Fribourg: Editions Universitaires and Göttingen: Vandenhoeck & Ruprecht.

Beal, Timothy K. (1994) "The System and the Speaking Subject in the Hebrew Bible: Reading for Divine Abjection," *Biblical Interpretation* 2: 171–89.

Beckwith, Roger (1985) *The Old Testament Canon of the New Testament Church and its Background in Early Judaism*, Grand Rapids: Eerdmans Publishing Company.

Benveniste, Emile (1971) *Problems In General Linguistics*, Coral Gables: University of Miami.

Berkowitz, M. (1993) *Zionist Culture and West European Jewry before the First World War*, Cambridge: Cambridge University Press.

Berlin, Adele (1989) "Lexical Cohesion and Biblical Interpretation," *Hebrew Studies* 30: 29–40.

Biale, David (1982) "The God With Breasts: El Shaddai in the Bible," *History of Religions* 21: 240–56.

—— (1994) *Eros and the Jews*, New York: Basic Books.

Bible and Culture Collective (1995) *The Postmodern Bible*, New Haven: Yale University Press.

Bird, Phyllis (1981) "'Male and Female He Created Them': Gen 1:27b in the Context of the Priestly Account of Creation," *Harvard Theological Review* 74: 129–59.

—— (1987) "Genesis 1–3 as a Source for a Contemporary Theology of Sexuality," *Ex Auditu* 3: 31–44.

—— (1989) "The Harlot as Heroine: Narrative Art and Social Presupposition in Three Old Testament Texts," *Semeia* 46: 119–40.

Black, Max (1962) *Models and Metaphors*, Ithaca: Cornell University Press.

Bloom, Harold (1976) "Poetic Crossing: Rhetoric and Psychology," *The Georgia Review* 30: 495–526.

—— (1986) "From J to K, or the Uncanniness of the Yahwist," in Frank McConnell (ed.) *The Bible and the Narrative Tradition*, Oxford: Oxford University Press.

—— (1990) "The Representation of Yahweh" and "The Psychology of Yahweh," in David Rosenberg and Harold Bloom, *The Book of J*, New York: Grove Weidenfeld.

Boyarin, Daniel (1990a) "The Eye in the Torah: Ocular Desire in Midrashic Hermeneutic," *Critical Inquiry* 16: 532–50.

—— (1990b) *Intertextuality and the Reading of Midrash*, Bloomington: University of Indiana Press.

—— (1992) "'This We Know to Be the Carnal Israel': Circumcision and the Erotic Life of God and Israel," *Critical Inquiry* 18: 474–505.

—— (1994a) "Freud's baby; Fliess's maybe: Male hysteria, homophobia, and the invention of the Jewish man," *GLQ* 2,1: 133.

—— (1994b) *A Radical Jew: Paul and the Politics of Identity*, Contraversions: Critical Studies in Jewish Literature, Culture, and Society, Berkeley and Los Angeles: University of California Press.

—— (forthcoming) "The Colonial Drag: Zionism, Gender, and Colonial Mimicry," in K. Seshadri-Crooks and Fawzia Afzal-Kahn (eds) *Dimensions of (So-called) Postcolonial Studies*, Durham: Duke University Press.

—— (forthcoming) "Bitextuality, Psychoanalysis, Zionism: On the Ambivalence of the Jewish Phallus," in C. Patton (ed.) *Queer Diasporas*, Series Q, Durham: Duke University Press.

Boyarin, Daniel and Boyarin, Jonathan (1993) "Diaspora: Generation and the Ground of Jewish Identity," *Critical Inquiry* 19: 693–725.

Brenkman, J. (1993) *Straight Male Modern: A Cultural Critique of Psychoanalysis*, New York: Routledge.

Brenner, Athalya (1989) *The Song of Songs*, Sheffield: Sheffield Academic Press.
—— (1993a) "On 'Jeremiah' and the Poetics of (Prophetic?) Pornography," in A. Brenner and F. van Dijk-Hemmes (eds) *On Gendering Texts: Female and Male Voices in the Hebrew Bible*, Leiden: Brill.
—— (ed.)(1993b) *A Feminist Companion to Genesis*, Sheffield: JSOT Press.
Brenner, Athalya and van Dijk-Hemmes, Fokkelien (1993) *On Gendering Texts*, Leiden: E. J. Brill.
Breuer, J. and Freud, S. (n.d.) *Studies on Hysteria*, ed. and trans., J. Strachey, New York: Basic Books.
Briggs, Sheila (1985) "Images of Women and Jews in Nineteenth- and Twentieth-Century German Theology," in C. W. Atkinson, C. H. Buchanan and M. R. Miles (eds) *Immaculate and Powerful: The Female in Sacred Image and Reality*, Boston: Beacon Press.
Bright, John (1967) *The Authority of the Old Testament*, Nashville: Abingdon.
Broome, E. C. (1946) "Ezekiel's Abnormal Personality," *Journal of Biblical Literature* 65: 277–92.
Brown, Peter (1988) *The Body and Society: Sexual Renunciation in Early Christianity*, New York: Columbia University Press.
Brueggemann, Walter (1982) *Genesis*, Interpretation, Atlanta: John Knox Press.
—— (1984) *The Message of the Psalms: A Theological Commentary*, Minneapolis: Augsburg.
—— (1985) "A Shape for Old Testament Theology II: Embrace of Pain," *Catholic Biblical Quarterly* 47: 407–15.
Buccellati, G. (1967) *Cities and Nations in Ancient Syria*, Rome: Instituto Di Studi Del Vincino Oriente, Universita Di Roma.
Budde, Karl (1917/18) "Das Rätsel von Micha I," *Zeitschrift für die alttestamtliche Wissenschaft* 37: 77–108.
Cady, Susan, Ronan, Marian, and Taussig, Hal (1989) *Wisdom's Feast*, San Francisco: Harper & Row.
Calvin, John (1950 [1559]) *Commentaries on the Twelve Minor Prophets, III: Jonah, Micah, Nahum*, trans. J. Owen, Grand Rapids: Eerdmans.
Camp, Claudia V. (1985) *Wisdom and the Feminine in the Book of Proverbs*, Decatur: Almond.
—— (1987) "Woman Wisdom as Root Metaphor: A Theological Consideration," in K. G. Hoglund *et al.* (eds) *The Listening Heart: Essays in Honor of Roland E. Murphy*, Sheffield: JSOT Press.
—— (1990) "The Female Sage in Ancient Israel and in the Biblical Wisdom Literature," in J. G. Gammie and L. G. Perdue (eds) *The Sage in Israel and the Ancient Near East*, Winona Lake: Eisenbrauns.
—— (1991) "What's So Strange about the Strange Woman?," in David Jobling *et al.* (eds) *The Bible and the Politics of Exegesis*, Cleveland: Pilgrim.
Campbell, K. M. (1972) "Rahab's Covenant," *Vetus Testamentum* 22: 243–44.
Carroll, Robert P. (1986) *Jeremiah: A Commentary*, London: SCM Press.
—— (1991) "Textual Strategies and Ideology in the Second Temple Period," in P. R. Davies (ed.) *Second Temple Studies. Vol 1: Persian Period*, Sheffield: Sheffield Academic Press.
Cassuto, Umberto (1983 [1967]) *A Commentary on the Book of Exodus*, trans. I. Abrahams, Jerusalem: The Magnes Press.
—— (1978) *A Commentary on the Book of Genesis* [Hebrew] Pt 1, Jerusalem: Magnes.
Charlesworth, James H. (ed.) (1983; 1985) *The Old Testament Pseudepigrapha*, 2 vols, Garden City, New York: Doubleday.

—— (1993) "In the Crucible: The Pseudepigrapha as Biblical Interpretation," in James H. Charlesworth and C. Evans (eds) *Pseudepigrapha and Early Biblical Interpretation*, Sheffield: JSOT Press.

Cheyne, T. K. (1882) *Micah*, Cambridge: Cambridge University Press.

Childs, Brevard S. (1974) *The Book of Exodus*, Philadelphia: Westminster.

Christ, Carol (1974) "Why Women Need the Goddess," in C. Christ and J. Plaskow (eds) *Womanspirit Rising*, San Francisco: Harper & Row.

Cixous, Hélène (1991) "Coming to Writing," in D. Jenson (ed.) *Coming to Writing and Other Essays*, trans. S. Cornell, D. Jenson, A. Liddle, and S. Sellers, Cambridge, MA and London: Harvard University Press.

—— (1993) "Without End no State of Drawingness no, rather: The Executioner's Taking Off," *New Literary History* 24: 91–103.

Clines, David J. A. (1990) *What Does Eve do to Help? and Other Readerly Questions to the Old Testament*, JSOT Supplement Series 94; Sheffield: JSOT Press [Sheffield Academic Press].

Coats, George (1988) *Moses: Heroic Man, Man of God*, Sheffield: JSOT Press.

Cohen, Jeremy (1989) *Be Fertile and Increase, Fill the Earth and Master It*, Ithaca: Cornell University Press.

Collins, John J. (1983) *Between Athens and Jerusalem*, New York: Crossroad.

Cornell, Drusilla (1992) *The Philosophy of the Limit*, New York and London: Routledge.

Cowley, A. E. (1923) *Aramaic Papyri of the Fifth Century BC*, Oxford: Oxford University Press.

Crenshaw, James L. (1981) "Sapiential Rhetoric and Its Warrants," *Vetus Testamentum Supplement* 32.

—— (1983) *Theodicy in the Old Testament*, London: SPCK.

Cross, E. (1988) *Theory and Practice of Sociocriticism*, Minneapolis: University of Minnesota Press.

Cross, Frank Moore (1973) *Canaanite Myth and Hebrew Epic*, Cambridge MA: Harvard University Press.

Culler, Jonathan (1982) *On Deconstruction: Theory and Criticism after Structuralism*, Ithaca: Cornell University Press.

Cyre, Susan (1994) "Fallout Escalates Over 'Goddess' Sophia Worship," *Christianity Today* 4-4-94.

Daly, Mary (1973) *Beyond God the Father*, Boston: Beacon.

Darr, Katheryn Pfisterer (1994) *Isaiah's Vision and the Family of God*, Literary Currents in Biblical Interpretation, Louisville: Westminster/John Knox.

Davies, Philip R. (1993) "Women, Men, God, Sex and Power: The Birth of a Biblical Myth," in A. Brenner (ed.) *A Feminist Companion to Genesis*, Sheffield: JSOT Press.

De Vaux, Roland O. (1961) *Ancient Israel: Its Life and Institutions*, New York: McGraw-Hill.

Derrida, Jacques (1976) *Of Grammatology*, trans. G. Spivak, Baltimore: Johns Hopkins University Press.

—— (1978) *Writing and Difference*, trans. A. Bass, Chicago: University of Chicago Press.

—— (1981) *Dissemination*, trans. B. Johnson, Chicago: University of Chicago Press.

—— (1982) *Margins of Philosophy*, trans. A. Bass, Chicago: University of Chicago Press.

—— (1985) "Letter to a Japanese Friend" in D. Wood and R. Bernasconi (eds) *Derrida and Différance*, Coventry: Parousia Press.

—— (1986) *Glas*, trans. J. P. Leavey and R. Rand, Lincoln: University of Nebraska Press.

—— (1988) *Limited, Inc.*, trans. S. Weber and J. Mehlman. Evanston, IL: Northwestern University Press.

—— (1991) "Interpretations at War: Kant, the Jew, the German," *New Literary History* 22: 39–96.

Dever, William G. (1984) "Asherah, Consort of Yhweh? New Evidence from Kuntillet 'Arjud," *Bulletin of the American Schools of Oriental Research* 255: 385–408.

Dijkstra, Bram (1986) *Idols of Perversity: Fantasies of Feminine Evil in Fin-de-siècle Culture*, New York: Oxford University Press.

Douglas, Mary (1966) *Purity and Danger*, London: Routledge & Kegan Paul.

Downing, Christine (1981) *The Goddess: Mythological Images of the Feminine*, New York: Crossroad.

Dragga, Sam (1992) "Genesis 2–3: A Story of Liberation," *JSOT* 55: 3–13.

Eilberg-Schwartz, Howard (1990) *The Savage in Judaism: An Anthropology of Israelite Religion and Ancient Judaism*, Bloomington: Indiana University Press.

—— (1992) "The Problem of the Body for the People of the Book," in H. Eilberg-Schwartz (ed.) *People of the Body: Jews and Judaism from an Embodied Perspective*, Albany: State University of New York Press [= *Journal of the History of Sexuality* 2 (1991) 1–24].

—— (1994) *God's Phallus and Other Problems for Men and Monotheism*, Boston: Beacon Press.

—— (forthcoming) "Damned If You Do and Damned If You Don't: Rabbinic Ambivalence Towards Sex and Body," in *Center for Hermeneutical Studies Protocol Series* 61.

Elliger, Karl (1934) "Die Heimat des Propheten Micha," *ZDPV* 57: 81–152.

Endres, John C. (1987) *Biblical Interpretation in the Book of Jubilees*, Washington: Catholic Biblical Association of America.

Eskenazi, Tamara C. and Judd, Eleanore P. (1994) "Marriage to a Stranger in Ezra 9–10," in T. C. Eskenazi and K. H. Richards (eds) *Second Temple Studies. Vol 2: Temple Community in the Persian Period*, Sheffield: Sheffield Academic Press.

Eslinger, Lyle (1989) *Into the Hands of the Living God*, Sheffield: Sheffield Academic Press and Almond Press.

Exum, J. Cheryl (1973) "A Literary and Structural Analysis of the Song of Songs," *Zeitschrift für Altentestamentliche Wissenschaft* 85: 47–79.

—— (1993) *Fragmented Women: Feminist (Sub)versions of Biblical Narratives*, Philadelphia: Trinity Press International.

Fanon, Frantz (1967) *Black Skins, White Masks*, trans. C. L. Markham, New York: Grove Press.

Feldman, David M. (1968) *Marital Relations, Birth Control and Abortion in Jewish Law*, New York: Schocken.

Felman, Shoshana (1985) *Writing and Madness [Literature/Philosophy/Psychoanalysis]*, Ithaca: Cornell University Press.

—— (1987) *Jacques Lacan and the Adventure of Insight: Psychoanalysis in Contemporary Culture*, Cambridge MA: Harvard University Press.

Fewell, Danna Nolan (1995) "Achsah and the (E)razed City of Writing" in G. Yee (ed.) *Judges and Method*, Minneapolis: Augsburg-Fortress.

Fewell, Danna Nolan and Gunn, David M. (1990) "Controlling Perspectives: Women, Men, and the Authority of Violence in Judges 4–5," *JAAR* 56: 389–411.

—— (1991) "Tipping the Balance: Sternberg's Reader and the Rape of Dinah," *Journal of Biblical Literature* 110: 193–211.

—— (1993) *Gender, Power, and Promise: The Subject of the Bible's First Story*, Nashville: Abingdon.

Fiorenza, Elisabeth Schüssler (1984) *Bread Not Stone: The Challenge of Feminist Biblical Interpretation*, Boston: Beacon Press.

Fishbane, Michael (1985) *Biblical Interpretation in Ancient Israel*, Oxford: Clarendon Press.

Fontaine, Carole (1987) "Proverbs," in J. L. Mays (ed.) *Harper's Bible Commentary*, San Francisco: Harper & Row.

—— (1988) "Queenly Proverb Performance," in K. G. Hoglund *et al.* (eds) *The Listening Heart: Essays in Honor of Roland E. Murphy*, Sheffield: JSOT Press.

Forsberg, M. (1988) "James Dearden: Life After 'Fatal Attraction,'" in *New York Times* 24, 7: 21.

Foucault, Michel (1972) *The Archeology of Knowledge*, trans. A. M. Sheridan Smith, New York: Pantheon.

Fout, J. C. (1992) "Sexual Politics in Wilhelmine German: The Male Gender Crisis, Moral Purity, and Homophobia" *Journal of the History of Sexuality* 2: 388–421.

Fox, R. (1967) *Kinship and Marriage*, London: Np.

Fretheim, Terence E. (1984) *The Suffering of God: An Old Testament Perspective*, Philadelphia: Fortress.

Freud, Sigmund (1896–) *The Standard Edition of the Complete Psychological Works of Sigmund Freud*, ed. and trans. J. Strachey in collaboration with A. Freud, see the following entries. London: The Hogarth Press.

—— (1896) "The Aetiology of the Neuroses," in *The Standard Edition*, vol. 3.

—— (1900) *The Interpretation of Dreams*, First Part, in *The Standard Edition* vol. 4.

—— (1900–1) *The Interpretation of Dreams*, Second Part, in *The Standard Edition* vol. 5.

—— (1908) "'Civilized' Sexual Morality and Modern Nervous Illness," in *The Standard Edition* vol. 9.

—— (1911) "Psycho-Analytic Notes on an Autobiographical Account of a Case of Paranoia [Dementia Paranoides]," in *The Standard Edition* vol. 12.

—— (1914a) "The Moses of Michelangelo," in *The Standard Edition* vol. 13.

—— (1914b) "On the History of the Psycho-Analytic Movement," in *The Standard Edition* vol. 14.

—— (1916–17) *Introductory Lectures on Psycho-Analysis*, in *The Standard Edition* vols 15 and 16.

—— (1918) "From the History of an Infantile Neurosis," in *The Standard Edition* vol. 17.

—— (1925a) "Note on the Mystic Writing-Pad," in *The Standard Edition* vol. 19.

—— (1925b) "An Autobiographical Study," in *The Standard Edition* vol. 20.

—— (1926) "The Question of Lay Analysis," in *The Standard Edition* vol. 20.

—— (1930) *Civilization and Its Discontents*, in *The Standard Edition* vol. 21.

—— (1931) "Female Sexuality," in *The Standard Edition* vol. 21.

—— (1937) "Analysis Terminable and Interminable," in *The Standard Edition* vol. 23.

—— (1939) *Moses and Monotheism: Three Essays*, in *The Standard Edition* vol. 23.

—— (1950) *Totem and Taboo: Some Points of Agreement between the Mental Lives of Savages and Neurotics*, trans. J. Strachey, New York: Norton.

—— (1962) *Three Essays on the Theory of Sexuality*, J. Strachey (ed. and trans.), New York: Basic Books.

—— (1963a) *Dora: An Analysis of a Case of Hysteria*, ed. P. Rieff, New York: Macmillan.

—— (1963b) "The Economic Problem in Masochism," in P. Rieff (ed.) *Freud: General Psychological Theory*, New York: Macmillan.

—— (1976) *The Interpretation of Dreams*, trans. J. Strachey, Harmondsworth, Middlesex: Penguin.

Friedman, Richard E. (1987) *Who Wrote the Bible?*, New York: Harper & Row.

Gallop, Jane (1985) *Reading Lacan*, Ithaca: Cornell University Press.

Gay, Peter (1987) *A Godless Jew: Freud, Atheism, and the Making of Psychoanalysis*, New Haven: Yale University Press.

Geller, Jay (1993) "A Paleontological View of Freud's Study of Religion: Unearthing the Leitfossil Circumcision," *Modern Judaism* 13: 49–70.

George, Mark K. (1995) *Body Works: Power, the Construction of Identity, and Gender in the Discourse on Kingship*, unpublished Ph.D. dissertation, Princeton Theological Seminary.

Gilman, Sander L. (1986) *Jewish Self-Hatred: Anti-Semitism and the Hidden Language of the Jews*, Baltimore: Johns Hopkins University Press.

—— (1991) *The Jew's Body*, London: Routledge.

—— (1993a) *The Case of Sigmund Freud: Medicine and Identity at the Fin de Siècle*, Baltimore: Johns Hopkins University Press.

—— (1993b) *Freud, Race, and Gender*, Princeton: Princeton University Press.

Gilroy, P. (1993) *The Black Atlantic: Modernity and Double Consciousness*, Cambridge, MA: Harvard University Press.

Girard, René (1977) *Violence and the Sacred*, trans. P. Gregory, Baltimore: Johns Hopkins University Press.

Gluckman, Max (1955) *Custom and Conflict in Africa*, Oxford: Blackwells.

Goldstein, B. (1992) *Reinscribing Moses: Heine, Kafka, Freud, and Schoenberg in a European Wilderness*, Cambridge: Harvard University Press.

Gordis, Robert (1978) *Love and Sex: A Modern Jewish Perspective*, New York: Hippocrene Books.

Gottwald, Norman (1954) *Studies in the Book of Lamentations*, Chicago: Alec R. Allenson, Inc.

Gould, E. (ed.) (1985) *The Sin of the Book*, Lincoln: University of Nebraska Press.

Goux, J.-J. (1990) *Symbolic Economies: After Marx and Freud*, trans. J. C. Cage, Ithaca: Cornell University Press.

Graves, Robert and Patai, Raphael (1983) *Hebrew Myths: The Book of Genesis*, New York: Greenwich House.

Greenberg, Irving (1977) "Cloud of Smoke, Pillar of Fire: Judaism, Christianity, and Modernity after the Holocaust," in E. Fleischner (ed.) *Auschwitz: Beginning of a New Era?*, New York: Ktav.

Griffiths, J. G. (1980) *The Origins of Osiris and his Cult*, Leiden: E. J. Brill.

Grosz, E. (1990) *Jacques Lacan: A Feminist Introduction*, London: Routledge.

Gruber, Mayer I. (1983) "The Motherhood of God in Second Isaiah," *Revue Biblique* 90: 351–59.

—— (1985) "Female Imagery Relating to God in Second Isaiah" (in Hebrew), *Beer Sheva* 2:75–84.

—— (1992) *The Motherhood of God and Other Studies*, Atlanta: Scholars Press.

Gunn, David M. (1987) "Joshua and Judges," in R. Alter and F. Kermode (eds) *The Literary Guide to the Bible*, Cambridge, MA: Belknap Press of Harvard University Press.

Habermas, Jürgen (1971) *Knowledge and Human Interest*, trans. J. J. Shapiro, Boston: Beacon.

Hagstrom, David G. (1988) *The Coherence of the Book of Micah: A Literary Analysis*, Atlanta: Scholars Press.

Hall, D. E. (1994) "Muscular Christianity: Reading and Writing the Male Social Body," in D. E. Hall (ed.) *Muscular Christianity: Embodying the Victorian Age*, Cambridge

Studies in Nineteenth-Century Literature and Culture 2, Cambridge, UK: Cambridge University Press.

Halperin, David J. (1993) *Seeking Ezekiel: Text and Psychology*, University Park: The Pennsylvania State University Press.

Handelman, Susan A. (1982) *The Slayers of Moses: The Emergence of Rabbinic Interpretation in Modern Literary Theory*, Albany: SUNY Press.

Harpham, G. G. (1994) "So . . . What *Is* Enlightenment? An Inquisition into Modernity," *Critical Inquiry* 20: 524–56.

Harrington, Daniel J. (1983) "Pseudo-Philo: A New Translation and Introduction," in James H. Charlesworth and C. Evans (eds) *Pseudepigrapha and Early Biblical Interpretation*, Sheffield: JSOT Press.

Hawk, L. Daniel (1991) *Every Promise Fulfilled: Contesting Plots in Joshua*, Literary Currents in Biblical Interpretation, Philadelphia: Westminster/John Knox.

Hayes, John H. (1979) "The Textual Criticism of the Old Testament," in *An Introduction to Old Testament Study*, Nashville: Abingdon.

Hendel, Ronald (1988) "The Social Origins of the Aniconic Tradition in Early Israel," *Catholic Biblical Quarterly* 50: 365–82.

Herodotus (1987) *The Histories, Book 2*, trans. D. Grene, Chicago: University of Chicago Press.

Hillers, Delbert R. (1965) "A Convention in Hebrew Literature: the Reaction to Bad News," *Zeitschrift für die alttestamentliche Wissenschaft* 77: 86–90.

—— (1984) *Micah*, Hermeneia, Philadelphia: Fortress.

—— (1992) *Lamentations*, Anchor Bible, New York: Doubleday.

Howie, C. G. (1950) *The Date and Composition of Ezekiel*, Philadelphia: Society of Biblical Literature.

Irigaray, Luce (1985) *Speculum of the Other Woman*, trans. G. G. Gill, Ithaca: Cornell University Press.

Ishida, Tomoo (1977) *Royal Dynasties in Ancient Israel: A Study of the Formation and Development of Royal-Dynastic Ideology*, Berlin and New York: Walter de Gruyter.

Jabès, Edmond (1985) "The Question of Displacement into the Lawfulness of the Book," in E. Gould (ed.) *The Sin of the Book*, Lincoln: University of Nebraska Press.

—— (1989) *The Book of Shares*, trans. R. Waldrop, Chicago: University of Chicago Press.

—— (1991 [Fr. 1963–65]) *The Book of Questions*, 7 books in 2 vols, trans. R. Waldrop, Hanover and London: Wesleyan University Press.

—— (1993) *The Book of Margins*, trans. R. Waldrop, Chicago: University of Chicago Press.

James, Henry (1934) *The Art of the Novel*, ed. R. Blackmur, New York: Scribner's.

Jay, Nancy (1985) "Sacrifice as Remedy for Having Been Born a Woman," in C. W. Atkinson (ed.) *Immaculate and Powerful*, Boston: Beacon.

—— (1988) "Sacrifice, Descent, and the Patriarchs," *Vetus Testamentum* 38: 52–70.

—— (1992) *Throughout Your Generations Forever: Sacrifice, Religion, and Paternity*, Chicago: University of Chicago Press.

Jobling, David (1986) *The Sense of Biblical Narrative: Structural Analyses in the Hebrew Bible, II*, JSOT Supplement Series 39; Sheffield: JSOT Press [Sheffield Academic Press].

—— (1991a) "Texts and the World – An Unbridgeable Gap? A Response to Carroll, Hoglund and Smith," in P. R. Davies (ed.) *Second Temple Studies. Vol 1: Persian Period*, Sheffield: Sheffield Academic Press.

—— (1991b) "Mieke Bal on Biblical Narrative," *Religious Studies Review* 17: 1–10.

Jobling, David and Catherine Rose (1996) "Reading as a Philistine: The Ancient and Modern History of a Cultural Slur," in M. G. Brett (ed.) *Ethnicity and the Bible*, Leiden: E. J. Brill, 381–417.

Johnson, Elizabeth A. (1992) *She Who Is*, New York: Crossroad.

Jordan, G. and Weedon, Chris (1995) *Cultural Politics: Class, Gender, Race and the Postmodern World*, Oxford and Cambridge: Blackwell.

Jung, Carl Gustav (1958) "A Psychological Approach to the Dogma of the Trinity," in *Psychology and Religion: West and East*, trans. R. F. C. Hull, London: Routledge & Kegan Paul.

Katz, R. (1987) *Love is Colder than Death: The Life and Times of Rainer Werner Fassbinder*, New York: Random House.

Kaufmann, Yehezkel (1972) *The Religion of Israel*, trans. and abridged M. Greenberg, New York: Schocken.

Keil, C. F. (1954 [1885]) *The Twelve Minor Prophets, I*, trans. J. Martin, Grand Rapids: Eerdmans.

Keller, Catherine (1994) "Inventing the Goddess," *The Christian Century 111*: 340–42.

Kennedy, James M. (1990) "Peasants in Revolt: Political Allegory in Genesis 2–3," *Journal for the Study of the Old Testament* 47: 3–14.

Kierkegaard, Søren (1985) *Fear and Trembling*, Harmondsworth, Middlesex: Penguin.

King, Philip J. (1989) "The Great Eighth Century," *Bible Review* 5/4: 23–33,44.

Klein, D. B. (1985) *Jewish Origins of the Psychoanalytic Movement*, Chicago: University of Chicago Press.

Koehler, L. and W. Baumgartner (eds) (1985) *Lexicon in Veteris Testament Libros*, Leiden: E. J. Brill.

Kolakowski, Leszek (1978) *Main Currents of Marxism I*, Oxford: Oxford University Press.

Kraeling, E. G. (1953) *The Brooklyn Museum Aramaic Papyri: New Documents of the Fifth Century from the Jewish Colony at Elephantine*, New Haven: Yale University Press.

Kristeva, Julia (1980) *Desire in Language: A Semiotic Approach to Literature and Art*, trans. L. S. Roudiez, T. Gora, and A. Jardine, New York: Columbia University Press.

—— (1982) *Powers of Horror: An Essay on Abjection*, trans. L. S. Roudiez, New York: Columbia University Press.

—— (1986a) "The System and the Speaking Subject," in T. Moi (ed.) *The Kristeva Reader*, New York: Columbia University Press.

—— (1986b) "Woman's Time," in T. Moi (ed.) *The Kristeva Reader*, New York: Columbia University Press.

—— (1986c) "A New Type of Intellectual: The Dissident," in T. Moi (ed.) *The Kristeva Reader*, New York: Columbia University Press.

—— (1987) *Tales of Love*, trans. L. S. Roudiez, New York: Columbia University Press.

—— (1995) *New Maladies of the Soul*, trans. R. Guberman, New York: Columbia University Press.

Kunin, Seth Daniel (1995) *The Logic of Incest: A Structuralist Analysis of Hebrew Mythology*, Sheffield: Sheffield Academic Press.

Lacan, Jacques (1977) *Ecrits: A Selection*, trans. A. Sheridan, New York: Norton.

—— (1982) *Feminine Sexuality*, trans. J. Rose and J. Mitchell, J. Rose (ed.), New York: W. W. Norton.

Lakoff, George and Johnson, Mark (1980) "Metaphors We Live By," in *Metaphors We Live By*, Chicago: University of Chicago Press.

Lakoff, George and Turner, Mark (1989) *More than Cool Reason*, Chicago and London: University of Chicago Press.

Landy, Francis (1983) *Paradoxes of Paradise: Identity and Difference in the Song of Songs*, Bible and Literature Series 7; Sheffield: Almond Press [Sheffield Academic Press].

Lanser, Susan (1988) "(Feminist) Criticism in the Garden: Inferring Genesis 2–3," *Semeia* 41: 67–84.

Laplanche, J. and Pontalis, J. B. (1973) *The Language of Psychoanalysis*, trans. D. Nicholson-Smith, Introduction by D. Lagache, New York: W. W. Norton.

Le Rider, J. (1993) *Modernity and Crises of Identity: Culture and Society in Fin-de-Siècle Vienna*, trans. R. Morris, New York: Continuum.

Lefebure, Leo D. (1994) "The Wisdom of God: Sophia and Christian Theology," *The Christian Century 111*: 951–56.

Lévi-Strauss, Claude (1966) *The Savage Mind*, Chicago: University of Chicago Press.

—— (1969) *The Raw and the Cooked*, trans. J. and D. Weightman, New York: Harper & Row.

—— (1973) *From Honey to Ashes*, trans. J. and D. Weightman, New York: Harper & Row.

—— (1975) *From Honey to Ashes*, trans. J. and D. Weightman, New York: Harper & Row.

—— (1978) *The Origin of Table Manners*, trans. J. and D. Weightman, New York: Harper & Row.

—— (1985) *The View from Afar*, New York: Basic Books.

Levinas, Emmanuel (1994 [1985]) *Ethics and Infinity: Conversations with Philippe Nemo*, trans. R. A. Cohen, Pittsburgh: Duquesne University Press.

Levine, B. A. and de Tarragon, J.-M. (1984) "Dead Kings and Rephaim: The Patrons of the Ugaritic Dynasty," *Journal of the American Oriental Society* 104: 649–59.

Lichtheim, Miriam (1976) *Ancient Egyptian Literature, II: The New Kingdom*, Berkeley: University of California Press.

Linafelt, Tod (1995) "Surviving Lamentations," *Horizons in Biblical Theology* 17: 45–61.

Lloyd, G. (1993) *The Man of Reason: "Male" and "Female" in Western Philosophy*, 2nd edn, Minneapolis: University of Minnesota Press.

Lowe, Walter (1993) *Theology and Difference: The Wound of Reason*, Bloomington: Indiana University Press.

Lyotard, Jean-François (1984) "Figure forclose. 1er janvier 1969," *L'écrit du temps* 5.

McCarter, P. Kyle (1980) *I Samuel. A New Translation with Introduction, Notes & Commentary*, Garden City: Doubleday & Company.

McCarthy, Dennis J. (1978) *Treaty and Covenant: A Study in Form in the Ancient Oriental Documents and in the Old Testament*, 2nd edn, Rome: Pontifical Biblical Institute.

McFague, Sallie (1982) *Metaphorical Theology*, Philadelphia: Fortress.

McKinlay, Judith (1994) *Wisdom the Host*, unpublished diss., University of Otago, New Zealand.

Manuel, F. E. (1992) *The Broken Staff: Judaism through Christian Eyes*, Cambridge MA: Harvard University Press.

Margalit, B. (1989) "The Meaning and Significance of Asherah," Vetus Testamentum 39: 264–97.

—— (1990) "Some Observations on the Inscription and Drawing from Khirbet el-Qom," *Vetus Testamentum* 40: 371–78.

Masson, Jeffrey Moussaieff (ed.) (1985) *The Complete Letters of Sigmund Freud to Wilhelm Fliess: 1887–1904*, Cambridge MA: Harvard University Press.

Mays, James L. (1976) *Micah*, Old Testament Library, Philadelphia: Westminster.

Meek, Theophilus (1956) "The Book of Lamentations," in *The Interpreter's Bible*, Nashville: Abingdon.

Mendenhall, George E. (1962) "Covenant," *Interpreters Dictionary of the Bible*.

Meyers, Carol (1987) "Temple," in P. J. Achtemeier (ed.) *Harper's Bible Dictionary*, San Francisco: Harper & Row.

—— (1988) *Discovering Eve: Ancient Israelite Women in Context*, New York and Oxford: Oxford University Press.

Milgrom, Jacob (1976) "Israel's Sanctuary: The Priestly Picture of Dorian Gray," *Revue Biblique* 83: 390–99.

Miller, J. Maxwell (1972) "In the 'Image' and 'Likeness' of God," *Journal of Biblical Literature* 91: 289–304.

Milne, Pamela J. (1989) "The Patriarchal Stamp of Scripture: The Implications of Structural Analyses for Feminist Hermeneutics," *Journal of Feminist Studies in Religion* 5: 17–34.

Mintz, Alan (1984) *Hurban: Responses to Catastrophe in Hebrew Scripture*, New York: Columbia University Press.

Miscall, Peter D. (1990) "Jacques Derrida in the Garden of Eden," *Union Seminary Quarterly Review* 44: 1–9.

Moeller, R. G. (1994) "The Homosexual Man Is a Man, the Homosexual Woman Is a Woman: Sex, Society, and the Law in Postwar West Germany," *Journal of the History of Sexuality* 4: 395–429.

Moi, Toril (1985) *Sexual/Textual Politics: Feminist Literary Theory*, London: Methuen.

Mopsik, Charles (1989) "The Body of Engenderment in the Hebrew Bible, the Rabbinic Tradition and the Kabbalah," in M. Feher with R. Naddoff and N. Tazi (eds) *Zone: Fragments for a History of the Human Body Part 1*, New York: Ozone.

Neumann, Erich (1955) *The Great Mother*, New York: Pantheon.

Neusner, Jacob (1987a) *Canon and Connection*, Lanham, MD: University Press of America.

—— (1987b) *Midrash as Literature*, Lanham, MD: University Press of America.

Newsom, Carol A. (1989) "Woman and the Discourse of Patriarchal Wisdom: A Study of Proverbs 1–9," in P. L. Day (ed.) *Gender and Difference in Ancient Israel*, Minneapolis: Fortress.

Norris, Christopher (1987) *Derrida*, Cambridge: Harvard University Press.

Nowack, W. (1903) *Die kleinen Propheten*, 2. Aufl, Göttingen: Vandenhoeck und Ruprecht.

Nye, M. (1993) "Throughout Your Generations Forever: Sacrifice, Religion, and Paternity," *Theology* 96: 227–28.

Ochshorn, Judith (1988) *The Book of the Goddesses: Past and Present*, New York: Crossroad.

Oden, T. C. (1994) "Confessions of a Grieving Seminary Professor," *Good News*: 10–13.

Olender, M. (1992) *The Languages of Paradise: Race, Religion, and Philology in the Nineteenth Century*, trans. A. Goldhammer, Cambridge MA: Harvard University Press.

Otwell, John H. (1977) *And Sarah Laughed: The Status of Woman in the Old Testament*, Philadelphia: Westminster.

Pagels, Elaine (1988) *Adam, Eve and the Serpent*, New York: Random House.

Pardes, Ilana (1992) *Countertraditions in the Bible: A Feminist Approach*, Cambridge: Harvard University Press.

Parkinson, R. B. (1991) *Voices from Ancient Egypt: An Anthology of Middle Kingdom Writings*, London: British Museum Press.

Patai, Raphael (1967) *The Hebrew Goddess*, New York: Ktav.

Pellegrini, A. (forthcoming) "*Without You I'm Nothing*: Performing Race, Gender, and Jewish Bodies," in *Jews and Other Differences: The New Jewish Cultural Studies*, Minneapolis: University of Minnesota Press.

Phillips, Gary A. (1994) "Drawing the Other: The Postmodern and Reading the Bible Imaginatively," in D. Jasper and M. Ledbetter (eds) *In Good Company: Essays in Honor of Robert Detweiler*, Atlanta: Scholars Press.

Plate, S. Brent (forthcoming) "Obfuscation: Blanchot's re-citation of the limits," *Literature and Theology*.

Plutarch (1936) *Moralia*, vol. 5, trans. F. C. Babbitt, Cambridge, MA: Harvard University Press.

Polzin, Robert (1980) *Moses and the Deuteronomist*, New York: Seabury.

Pressler, Carolyn J. (1993) *The View of Women Found in the Deuteronomic Family Law*, Berlin and New York: Walter de Gruyter.

Provan, Iain W. (1991) *Lamentations*, New Century Bible Commentary, Grand Rapids: Eerdmans.

Ragland-Sullivan, Ellie (1986) *Jacques Lacan and the Philosophy of Psychoanalysis*, Urbana: University of Illinois Press.

Ramsey, George W. (1988) "Is Name-Giving an Act of Domination in Genesis 2:23 and Elsewhere?" *Catholic Biblical Quarterly* 50: 24–35.

Rank, Otto (1985) "The Essence of Judaism (1905)," in D. B. Klein (ed.) *Jewish Origins of the Psychoanalytic Movement*, Chicago: University of Chicago Press.

Rashkow, Ilona N. (1990) "Adam and Eve," in *Upon the Dark Places: Anti-Semitism and Sexism in English Renaissance Biblical Translation*, Bible and Literature Series 28; Sheffield: Almond Press [Sheffield Academic Press].

—— (1993) *The Phallacy of Genesis: A Feminist-Psychoanalytic Approach*, Louisville: Westminster/John Knox.

Richardson, P. and Granskou, D. (eds) (1986) *Paul and the Gospels (Anti-Judaism in Early Christianity, I)*, Waterloo: Wilfrid Laurier University Press.

Robert, Marthe (1976 [1974]) *From Oedipus to Moses: Freud's Jewish Identity*, trans. R. Mannheim, New York: Doubleday.

Rorty, Richard (1992) "The Pragmatist's Progress," in U. Eco (ed.) *Interpretation and Overinterpretation*, Cambridge: Cambridge University Press.

Rose, Jacqueline (1982) "Introduction," in J. Lacan, *Feminine Sexuality*, trans. J. Mitchell and J. Rose (ed.) New York: Norton.

Rosenberg, Joel (1986) "The Garden Story Forward and Backward: The Non-Narrative Dimension of Gen. 2–3," in *King and Kin: Political Allegory in the Hebrew Bible*, Indiana Studies in Biblical Literature; Bloomington: Indiana University Press.

Rowlett, Lori (1992) "Inclusion, Exclusion and Marginality in the Book of Joshua," *Journal for the Study of the Old Testament* 55: 15–23.

Rubenstein, Richard L. (1966) *After Auschwitz: Radical Theology and Contemporary Judaism*, New York: Macmillan.

—— (1972) *My Brother Paul*, New York: Harper.

Rubin, N. (1988) "Body and Soul in Talmudic and Mishnaic Sources," *Koroth* 9: 151–64.

Rudolph, Wilhelm (1975) *Micha – Nahum – Habakuk – Zephanja*, Gütersloh: Gütersloher Verlagshaus Gerd Mohn.

Ruether, Rosemary Radford (1983) *Sexism and God-Talk: Toward a Feminist Theology*, Boston: Beacon Press.

Russell, Letty (ed.) (1976) *The Liberating Word: A Guide to Nonsexist Interpretation of the Bible*, Philadelphia: Westminster Press.

Ryle, Herbert Edward (1899 [1892]) *The Canon of the Old Testament. An Essay on the Gradual Growth and Formation of the Hebrew Canon of Scripture*, 2nd edn, London: Macmillan.

Santner, E. (1996) *My Own Private Germany: Daniel Paul Schreber's Secret History of Modernity*, Princeton: Princeton University Press.

Sapp, Stephen (1977) *Sexuality, the Bible and Science*, Philadelphia: Fortress.

Sarna, Nahum M. (1970 [1966]) *Understanding Genesis*, New York: Schocken.

—— (1991) *Exodus*, The JPS Torah Commentary, Philadelphia: Jewish Publication Society.

Sawyer, John F. A. (1974) "The Meaning of 'In the Image of God' in Genesis I–XI," *Journal of Theological Studies* 25: 418–26.

Scarry, Elaine (1985) *The Body in Pain*, New York: Oxford University.

Schalit, A. (1971) "Elephantine," in *Encyclopaedia Judaica*.

Schüngel-Straumann, H. (1986) "Gott als Mutter in Hosea 11," *Tübinger Theologische Quartalschrift* 166: 119–34.

Sedgwick, Eve Kosofsky (1985) *Between Men: English Literature and Male Homosocial Desire*, New York: Columbia University Press.

Seeberg, R. (1923) "Antisemitismus, Judentum und Kirche," in *Zum Verstandnis der gegenwartigen Krisis in der europaischen Geisteskultur*, Leipzig: A. Deichert.

Seshadri-Crooks, K. (1994) "The Primitive as Analyst," *Cultural Critique* 28: 175–218.

Setel, T. Drorah (1985) "Prophets and Pornography: Female Sexual Imagery in Hosea," in L. M. Russell (ed.) *Feminist Interpretations of the Bible*, Oxford: Blackwell.

Shaw, Charles S. (1990) *The Speeches of Micah: A Rhetorical-Historical Analysis*, Ph.D. dissertation, Emory University.

Silverman, Kaja (1983) *The Subject of Semiotics*, New York: Oxford University Press.

—— (1988) *The Acoustic Mirror: The Female Voice in Psychoanalysis and Cinema*, Bloomington: Indiana University Press.

—— (1992a) *Male Subjectivity at the Margins*, New York and London: Routledge.

—— (1992b) "The Lacanian Phallus," *Differences* 4: 84–115.

Skehan, Patrick (1971) *Studies in Israelite Wisdom and Poetry*, ed. J. A. Fitzmyer, Worcester MA: Heffernan.

Small, J. D. and Burgess, J. P. (1994) "Evaluating 'Re-Imagining,'" *The Christian Century 111*: 342–44.

Smith, George Adam (1928) *The Book of the Twelve Prophets, I: Amos, Hosea, and Micah*, rev. edn, New York: Harper & Brothers.

Speiser, E. A. (1964) *Genesis*, The Anchor Bible, Garden City: Doubleday.

Spiro, Melford (1961) "An Overview and a Suggested Reorientation," *Context and Meaning in Cultural Anthropology*, F. I. K. Hsu (ed.) Homewood: Dorsey Press.

—— (1987) *Culture and Human Nature*, B. Kilborne and L. L. Langness (eds) Chicago: The University of Chicago Press.

Sprengnether, M. (1990) *The Spectral Mother: Freud, Feminism, and Psychoanalysis*, Ithaca: Cornell University Press.

Stansell, Gary (1988) *Micah and Isaiah: A Form and Traditional Historical Comparison*, Atlanta: Scholars Press.

Sternberg, Meir (1985) *The Poetics of Biblical Narrative: Ideological Literature and the Drama of Reading*, Bloomington: Indiana University Press.

Stevens, W. (1951) "The Noble Rider and the Sound of Words," in *The Necessary Angel: Essays on Reality and the Imagination*, London: Faber & Faber.

Stone, L. (1991) "Ethical and Apologetic Tendencies in the Redaction of the Book of Joshua," *Catholic Biblical Quarterly* 53: 25–36.

Stone, M. (1977) *The Paradise Papers*, London: Virago.

Stulman, Louis (1990) "Encroachment in Deuteronomy: An Analysis of the Social World of the D Code," *Journal of Biblical Literature* 109: 613–32.

Talmon, Shemaryahu (1975a) "The Old Testament Text," in F. M. Cross and S. Talmon (eds) *Qumran and the History of the Biblical Text*, Cambridge: Harvard University Press.

—— (1975b) "The Textual Study of the Bible – A New Outlook," in F. M. Cross and S. Talmon (eds) *Qumran and the History of the Biblical Text*, Cambridge: Harvard University Press.

—— (1991) "Between the Bible and the Mishnah: Qumran from Within," in S. Talmon (ed.) *Jewish Civilization in the Hellenistic Roman Period*, Sheffield: JSOT Press.

Theissen, Gerd (1978) *Sociology of Early Palestinian Christianity*, trans. J. Bowden, Philadelphia: Fortress.

—— (1985) *Biblical Faith: An Evolutionary Approach*, trans. J Bowden, Philadelphia: Fortress.

—— (1987) *Psychological Aspects of Pauline Theology*, trans. J. P. Galvin, Philadelphia: Fortress.

Torgovnick, M. (1990) *Gone Primitive: Savage Intellects, Modern Lives*, Chicago: University of Chicago Press.

Tov, Emanuel (1982) "A Modern Textual Outlook Based on the Qumran Scrolls," *Hebrew Union College Annual* 53: 11–27.

—— (1992) "The Unpublished Qumran Texts from Caves 4 and 11," *Journal of Jewish Studies* 43: 101–36.

Trible, Phyllis (1973) "Depatriarchalizing in Biblical Interpretation," *Journal of the American Academy of Religion* 41: 30–48.

—— (1978) *God and the Rhetoric of Sexuality*, Philadelphia: Fortress.

Turner, Bryan (1984) *The Body and Society: Explorations in Social Theory*, Oxford: Oxford University Press.

Turner, Victor (1967) *The Forest of Symbols*, Ithaca, NY: Cornell University Press.

Ulrich, Eugene (1992) "Pluriformity in the Biblical Text, Text Groups, and Questions of Canon," in Julio Trebolle Barrera and Luis Vegas Montaner (eds) *The Madrid Qumran Congress*.

Ungern-Sternberg, R. F. von (1958) *Der Rechtsstreit Gottes mit seiner Gemeinde: Der Prophet Micha*, Stuttgart: Calwar Verlag.

Urbach, Ephraim E. (1987) *The Sages: Their Concepts and Beliefs*, Boston: Harvard University Press.

van Dijk-Hemmes, Fokkelien (1993) "The Metaphorization of Woman in Poetic Speech: An Analysis of Ezekiel 23," in A. Brenner and F. van Dijk-Hemmes (eds) *On Gendering Texts: Female and Male Voices in the Hebrew Bible*, Leiden: Brill.

Van Herik, Judith (1982) *Freud on Femininity and Faith*, Berkeley and Los Angeles: University of California Press.

Voltaire (1906) "Ezekiel," in *Philosophical Dictionary*, vol. 4, trans. W. F. Fleming, Acron: Werner.

von Rad, Gerhard (1966) *Deuteronomy*, trans. D. Barton, Philadelphia: Westminster.

—— (1972) *Genesis*, Old Testament Library; Philadelphia: Westminster Press.

—— (1976) *Genesis*, trans. J. H. Marks, Philadelphia: Westminster.

Weinberg, Joel (1992) *The Citizen-Temple Community*, trans. D. L. Smith-Christopher, Sheffield: Sheffield Academic Press.

Weininger, Otto (1975 [1906]) *Sex and Character*, 6th edn, New York: AMS.

Weiser, Artur (1959) *Das Buch der zwölf Kleinen Propheten, I*, 3. Aufl., Göttingen: Vandenhoeck & Ruprecht.

Wenham, G. J. (1979) *The Book of Leviticus*, Grand Rapids: William B. Eerdmans.

Westermann, Claus (1969) *Isaiah 40–66*, Old Testament Library, Philadelphia: Westminster.
—— (1980) *The Psalms: Structure, Content, and Message*, Minneapolis: Augsburg.
—— (1984) *Genesis 1–11*, trans. J. J. Scullion, Minneapolis: Augsburg.
Wilson, S. G. (ed.) (1986) *Separation and Polemic (Anti-Judaism in Early Christianity, II)*, Waterloo: Wilfrid Laurier University Press.
Wink, Walter (1989a) Review of Gerd Theissen, *Psychological Aspects of Pauline Theology*, *Religious Studies Review* 15: 40–42.
—— (1989b) *Transforming Bible Study*, Nashville: Abingdon.
Wolff, Hans Walter (1990 [1982]) *Micah*, trans. G. Stansell. Minneapolis: Augsburg.
Younger, K. Lawson, Jr. (1995) "The Configuring of Judicial Preliminaries: Judges 1:1–2:5 and its Dependence on the Book of Joshua," *Journal for the Study of the Old Testament* 68: 75–92.

INDEX OF AUTHORS

INDEX OF SUBJECTS

INDEX OF ANCIENT SOURCES

19:6 80
19–24 59
20:2–4 43, 70
20:2–6 56, 70, 165, 189
20:23 43
22:16 162
24:9–11 45
32 59
33:17–23 45–46, 54
34:6–7 56
34:17 43

Leviticus
7:11–21 93
11:16 8
11:42–44 37
12, 10 37
13–14 7, 8, 37
15:30 37
15:16–18 52
18 37
19:27 37
20:10–26 37
21:5 37
21:16–23 37

Numbers
5:13 162
11:12 69
14:2–4 162
14:13–35 159
21:4–9 82
21:32 151
25:1 91
32:1–33 163
32:39–42 151
34:1–12 163

Deuteronomy
1:6–8 163
4:11–24 43, 46
4:15–20 165
5:8–9 43, 165, 170
7:1–26 153, 158
7:6 154
8:19–20 153
9:3 158
9:5 161
12:29–32 153
14–15 8
16:21 67
21:23 160

22:23 162
27:15 43
28:36 162
29:11 161
32:6 67
32:33 77

Joshua
1:5 158
1:12–18 163
2–11 153
2 140
2:1 157
2:6 151
2:8–9 157–58
2:12, 17, 20 155–56
2:15 157
2:19 161
2:1–24 155
2:9–11 157
2:12–13 148
6:1–25 155
6:16 157
6:20–21 157
6:25–26 156, 160
7:1, 11 162
7:1–5 158
7:1–8:29 158
7:7–9 162
7:11 159
7:19 159
7:20 162
7:25 159
7:26 160
8:1–29 151, 158, 160
9:1–10:15 155
9:1–27 155, 160
9:9–10 157
9:19, 20 155
10:1, 28, 31–39 151
10:2 158
10:8 157
10:14 157
10:16–39 157
11:10, 17 151
13:13 142
18:9ff 161
22:1–34 163

Judges
1 140, 143
1:8 142

Writing bodies?
Only half the story.
Come close
and I will tell you
the rest:
Your pen dips
into my ink
and scrawls the invisible
word of God
across the face
of creation:
bodies
writing bodies.

Claudia Camp